Natural History of Nova Scotia

Produced by the Nova Scotia Museum, the Department of
Education and Culture, Province of Nova Scotia.
Minister: Honourable Robbie Harrison
Deputy Minister: Lloyd Gillis

The first edition of The Natural History of Nova Scotia was written by
Michael Simmons, Derek Davis, Lesley Griffiths and Ann Muecke and
published in 1984 as a joint project by the Department of Lands and
Forests (now the Department of Natural Resources) and the Nova
Scotia Museum. The first edition was reprinted in 1989.

This revised edition is based extensively on the first edition and was
produced by the Nova Scotia Museum in partnership with Communications Nova Scotia and with the financial assistance of the Canada/
NovaScotia Cooperation Agreement on Sustainable Economic
Development.

This project was partially funded by
The Canada-Nova Scotia
COOPERATION Agreement on
Sustainable Economic Development

Canadä

NOVA SCOTIA
Department of Education and Culture

Editors: Derek S. Davis
                    Sue Browne
Graphic Designer: David MacDonald
Production: Derek Cowie Design
Scans: Image House Digital

Co-published with Nimbus Publishing.
A product of the Nova Scotia Government
Co-publishing Program.

Cover photographs: Ballantynes Cove, Antigonish Co.:
Roger Lloyd; Dover Island beach near Canso, Guysborough Co.:
Oliver Maass; Cape Breton Highlands: Alex Wilson; Cheticamp
Causeway, Inverness Co.: Alex Wilson.

Canadian Cataloguing in Publication Data
Main entry under title:
    The natural history of Nova Scotia

    Rev. ed.
    Co–published by the Nova Scotia Museum.
    Includes index.
    Contents: V. 1. Topics and habitats — v. 2. Theme regions.
    ISBN 1-55109-236-0 (v.1)
    ISBN 1-55109-238-7 (v.2)

1. Natural history — Nova Scotia. I. Davis, Derek S. II. Browne,
Sue. III. Nova Scotia Museum.

QH106.2.N68N27 1997 508.716 C95–966009–7

Printed on papers that
contain recycled fibre

TABLE OF CONTENTS

**TABLE OF
CONTENTS**

continued

ACKNOWLEDGEMENTS

This revision of the *Natural History of Nova Scotia* was made possible through the perseverance and vision of Dr. Derek S. Davis, until recently Chief Curator of Natural History at the Nova Scotia Museum.

The project was built on the work of hundreds of people who have worked and are working in Nova Scotia. In an attempt to synthesize the work, we have particularly relied on the expertise of a number of people in the civil service and the academic community as well as field naturalists. Some of these people have reviewed drafts of the manuscript, but the final decisions are those of the project team. We wish to acknowledge with deep gratitude the contributions of those people listed below, but we do not hold them responsible for any errors or omissions. We apologize if we have missed anyone who contributed to the project.

The project was funded under the Canadian–Nova Scotia Agreement on Sustainable Economic Development and was based at the Nova Scotia Museum of Natural History.

The following people helped produce this revised edition of the *Natural History of Nova Scotia:*

VOLUMES I AND II PROJECT TEAM:

PROJECT COORDINATOR
Sue Browne

PROJECT ADMINISTRATOR
Derek Davis

DATA MANAGER
Maria Hartery

GRAPHIC DESIGN
David MacDonald

RESEARCHERS
Ron Loucks, Loucks Oceanology Ltd.
Bernie McGuire   Heather MacLeod
Pat Stewart, Envirosphere Consultants Ltd.

TECHNICAL EDITING
Sue Browne   Susan Lucy
Derek Davis

COPY EDITING
Douglas Beall   Nicole Watkins Campbell
Iris Coupe   Rebecca Fleming
Peter King   Robbie Rudnicki
Susan Lucy

ORIGINAL ILLUSTRATIONS
Derek Davis   Gary Patterson
Barry Donovan   Robert Raeside
Barbara Lock   Fred Scott
Clinton Milligan   Jeffrey Ward

MAP
Nova Scotia Geomatics Centre
Tod Burt   Lee MacNeill
Gordon Cranton

SUPPORT DESIGN
Neil Meister   Kevin Sollows

PRODUCTION ART
Derek Cowie Design   Sherry Laidlaw

PRODUCTION MANAGER
John Hennigar-Shuh

PHOTOGRAPHS FROM THE COLLECTIONS OF:
Phyllis Blades, Bob Bancroft, Karen Casselman, Alan Dauphinee, Mark Elderkin, Carl Haycock, Oliver Maass, Linda Morris, Tim Randall, Nova Scotia Department of Education and Culture, Nova Scotia Department of Natural Resources, and the Bedford Institute of Oceanography (BIO).

THE FOLLOWING PROVINCIAL AGENCIES CONTRIBUTED TO THE REVISION:

Department of Agriculture and Marketing—with special thanks to Ken Beesley, Rob Gordon, Mike Langlands, Phil Warman, Ken Webb

Department of Education and Culture—with special thanks to Penny Brown, Angéline Doucet, John Gilhen, Bob Grantham, Debra McNabb, Scott Robson, Fred Scott, Sheila Stevenson, Alex Wilson, Ruth Whitehead, Barry Wright, John Hennigar-Shuh

Department of the Environment—with special thanks to Dave Briggens, Andrew Cameron, Herb Doane, Darryl Taylor

Department of Fisheries—with special thanks to Bob Bancroft, Kim Kelsey, Don MacLean

Department of Municipal Affairs—with special thanks to Brian Cuthbertson

Department of Natural Resources—with special thanks to Sandy Anderson, Dan Banks, Bob Boehner, Fred Boner, Colleen Brothers, John Calder, Howard Donahoe, Tony Duke, John Gillis, Ross Hall, Andrew Hanam, Paul Harvey, Dave Harris, David Hopper, Chris Kavanaugh, Duncan Keppie, John Leduc, Art Lynds, Jack MacDonald, Randy Milton, Peter Neiley, Tony Nette, Mike O'Brien, Garth Prime, Mark Pulsifer, Peter Rogers, Barry Sabean, Dale Smith, Ken Snow, Ralph Stea, Chris Trider, Paul Tufts

Department of Supply and Services—with special thanks to Susan Lucy and Nicole Watkins Campbell

THE FOLLOWING FEDERAL AGENCIES CONTRIBUTED TO THE REVISION:

Atlantic Geoscience Centre—with special thanks to Gordon Fader, Don Forbes, Peter Giles, Gary Grant, Lubomir Jansa, Bob Miller, David Piper, Bob Taylor, John Wade

Canada/Nova Scotia Offshore Petroleum Board—with special thanks to Dave Brown

Canadian Wildlife Service—with special thanks to Diane Amirault, Dick Brown, Tony Erskine, Steffan Gerriets, Peter Hicklin, Joe Kerekes, Tony Lock, Al Smith

Department of Agriculture—with special thanks to Gary Patterson

Department of Canadian Heritage—with special thanks to James Bridgeland, David Lawley, Neil Munro, Judith Tulloch

Department of National Defense—with special thanks to Wayne Lumpsdon

Department of Fisheries and Oceans—with special thanks to Don Gordon, Barry Hargrave, Brian Petrie, Gerald Seibert, Wes White

Environment Canada—with special thanks to Don Ambler, Tom Clair, John Dublin, Colleen Farrell

National Resource Council of Canada—with special thanks to Carolyn Bird

THE FOLLOWING ACADEMIC INSTITUTIONS CONTRIBUTED TO THE PROJECT:

Acadia University—with special thanks to Graham Daborn, Mike Dodswell, Sherman Bleakney, Tom Herman, Redge Newell, Ruth Newell, Bob Raeside

Dalhousie University—with special thanks to Barry Clark, Bill Friedman, Martin Giblin, Paul Schenk, Bob Scheibling, Dave Scott, Pierre Taschereau

Mount Allison University—with special thanks to Laing Ferguson

Nova Scotia College of Art and Design—with special thanks to Pat Manuel

St. Francis Xavier University—with special thanks to Tony Davis

Saint Mary's University—with special thanks to Terrence Day, Greg Klassen, Henrietta Mann, Hugh Millward, David Richardson, Doug Strongman, John Waldron

Technical University of Nova Scotia—with special thanks to Terry Hennigar

University College of Cape Breton—with special thanks to Don Arseneau, Charles Taylor

SPECIAL THANKS TO THE FOLLOWING INDIVIDUALS WHO CONTRIBUTED TO THE PROJECT:

Peter Austin-Smith
Norval Balch
John Brett
Paul-Michael Brunelle
Karen Casselman
Con Desplanques
Arlene Diepenbrock
Shauna Henderson
David Hope-Simpson
Robert Ireland
Carole Jacquard
Lewis King
Alan Knockwood

Zoe Lucas
Mary Lynack
Clinton Milligan
Wallace Niven
John Parsons
Alan Ruffman
Gary Saunders
Ruth Smith
Harry Thurston
Mike Wamboldt
Howard Williams
Mary Williams

INTRODUCTION

THE THEME REGIONS
GEOGRAPHICAL CLASSIFICATION SYSTEM

Volume I of the *Natural History of Nova Scotia, Topics and Habitats*, provides a description of the non-living and living elements of the natural environment of the province. In Volume II, *Theme Regions*, the relationships between these elements are described as they actually occur in the landscape. This is achieved by use of a geographical classification system of Regions, Districts, and Units that are defined according to distinctive landscape characteristics. We hope the reader will be able to identify these Regions, Districts, and Units in the field, know when a boundary or transition zone has been crossed, and identify the distinctive environmental relationships that occur.

A map accompanies the description of each Region and shows its component Districts. Figures 1 and 2 are more detailed maps showing Units, and a larger folded 1:500,000 map is included in the back pocket of this volume. Boundaries are necessarily approximate and should be regarded as narrow zones rather than lines.

CLASSIFICATION SYSTEM

A hierarchical system has been developed to demonstrate how these geographical entities have been determined. This approach closely follows the Biophysical Land Classification System that has been widely applied to terrestrial areas since the mid-1960s.[1,2] It has been extended to include the marine areas adjacent to Nova Scotia.[3]

The three levels of the hierarchy are as follows:
1. Regions: eight on land and one in the sea
2. Districts: 33 on land and four in the sea
3. Units: 65 on land and 11 in the sea

In some cases Units are geographically dispersed and are coded with letters as sub-Units.

TERRESTRIAL THEME REGIONS

Nova Scotia has eight terrestrial Regions that have been divided into 33 Districts and 65 Units (see Figure 1).

In the Biophysical Land Classification System, land regions are defined on the basis of "regional climate as expressed through regional vegetation." The classification adopted here recognizes six regional climates in Nova Scotia but further divides two of these climatic areas on the basis of regional geology to create eight Regions, as shown in Table 1.

The different Districts within a given Region are defined by "a distinctive landscape pattern." This pattern may be a reflection of geology, surficial materials, soils, hydrology, relief, or vegetation. In each case, one dominant element has been selected as the defining characteristic; other elements are usually closely related. This definition of Districts corresponds closely to the definition of land districts adopted in the Biophysical Land Classification System.

Units are generally fairly homogeneous areas within Districts. Landscapes may vary within them, but they reflect a recurring pattern of landforms, soils, or vegetation. Habitats can be identified and mapped within Units and used as a basis for detailed studies of species association and inventory (see Table 2).

The following example is presented as an aid to the interpretation of the geographical divisions. Looking at the map, one finds:

313a
This area known as the Creignish Hills is located northwest of Bras d'Or Lake on Cape Breton Island.

The number 313a stands for several things:

Theme Region 300
The first number, 3, refers to the Avalon Uplands (Region 300). These upland areas experience more severe winters, with greater amounts of precipitation and shorter growing seasons than the surrounding lowlands. Climatic conditions are not as harsh as in the Cape Breton highlands. This climate is reflected in the dominant hardwood vegetation characterized by a Sugar Maple, Yellow Birch–Fir association.

District 310
The second number, 1, refers to the distinctive geology and landforms found in District 310. This

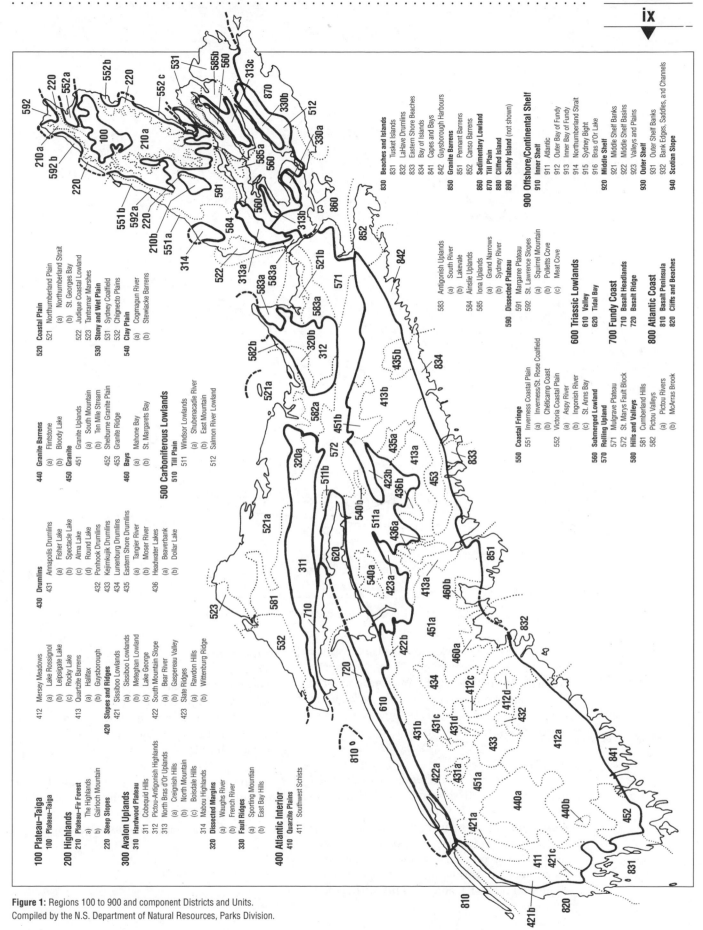

Figure 1: Regions 100 to 900 and component Districts and Units.
Compiled by the N.S. Department of Natural Resources, Parks Division.

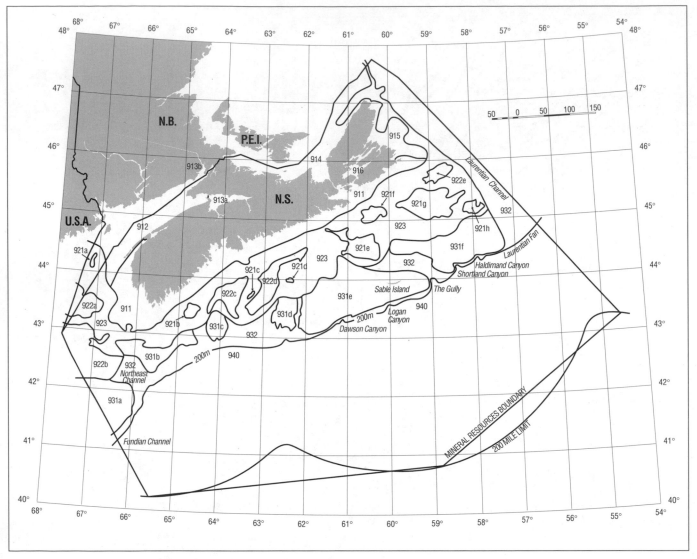

Figure 2: Region 900, Offshore/Continental Shelf, and component Districts and Units. Nova Scotia Geomatics Centre, Amherst, N.S.

District encompasses six of the ten plateaus which make up Theme Region 300. These six plateaus are all sharply defined, with level plateau surfaces at elevations between 200 and 300 m. Margins of the plateaus generally fall abruptly for 150 m or more, with little dissection by stream valleys.

Unit 313

The third number, 3, differentiates the three hill masses on the north shore of Bras d'Or Lake from two larger Units in District 310, one of which is located on the mainland and the other on Cape Breton Island. Differences in geology, glacial history, and soils combine to define the unique combination of features found in Unit 313 from the somewhat similar features found in Units 311, 312, and 314.

sub-Unit 313a

Three hill masses—Creignish Hills, North Mountain, and Boisdale Hills—comprise Unit 313. The hills are separated by the lowland fringes of the Bras d'Or Lake and are differentiated by the suffixes a, b, and c. Thus, sub-Unit 313a is the Creignish Hills.

Note: In some cases, Districts are not divided into Units but into sub-Districts. In these cases the reference number ends with a zero and a letter, for example, Gairloch Mountain (sub-District 210b).

BOUNDARIES

In this classification system, boundaries are defined by biophysical characteristics. For example, the rock types found in Region 300 are more resistant than those in surrounding Regions. As a result, isolated and well-defined hill masses have been formed by differential erosion of the soft and hard rocks. These hill masses are sufficiently elevated above the surrounding landscape to create distinctive climates. The more severe climate of the hills has led to the dominance of forest types quite different from the surrounding lowlands. Bedrock geology is also reflected in the generally thin soils over bedrock.

In the case of Theme Region 300, the distinctive regional climate is created by the elevation, which has evolved from differences in bedrock geology, which in turn have determined the nature of surficial materials. Climatic boundaries are therefore sharply defined and coincide with topography, bedrock geology, and soil boundaries.

Theme Regions

Among the eight Regions, only two sets of boundaries are ill-defined. Both are cases where regional climate is not determined by topographical and geological breaks in the landscape. All other boundaries of regions are easily identified by abrupt topographical breaks attributable to underlying geological structure. The two ill-defined boundaries are:

1. Atlantic Coast (Region 800): Wind and salt spray prevent normal growth of trees along the exposed Atlantic coast. Headlands and islands are frequently barren of trees. Inland, spruce is the most hardy tree and may dominate the forest for up to 8 km from the coast. As conditions become kinder inland, maple and birch begin to appear; other species grow according to local conditions. The inland boundary of the coastal forest varies considerably and cuts across all geological and topographical features. The high water mark provides boundaries with Region 900.

2. Plateau-Taiga (Region 100): Extreme exposure to

No.	Name	Regional Climate	Regional Vegetation	Regional Geology
100	Plateau-Taiga	exposed plateau —high winds	taiga-spruce	ancient high plateau
200	Highlands	highlands—short summers	fir	ancient high plateau
300	Avalon Uplands	uplands—high precipitation	maple-birch-fir	resistant fault blocks
400	Atlantic Interior	interior— warm summers	spruce (maple)- hemlock-pine	Meguma Group and granitic intrusions
500	Carboniferous Lowlands	interior— warm summers	spruce (maple)- hemlock-pine	Carboniferous sediments
600	Triassic Lowlands	interior— warm summers	spruce- hemlock-pine	Triassic sandstones
700	Fundy Coast	Fundy— moderated interior	transition	Basalt and fault blocks
800	Atlantic Coast	Atlantic coast—mild winters, high winds	spruce, barrens, and dunes	Meguma Group and granitic intrusions

Table 1: Terrestrial Theme Region climate, vegetation, and geology.

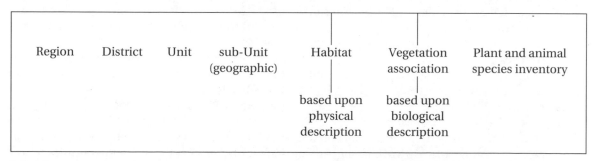

Table 2: The hierarchical system used in the *Natural History of Nova Scotia* allows landscape features to be mapped at various levels of detail.

winds stunts tree growth on the highest parts of the Cape Breton highlands. Although a large area is identified as taiga in the vicinity of the National Park, a variety of smaller areas of taiga occur in exposed locations to the north and south. Occurrence of wind-dominated taiga does not reliably correlate with topographical conditions.

Districts

Various dominant environmental criteria are used to define Districts. Each District has one defining characteristic, which is usually an element of the physical environment, most often bedrock geology. Surficial materials, landforms, and vegetation are also used in some circumstances. Frequently, the occurrence of the dominant factor is closely linked with other environmental conditions. For example, within the Carboniferous Lowlands (Region 500), a very distinct District (540) is defined by Kingsville soils. These soils are derived from the Scotch Village Formation in which flat-lying strata give a very level surface. The formation produces heavy clay soils which have very poor surface drainage and slow internal drainage. As a result, large organic deposits have accumulated. The Scotch Village Formation occurs over an area wider than the District, and the peat bogs cover an area smaller than the District. Therefore, the District boundary in this case is a compromise between the two soil formations.

The selection of the dominant characteristic on which a District's definition depends is thus a matter of judgement.

Units

Most major environmental factors do not vary within each Unit. A significant change in any one of these factors is in fact what differentiates one Unit from another. This does not imply that Units are homogeneous, but that environmental conditions create recurring patterns. For example, within the Atlantic Coast Region (800), a District with a dominance of abundant coastal sediment (District 830) is recognized; in turn, four Units are recognized as follows:

831 long, shallow estuaries with extensive salt marshes

832 eroding drumlins, islands, and isolated sand beaches

833 shallow large estuaries, salt marshes, and sand beaches

834 coastal islands

These Units have many similarities, but at least one major factor is different in each. Within the Unit, a repetitive, recognizable sequence of major environmental factors occurs. Boundary conditions are usually well defined as, for example, between Units 833 and 834: coastal islands occur east of Owls Head, and sandy beaches occur west of Owls Head. Estuaries to the west are characterized by salt marshes, but those to the east of Ship Harbour are generally smaller and without significant salt marshes.

OFFSHORE THEME REGIONS

Classification of the Offshore/Continental Shelf (which includes the continental slope) follows a similar approach, using a hierarchy of Districts, Units, and sub-Units (see Figure 2). The Nova Scotia offshore is part of the North Atlantic Ocean, with which it shares broad similarities in physical oceanography, and plant and animal communities. Local variations within the Region principally reflect changes in productivity of the biological communities (e.g., upwelling or mixing zones) or localization of species (e.g., stocks, or localized warm-water fauna). The foot of the continental slope and the area just beyond, as included within political boundaries, has been chosen as a convenient limit of the Region, but, as noted, many of the features of the biological communities can be extended to cover the rest of the North Atlantic. This approach is consistent with biological classification systems for oceans previously developed for marine conservation[4,5] in which the whole of the Nova Scotia continental shelf falls into the Acadian-Boreal Zone, one of several broad divisions of the ocean based on animal and plant distributions. The Acadian-Boreal Zone extends from Newfoundland to Cape Cod and includes the Gulf of St. Lawrence. The biota is essentially boreal (between tropical and subarctic) in character.

Districts in Region 900 are geographically distinct areas based principally on depth and the topographical divisions of the continental shelf and slope.[6] The divisions of Inner, Middle, and Outer Shelf have been extended to include parts of the Gulf of Maine and Northumberland Strait. These are areas broadly similar in topography and geological origin and are thus consistent with the "District" definition used for the Nova Scotia landmass. As well, the Districts tend to have distinctive physical oceanographic and biological features, although boundaries often do not exactly coincide, owing to the mobile and variable nature of the ocean. For instance, the waters immediately adjacent to the coast and falling within the Inner Shelf District are biologically different from waters in the Middle Shelf District, owing to freshwater influences and temperature extremes. Similarly, the Outer Shelf and Scotian Slope districts have distinctive physical and biological processes.

Units within Districts are based on both geological and biophysical features. In the Inner Shelf District, Units have a highly local nature, with characteristics reflecting special geological or biological features. The six Units are defined by features such as tidal regime, degree of circulation and heating, and local sediment and bedrock conditions. Districts further offshore (the Middle Shelf and Outer Shelf) have less of a local character, but they are usually distinct in terms of topography and depth (e.g., banks, basins, saddles) and have distinct biological features related to depth and sediment type. For example, banks tend to have significant populations of suspension-feeding organisms such as Sea Scallop and Ocean Quahog that are not present in the deeper areas surrounding the banks.

Many of the Unit divisions support recognized habitat classifications[6] such as soft bottom, corresponding to the bottoms in basins and deeper areas of the continental shelf (Units 922 and 932); insular environments (Sable Island, District 890, on Sable Island Bank, Unit 931e); submarine canyons (Unit 932); upwelling areas (included in Units 911, 912, and 931); topographic highs (offshore banks, Units 921 and 931); naturally deep holes (basins, Unit 922); and water-circulation bodies (gyres, District 940).

COMPARISON WITH OTHER SYSTEMS

During the preparation of the biophysical classification used in the *Natural History of Nova Scotia*, reference was made to other systems under development. Some apparent differences require explanation.

Systems Plan for Provincial Parks and Protected Areas

The revision of the *Natural History of Nova Scotia* was planned as a parallel and coordinated project with systems planning for provincial parks and protected areas. As the work proceeded, it was found that in some areas the boundaries of Districts and Units on the land were not sensitive enough to adequately meet planning requirements. As a result, some boundary changes were made, and all of the Regions, Districts, and Units were renumbered in a way different from the Theme Regions numbering. The 77 "Natural Landscapes" that have been identified and named for parks planning purposes have been identified at the end of each District or Unit description. Information used to define these "Natural Landscapes" is on file with the Parks and Recreation Division of the Nova Scotia Department of Natural Resources. This information is the basis of a major initiative for new parks and protected areas in the province.[7,8,9]

Federal Ecozone and Ecoregion Mapping

The Centre for Land and Biological Resources Research of Agriculture Canada has recently[10] brought together a summation of several years of work by federal agencies through publication of a provisional map of "Terrestrial Ecozones and Ecoregions of Canada." Under this system, Nova Scotia is described as part of the "Atlantic Maritime Ecozone," and the province is further divided into eight "Ecoregions":

137 Atlantic Coast
141 Cape Breton Highlands
142 Nova Scotia Highlands
143 Maritime Lowlands
145 Annapolis-Minas Lowlands
150 Fundy Coast
153 Southwest Nova Scotia Uplands

These "Ecoregions" are further subdivided into 25 "Land Resource Areas" (LRAs) which in some cases are the same as the Districts used in the *Natural History of Nova Scotia*. The differences between the two systems result from the level of detail required at the national and provincial levels. The two systems are sufficiently similar to be used together without much difficulty.

Federal Marine Region Mapping

Mapping and description of "Marine Regions" was initiated by Parks Canada as a basis for national marine parks planning and has since been considered for marine environmental quality monitoring by Environment Canada. This work was carefully considered when describing the components of Region 900 of the *Natural History of Nova Scotia*. In the federal system, Nova Scotia waters fall within two "Marine Realms" (26 Gulf of St. Lawrence and 27 Atlantic) or within four "Marine Regions" (4 Gulf of St. Lawrence, 5 Atlantic, 6 Bay of Fundy, and 7 Magdalen Shallows). *Natural History of Nova Scotia* provides detailed descriptions of these areas.

REGIONAL DESCRIPTIONS

Each regional description includes information on the Region's character, geology, landscape development, climate, soils, vegetation, fauna, sites of special interest, associated topics and habitats. Additional subjects are included as required, and in some cases headings are combined.

As previously described, a hierarchical approach is used. For any particular Unit, the reader would want to first read the Region description, then the District description, and finally the Unit description; more specific information will be found at each succeeding level of description. Associated Topics and Habitats are not repeated in the District and Unit descriptions if they were first noted in the Region description.

Twenty-one figures illustrate the relationship of the Regions, Districts, and Units to each other, to-pography, and geological structure. The block dia-grams are schematic depictions of the landscape; particular locations are used to assist the reader's orientation.

Much is still to be learned about the natural his-tory of Nova Scotia. Readers are encouraged to sub-mit any information that might contribute to a fuller understanding of the Units.

"Sites of Special Interest" listed in each Unit or sub-District description are drawn from several sources: the final report of the International Biologi-cal Programmes' Conservation of Terrestrial Envi-ronments, Maritime Provinces Committee, which identifies proposed ecological conservation sites; a list of provincial parks and park reserves (where each is named, but for many no detailed information is available); and the personal knowledge of many of the reviewers listed in the acknowledgements.

The information under the "Proposed Parks and Protected Areas System" is a cross-referencing of numbered "Natural Landscapes" and names of "Can-didate Protected Areas" currently in use by the Nova Scotia Department of Natural Resources.

"Associated Offshore Units" are offshore areas abutting the coastal part of the District or Unit. "As-sociated Coastal Units" are land areas abutting off-shore Units.

"Associated Topics" are Topics described in Vol-ume I that are of particular relevance to the Region, District, or Unit.

"Associated Habitats" are Habitats that are of particular importance in the Region, District, or Unit.

• • • • • • • •

References

1 Lacate, D.S. (compiler) (1969) *Guidelines for Biophysical Land Classification.* Publication 1264. Department of Fisheries and Forestry, Canadian Forestry Service, Ottawa.

2 Wiken, E. (1986) *Terrestrial Ecozones of Canada.* Ecological Land Classification Series 19. Lands Directorate, Environment Canada, Ottawa, 26 pp.

3 Davis, D.S., P.L. Stewart, R. Loucks, and S. Browne (1994) "Development of a Biophysical Classification of Offshore Regions for the Nova Scotia Continental Shelf." In *Cooperation in the Coastal Zone,* edited by P.G. Wells and P.J. Ricketts. Coastal Zone Canada '94 Conference Proceedings, vol:5:2149–57. Coastal Zone Canada Association, Bedford Institute of Oceanography, Dartmouth, N.S.

4 Ray, G.C., B.P. Hayden, and R. Dolan (1982) *Development of a Biophysical Coastal and Marine Classification System.* In *National Parks, Conservation and Development: The Role of Protected Areas in Sustaining Society,* edited by J.A. Mcneely and K.R. Miller. Proceedings of the World Congress on National Parks, Bali, Indonesia, Smithsonian Institution Press, Washington, D.C., 39–44.

5 Salm, R.V., and J.R. Clarke (1984) *Marine and Coastal Protected Areas: A Guide for Planners and Managers.* International Union for the Conservation of Nature and Natural Resources, Gland, Switzerland.

6 King, L.H., and B. MacLean (1976) "Geology of the Scotian Shelf." Marine Sciences Paper 7. Geological Survey of Canada Paper 74–3. Canadian Hydro-graphic Services, Department of the Environment and Geology, Survey of Canada, Ottawa.

7 Lynds, A., and J.M. LeDuc (1993) "Understanding and Protecting Biodiversity at the Landscape Level in Nova Scotia." In *Protecting Our Natural Heritage,* proceedings of a workshop on biodiversity and protected areas in Atlantic Canada, Environment Canada, Dartmouth, N.S., 15–19.

8 Leduc, J.M., and A.D. Smith (1992) "System planning for protection-oriented provincial parks in Nova Scotia." In *Science and the management of protected areas,* edited by J.H.M. Willison, S. Bondrup-Nielsen, C. Drysdale, T.B. Herman, N.W.P. Munro, and T.L. Pollock, proceedings of an international conference, Acadia University, Wolfville. Elsevier, Amsterdam, 139–144.

9 Nova Scotia Department of Natural Resources (1994) *A Proposed Systems Plan for Parks and Protected Areas in Nova Scotia.* Nova Scotia Department of Natural Resources, Parks Division, Halifax, N.S. 20 pp.

10 Ecological Stratification Working Group (1993) "Ecoregions of Canada," provisional map, scale 1:7,500,000. Agriculture Canada, Research Branch, Centre for Land and Biological Resources Research, and Environment Canada, State of the Environment Reporting, Ottawa.

A note to the reader

The following list of references is by no means comprehensive, but will assist the reader in finding additional information related to the topics discussed in Volume II of the *Natural History of Nova Scotia*. Readers are also encouraged to refer to "Associated Topics" and "Associated Habitats" in Volume I, as listed at the end of each of the Unit descriptions in Volume II.

Additional References

Benson, D.W. and G.D. Dodds (1977) *The Deer of Nova Scotia*. Department of Lands and Forests, Province of Nova Scotia. Halifax. 92 pp.

Banfield, A.W.F. (1974) *The Mammals of Canada*. University of Toronto Press, Toronto. 438 pp.

Catling, P.M., B. Freedman and Z. Lucas (1984) *The Vegetarian and Phytogeography of Sable Island, N.S.* Proceedings of the Nova Scotian Vol.34:181-247. Halifax.

Erskine, A.J. (1992) *Atlas of Breeding Birds of the Maritime Provinces*. Nimbus Publishing Ltd, and the Nova Scotia Museum. Halifax. 270 pp.

Gilhen, J. (1974) *The Fishes of Nova Scotia's Lakes and Streams*. The Nova Scotia Museum, Halifax. 192 pp.

Gilhen, J. (1984) *Amphibians and Reptiles of Nova Scotia*. The Nova Scotia Museum, Halifax. 162 pp.

Howe, C.D. (1912) in Fernow, B.E. (1912) *Forest Conditions of Nova Scotia*. Commission of Conservation, Ottawa. (Published by permission of the Department of Crown Lands, Nova Scotia)

Loucks, O.L. (1962) *A Forest Classification For the Maritime Provinces*. Proceedings of the Nova Scotia Institute of Science, Vol.25: 85-167. Halifax.

Peterson, R.L. (1966) *The Mammals of Eastern Canada*. Oxford University Press, Toronto. 465 pp.

Rowe, J.S. (1972) *Forest Regions of Canada*. Canadian Forestry Service Bulletin 1300. Ottawa.

Scott, W.B. and M.G. Scott (1973) *Freshwater Fishes of Canada*. Fisheries Research Board of Canada, Bulletin 184, Ottawa. 966 pp.

Scott, W.B. and M.G. Scott (1988) "Atlantic Fishes of Canada" In *Canadian Bulletin of Fisheries and Aquatic Sciences No. 219*. Ottawa. 713 pp.

Wright, B. (1989) *The Fauna of Sable Island*. Curatorial Report #68. The Nova Scotia Museum, Halifax.

Theme Regions

100
Plateau–Taiga

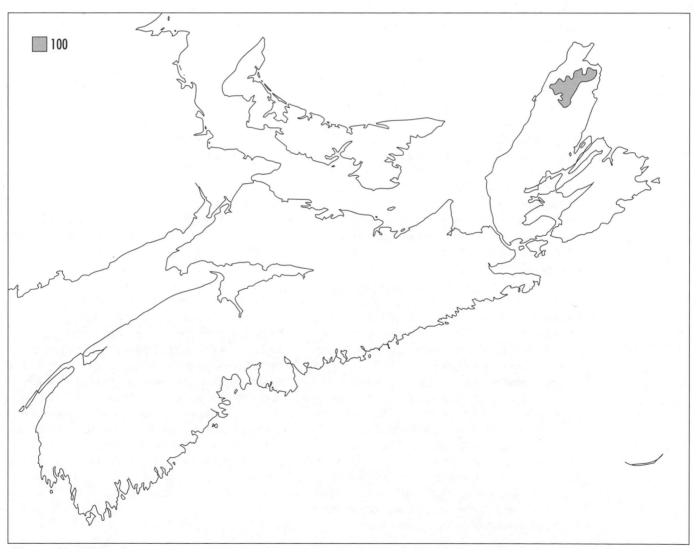

Figure 3: Region 100, Plateau–Taiga.

100 PLATEAU–TAIGA

REGIONAL CHARACTERISTICS

The plateau surface is more than 500 m in elevation and is the highest part of Nova Scotia. Its height results in a harsh climate with extreme exposure to winds and a very short growing season. Dwarfed spruce–taiga—a combination of dense spruce, blanket bogs, and barrens—dominates the vegetation, providing summer moose habitat.

GEOLOGY

Some of the oldest rocks in Nova Scotia are found in the Plateau–Taiga Region. Over a long history characterized more by periods of erosion than deposition, these previously deeply buried rocks which now form the highest elevations in the province were exposed.

Geologically the Plateau–Taiga is part of the Cape Breton highlands fault block, and it has only a few of the several rock types which are found in complex relationships throughout the larger area. The bedrock is predominantly composed of severely altered rocks, some of which have been distinguished as the George River Group. These rocks were originally deposited during Precambrian times, possibly as marine sediments. During subsequent deep burial, they were severely altered by heat and pressure to form hard, banded crystalline rocks called schists and gneisses.

The schists and gneisses are cut by granites in a complex way. The granites range in age from Precambrian to Devonian-Carboniferous. The intrusive nature of the granite, and especially its crosscutting contact with surrounding rocks, can be seen in several places (see Figure 5).

Any sediments deposited above these basement rocks were long ago removed by erosion. Almost certainly, Carboniferous sediments thickly covered this area at one time. Carboniferous cover is still found as patches on the slopes of the Cape Breton highlands block and as a more or less continuous fringe at lower elevations. This indicates that the present landscape was created prior to the Carboniferous, and that the cliffs, slopes, and plateau are all exhumed features of an ancient landscape.

Because sedimentary rocks younger than Precambrian are absent, there is no evidence of paleo-environments that may have existed in this area during the period of about 600 million years before the Pleistocene glaciation.

LANDSCAPE DEVELOPMENT

Uplift and Erosion
The Plateau–Taiga Region represents an ancient, deeply eroded landscape that is presently undergoing imperceptibly slow morphological change. However, despite being eroded, it is not low-lying but includes the highest elevations in the provincial landscape. This is attributable to several causes:
- the plateau is on the highest side of the tilted planation surface or peneplain
- the hard mass of the Cape Breton highlands was very resistant and less affected by the renewed cycle of erosion in the Tertiary than the surrounding softer sediments
- the block itself appears to have moved vertically upwards after the overlying Carboniferous strata were deposited

Glaciation
Glaciation during the past one million years has left a veneer of compacted glacial till over about 50 per cent of the Plateau–Taiga Region but no stratified ice-contact deposits or glacial outwash material. The ice cover which engulfed the Cape Breton highlands during the last phase of ice advance (the Wisconsinan) was reduced to an ice-cap in the later stages. From this relatively static ice-cap, glaciers radiated down the steep slopes of the highlands, scouring the surface, reworking and redepositing rock debris. The surface underneath the ice-cap itself appears to have been relatively protected. Evidence of permafrost in the area of the Plateau–Taiga indicates that deep freezing was more significant than scouring in this region. Evidence of some glacial movement is found, however, in the form of glacial striae and plucked bedrock.

Plate 1: Region 100. Oblique aerial view of the Plateau–Taiga landscape showing the mosaic of small lakes, bogs and scrub spruce forest. Photo: A. Wilson.

Recent Evolution

The surface of the Plateau–Taiga is undulating, with low hills and shallow valleys, and it is exposed and barren. There are large areas of bare bedrock, but little evidence of active erosion. The gradients are such that streams are sluggish and have little erosive power. Material loosened by seasonal freezing and thawing tends to remain in place.

CLIMATE

The elevation of the Plateau–Taiga Region influences its climate, which features harsh winters, short summers, exposure to almost constant winds, and high precipitation.

Because of an absence of weather stations in this area, precise weather records are not available. In general, winters are long and cold. Spring is very late, and summer is cool and short. Although the estimated mean annual temperature, less than 5°C, is not markedly colder than other areas in the Maritimes, the daily temperature range is considerably greater. Short-term observations in summer indicated that daily minimum temperatures were from 10° to 14°C lower on the plateau than along the coast. The first freezing temperatures were recorded as early as September 8. There is good reason to believe that in some years minimum temperatures will drop below freezing during every month.

Total annual precipitation is more than 1600 mm a year, the highest in the province. More than a quarter of this falls as snow—more than 400 cm. However, snowfall accumulations are not as great as might be expected. For example, at the end of February the Cape Breton highlands have a median snow cover in excess of 50 cm, while northern New Brunswick, where the total annual snowfall is similar, has a median snow cover greater than 100 cm. The presence of crusted layers within the snow cover indicates frequent episodes of rain and thaw through the winter.

The snowpack stays for a long time. In some north-facing hollows it may still be present in July. The peak runoff period in the Cape Breton highlands is in May. Elsewhere in the province, peak runoff occurs in March and April.

Wind records suggest that strong winds blow in northern Cape Breton during much of the year. The Plateau–Taiga Region is an exposed plateau that offers very little shelter. Low cloud cover or fog is common, and relative humidities are high.

The Plateau–Taiga Region has a very short growing season, probably six to eight weeks shorter than adjacent areas on the coast. The frost-free period is substantially shorter than 100 days. The winds have a very adverse impact on the growth of vegetation. Ice blasting causes trees to be dwarfed and stunted. Organic matter tends to accumulate, partly because the time available for decomposition is so short.

FRESH WATER

Region 100 may be divided into two major watersheds. The western portion of the Region is the headwater of the Chéticamp River and has relatively few lakes. The eastern portion contains many small glacial lakes. Streams that drain the Plateau–Taiga have a radial pattern overall and tend to meander on the plateau. Streams maintain a somewhat irregular or deranged character individually until steeper gradients are reached at margins of the plateau, where the water falls into steep brooks. Productivity is low, and pH ranges between 5.2 and 6.2. Conductivity is also low, averaging 30 micromhos/cm.

The shallow lakes are margined by bog vegetation and tend to have high peat accumulations. Small islands and sloped and raised bogs are common. In many cases, the bogs contain ponds arranged in a concentric configuration around a domed centre, or in a random pattern on a flat surface.

SOILS

This area was not mapped in the soil survey of Cape Breton Island because of its inaccessibility. However, it is now known that the gneisses and other metamorphic rocks which predominate have produced sandy loams that vary in depth from zero on rock outcrops to almost 1.5 m over much of the area. Soil depth is not the factor limiting tree growth. Soils are usually ferro-humic podzols, gleysols, or organic, according to drainage conditions. Surface organic layers are deep, and many areas are covered by several decimetres of dry, semi-decomposed organic material. The most significant features are the major accumulations of sphagnum and sedge peat. These peat accumulations grow both horizontally and vertically.

PLANTS

The Plateau–Taiga Region corresponds to Loucks' Spruce–Taiga Zone. The main influences on regional vegetation are the harsh winter climate, the high precipitation, and the poorly drained terrain. The cold, wet conditions favour conifers and other bog and barren vegetation. Winds and ice blasting result in stunted krummholz. Short, dense spruce and fir alternate with shrub barrens and peat bogs (see Figure 5).

In the few areas where soils are deep and well drained, a relatively stable association of stunted Black Spruce, White Spruce, Balsam Fir, and White Birch occurs. Mountain Ash is scattered along stream sides, and Balsam Fir forms almost pure stands. Barrens occur on shallow soils on low ridges, while sedge and sphagnum bogs occur in depressions and on seepage slopes. The high plateau barrens are characterized by exposed and stunted Black Spruce and Balsam Fir, Reindeer Moss and other lichens, blueberry, Sheep Laurel and deep surficial humic layers. Although it is quite possible that fires were originally an important factor in the development of the Taiga barrens, the presence of advanced barren vegetation indicates that fires have not occurred for a long period of time. Peat bogs are characterized by a variety of sphagna species, bulrushes, beak rush, cranberry, mosses, and liverworts.

Relict arctic-alpine plants are an important feature of this Region's vegetation. Dwarf birches and the Alpine Whortleberry are particularly associated with this area.

ANIMALS

The barren and bog vegetation in this Region does not support a large or diverse fauna. Small mammals present in the bogs and barrens include the Common Shrew and Red-backed Vole. The Region provides some lynx habitat. Moose sometimes use the area. Black Bear are common in the fall when blueberries are abundant. Although breeding birds are not abundant in this Unit, they include the Greater Yellow-legs and Grey-cheeked Thrush. Relict arctic aquatic animals are found in the small dystrophic lakes. The area harbours abundant populations of amphibians such as Mink Frog and Yellow-spotted Salamander. Freshwater fishes include White Perch, Brook Trout, and American Eel.

SCENIC QUALITY

This high plateau, with its stunted forest and few lakes, offers unique but often bleak scenery. It generally rates as medium in scenic value, although it is moderately high at the interface of forest, bog, and barrens. Where it overlooks deeper river valleys (e.g., Chéticamp River, North Aspy River) the scenic potential is occasionally very high. However, with no road access and few trails, there is little opportunity to view the area.

CULTURAL ENVIRONMENT

The Plateau–Taiga is best known as a conservation area since it is part of the Cape Breton Highlands National Park, established in 1936. Recreational fishing takes place at several lakes in the Region. In the past, moose and Woodland Caribou were decimated by indiscriminate slaughter. In 1947, moose from Alberta were successively introduced into the park to restore populations; Woodland Caribou were unsuccessfully reintroduced in 1968. The construction of the Wreck Cove Hydro Power Plant in the early 1970s directed the waters of Chéticamp Lake into a hydro power reservoir.

● ● ● ● ● ● ● ●

Sites of Special Interest
- Sunday Lake (IBP Proposed Ecological Site 20)— an example of high plateau with boreal forest, bogs, and barrens with rare arctic-alpine plants
- Chéticamp River (nominated as a Heritage River)

The Proposed Parks and Protected Areas System includes Natural Landscapes 64c, 72a, 72b, and 72c. Most of this area is protected within Cape Breton Highlands National Park.

Associated Topics
T2.2 The Avalon and Meguma Zones, T2.3 Granite in Nova Scotia, T2.4 The Carboniferous Basin, T3.1 Development of the Ancient Landscape, T3.2 Ancient Drainage Patterns, T3.3 Glaciation, Deglaciation and Sea-level Changes, T3.4 Terrestrial Glacial Deposits and Landscape Features, T4.1 Post-glacial Climatic Change, T4.2 Post-glacial Colonization by Plants, T5.2 Nova Scotia's Climate, T10.6 Trees, T10.12 Rare and Endangered Plants, T12.11 Animals and Resources, T12.13 Recreational Resources.

Associated Habitats
H4.1 Bog, H5.1 Barren, H6.2 Softwood Forest (Balsam Fir Association; Spruce, Fir Association), H6.3 Mixedwood Forest (White Spruce, Fir–Maple, Birch Association).

200
Highlands

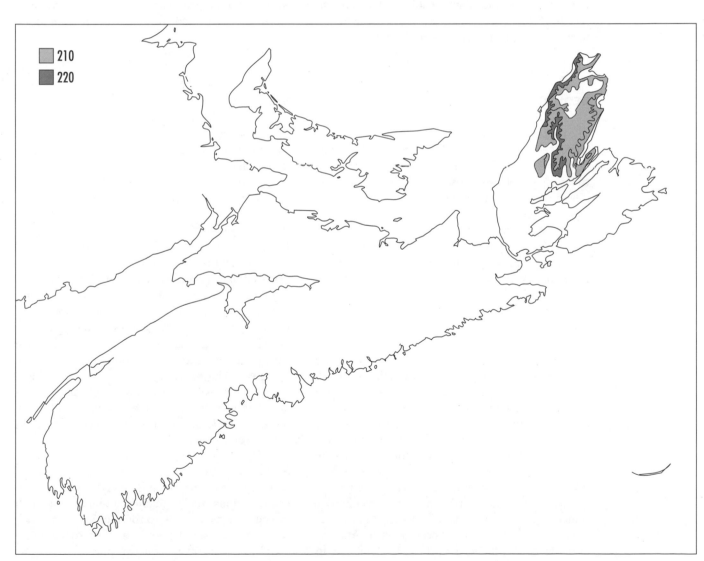

210
220

Figure 4: Region 200, Highlands, and its component Districts.

200 HIGHLANDS

The Highlands Region is divided into Districts and sub-Districts as follows:

210 Plateau–Fir Forest
    (a)   The Highlands
    (b)   Gairloch Mountain
220 Steep Slopes

REGIONAL CHARACTERISTICS

Northern Cape Breton Island is dominated by a highland block of ancient metamorphic and granitic rocks. Deep valleys, which dissect all sides of the block, are habitat for damp, cool deciduous forests (District 220). On the southward-sloping plateau surface, generally above 300 m, the short growing season and severe climate allow only a Balsam Fir forest to grow (District 210).

GEOLOGY

The rocks of the Highlands reflect a long and complicated geological history. The oldest rocks, located north of Pleasant Bay and the Cabot Trail, are similar to strongly metamorphosed rocks of the Canadian Shield and are about as old (about 1.2 billion years old). The central part of the Highlands contains younger Precambrian and Middle Paleozoic volcanic and sedimentary rocks. Deformation (folding) and metamorphism vary in intensity. The Precambrian rocks include marbles and quartzites, as well as volcanic rocks that were mapped as the George River Group. Late Devonian and Carboniferous rocks rest unconformably on the older rocks.

1. Oldest Rocks in Cape Breton

The Precambrian geological history of the Highlands is complex and represents many periods of deformation and metamorphism. Precambrian rocks were deformed and metamorphosed approximately one billion years ago, and again about 600 to 570 million years ago. Many geologists believe the very high temperature-and-pressure metamorphic rocks of the northwest Highlands, the Blair River Complex, belongs to ancestral "North America." Precambrian metamorphic rocks of the central Highlands were deposited prior to the Late Precambrian deformation and metamorphism of about 600 to 570 million years ago. Late Precambrian to early Cambrian diorites and granites were intruded into the older rocks.

2. Pre–Middle Devonian

The Early and Middle Paleozoic history of the Highlands is somewhat clouded by variable amounts of deformation and metamorphism. Where rocks are somewhat undeformed, the original textures of volcanic and clastic sedimentary rocks are visible. Radiometric dating of the volcanic units show their ages to range from Middle Ordovician and Late Silurian. Granites were intruded in the Ordovician and Late Silurian. Middle Devonian and younger periods of erosion have stripped away some of the older rocks.

3. Middle to Late Devonian

The lack of a strong indication for the Middle to Late Devonian Acadian Orogeny is unique to the Cape Breton Highlands. Elsewhere in Nova Scotia, the Acadian Orogeny was a major folding event created as continental plates collided in the formation of the supercontinent Pangaea. Study of the Highlands indicates that its rocks were deformed and metamorphosed in the Late Silurian, which is not the "usual" Acadian time.

4. Carboniferous Sea

During the long period that Nova Scotia was part of Pangaea, sediments deposited in the Carboniferous Sea eventually covered most or all of the Highlands Region and the adjoining Plateau–Taiga Region. Only occasional remnants of these strata are now found on the highland plateau, such as the late Carboniferous block of Canso sandstone that can be seen near the western entrance to Cape Breton Highlands National Park. During the late Carboniferous, the highland block appears to have moved vertically upwards and deformed the Carboniferous strata. In places, these Carboniferous rocks are domed upward at the margins of the Highlands.

5. Mesozoic Erosion

During the time between the Permian and Cretaceous periods, the Highlands underwent another period of erosion. The Carboniferous strata were stripped from the older rocks and the area now occupied by Region 100 and 200 was part of a planation surface that extended across the Maritimes.

6. Tertiary Uplift and Erosion

During the Tertiary, the planation surface was uplifted and tilted. After that, another period of erosion once more exploited variations in rock resistance across the flat eroded surface. The Cape Breton Highlands are situated on the highest part of the tilted plain and have thus been subjected to the greatest degree of erosive attack.

LANDSCAPE DEVELOPMENT (FAULTING)

Another important element of the morphological character of the Highlands block is the combination of faults found around its margin and crosscutting its interior. The boundaries of the Highlands are in places depositional (where softer Carboniferous strata have been deposited directly onto older metamorphosed rocks) and in places faulted. In either case, erosion has preferentially exploited the softer material and exposed a steep scarp slope at its margins. Faulting has defined the straight sides of the Highlands on the east and west, influencing the angular drainage patterns of many rivers and streams. The two main fault directions are north-northeast and west-northwest, with the former predominating.

The principal fault in the Highlands is the Aspy Fault, which runs southwards from Cape North (see Figure 5). For 40 km its position is shown by a straight escarpment that continues across the Highlands as a straight line of river valleys and reappears on the south side of the Margaree River Valley. The ancient Aspy Fault shows evidence of movements dating back to the Ordovician period. Other faults have also been exploited by rivers which rise well towards the interior of the Highlands and form long, steep-sided and V-shaped valleys at the margins, e.g., Grand Anse River, Ingonish River.

Some upland masses are isolated by faults, for example, Sugar Loaf Mountain in the interior, and Gairloch Mountain on the southerly margin of the Highlands.

CLIMATE

The climate of the Boreal Forest Region in the Cape Breton Highlands is influenced by elevation and by winds blowing off adjacent ocean waters. Its main features are cold long winters, short cool summers, and high precipitation. It differs from the climate of the Plateau–Taiga Region mostly as a result of the lesser impact of the wind (see Region 100).

Because there are no weather stations in the Region, detailed climatic information is not available.

Although the mean annual temperature of less than 5°C is not markedly colder, the daily temperature range is considerably greater than in other areas in the Maritimes. The beginning of winter, as marked by a continuous layer of snow 2.5 cm deep, usually occurs in the Highlands in early or mid-November. Snowfall is heavy, but accumulations are limited by frequent episodes of rain and thawing. Records for weather stations in an adjacent Region at Chéticamp and Ingonish Beach show that mean daily temperatures in January, February, and March are consistently lower at Chéticamp, reflecting the influence of winds that blow mainly from the north and northwest over the frigid, ice-covered waters of the Gulf of St. Lawrence. This east-west difference is also noticeable in parts of the Highlands.

Summer temperatures start to rise sharply in May and fall abruptly in September. Mean daily temperatures in July are somewhat cooler in the Highlands than in most other interior areas of the province.

More than 1600 mm of precipitation falls each year in the highest areas of the Region. Elsewhere, amounts range between 1400 and 1600 mm. The higher precipitation recorded on the eastern side of the Region is evidence of the effects of an Atlantic rain shadow. More than 400 cm of snow falls on most of the area, with lesser amounts being recorded on the Atlantic side because of the slightly warmer winter temperatures. The snow cover melts in late April or May.

This Region is shrouded in fog or low-level clouds many days of the year, and relative humidities are high. Interesting microclimatic features include cold-air drainage and fog in the canyons, and high relative humidity and low sunlight exposure for north-facing cliffs in steep-walled canyons.

The growing season is short, but tree growth is rapid, except where strong winds stunt growth on exposed ridges.

FRESH WATER

The main drainage pattern is radial, and rivers follow the fault lines in the bedrock. The steep-sided river valleys do not develop floodplains or wide intervales until they leave the Highlands; however, an exception to this general rule is the Margaree River, which has a broad intervale extending well into the Highlands.

The few small glacial lakes and wetlands are dystrophic and have low conductivity levels. Biological diversity is also low.

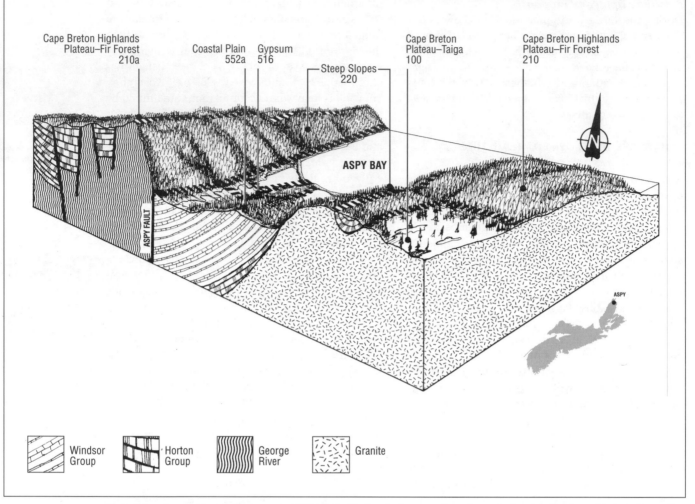

Cape Breton Highlands
Plateau–Fir Forest
210a

Coastal Plain
552a

Gypsum
516

Steep Slopes
220

Cape Breton
Plateau–Taiga
100

Cape Breton Highlands
Plateau–Fir Forest
210

ASPY FAULT

ASPY BAY

N

ASPY

Windsor Group

Horton Group

George River

Granite

Figure 5: Aspy Bay area. The straight, steep scarp (District 220) of the Aspy Fault separates the northern extension of the Cape Breton Highlands Plateau–Fir Forest (District 210) from the Coastal Plain (Unit 552). In the foreground the vegetation of the Cape Breton Plateau–Taiga (Region 100) above 500 m is seen on the granite massif which dominates northern Cape Breton Island.

SOILS

This area was not mapped in the soil survey of Cape Breton Island because of its inaccessibility. However, it is now known that the soils are considerably better than the blanket designation "Rough mountain land" would suggest. The soils are mostly heavily podzolized sandy loams, which are surprisingly deep considering that the underlying rocks are highly resistant. The depth of the soils suggests that the Highlands were protected by a static ice cover during the last glaciation. One interesting feature is the steep slope of the sides of the Highlands plateau surface.

PLANTS

The Cape Breton Highlands Region falls within Loucks' Gaspé–Cape Breton Ecoregion. Balsam Fir, White Birch, and White Spruce are the main species, forming what is essentially the true Boreal Forest Region in Nova Scotia. The main influences on the regional vegetation are cool temperatures, high precipitation, and the effects of wind and insect damage. Because of inaccessibility, cutting was not a major disturbance factor until the 1970s. Since the Spruce Budworm salvage project, large areas of dead Balsam Fir have been removed. Replanting with Black Spruce is taking place in some areas. Stands of fire origin are present but uncommon.

On the slopes fringing the plateau the true boreal forest is replaced by the Acadian Forest association—

shade-tolerant hardwoods along the steep-walled canyons on the eastern and western coasts, and predominantly softwoods on the Atlantic slope in the northeast corner of the Region. The shade-tolerant hardwoods—Yellow Birch, White Birch, and Sugar Maple—are mainly found between 200 m and 300 m above sea level. On the plateau, barrens and bogs are common.

This Region is interesting because of the diversity of floral elements represented. The northernmost limit for Alleghanian tree species (for example, Sugar Maple) in the Atlantic Provinces is found here. Also represented are the arctic-alpine and the Cordilleran elements. The Cordilleran flora in Cape Breton is usually restricted to wooded ravines, or damp, cool deciduous and mixed woods; it is more commonly found in similar cool, moist habitats on the Pacific coast or along the Rocky Mountains.

ANIMALS

The fauna of the Highlands reflects this Region's boreal character and its status as one of the few large areas in Nova Scotia which remain relatively inaccessible. Boreal species such as the moose, Snowshoe Hare, and lynx are found here. Larger carnivores such as bear and perhaps cougar have a large range of undisturbed habitat. Deer are present during summer and fall but are restricted in distribution by the deep snow in winter and spring. Also present here are disjunct species with a generally northern or mountain distribution elsewhere, for example, the Rock Vole and the Gaspé Shrew. Region 200 offers a wide range of habitats, which include more areas of mature woodland, both hardwoods and softwoods, than are found in the other Regions. Other habitats include bogs, barrens, cliffs, and talus slopes.

CULTURAL ENVIRONMENT

The Highlands form a distinct landscape component of Cape Breton, and its many communities are largely of Scottish descent. Where soil was good, farming was undertaken in the early 1800s; however, by 1820 only marginal farmlands were available. Many Scottish migrants later abandoned these less-productive soils, permitting successional forest regeneration. Today, only the best land in this area is farmed, and many communities depend on the sea for a living. Balsam Fir forests on the plateau have been impacted by fires, Spruce Budworm, and, more recently, clearcutting to salvage timber ravaged by budworm infestations. Seasonal hunting continues in this area; however, tourism and recreational activities predominate because of the impressive scenery and wildlife attractions of the Cabot Trail and Cape Breton Highlands National Park. Highlands watersheds were harnessed to create a major hydroelectric power plant in Wreck Cove in the early 1970s.

• • • • • • • •

Associated Topics
T2.1 Introduction to the Geological History of Nova Scotia, T2.3 Granite in Nova Scotia, T3.1 Development of the Ancient Landscape, T5.2 Nova Scotia's Climate, T9.1 Soil-forming Factors, T10.4 Plant Communities in Nova Scotia, T11.9 Carnivores, T11.10 Ungulates.

Associated Habitats
H3 Fresh Water, H4.1 Bog, H5.1 Barren, H5.3 Cliff and Bank, H5.4 Talus Slope, H6.1 Hardwood Forest (Sugar Maple, Yellow Birch, Beech Association), H6.3 Mixedwood Forest (Spruce, Fir–Maple, Birch Association).

210 PLATEAU–FIR FOREST

The Plateau–Fir Forest District is divided into two sub-Districts:
  (a) The Highlands
  (b) Gairloch Mountain

GEOLOGY AND LANDSCAPE DEVELOPMENT

The undulating plateau crest of the Cape Breton Highlands is dissected by faults into two parts: the Highlands (including part of Kellys Mountain) and Gairloch Mountain (an isolated section on the southern fringe). The plateau surface is tilted to the southeast, and the average elevation drops from about 500 m to about 400 m at the edge of the Highlands. This may represent the slope of the original upland surface.

Long periods of erosion on the Cape Breton Plateau have uncovered severely altered rocks which were once deeply buried. These rocks are very hard and resistant, and at present are being eroded very slowly. Even the last glaciation did little to modify the plateau surface. There is some controversy about the exact sequence of events during the Wisconsinan ice advance across Cape Breton, but it appears that the Highlands was covered by an ice-cap at least during the later stages. This ice-cap may have protected the underlying plateau but generated glaciers which radiated down the marginal slopes. The glacial deposits on the plateau surface are dominated by compacted subglacial till. Exposed bedrock may be ice-plucked or display striations. Erratics are common.

Gairloch Mountain is cut off from the southern part of the Highlands by two major faults. The boundaries of this block are sharp and steep where softer rocks have been eroded away. In the northwest, where metamorphic rocks are faulted against resistant early Carboniferous Horton deposits, no steep scarp slope is present. Similarly, on the south side, where there is a depositional boundary with resistant Devonian-Carboniferous rocks, the contact is not topographically distinctive (see Figure 21). However, on the north side, where easily eroded Windsor deposits are set against the metamorphic rocks, a pronounced scarp slope is found.

The maximum elevation of Gairloch Mountain is almost 430 m, about 100 m less than the highest part of the Highlands. This reflects its more southerly, and therefore lower, position on the tilted planation surface.

FRESH WATER

The drainage pattern across the Cape Breton Highlands is radial. Streams flowing on the plateau surface are relatively slow-moving but in their middle sections cascade down the scarp slopes. In many cases the tributary streams appear to follow joint and fault directions very closely; e.g., North Aspy River. Individual brooks flowing down the scarp slopes on the north side are short and straight, whereas those in the south, where there is no escarpment, tend to have branching tributary patterns.

District 210 contains relatively few glacial lakes. Conductivity averages 33 micromhos/cm. The pH in Warren Lake averages 5.8.

Blanket bogs are typical of sub-District 210a; the systems form concentric patterns with some flow between adjacent bogs. Ribbed fens are associated with this type of formation.

PLANTS

The vegetation of the Highlands is characterized by largely even-aged boreal forest, with Balsam Fir, White Birch, and White Spruce as the main species. The main successional agents are windthrow and insect damage, particularly Spruce Budworm. Fire influences are mainly restricted to the area behind Neils Harbour, where pure stands of Jack Pine are found. Elsewhere in the District, pine is uncommon.

Typically, in the central and western Highlands, the Balsam Fir is 50–75 years old. White Birch readily colonizes openings caused by windthrow, but fir eventually reasserts itself. White Spruce is scattered through the forest, and often individual trees are much older (150 years) than the surrounding fir. Most of the Balsam Fir has died following Spruce Budworm infestation in the late 1970s and was replaced by a dense growth of raspberries with some Elderberry. The only tree species able to survive this competition are White Birch, Mountain Ash and Pin Cherry. Eventually the birch shades out the raspberry, enabling Balsam Fir to re-establish itself. Ground vegetation in the mature Balsam Fir forest is often luxuriant. Mountain Maple and Hobblebush frequently form a dense shrub canopy, with ferns, Wood-sorrel, and mosses below. South of the South Aspy River an area dominated by crescent-shaped granite ridges produces a vegetation pattern similar to that found in the Plateau–Taiga Region: barrens on the dry ridge tops, bogs in the depressions, and open stands of Balsam Fir in between.

On the broad, flat plain which slopes down to the Atlantic Ocean between Neils Harbour and Broad Cove, the vegetation has been more influenced by fire and cutting, and is therefore at an earlier successional stage. On the shallow granitic soils, Balsam Fir, Black Spruce, Jack Pine, and White Pine form younger stands, with Bracken Fern underneath.

ANIMALS

The fauna found in this District is, for the most part, characteristically boreal. The Snowshoe Hare is common, but it is subject to cyclic population fluctuations. The Highlands provide one of the last significant refugia for its predator, the lynx. The bobcat is rarely found in the area, and unconfirmed sightings of cougar have been reported. Deer and moose are both present. The moose subspecies *Alces alces andersoni* was introduced to the area and is flourishing. Deer use the area for summer range but generally move to sheltered lower slopes in winter. The brain parasite *Parelaphostrongylus tenuis* has been identified in deer, but the seasonal separation of moose and deer during concentration periods has apparently helped retard its transfer between the species.

A small relict population of Pine Marten existed in northern Cape Breton in the 1980s, but no recent reports are available to confirm its continued existence. The boreal forest does not support large or diverse populations of small mammals.

Spruce Budworm has resulted in many dead and dying trees, changing the habitat structure. Birds that bore into dead wood for insects, particularly woodpeckers, are abundant. Nuthatches are also common. Fish species include Brook Trout and Gaspereau.

SCENIC QUALITY

This area can often appear bleak and forbidding, and where the fir forest is unbroken there is little visual diversity. The infestation of Spruce Budworm is still apparent in many areas. Nevertheless, the presence of bogs and barrens adds variety, and the crests overlooking the deeper valleys have great scenic potential. Those areas accessed by the Cabot Trail and Trans-Canada Highway provide some spectacular viewpoints (see Sites of Special Interest).

CULTURAL ENVIRONMENT

Various parts of the Plateau–Fir Forest have experienced the impact of major fires and heavy Spruce Budworm infestation. Large expanses of affected trees were clearcut as part of a salvage operation in the early 1990s. Although woodlot lumbering has been practised by some residents of these areas, most communities are focused on the resources of the surrounding sea. Seasonal hunting also characterizes land use. The Cabot Trail and the Cape Breton Highlands National Park are key tourism and recreational attractions. Peat resources underlie large expanses of the Plateau–Fir Forest.

• • • • • • • •

Sites of Special Interest
The geological and geomorphological features of most interest in the Cape Breton Plateau–Fir Forest District are:
- the relationships between the metamorphic rocks and intrusive igneous rocks
- the banded schists and gneisses
- faults, fault scarps, and fault valleys
- waterfalls, coastal cliffs, and narrow beaches
- *Geological Highway Map of Nova Scotia* (1980) references:
  68 Near Fox Back Lake—Precambrian granitic rocks and a view of intruding gneisses
  69 Aspy Fault scarp
  71 Green Cove—gneisses intruded by pink and white granites
  73 Cape Smokey Lookoff—Precambrian granite intruded by dark-coloured diabase dykes
  74 Kellys Mountain Viewpoint (St. Anns Lookoff)—a road cut through Precambrian high-grade gneisses from which one can look across fault-controlled St. Anns Harbour to the main mass of the Highlands
- Bras d'Or Lookoff—on Kellys Mountain overlooking Bras d'Or Channel and the Sydney area
- Cabot Trail between Jumping Brook and Pleasant Bay—view of the plateau and an exposure of granite
- North of Chéticamp, near Jerome Mountain—a faulted contact between granite and gneiss
- Cabot Trail, west park entrance—a cliff of Precambrian granite veined with quartz
- Ingonish, Middle Head peninsula—pink granite cutting dark rocks
- Sugar Loaf Mountain—a granite mass rising to more than 460 m

**210
Plateau–Fir
Forest**

- French Mountain Lake (IBP Proposed Ecological Site 17)—raised and sloping bogs, dystrophic lake
- French Mountain Bog (IBP Proposed Ecological Site 18)—good example of species-rich minerotrophic bog

Provincial Parks and Park Reserves
- Kellys Mountain

Proposed Parks and Protected Areas System includes Natural Landscapes 64a, b, c, d, and e and Candidate Protected Areas 1 Pollet Cove–Aspy Fault, 2 Jim Campbells Barren, and 4 French River.

Associated Offshore Unit
915 Sydney Bight.

Associated Topics
T2.4 The Carboniferous Basin, T3.2 Ancient Drainage Patterns, T3.3 Glaciation, Deglaciation and Sea-level Changes, T3.4 Terrestrial Glacial Deposits and Landscape Features, T10.1 Vegetation Change, T10.2 Successional Trends in Vegetation, T10.6 Trees, T10.7 Ferns and Their Allies, T11.2 Forest and Edge-habitat Birds, T11.16 Land and Freshwater Invertebrates, T11.17 Marine Invertebrates, T12.10 Plants and Resources, T12.11 Animals and Resources, T12.12 Recreational Resources.

Associated Habitats
H3.1 Freshwater Open-Water Lotic, H3.3 Freshwater Bottom Lotic, H4.1 Bog, H5.1 Barren, H6.2 Softwood Forest (Pine Association; Balsam Fir Association).

220 STEEP SLOPES

GEOLOGY AND LANDSCAPE DEVELOPMENT

The margins of the Cape Breton Highlands are, for the most part, clearly visible and are marked by steep slopes and deep valleys. In many cases these slopes and valleys have formed along faults where rubbly rocks in the zone of movement have been washed away (see Figure 21).

In those places where the metamorphic rocks of the Highlands have a depositional contact with softer, erodible strata, an abrupt change of relief is produced by differential erosion; e.g., North Bay Ingonish, St. Lawrence Bay, south of the Middle Aspy River. In each of these examples the situation is complicated by faulting.

Unlike the plateau, where the undulating terrain is undergoing little modification, erosion is very active in the slopes and valleys. The steep slopes are frequently covered by talus, the product of cryogenic (freeze-thaw) action. The angle of repose of the talus varies according to its texture and coarseness. Rapid downslope wasting is generally impeded by vegetation, particularly where trees and ground cover stabilize the slope. Slumping occurs in some places where abundant material is present; in other places, downslope movement has produced a line of boulders.

Steep cliffs which rise almost directly from the sea occur where District 220 intersects the coastline. Sediment supply is very sparse and beaches are few and narrow.

**220
Steep
Slopes**

Plate 2: Region 200. Oblique aerial view of the deeply dissected slopes (District 220) of the Cape Breton Highlands landscape in winter. Photo: O. Maass.

FRESH WATER

The drainage pattern is dendritic. Several important rivers flow in fault-controlled valleys; e.g., Margaree, Grand Anse, North Aspy, Warren Brook, Clyburn Brook. Waterfalls are common at the edge of the scarp slopes. The pH levels in Kellys Mountain Brook average between 6.5 and 8.5. Groundwater in the bedrock is soft and corrosive. Groundwater comes to the surface in the colluvial deposits as seeps and springs.

PLANTS

The vegetation of this District is characterized by deciduous woodlands on steep slopes. Eastern Hemlock and White Pine are dominant on the slopes, giving way to early successional White Birch, White Spruce, and Balsam Fir on unstable slopes or valley bottoms. Canyon systems are an important feature of this District. The canyon slopes are often covered with a mantle of colluvial material in which White Birch, Yellow Birch, Sugar Maple, and Balsam Fir grow. Along the western coast, the steep slopes are exposed to the influence of the Gulf of St. Lawrence. White Birch, Yellow Birch, White Spruce, and Pin Cherry are often stunted by salt spray–laden winds. Insects and diseases have dramatically reduced the American Beech in this District.

Where Eastern Hemlock stands occur, usually on the upper slopes, mosses dominate the ground vegetation. Under mature hardwood stands the fern–Striped Maple association is found with a rich diversity of species.

Arctic-alpine and Cordilleran disjunct plants are found in this District, especially on wet, north-facing canyon rock walls and in other shady, moist habitats. These include Rusty, Smooth, and Alpine Woodsia; Common Bladderfern; Willowherb; Western Rattlesnake-plantain; Northern Bedstraw; and Sweet Cicely.

ANIMALS

Habitats for fauna in this District are varied and relatively productive, including mature hardwood forest, conifers, talus slopes, cliffs, and moist valley bottoms. The rich, well-drained soils, deep leaf litter, and varied ground vegetation in the predominantly hardwood district create ideal habitat for small mammals. In fact, the most diverse small-mammal fauna in the entire province is found in the hardwood forests growing on talus slopes. Fourteen of the seventeen insectivore and rodent species known to occur on

Cape Breton Island are found here. These include the Gaspé Shrew and the Rock Vole, relict species normally limited to more northerly regions and higher altitudes. The Rock Vole and Southern Bog Lemming are particularly associated with a combination of talus slope and hardwood forest habitats, like those most frequently found along the eastern side of the District. Although small-mammal populations are diverse, they do not tend to exist in large numbers. However, the weasel is one predator that occurs frequently.

The coniferous forests more commonly found on the western side of the District do not provide good small-mammal habitat.

The steep slopes of 40–45° inhibit the movements of larger mammals, although deer make use of the hardwood browse in more accessible areas.

The diversity of vegetation and the well-developed structural profile of the mature hardwood forest ensure a rich avifauna, dominated by warblers, nuthatches, and woodpeckers. Bald Eagles are common in the eastern areas.

SCENIC QUALITY

This District boasts some of the most spectacular scenery in the province, owing largely to its tremendous range of elevation over short distances (as much as 300 m over one kilometre). Where the mountains meet the sea, as at Jerome Mountain and Cape Smokey, there are excellent coastal panoramas. Fortunately, many of these may be viewed from scenic lookoffs along the Cabot Trail. The deep interior valleys of the Aspy, Chéticamp, Ingonish, Northeast Margaree, and other major rivers and streams provide drama and mystery, and offer waterfalls and rapids. Mature deciduous stands, particularly those of beech, are an added attraction. Only the Aspy River valley is accessible by paved road.

CULTURAL ENVIRONMENT

Forests of the Steep Slopes have been impacted by fire. The Pleasant Bay fire of 1947 transformed much of this landscape for a period of time. Steep highland inclines proved a major challenge to the construction of the Cabot Trail, which was completed in 1932 but later considerably upgraded and improved. Slopes buttressing river-valley farmlands were sometimes cleared for pastureland; however, much of this farmland was abandoned and subsequently experienced oldfield regeneration to White Spruce. The old French name for Cape Smokey was "Cape Enfumé," so named because of the clouds of mist which often cloak this area. Northern slopes of Cape Smokey were cleared to build a ski hill in 1970. In the early 1970s the Wreck Cove power plant was built, harnessing the hydro power of highland watersheds. In Mi'kmaq culture, the Fairy Hole cave in Kellys Mountain is believed to be Kluscap's (Glooscap's) final home before he left the Earth World behind.

• • • • • • •

Sites of Special Interest
- Indian Brook—waterfall
- Grand Anse River (IBP Proposed Ecological Site 19)—old Sugar Maple stand in the steeply sloping valley (possibly typical of pre-settlement forest); rare arctic-alpine plants including Green Spleenwort
- North Aspy River (IBP Proposed Ecological Site 21)—old Sugar Maple forest
- French River (IBP Proposed Ecological Site 22)—old mixedwood forest, cliffs, and talus slopes
- Oregon (IBP Proposed Ecological Site 23)—old Eastern Hemlock stand above North River
- Second Fork Brook (IBP Proposed Ecological Site 15)—old Sugar Maple stand, waterfall (Margaree River)
- Lone Shieling Black House—trail system through hardwood forest

Provincial Parks and Park Reserves
- Cape Smokey
- North River
- South Lake-O-Law

Proposed Parks and Protected Areas System includes Natural Landscapes 69, 70, 71, and 76, and Candidate Protected Areas 1 Pollets Cove–Aspy Fault, 3 Margaree River, 4 French River, 5 Sugarloaf Mountain, 6 Middle River, and 7 North River.

Scenic Viewpoints
- Cabot Trail (paved road): Lookoffs at Presqu'ile, Cap Rouge, Pleasant Bay, Aspy River, Cape Smokey
- Trails: Chéticamp River, Aspy River, Clyburn Brook, Cape Smokey, North River

Associated Offshore Units
914 Northumberland Strait, 915 Sydney Bight.

Associated Topics
T2.2 The Avalon and Meguma Zones, T2.3 Granite in Nova Scotia, T2.4 The Carboniferous Basin, T3.1 Development of the Ancient Landscape, T4.2 Post-glacial Colonization by Plants, T7.3 Coastal Landforms, T8.1 Freshwater Hydrology, T8.2 Freshwater Environments, T9.1 Soil-forming Factors, T10.4 Plant Communities in Nova Scotia, T10.6 Trees, T10.7 Ferns and Their Allies, T10.8 Mosses, Liverworts and Hornworts, T10.12 Rare and Endangered Plants, T11.2 Forest and Edge-habitat Birds, T11.3 Open-habitat Birds, T11.10 Ungulates, T11.11 Small Mammals, T.12.8 Fresh Water and Resources.

Associated Habitats
H3.1 Freshwater Open-Water Lotic, H3.3 Freshwater Bottom Lotic, H4.1 Bog, H5.3 Cliff and Bank, H5.4 Talus Slope, H6.1 Hardwood Forest (Maple, Oak, Birch Association; Sugar Maple, Yellow Birch, Beech Association), H6.2 Softwood Forest (Spruce, Hemlock, Pine Association; Balsam Fir Association), H6.3 Mixedwood Forest (White Spruce, Fir–Maple, Birch Association).

220 Steep Slopes

300
Avalon Uplands

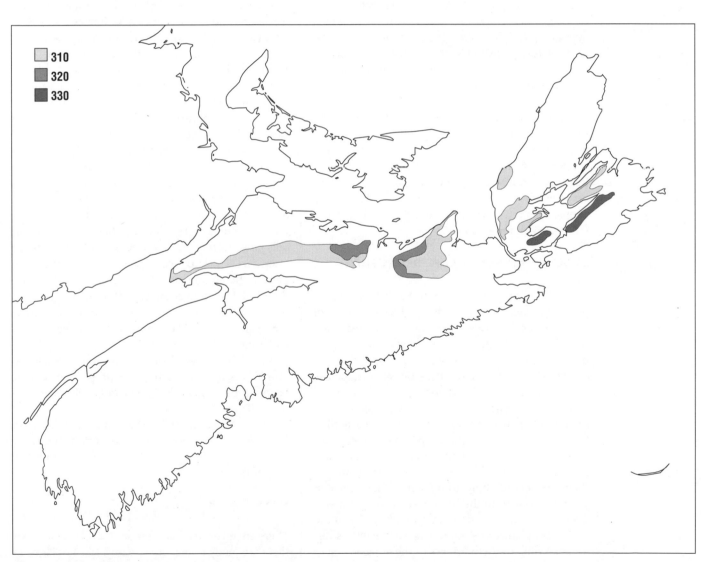

310
320
330

Figure 6: Region 300, Avalon Uplands, and its component Districts.

300 AVALON UPLANDS

Region 300 is divided into three Districts on the basis of geology, geomorphology, elevation, and climate:

310 Hardwood Plateau
320 Dissected Margins
330 Fault Ridges

REGIONAL CHARACTERISTICS

These uplands experience more severe winters, greater precipitation, and shorter growing seasons than the surrounding lowlands, but climatic conditions are not as harsh as in the Cape Breton highlands. The climate of this Region is reflected in the dominant hardwood vegetation characterized by a Sugar Maple, Yellow Birch–Fir association. Six of the eight plateaus (District 310) which compose the Region are sharply defined, with level plateau surfaces at elevations between 100 and 300 m above sea level. Margins of the plateaus generally fall abruptly, 100 m or more, with little dissection by stream valleys. The remaining two uplands (District 330) are at lower elevations and have a less severe climate and a greater proportion of softwood trees. Mainland parts of this Region are bordered by ancient sedimentary rocks on which soils are deeper and river valleys more deeply carved (District 320). All of these uplands provide excellent moose ranges.

GEOLOGY AND LANDSCAPE DEVELOPMENT

The blocks are made up of very resistant metamorphic and igneous rocks, among which are some of the most ancient rocks in Nova Scotia. In most cases, the blocks are bounded and crosscut by faults. At the margins these give steep scarp slopes; within the blocks, where harder and softer strata are juxtaposed, they produce rugged hills and valleys.

The crests of the blocks are often narrow and dissected but are usually uniform in height along their length. Their height relationship is cited as evidence for a Cretaceous planation surface. The crests progressively decrease in elevation southeastwards as they intersect an almost uniform surface now dissected and tilted to the southeast. Subsequent erosion has removed soft strata and left the resistant blocks as uplands. The prominence of the blocks varies according to the hardness of the adjacent rocks and their position on the tilted peneplain.

CLIMATE

Elevation is the dominant influence on the climate of this somewhat diverse Region. The climate in different areas is modified by proximity to water masses. The main climatic features are wide daily and seasonal temperature ranges, and high precipitation, especially snowfall.

Winters are generally long and cold. Because of their greater elevation, the Cobequids record the coldest temperatures within the Region. The uplands south and east of the Bras d'Or Lake are slightly warmer than the rest of the Region because of lower elevations and the moderating influence of the Bras d'Or Lake and the Atlantic Ocean. Spring is late, although somewhat earlier in the Bras d'Or area. Mean temperatures do not rise above 0°C until April. Summer temperatures are cool at the higher elevations, but warmer towards Cape Breton. Freezing temperatures return before the end of November in the Cobequid Hills and Antigonish Highlands, and one or two weeks later in Cape Breton.

Total annual precipitation exceeds 1200 mm in the mainland. The Region is noticeably wetter in Cape Breton, where precipitation exceeds 1400 mm. Snowfall is greatest on the highest parts of the Mainland, exceeding 300 cm. In Cape Breton, 200–250 cm falls close to the Bras d'Or Lake, and over 250 cm elsewhere. The snow-cover season follows the same pattern, being longer in the mainland areas (more than 140 days) and somewhat shorter (130 days) in the rest of the Region. In midwinter, snow accumulations of more than 40 cm occur in the Cobequid Hills and Antigonish Highlands.

Cloud cover occurs frequently, and the relative humidity is high. Exposure to wind is an important factor at the highest elevations and in areas close to the Gulf of St. Lawrence.

The main features of the bioclimate of the Avalon Uplands are the short frost-free period, the short growing season, cool moist summers, and low evapotranspiration.

FRESH WATER

There are relatively few lakes across this Region, but there are many rivers and streams. Most uplands in this Region tend to function as drainage divides for watershed areas. The headwaters are not especially productive.

SOILS

The main influences on soils in this Region are the high precipitation, the presence of somewhat more basic igneous rocks, steep terrain that provides good drainage, and a prevalence of deciduous trees. Soils here are strongly leached but in many areas have higher natural fertility than soils found on the more acid upland rock. Soils are usually well-drained, shallow, and stony sandy loams, often of the Ferro-Humic Podzol Great Group. Because of low evapotranspiration, substantial levels of organic matter accumulate in the upper layers. Leaf litter from the hardwood forests develops into a mull or moder humus form.

C.D. Howe made the following observations on soil-forest relationships in 1912: "The felsites and syenites are similar to granites ... they vary in hardness, and the softer forms give rise to very vigorous soils which rank with alluvial soils in fertility, while the harder forms results in a soil similar in fertility to that of the more compact sandstones. They are, therefore, feeble soils."

The more recent Cumberland County Soil Survey (1973) reports: "The somewhat higher base status derived from ferro-magnesian minerals may have something to do with the prevalence of hardwood trees in the Cobequid Mountains and the rich undergrowth there, but this effect is difficult to separate from the adverse effect of exposure on the conifers."

PLANTS

Most of the Region falls within Loucks' Sugar Maple, Yellow Birch–Fir Zone and these are the predominant species. Parts of the Region south and east of the Bras d'Or Lake are in the Sugar Maple–Hemlock, Pine Zone. The major influences on the regional vegetation are the fertile soils, cold winters and cool summers, good drainage, and relative lack of disturbance. The high elevation and well-drained fertile sites favour hardwoods or mixed woods, with softwoods appearing on poorly drained sites and cool, moist ravine slopes and valley bottoms. Shallow soils on parts of the plateau surfaces support only Balsam Fir with lesser amounts of spruce.

Sugar Maple, American Beech, and Yellow Birch are the main species on the hills. White Spruce, Red Spruce (mainly in the Cobequid Hills), and Balsam Fir form mixed or softwood stands on valley slopes, while Black Spruce, White Spruce, scattered Eastern Hemlock, and White Pine predominate on the valley bottoms. A prominent feature in this Region is the vigorous shrub growth, particularly of Mountain Maple, Witch Hazel, and Hobblebush. This shrub community develops in cut-overs and insect-killed stands, with the prominent addition of *Rubus* spp. Following disturbance, shade-intolerant hardwoods are found throughout but are more prevalent on lower slopes, mixed with spruce and fir. There are few bogs in this Region, but seepage sites are common.

Plants of the Alleghanian floral element, whose main range is further south, are associated with intervale habitat in this Region.

ANIMALS

This Region provides a range of forested habitats but does not have significant aquatic habitats. It includes large areas which are relatively undisturbed and inaccessible, and provide good habitat for ungulates, bears, and the larger carnivores.

CULTURAL ENVIRONMENT

Specific sites by the Bras d'Or Lake were Mi'kmaq burial grounds, and these spots continue to be important to the Mi'kmaq today. In general, highland areas such as the Avalon Uplands were settled by Scots in the first half of the nineteenth century, when fertile valley lands were no longer available. Farmlands were established as forests were cleared; however, most emigrants were squatters on the land. According to the 1851 census, many backland settlers had cleared 10–20 acres, enough to pasture cows, sheep, goats and horses and to grow essential crops. Soils were often only marginally productive. For the majority of these highland emigrants, seasonal employment was sought in the Sydney coal mines, the fishery (particularly with American vessels fishing in the Gulf), and selling timber stripped from unprotected Crown land. Poor livelihoods and meagre agricultural potential led backland settlers to abandon their farmlands; consequently, successional forest regeneration of the land took place. Today, a limited amount of farming is practised. A century ago, 100,000 sheep roamed the uplands and meadows of Cape Breton but, with the waning of rural life, by the 1970s only 2,700 animals remained. Upland areas are now used for commercial maple syrup production and mining ventures; however, forestry is the dominant economic land use. The impressive upland scenery of these environs has attracted recreation and tourism.

**300
Avalon
Uplands**

• • • • • • • •

Associated Topics

T2.1 Introduction to the Geological History of Nova Scotia, T2.2 The Avalon and Meguma Zones, T2.4 The Carboniferous Basin, T3.1 Development of the Ancient Landscape, T4.2 Post-glacial Colonization by Plants, T5.2 Nova Scotia's Climate, T9.1 Soil-forming Factors, T10.4 Plant Communities in Nova Scotia, T10.6 Trees, T11.10 Ungulates, T12.2 Cultural Landscapes, T12.10 Plants and Resources.

Associated Habitats

H3.1 Freshwater Open-Water Lotic, H3.3 Freshwater Bottom Lotic, H6.1 Hardwood Forest (Sugar Maple, Yellow Birch, Beech Association), H6.2 Softwood Forest (Spruce, Fir, Pine Association; Spruce, Fir Association), H6.3 Mixedwood Forest (Spruce, Fir, Pine–Maple, Birch Association).

310 HARDWOOD PLATEAU

District 310 has four Units, two on the mainland and two in Cape Breton, each with its own distinctive geological and geomorphological features:

311 Cobequid Hills
312 Pictou-Antigonish Highlands
313 North Bras d'Or Uplands
   (a)   Creignish Hills
   (b)   North Mountain
   (c)   Boisdale Hills
314 Mabou Highlands

GEOLOGY

A number of fault blocks are grouped within this District in northern mainland Nova Scotia and Cape Breton, and are positioned on the up-tilted, northern side of the planation surface. The highest elevations of each block are between 275 and 340 m. A similar elevation and northerly position on the planation surface give areas within the District common climatic characteristics. At these elevations the plateau is characterized by hardwoods. This District also includes areas of lower elevation, down to 200 m, in which softwoods occur.

SCENIC QUALITY

These plateaus have similar qualities, because they possess similar topography, range of relief, and vegetation. The smaller units (Mabou Highlands and North Mountain) possess little or no plateau top and thus offer throughout what is available only on the margins of the other uplands: high relief, incised river valleys, and panoramic views of surrounding lowlands. Though the forest land cover is unrelieved by lakes or fields, the broadleaf trees are scenically distinctive and display spectacular autumn colour. Waterfalls are another interesting landscape element and occur most frequently in the Mabou Highlands and on the faulted southern scarp of the Cobequid Hills. Scenic quality is very high where these uplands overlook the ocean or large lakes, as on the Mabou coast, along the West Bay of Bras d'Or Lake, and along the shores of Cobequid Bay and Minas Channel.

Plate 3: Region 300. View from the Parrsboro area looking north towards the Cobequid Hills (Unit 311). The uniform hilltops of this landscape represent the ancient erosion surface. Photo: R. Lloyd.

311 COBEQUID HILLS

GEOLOGY

The Cobequid Hills are the surface expression of a steep-sided, elongated fault block—a slice of Avalon crust—which forms a highland on the north side of the Minas Basin. It is a resistant massif surrounded by more easily eroded and low-lying Carboniferous and Triassic sediments (see Figure 19). The geology of the Cobequid Hills is dominated by metamorphosed sediments, granites, and volcanic deposits which range in age from Precambrian to Devonian. These have been crushed, folded, and faulted. Geological complexity is manifest in the rapid changes of rock type within short distances.

Precambrian Basement Rocks

The oldest rocks are those of the Bass River Complex, found from Economy River to Nuttby and in the Central New Annan area, and the Mount Thom Complex, exposed at Mount Thom. These rocks were originally sedimentary and volcanic deposits but have been metamorphosed to schists and gneisses. They form part of the Precambrian basement upon which deposition took place in the Silurian. Included in this basement are altered granites which were intruded during obscure early phases of crustal upheaval.

Overlying Sedimentary Rocks

There are no Cambrian strata in the Cobequid Hills, but deposition appears to have been continuous from the Silurian through the Devonian and Carboniferous.

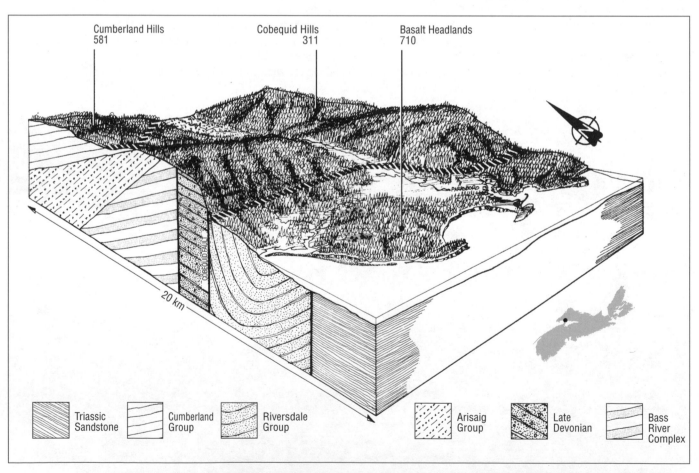

Cumberland Hills
581

Cobequid Hills
311

Basalt Headlands
710

20 km

| Triassic Sandstone | Cumberland Group | Riversdale Group | Arisaig Group | Late Devonian | Bass River Complex |

Figure 7: Parrsboro shore area. The Cobequid Hills (Unit 311), part of the Avalon Uplands, descend abruptly along the Cobequid Fault to the lowlands fringing the Minas Basin. To the north, in contrast, the Cobequids merge gradually into the Cumberland Hills (Unit 581). Headlands of basalt along the Minas Basin separate bays carved from the less-resistant Riversdale shales and Triassic sandstones of the Fundy Coast (District 710).

Many different rock types are present. The earlier, Silurian deposits of fossiliferous siltstone and shale are interleaved with various types of volcanic deposits such as ash (tuff) and flows (ignimbrites and lavas). These give way to younger (Devonian) non-fossiliferous red beds, which can be correlated to the Knoydart Formation in the Pictou-Antigonish area. The red beds were deposited in shallow, fresh water and are thought to represent the retreat of the sea prior to the Acadian crustal collision which led to the formation of Pangaea. Middle Devonian deposits include more volcanic rocks. Late Devonian strata include coarse sediments which continue into the Carboniferous.

Acadian Orogeny

The Acadian Orogeny caused the crushed and folded sediments to begin melting and mobilizing deep within the crust. The resulting granitic liquid rose and cooled, forming large intrusive bodies. These granites, together with their older counterparts, now represent more than 40 per cent of the bedrock underlying the Cobequid Hills.

Surface Exposure of the Fault Block

Although the Cobequid Hills have ancient origins, they did not become a topographic feature until after the Cretaceous. The block appears to have begun moving vertically upwards via fault movement during the Carboniferous, but was deeply covered by sediment at that time. Unlike other areas in the Avalon Uplands, it did not form an island in the Carboniferous Sea.

The block lies on the upper side of the uplifted planation surface and has remained as a resistant highland while the surrounding softer Carboniferous and Triassic sediments have been stripped away (see Figure 7).

LANDSCAPE DEVELOPMENT

The Cobequid Hills form a cigar-shaped block about 120 km long, 15 km wide, and on average 275 m high. The crest is a narrow, featureless plateau which ends abruptly at faulted margins on both the north and south sides. The western extremity is the granite headland of Cape Chignecto (see Figure 9).

Faults

The southern boundary is the scarp of the Cobequid Fault, which is the westerly continuation of the Chedabucto Fault. This fault, which can be traced from Truro to Cape Chignecto, is obscure in the east, but in the west it has a steep and prominent scarp

slope. The fault zone is best exposed along the beach just west of Port Greville. It is also visible at Bass River as a 100-m band of crushed rock. East of Parrsboro it appears as a series of high cliffs and steep hills that are skirted by the road. From Parrsboro to Diligent River, the highway follows the contact between the resistant older rocks on the north side and the Carboniferous lowlands to the south. Beyond Fox River, the fault follows the north shore of the Minas Channel, becomes obscure around Advocate, and runs seaward off high cliffs at Cape Chignecto.

The northern boundary of the Cobequid Hills runs from Earltown to River Philip. Although there is an abrupt drop to the rolling northern plain, the slope descends more by a series of steps than as high cliffs. The fault on the northern side is covered by Carboniferous deposits.

Within the Cobequid Hills, other east-west faults divide the block into long slices, but these have little topographic expression because they are juxtaposed rocks of similar hardness.

The crest of the Cobequid Hills is relatively even and undissected, except for two places where it is crosscut by major valleys: the Parrsboro and Folly gaps. The Parrsboro and Folly gaps are believed to be the abandoned valleys of rivers which at one time may have flowed southwards from the Gulf of St. Lawrence. They were superimposed upon the massif as it rose and became exposed, and they cut deep channels across its surface. The remnants of these rivers now flow northwards and may be represented by River Hebert and the Wallace River. The floors of the Parrsboro and Folly gaps are covered by glacial debris, including thick deposits of gravel. Folly Lake has formed between dams of gravel at either end of the valley. Water seeps through on both sides to form the headwaters of the Wallace and Folly rivers.

Along the sides of the Parrsboro Gap are glacio-fluvial gravel terraces and kames. Other kames and kame terraces in the centre of the valley cut off several small lakes.

FRESH WATER

The Cobequid Hills form a drainage divide across northern mainland Nova Scotia. Primary tributaries tend to run north-south. The Region contains the headwaters for many watercourses draining to the Bay of Fundy and the Northumberland Strait, including the Folly, Portapique, Economy, and Chiganois rivers. The streams rise in the lakes and bogs on the till-blanketed crest and then plunge down the scarp slopes in waterfalls, cascades, and straight, steep-sided gorges. The falls and gorges are most spectacular on the south side; e.g., along the Economy, Moose, Bass, and Portapique rivers. On the north side, falls can be seen east and west of New Annan. The valleys tend to be wider on the north side. In some cases, a new channel has been cut in the centre of a wider, shallow valley; e.g., along the Folly River where the river occupies a central narrow gorge 20–30 m deep.

The small headwater lakes, bogs, and swamps are relatively infertile. Conductivity ranges between 16 and 62 micromhos/cm and pH averages 6.8.

SOILS

The soils derived from the igneous and metamorphic rocks in this Unit are stony, usually shallow, and extremely acidic, gravelly, sandy loams. Over large areas the bedrock is within 0.5 m of the surface, and rock outcrops are common. The Cobequid series covers most of the area. This well-drained, sandy loam is an excellent forest soil, providing a porous but solid rooting medium. The cool, moist climate is responsible for the accumulation of colloidal organic matter in these soils. Wyvern soils are found along the northern edge of the Cobequid Hills. These soils are similar in many ways to the Cobequid series. Significant areas of Wyvern soils were accessible to early settlers who cleared the land; some is now reverting to forest while the rest is being used for blueberry production. Small areas of Hebert soils (well to excessively drained gravelly, sandy loams) are found on glacio-fluvial sands and gravels around lakes.

PLANTS

The plateau top of the Cobequids now supports a Sugar Maple, Yellow Birch, and American Beech forest interlaced on shallow soils with Balsam Fir and Red and Black Spruce. The poorly drained depressions support Balsam Fir and Black Spruce.

The northern part of the plateau has the purest stands of hardwoods. Conifers become increasingly common to the south, especially Red Spruce and Balsam Fir. The influence of the Bay of Fundy can be seen towards the west where extensive stands of Red Spruce thrive up to 200 m above sea level. Parts of the plateau in Cumberland County that were once cleared for agriculture are now blueberry fields. Other fields were created recently by clearing woodlands. Oldfields have come back in coniferous stands dominated by White Spruce.

Eastern Hemlock is common in ravines. White Spruce, Red Spruce, and Balsam Fir form mixed woods with Sugar Maple, Yellow Birch, and Red Ma-

ple on the slopes, becoming softwood forests of Black Spruce, White Spruce, and White Pine in the valley bottoms.

Exposure to wind affects a large part of the Unit. Red Spruce and Yellow Birch are particularly susceptible and may be stunted.

In 1912, C.D. Howe observed: "On the granite north of Advocate bay [there is] a luxuriant forest which contains 75 percent red spruce. The same type is found on the granite mass north of Greville bay. From there, the outcrops of this group of rocks occur only in small patches, until the Cobequid hills are reached, where they are found in largest mass. The northern slopes of the Cobequid hills in the neighborhood of Wentworth, for example, support at the base a mixed forest of hardwoods and red spruce, fir and hemlock, in which softwoods originally predominated. As one ascends the slopes the forest becomes prevailingly of the hardwood type. In some places it is two-thirds yellow birch; in other places it is about equally divided between yellow birch, hard maple and beech. Near the top of the slopes one often finds narrow ridges which are covered to the extent of ninety percent with beech of inferior quality. In the higher levels frequently immense hopper-like basins are found nearly enclosed by ridges. In these, the forest is composed in nearly equal proportions of balsam fir, red spruce and the hardwoods. In the narrow valleys of the streams on the other hand, hemlock, spruce and fir prevail in the order named, so that looking at the northern slopes of Cobequid from a distance, one sees the green of the prevailing hardwoods interspersed with black bands of coniferous softwood foliage."

Ground and shrub vegetation is usually varied and luxuriant. A number of unusual arctic-alpine and Alleghanian plant species may be found in cool, moist ravines and in rich Sugar Maple woods.

ANIMALS

In winter, the accumulation of snow and the more-open deciduous forest forces deer to migrate off the Cobequid Hills to the south-facing lower slopes. The deer then return in May to mature hardwood habitats to feed on spring flowers. The Cobequid Hills support good moose populations year-round. Softwood forests on poorly drained soils are used by moose for winter cover. It is thought that the winter separation of moose and deer lessens the transfer of a central-nervous-system nematode parasite from deer carriers to the moose.

Animals and plants characteristic of fertile wetlands are not abundant in this Region. Steep watercourses and small, relatively unproductive headwater ponds and bogs disfavour their establishment. Low-energy drainage systems on the crest are inhabited by beaver, but sparse food and harsh climate usually limit populations. Bobcats and, more recently coyotes, hunt the softwood swamps for Snowshoe Hare.

Maple and Yellow Birch forests provide an excellent opportunity for animals dependent on tree cavities and fallen logs. The erythristic (all-red) colour phase of the Eastern Redback Salamander is commonly found in the hardwood forest.

The scarcity of active farmland results in the virtual absence of most open-country birds, and the predominance of hardwoods may restrict the occurrence of some birds characteristic of softwood forests. However, the Great Horned Owl is known to nest in the softwoods on top of the hills and in the hardwood slopes below them. Goshawk, Red-tailed Hawk, and Barred Owl also nest in this Unit. In winter, bird life is relatively scarce except for possible sightings of Common Raven, Pileated Woodpecker, and Ruffed Grouse in the hardwoods. Grey Jay and chickadees proliferate in the softwoods. Many species of warbler and other insectivorous birds can be seen here in the summer.

Brook Trout is the predominant fish species, but Brown Trout and Atlantic Salmon are also found in many small headwater streams.

Unit 311 meets the coast at Cape Chignecto, where one sees various marine birds and Grey Seal. Cliffs in this area are monitored as possible nesting sites for Peregrine Falcon.

CULTURAL ENVIRONMENT

Much of the Cobequids Hills was logged in the early 1900s. A second wave of forestry is now occurring with increasing construction of forest-access roads and clearcuts. The new route for the Trans-Canada Highway also passes through this Unit. Such activity may favour some wildlife species and possibly negatively affect some other, old forest–dependent species. Sugar Maple stands in the Cobequid Hills have also been used for the commercial production of maple syrup. In some areas, such as Mount Thom, forests were cleared for farmlands that are still in use. Road construction has been challenged by the Cobequid Hills, with passages like the Folly Gap providing important routing points. Tracts of woodland have been cleared for commercial blueberry production.

• • • • • • • •

Sites of Special Interest
• Road from Highway 104 to Lornevale—shallow iron deposits 800 m north of Cobequid Fault
• Londonderry—iron-bearing carbonates formed the foundation of an iron industry in the nineteenth century
• Folly Gap—U-shaped glaciated valley best seen near Wentworth is a relic of the ancient drainage system
• Folly Lake—glacial lake
• Parrsboro Gap—the channel cuts Unit 311, draining the River Hebert north and the Parrsboro River south; glacial terraces and kames
• Economy River, Bass River, Moose River, Tatamagouche—waterfalls
• Portapique River—cascades and gorge
• Nuttby Mountain—lookoff
• Bass River—Cobequid Fault zone of crushed rock
• Greville Bay and Cape Chignecto—cliff exposure of Cobequid Fault
• Lynn Mountain—mature deciduous forest with characteristic flora
• Eatonville—junction of Units 311, 532, and 581

Provincial Parks and Park Reserves
• Simpson Lake, Cape Chignecto

Proposed Parks and Protected Areas System includes Natural Landscape 23, and Candidate Protected Areas include 24 Economy River and 25 Portipique River.

Scenic Viewpoints
• Wentworth Valley, Sugarloaf Mountain, Parrsboro Valley, Greville Bay, Five Islands Provincial Park, Portapique River, Economy River (falls), Moose River (falls).

Associated Offshore Unit
912 Outer Bay of Fundy.

Associated Topics
T2.2 The Avalon and Meguma Zones, T2.4 The Carboniferous Basin, T3.2 Ancient Drainage Patterns, T3.4 Terrestrial Glacial Deposits and Landscape Features, T8.1 Freshwater Hydrology, T10.12 Rare and Endangered Plants, T11.4 Birds of Prey, T11.12 Marine Mammals, T12.10 Plants and Resources.

Associated Habitats
H3.1 Freshwater Open-Water Lotic, H3.3 Freshwater Bottom Lotic, H5.2 Oldfield, H6.1 Hardwood Forest (Sugar Maple, Yellow Birch, Beech Association).

312 PICTOU-ANTIGONISH HIGHLANDS

GEOLOGY

The Pictou-Antigonish Highlands are underlain by a block of old crustal rocks which are bounded and transected by numerous faults. The Unit stands at an average elevation of 245 m but is dissected into steep-sided hills and valleys where faults cut across the resistant massif. The two most important faults are the Hollow Fault in the northwest and the Cobequid-Chedabucto Fault on the south. These two faults accommodated extensive lateral slip motion as the crustal sections were slipping into place during the formation of Nova Scotia.

The strata within the Pictou-Antigonish fault block are dislocated and do not form a neat succession. However, when pieced together like a jigsaw puzzle, they provide an almost continuous record of the geological evolution of this section of Nova Scotia. This can be correlated with parts of Cape Breton, the Cobequid Hills, and other areas further south along the Atlantic seaboard.

Early Geological Events
The oldest strata are of the Precambrian Georgeville Group, which consists of volcanic and sedimentary rocks many thousands of metres thick. These rocks are intruded by fine-grained igneous rocks that are believed to be the necks of ancient volcanoes. Sugarloaf Hill south of Malignant Cove is an example of a volcanic neck. This early period of vulcanism ended with crustal disturbance and metamorphism that may have been part of the Taconic Orogeny during the Ordovician.

Marine Sediments at Arisaig
Between the Taconic and Acadian orogenies (Silurian to Devonian) came a period of continuous deposition in a shallow sea. During this time the Avalon Zone was developing far distant from the Meguma sediments, which had already accumulated off the coast of Africa (or South America). The richly fossiliferous strata which accumulated in this shallow sea are exposed west of Arisaig Point and contain brachiopods, graptolites, pelecypods, trilobites, crinoids, cephalopods, ostracods, and bryozoans. These fossils are well preserved and have been very significant in tracing the history of the Avalon Zone and relating it to other parts of eastern North America.

Freshwater Deposits
The succession of strata ended with the shallow accumulation of water-lain deposits. The youngest are the red beds of the Knoydart Formation (exposed along the road between McArras Brook and Dunmaglass, 5 km to the south). These contain the remains of freshwater fish which have been correlated with similar strata in Europe. It appears that the North American and European crustal plates may have drifted together by this time, initiating the formation of Pangaea and the onset of the Acadian Orogeny.

Acadian Orogeny
During this orogeny, the pile of sediments was uplifted and granite was intruded. The Pictou-Antigonish block rose along the major fault lines and initially formed a topographic high. Later it became an island in the Carboniferous Sea and was eventually engulfed by Carboniferous sediments. Still later, erosion caused readjustment to take place along the numerous fault lines, which in turn produced a "jumbling" of the strata.

LANDSCAPE DEVELOPMENT

The northern border of the Pictou-Antigonish Highlands is the scarp of the Hollow Fault, which extends from Cape George almost to New Glasgow. Beyond this to the west it joins the Cobequid-Chedabucto Fault. Along the Hollow Fault is a 200-m scarp which has developed as a result of differential erosion since the Tertiary. The old strata of the highlands are much more resistant to erosion than those surrounding them. The scarp is conspicuous south of Piedmont. Further northeast, between Baileys Brook and Doctors Brook, the fault lies in a long, straight valley with a very high, steep southern margin. Along the valley flow the tributaries of several rivers, which turn abruptly northwestwards and drain into the Northumberland Strait. The valley, called "The Hollow" or "Bruin's Highway," has eroded from the softer or broken strata within the fault zone. From Malignant Cove to Cape George, the Hollow Fault forms high cliffs along the straight coastline.

Within the body of the fault block many subsidiary faults crosscut in north-south and northeast-southwest directions. Narrow valleys have formed along some of these lines, particularly where softer strata have been downfaulted, for example, east from Kenzieville. This valley was deepened during the Pleistocene and now contains deposits of sand and gravel which create a uniform grade. Some valleys are ancient landscape features which are now being exhumed as the Carboniferous infilling strata are being stripped away. An example of such a fossil valley is found at Marshy Hope and along the Eden River. Another valley near Kenzieville lies along the length of the Kenzieville Trough—a downfolded section of the Arisaig Formation.

Around the borders of the Pictou-Antigonish Highlands, the prominence of the scarp slope reflects the different hardnesses of adjacent strata. Where soft Windsor sediments are set against the resistant block, the scarp is prominent; where harder Horton strata are juxtaposed, the scarp has a diminished expression.

The southern boundary of the Highlands is the Cobequid-Chedabucto Fault; here the block is set against Horton strata (see Figure 18). The topography of this margin is rugged. The scarp reaches 180 m in places and is cut by deep valleys where other fault lines create lines of weakness; e.g., along Garden River to Eden Lake, and along Moose River, Beaver River, and Campbells Brook. The height of the scarp in part reflects the vertical movement (in addition to the extensive horizontal movement) along this major fault.

FRESH WATER

The drainage pattern is generally dendritic but is heavily influenced by fault lines. Along the margins, streams and rivers flow down the scarp slope in straight narrow channels. Unlike the Cobequid Hills, there are no wind gaps across the Pictou-Antigonish Highlands as evidence of superimposed drainage. Surface water consists mainly of rivers and streams; there are very few lakes. Conductivity in the streams ranges between 28 and 54 micromhos/cm and pH averages 6.4.

SOILS

Four major soil associations occur in this area. Cobequid soils occupy the southeastern sector of Pictou County. These are stony loams or sandy loam soils developed on a variety of tills derived from diorite, felsite, syenite, and granite. Barney River soils have developed on shaly loam tills derived principally from Silurian shales, while Kirkmount soils around North Bloomfield have developed on tills derived from schists, hard sandstones, and slates. Well-drained Thom soils have developed on tills derived from sandstone and hard metamorphic rocks.

Because of the elevation and low evapotranspiration, all these soils tend to have accumulated substantial levels of organic matter in the surface layers. Most are stony and shallow to bedrock. The Barney series is somewhat less stony and is also somewhat finer textured than the others.

PLANTS

Mainly shade-tolerant hardwood forest covers this Unit, with Yellow Birch, Sugar Maple, and American Beech being most common. Red Spruce, White Spruce, Eastern Hemlock, and Balsam Fir are scattered on the upland surfaces and form coniferous stands on the lower slopes and valley bottoms. Red Spruce is less common towards the eastern side of the Unit. White Spruce has colonized old farmlands in the area. As in Unit 311, the shrub layer is diverse and vigorous.

An historical perspective on the evolution of the forests is supplied by C.D. Howe, who wrote in 1912: "This large mass of felsites and syenites ... supports a mixed, thoroughly culled forest. The eastern slopes along the Upper Ohio river southeast of Antigonish are quite abrupt and are covered with a mixed coniferous and hardwood forest in which the hardwoods predominate. On some of the slopes they are in pure stands. The broad tableland between the headwaters of the Ohio river and Black brook is made up of low ridges and depressions, the former being covered chiefly by yellow birch and the latter by rather inferior red spruce. The soil is thin, and large areas are covered with rock fragments. The flats about the lakes, however, support nearly pure stands of good spruce. The tableland also contains frequent black spruce-fir swamps. The western third of the area is three-quarters hardwood, over half of which is yellow birch, and the remaining portion is about equally divided between red spruce and fir."

ANIMALS

This Unit provides a mixture of mature hardwood and softwood habitats and oldfields, with few bogs or lakes. Like the Cobequid Hills, the Pictou-Antigonish Highlands provide very good moose habitat. The Fisher has been reported from this Unit. Although little appears to be known about this area, it may be assumed that wildlife will be relatively abundant.

Freshwater fishes include White Sucker, Brook Trout, sticklebacks, Golden Shiner, Yellow Perch, and Banded Killifish.

CULTURAL ENVIRONMENT

Highland Scots settled in various locales in this highland area, practising subsistence farming on marginally productive soils. Many of these farmlands were later abandoned and regenerated into the regional forest of the area. Much of this area is managed for forestry.

• • • • • • • •

Sites of Special Interest
- Sugarloaf Hill (south of Malignant Cove)— ancient volcanic neck
- Arisaig Point westwards—well-preserved fossils of brachiopods, graptolites, clams, trilobites, crinoids, cephalopods, ostracods, bryozoans
- Knoydart—fossil fish, ostracods, and plant remains in ancient coastal floodplain
- Cape George to Malignant Cove—cliffs along the Hollow Fault
- Marshy Hope, Eden River—fossil valleys with remnant Carboniferous infilling
- Blue Mountain—good lookoff north along French River
- Clydesdale (IBP Proposed Ecological Site 11)— mature, relatively undisturbed Sugar Maple forest
- the road between McArras Brook and Dunmaglass exposes red beds of the Knoydart Formation

Provincial Parks and Park Reserves
- Beaver Mountain
- James River
- Cape George

Proposed Parks and Protected Areas System includes Natural Landscapes 44a and 44b.

Scenic Viewpoints
- Highway 347 at Blue Mountain, Highway 104 along Barneys River, Beaver Mountain Provincial Park

Associated Offshore Unit
914 Northumberland Strait.

Associated Topics
T2.2 The Avalon and Meguma Zones, T3.1 Development of the Ancient Landscape, T11.10 Ungulates, T12.9 Soil and Resources, T12.10 Plants and Resources.

Associated Habitats
H5.2 Oldfield, H6.1 Hardwood Forest (Sugar Maple, Yellow Birch, Beech Association), H6.2 Softwood Forest (White Spruce Association; Spruce, Fir Association).

313 NORTH BRAS D'OR UPLANDS

This Unit is divided into three sub-Units:
    (a)   Creignish Hills
    (b)   North Mountain
    (c)   Boisdale Hills

GEOLOGY AND LANDSCAPE DEVELOPMENT

The North Bras d'Or Uplands are a series of elongated northeast-southwest oriented fault blocks situated on the north side of Bras d'Or Lake. They are composed of Avalon crustal material, predominantly Precambrian in age, which has risen in the landscape. The blocks have moved vertically along fault boundaries and have domed and tilted the surrounding Carboniferous strata (see Figures 8 and 19).

The blocks occupy a central position along the tilted planation surface and generally achieve average elevations which are consistent with that position, about 245–310 m. The elevations are greatest on the southeast side where movement was along faults. They then tilt towards the northwest, declining in elevation and ending in relatively shallow dip-slopes on the northern margins.

The relief along the boundaries of the blocks depends upon the nature of the adjacent Carboniferous deposits. The North Bras d'Or Uplands were once islands in the Carboniferous Sea, were probably engulfed by sediment, but are now eroded out as topographic highs. Some parts of the margins are set against resistant early Carboniferous Horton grits,

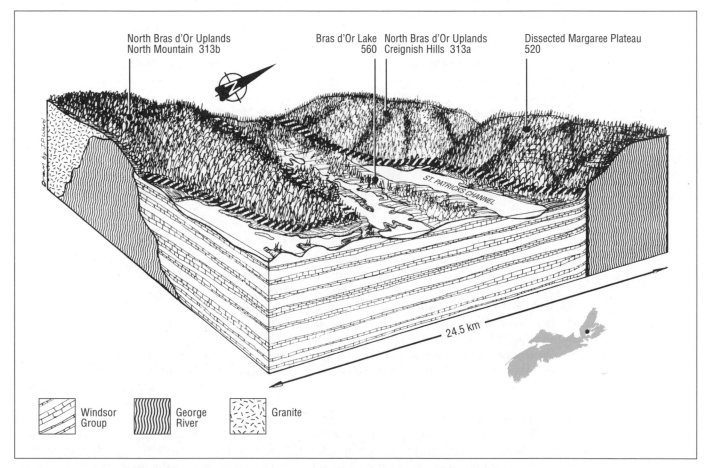

Figure 8: North Bras d'Or Uplands area. Fault-bounded blocks of resistant metamorphic and granitic rocks form the North Bras d'Or Uplands (Unit 313). The easily eroded Windsor Group rocks remain only as a partly submerged lowland fringe around the Bras d'Or Lake (District 560). More resistant Horton sandstones remain as the dissected Margaree Plateau (Unit 591).

whereas others lie against the Windsor Group deposits. These softer sediments are easily eroded and expose the resistant Precambrian rocks in maximum relief. Horton sandstones, in contrast, form a resistant continuum and mask the boundary with the older rocks.

Creignish Hills (sub-Unit 313a)

The Creignish Hills occupy the same relative position on the planation surface as the Pictou-Antigonish Highlands and achieve an average elevation of 275 m. This block is divided into two almost equal sections of metamorphosed volcanic and sedimentary rocks and granite; the former is Precambrian and the latter is Ordovician.

The northern margin is against Horton grits, which form a rolling upland and topographically mask this boundary. The southern boundary is faulted from Whycocomagh Bay to River Denys Mountain and forms a steep scarp slope against the adjacent Windsor Group deposits.

The profile of the North Bras d'Or Uplands as seen from near Port Hawkesbury is relatively even and dominates the first view of Cape Breton from the causeway.

North Mountain (sub-Unit 313b)

North Mountain lies on the west side of Bras d'Or Lake between Denys Basin and West Bay. It is about 260 m high and is composed of Precambrian granitic and George River Group rocks. The latter originally contained limestone bands, which have been metamorphosed into marble. Some marble is still quarried at Marble Mountain.

The North Mountain block was outside the early Carboniferous basin where the Horton strata were deposited. Later on, during Windsor time, when the sea covered a wider area, the North Mountain block became an island against which Windsor Group strata accumulated. The block is now almost entirely surrounded by Windsor deposits, which are deeply eroded and give maximum relief on both the north and south sides. The scarp is steepest on the south side and forms cliffs along West Bay. The more gentle dip-slope reaches Denys Basin at a shallower angle. The block is crosscut by a fault, forming a narrow, steep-sided valley.

Boisdale Hills (sub-Unit 313c)

This part of the North Bras d'Or Uplands lies on the east side of Bras d'Or Lake and has a more complex geological composition than either the Creignish Hills or North Mountain. The strata include late Precambrian sediments and volcanics, granites of Precambrian and Devonian age, and younger volcanic and sedimentary rocks.

This upland block is crosscut by northeast–southwest oriented faults which divide it into a series of strips. Precambrian granites and George River Group rocks are thus juxtaposed against Cambrian and middle Devonian strata. The fault lines are eroded to form scarp slopes in several places along the coast and inland. A well-developed fault scarp can be seen at Eskasoni; another is aligned southwest and northeast along East Bay.

The Carboniferous strata immediately adjacent to the older rocks are the sandstones and shales of the Grantmire Formation. These are intermediate in erodibility and provide moderate relief next to the harder upland strata.

FRESH WATER

There are few lakes, and most of the streams and rivers are tributaries feeding larger rivers in the surrounding District 560. Colluvial deposits in stream valleys are zones of springs and groundwater seeps.

Creignish Hills (sub-Unit 313a)

The hills form a divide across western Cape Breton. Both the south-flowing Inhabitants River and the north-flowing Mabou River rise in these hills.

North Mountain (sub-Unit 313b)

The valley is occupied by two streams, Kennedys Brook and MacIntyres Brook. Lakes, bogs, and wandering streams are found on the relatively flat crest of North Mountain, but once the marginal slopes are reached, the streams become straight and fast flowing.

Boisdale Hills (sub-Unit 313c)

The landscape is divided into numerous tertiary watersheds that drain many short streams and small lakes.

SOILS

A wide variety of metamorphic and granitic rocks occurs in this Unit, but the strong podzol development and the presence of a thick iron humate B horizon typical of ferro-humic podzols tend to mask the diversity of the parent materials. The principal soil, which has developed from the thin mantle of stony loam till is Thom—a well-drained, stony, sandy loam. Small areas of peat are found in depressions. On the Boisdale Hills (sub-Unit 313c), Mira soils (mottled, sandy loam) have developed where drainage is impeded by relief. There are also some coarse-textured Debert soils. Shallow soils occur on ridges and steep slopes.

PLANTS

Sugar Maple, Yellow Birch, American Beech, and shade-intolerant hardwoods occupy the upper slopes and high ridges, while Balsam Fir, White Spruce, and Black Spruce cover the upland flats and ravine slopes. On the Boisdale Hills (sub-Unit 313c), where elevations are somewhat lower (200 m), mixedwoods become more prevalent.

ANIMALS

Little direct study has been done in this Unit, but the small amount of information available for sub-Unit 313c indicates the fauna in Unit 313 is not necessarily similar to that in Units 311 and 312.

Of special note are the large number of eagle nests in stream ravines in sub-Unit 313c. Deer use the side slopes for winter yards; the slopes shelter them, especially on sunny days when the slopes block winter winds. There are few to no moose in this area. Fish include Brook Trout, Golden Shiner, White Sucker, White Perch, sticklebacks, and Banded Killifish.

CULTURAL ENVIRONMENT

Creignish Hills (sub-Unit 313a)
Bornish Hills, a section of the Creignish Hills, is a protected site under the Special Places Act administered by the Department of Natural Resources.

North Mountain (sub-Unit 313b)
North Mountain was well known for its Marble Mountain limestone quarry. The story of this limestone and marble quarry industry of the late 1800s and early 1900s is documented at the Marble Mountain Museum. After limestone was extracted from the quarry, it was crushed, slaked, and shipped to Prince Edward Island, where farmers used it to lime soils. Important Mi'kmaq burial sites are found in North Mountain cliffs bordering the Bras d'Or Lake.

Boisdale Hills (sub-Unit 313c)
Forestry has been one of the dominant land uses in the Boisdale Hills. A limestone quarry once operated here.

• • • • • • • •

Sites of Special Interest
• Marble Mountain—marble quarry

Provincial Parks and Park Reserves
• Marble Mountain
• Barachois
• Eskasoni fault scarp
• East Bay fault scarp
Proposed Parks and Protected Areas System includes Natural Landscapes 49a and 49b.

Ecological Reserves
• Bornish Hill Nature Reserve (sub-Unit 313a)

Scenic Viewpoints
• Marble Mountain (sub-Unit 313b)

Associated Topics
T2.2 The Avalon and Meguma Zones, T2.4 The Carboniferous Basin, T3.1 Development of the Ancient Landscape, T11.4 Birds of Prey, T12.3 Geology and Resources.

Associated Habitats
H3.1 Freshwater Open-Water Lotic, H3.3 Freshwater Bottom Lotic, H3.5 Freshwater Water's Edge Lotic, H4.1 Bog, H6.1 Hardwood Forest (Maple, Oak, Birch Association; Sugar Maple, Yellow Birch, Beech Association), H6.2 Softwood Forest (Spruce, Fir Association).

**313
North
Bras d'Or
Uplands**

314 MABOU HIGHLANDS

GEOLOGY AND LANDSCAPE DEVELOPMENT

The Mabou Highlands lie southwest of the Cape Breton highlands on the Northumberland Strait. They form a rounded knoll 15 km by 8 km which reaches an elevation of 335 m at the north end and 320 m at the south end. The surface of the Mabou Highlands is highly dissected, and little remains of the original plateau. The sides are deeply eroded. The area is underlain by two rock types: one is a series of metamorphosed sedimentary and volcanic rocks, and the other is a gneiss complex. Both are probably Precambrian in age and are comparable to similar rocks found in the Cape Breton highlands (Regions 100 and 200). Both are very resistant to erosion. The western boundary of this block of Avalon crust is a north-south fault which has set Devonian-Carboniferous sandstones against the Precambrian strata.

The Mabou Highlands are almost entirely surrounded by Horton strata, but unlike other sections of the Avalon Uplands, they stand out in high relief against these rocks. At the boundaries the hills rapidly climb to 200 m above the Horton deposits. There are steep cliffs along the rather even Northumberland coastline from Port Ban to Cape Mabou.

Coarse glacial deposits lie against the lower slopes of the Mabou Highlands south of Inverness. Other finer sandy deposits are found on the banks of Broad Cove, ascending to more than 150 m above sea level.

FRESH WATER

Streams that flow in wide valleys near the crest of the Mabou Highlands occupy deep gorges further down the slopes and are separated by rounded valley shoulders. The drainage exhibits a radial pattern, with stream systems draining outwards from the rounded crest.

Groundwater springs and seeps can be found in areas with colluvial deposits.

SOILS

The main soil series is Thom, a well-drained, stony, sandy loam. Thom soils are heavily podzolized, with a thick iron humate B horizon. Small areas of peat are common in depressions.

PLANTS

Away from the immediate influence of the winds off the Gulf of St. Lawrence, shade-tolerant hardwoods dominate the upland plateau in this Unit, with Sugar Maple, Yellow Birch, and American Beech being the main species. White Spruce and Balsam Fir are found on coastal sites, while Balsam Fir, spruce, and Eastern Hemlock form softwood stands or mixedwood stands with Red Maple and birch on the lower slopes. A large area around South Cape Mountain has been cleared for use as a community pasture.

ANIMALS

Trapping in the northern part of the Mabou Hills in July and September 1982 revealed that no Rock Voles or Gaspé Shrews were present, but otherwise the small-mammal fauna was diverse. Bald Eagles are frequently seen near Mabou Harbour.

CULTURAL ENVIRONMENT

The marginal farmland of the Mabou Highlands was settled by Scots in the mid-nineteenth century, with subsistence agriculture and sheep farming forming much of the economic base, together with the timber trade and mining nearby. Many of these farms were later abandoned, and forest succession ensued. However, sheep farming is still practised here today. The Sight Point Walking Trail has long been a recreational attraction here. Seasonal hunting also takes place in these highlands.

• • • • • • • •

Sites of Special Interest
• Sight Point—exposures of Precambrian intrusive rocks
• Inverness and Broad Cove—raised beaches

Provincial Parks and Park Reserves
Proposed Parks and Protected Areas System includes Natural Landscape 60.

Scenic Viewpoints
• Sight Point, Glenora Falls

Associated Offshore Unit
914 Northumberland Strait.

Associated Topics
T2.2 The Avalon and Meguma Zones, T3.4 Terrestrial Glacial Deposits and Landscape Features, T11.4 Birds of Prey, T12.9 Soil and Resources, T12.11 Animals and Resources, T12.12 Recreational Resources.

Associated Habitats
H6.1 Hardwood Forest (Sugar Maple, Yellow Birch, Beech Association), H6.3 Mixedwood Forest (Spruce, Fir, Pine–Maple, Birch Association).

**314
Mabou
Highlands**

320 DISSECTED MARGINS

This District is divided into two sub-Districts:

(a) Waughs River
(b) French River

GEOLOGY AND LANDSCAPE DEVELOPMENT

At the margins of the Cobequid Hills and the Pictou-Antigonish Highlands in Pictou County are foothills which lie between the uplifted plateaus and the relatively undisturbed surrounding lowlands (see Figure 18). Kame fields and esker systems are evident in the landscape. The two main areas are Waughs River (sub-District 320a) and French River (sub-District 320b).

Waughs River (sub-District 320a)

East of Warwick Mountain on the north side of the Cobequid Hills are a number of small faults which lie broadly parallel to the Cobequid Fault. These create a series of slices at the margin of the upland, and these slices form dissected steps down to the Northumberland Plain (see Figure 9). Numerous rivers and streams create attractive and varied hill and valley topography.

French River (sub-District 320b)

The north and west margins of the Pictou-Antigonish Highlands are broken into numerous blocks by two sets of faults running north-south and east-west. Strata of varying hardness have been juxtaposed and

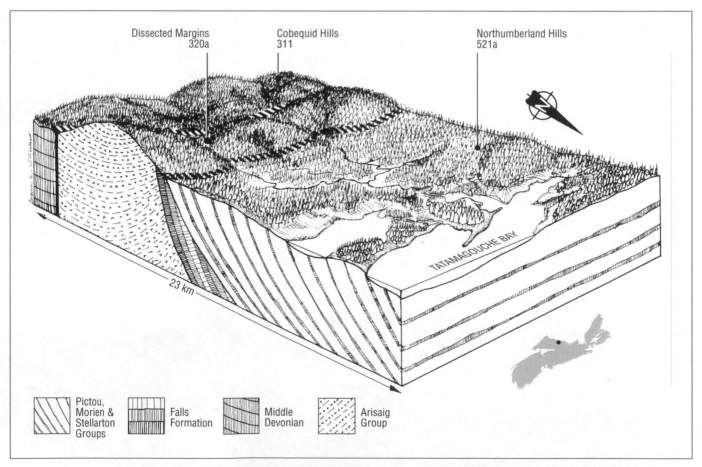

Dissected Margins
320a

Cobequid Hills
311

Northumberland Hills
521a

23 km

TATAMAGOUCHE BAY

Pictou, Morien & Stellarton Groups

Falls Formation

Middle Devonian

Arisaig Group

Figure 9: Northumberland Plain area. The wide coastal plain (Unit 521) with low sandstone ridges nearly parallel to the coast is terminated abruptly by the Dissected Margins (District 320) of the Avalon Uplands which are underlain by older, more resistant sedimentary rocks. The distant Cobequid Hills (Unit 311) grade subtly into the foothills.

the area has been dissected by many streams and rivers. The landscape is hilly with steep narrow valleys occupied by branches of the French River.

SOILS

In both parts of this District the soils reflect the contributions of both varied bedrock and Carboniferous glacial material brought in from the north.

Waughs River (sub-District 320a)
Well-drained Cobequid soils derived mainly from granitic materials occur at the higher elevations. In the Pictou County part of the sub-District, Westbrook soils (well-drained loam) have developed from a gravelly loam till which was derived from Carboniferous conglomerates of the Horton Group. In Colchester County, Wyvern soils, which are similar to Cobequid soils, have developed on granite-rich tills.

French River (sub-District 320b)
Thom and Cobequid soils (typical highland soils) again occur at higher elevations. Elsewhere Barney soils (well-drained loam) have developed on shaly clay loams derived from Silurian shales.

PLANTS

Mixed forest covers most of this District, with hardwood stands on well-drained ridges. Balsam Fir, Red Spruce, White Spruce, Red Maple, and birch are the common trees.

ANIMALS

This District shares many of the faunal characteristics of the Cobequid Hills (Unit 311). Brown Trout and Brook Trout are common fish species in the smaller tributaries that feed the French and Waugh rivers.

SCENIC QUALITY

When compared with District 310, scenery is often less spectacular but more intimate and varied. The many hills, knolls, and small river valleys, combined with more frequent evidence of human settlement (roads, farms, and small clearings), add much variety and interest. Scenic ratings vary from medium to moderately high. Particularly attractive are the valleys of MacKays Brook and Waughs River (sub-District 320a), Barneys River, West Barneys River, and the East French River (sub-District 320b). Numerous viewpoints from the roads travelling down to Tatamagouche provide vistas of the slopes and the plain beyond.

CULTURAL ENVIRONMENT

Waughs River (sub-District 320a)
Forestry characterizes land use. Scots settled in these upland areas, later abandoning some settlements. Waterways were utilized downstream to power grist mills such as the Balmoral Mill, which is now a museum site.

French River (sub-District 320b)
The dominant land use in this area is woodland management. Sparse settlement occurs along river intervales.

• • • • • • • •

Sites of Special Interest
• Four Mile Brook near Tatamagouche Mountain—waterfall
• Balmoral Mills—picnic park and historic site (Grist Mill)

Provincial Parks and Park Reserves
Proposed Parks and Protected Areas System includes Natural Landscape 42.

Associated Topics
T2.2 The Avalon and Meguma Zones, T3.4 Terrestrial Glacial Deposits and Landscape Features, T12.10 Plants and Resources.

Associated Habitats
H6.3 Mixedwood Forest (Spruce, Fir, Pine–Maple, Birch Association).

320
Dissected
Margins

330 FAULT RIDGES

This District is divided into two sub-Districts:
  (a)   Sporting Mountain
  (b)   East Bay Hills

GEOLOGY AND LANDSCAPE DEVELOPMENT

The Fault Ridges lie on the south side of West Bay, Cape Breton. The District is made up of two elongated blocks of Precambrian rocks: Sporting Mountain and East Bay Hills. Each block is composed of the same two rock types: volcanic deposits of the Fourchu Group (ash and lava interleaved with marine sediments) and granites, but in different proportions. Sporting Mountain is predominantly composed of granites, whereas the East Bay Hills have more Fourchu Group rocks (see Figure 29).

Both blocks are elongated northeast-southwest in accordance with the same prevailing trend of faults which dominates the geomorphology of the North Bras d'Or Uplands. The southeastern margins are also faulted, in this case bringing the resistant Precambrian strata against late Carboniferous sandstones and siltstones. On the northeastern side the contact is with easily eroded Carboniferous Windsor Group strata, which were deposited directly against the blocks when they stood as islands in the Carboniferous Sea.

Morphologically, the relief and elevations of Sporting Mountain and East Bay Hills reflect not only their geological setting, surrounded by rocks of varying resistance, but also their position on the low side of the planation surface. Both blocks rise to little more than 180 m, forming low ridges in an otherwise lowland landscape. Precambrian rocks of equivalent resistance have created dominant uplands further north, but here, where there was little uplift during the Tertiary, there was also minimal rejuvenation of erosional action and limited exposure of this hard core of old rocks.

The steepest slopes are found on the northwest side of both Sporting Mountain and East Bay Hills, where soft Windsor Group rocks form a narrow band along the shore. The valley of Breac Brook, at the north end of East Bay Hills, appears to be an ancient coastal valley which was filled by Windsor Group deposits and is now being exhumed. The fault line on the southeastern margin can be seen in some areas (e.g., northeast of Oban) but in general does not form a prominent scarp slope.

In this part of Cape Breton south of Bras d'Or Lake, glaciation more than geological structure appears to have influenced drainage patterns. South of East Bay Hills the glacial direction is strongly northeast-southwest, in this case parallel to the fault which defines their southern boundary.

FRESH WATER

Both Sporting Mountain and East Bay Hills have relatively flat plateau-like crests which are poorly drained. The streams flowing towards West Bay become straight and fast-flowing once the coastal slopes are reached, but those flowing southeast retain a dendritic-to-deranged (or disorganized) pattern. Most streams are located on the margins. In the eastern part of this District, the streams are aligned northeast, reflecting the glacial direction. The District contains several large lakes and a few scattered raised bogs.

SOILS

Heavily podzolized Thom soils with a thick iron humate B horizon cover most of this District. They are associated with Arichat soils (poorly drained, mottled, sandy loams), found where the relief is gently undulating or depressional. There are also small areas of peat.

PLANTS

The two parts of this District are somewhat lower than the North Bras d'Or Hills and shade-tolerant hardwoods, although present, are no longer dominant. The South Bras d'Or Hills support instead mixed stands of Red Maple, White Birch, Yellow Birch, American Beech, Balsam Fir, and White Spruce.

ANIMALS

There are few moose in this area. Deer are found on side slopes in winter yards. There are a large number of eagle nests in stream ravines.

SCENIC QUALITY

These two plateau blocks have less relief than District 310, even on their north-facing scarps, and they lack the visual interest of pure hardwood stands. Nevertheless, they offer some spectacular views north over Bras d'Or Lake, for example, where Highway 4 climbs above shore level near Irish Cove and Middle Cape.

CULTURAL ENVIRONMENT

Small-scale farming is practised in some areas of Sporting Mountain (sub-District 330a) and the East Bay Hills (sub-District 330b). Fishing the waters of the Bras d'Or Lake and sporadic forestry have been economic activities in the past. Much of this area is now cottage country, and tourism plays a significant role in the local economy. In the early 1900s the mineral springs at Glengarry in Irish Cove were well known for their perceived healing properties, which drew local people as well as distant travellers.

• • • • • • • •

Sites of Special Interest
- Irish Cove Park (East Bay Hills)—view of East Bay and road-cut exposure of Precambrian ash (tuff) deposits
- Breac Brook, an ancient coastal valley filled with deposits, now being exhumed

Provincial Parks and Park Reserves
- Ben Eoin
- Big Pond

Proposed Parks and Protected Areas System includes Natural Landscape 50.

400
Atlantic Interior

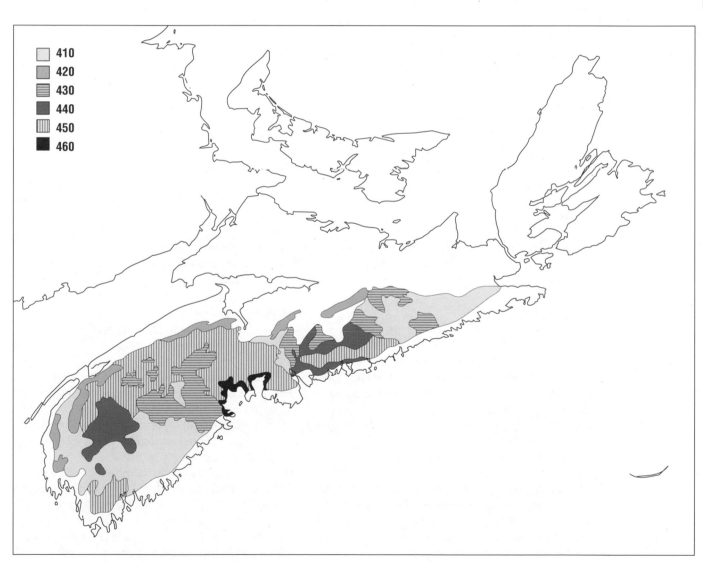

410
420
430
440
450
460

Figure 10: Region 400, Atlantic Interior, and its component Districts.

400 ATLANTIC INTERIOR

The Atlantic Interior is divided into six Districts on the basis of morphology, surficial deposits, and vegetation characteristics:

410 Quartzite Plains
420 Slopes and Ridges
430 Drumlins
440 Granite Barrens
450 Granite
460 Bays

REGIONAL CHARACTERISTICS

Inland from the coastal forest, the immediate climatic influence of the Atlantic Ocean is replaced by slightly warmer summers and cooler winters with much less wind exposure. The planed surface of the old, hard rocks is tilted gently to the southeast, and some of Nova Scotia's longest rivers flow across this surface. Most of the province's lakes have been created by glacial action on the relatively flat surface. Vegetation varies from the mature spruce-hemlock-pine forests common on the Kejimkujik Drumlins (Unit 433) to the heath vegetation on the Granite Barrens (District 440) (see Figure 11).

GEOLOGY

The Atlantic Interior has three main groups of rocks: slate and greywacke (the Meguma Group); lava and ash (the White Rock Formation); and granite.

Meguma Group
The rocks of the Meguma Group are Cambrian to Silurian in age. This group has been divided into the Goldenville Formation (after a mining area in eastern Nova Scotia where the strata are well exposed) and the Halifax Formation. The Goldenville Formation is made up of greywacke (a quartz-rich rock containing some clay), and the Halifax Formation is made up of slates.

Meguma Group strata are widely exposed across the Region and underlie about half of the terrain. They were deposited in an extensive offshore basin in which conditions stayed the same over wide areas and for long time intervals; consequently, they are rather uniform in colour and texture wherever they are found.

Gold deposits have formed within the Meguma on domes and plunging anticlines where the strata became fractured by folding. The richest veins usually occur in the zone of maximum curvature, with the largest veins in tightly folded anticlines. The veins were apparently deposited from solutions that arose deep within the lower areas and penetrated up through the fractures and along the bedding planes.

The entire thickness of the Meguma Group is unknown, because its base cannot be seen and its top has been eroded away. A section of Goldenville about 5,650 m thick has been measured between Sissiboo Falls and Weymouth in Unit 411; this appears to be close to the maximum exposed at present. Similar thicknesses are indicated in eastern Nova Scotia. About 3,650 m of the Halifax Formation have been deposited, and perhaps much more in the vicinity of Halifax. This thins out to a maximum of 1,225 m or less in southwestern Nova Scotia.

White Rock Formation
In the Silurian, following the deposition of the Meguma Group, one or more volcanic centres developed, probably close to what is now the coastal area near Yarmouth. A series of strata composed of (about 50 per cent) lavas and ash and (about 50 per cent) sandstone and mudstone built up. These strata are jointly called the White Rock Formation today. They are preserved in a series of synclines in the Yarmouth area, at Cape St. Mary, along the Sissiboo River, at Bear River, and in the Gaspereau area. The White Rock Formation is thickest at Yarmouth, where 3,000 m have been measured with only the bottom exposed, and it becomes progressively thinner to the north.

During the Late Silurian to Early Devonian period, the Meguma and White Rock strata were folded and changed by heat and pressure during the crustal disturbance called the Acadian Orogeny. The strata folded much as a rug would if its edges were pushed together. For the most part, the axes of the folds lie parallel to the long axis of the province and form an arc from Yarmouth to Canso. They lie an average of 5 km apart and can be traced lengthwise for up to 150 km. The folds are sometimes symmetrical, but they are often asymmetrical and often so tight that the crests have turned sideways and become overturned.

While lateral pressure was exerted, the temperature rose to a maximum of 650°C and the character of the original strata was changed. Under these conditions, the chemical elements of the rocks recombined to form a characteristic series of minerals: garnet, staurolite, andalusite, and sillimanite. The temperature and pressure conditions of this regional metamorphism can be estimated by examining the minerals that formed, because each only forms when certain temperatures and pressures exist.

Surveys carried out in the 1950s and 1960s reported soils developed from mica and hornblende schists, particularly in Yarmouth and Digby counties. Correlation of these soils with the geology is unclear, because zones of intense metamorphism of the quartzites are as frequent in Unit 412 as in Unit 411.

Granite

The third main group of rocks in the Atlantic Interior falls under the name "granite." This familiar, coarse-textured rock actually includes a whole range of related but different rock types. They have a variety of colours, textures, and compositions but commonly contain large greyish or pink crystals of potash feldspar in a matrix of smaller crystals dominated by quartz and mica.

Most of the granite lies in a huge body called the South Mountain Batholith, which is exposed in a giant arc from Yarmouth County northwards to the edge of the Annapolis Valley and around to Halifax. This batholith intruded during the late stages of the Acadian Orogeny as a hot, thick liquid. This magma rose by penetrating the overlying Meguma strata, broke off blocks, and assimilated them. In places near the contact, blocks of Meguma country rock can be seen in various stages of assimilation, as xenoliths. In some places they look almost unchanged, whereas in others they have been almost entirely absorbed and can be seen only as ghosts.

The heat given off during the intrusion, and later as the magma cooled, baked the surrounding Meguma strata and created a narrow contact aureole. In this aureole characteristic minerals have developed, in particular cordierite which is round and black and gives the slates a spotted appearance. Good examples of the changes that took place close to the contact can be seen west and north of the Northwest Arm near Halifax.

Pre-Carboniferous Erosion

Following the Acadian Orogeny and the emplacement of the granite came a period of very rapid erosion. Material several miles thick was removed within about 10 million years and the granite was exposed.

The sediments generated during this erosion were carried off and deposited elsewhere. The erosion surface was later to form the basement upon which Carboniferous strata were deposited.

Development of the Present Topography

Probably during the Cretaceous the whole area was eroded down to a fairly level surface, which is now more or less coincident with the overall level of the Atlantic Interior. Large areas of granite became exposed, some of which now form domes or high, rounded hills. The overlying, folded greywacke and slates were eroded away and are now found mainly around the edges of the granite, or in what were the lower areas between the granite cupolas and domes. The slates, being the uppermost strata, were worn away when the Meguma folds were planed off, and the greywacke was exposed underneath. The slates are still preserved in many places in the synclinal troughs and now occur as long, narrow bands running east and west. The folds are steeper and more compressed east of Halifax than to the west, so that the slates between Halifax and central Guysborough County are in rather narrow bands, while northward in Hants County they form wide zones. The general pattern can be seen on the geological maps. Only in western Lunenburg County, and in adjacent Queens and Annapolis counties, are large areas of slate found.

Faults

The topography of southwestern Nova Scotia has not been influenced significantly by faults. However, east of Halifax, where there are many faults and the strata are also more intensely folded, the opposite is true. From St. Margarets Bay to Guysborough, the Meguma strata are shattered by innumerable faults, a number of which affect the outline of the coast and the topography inland. One at Cole Harbour continues inland up the valley of Lake Major; another at Sheet Harbour controls the upper bend of the harbour, continues up the deep valley of the West River, and stretches inland practically across the entire Southern Upland. The long, straight harbours at Indian Harbour, Country Harbour, and New Harbour in eastern Guysborough County are also determined by faults. The fault at Country Harbour is the most prominent: there, a deep, straight-sided channel penetrates inland about 25 km to form one of the best natural harbours in the world.

Topography

When viewed from North Mountain across the Annapolis Valley, or from an elevation looking south towards the escarpment of Guysborough County, the surface of the Atlantic Interior presents an almost even, level skyline. This uniform surface is also evident inland, as in northern Annapolis County. There the upland surface is around 150 m above sea level and has a relief of barely 15 m. East of Halifax, near the coast, the river valleys are deep and cut far below the surface, but even here the uniform height of the upland surface is evident from a distance. In the southwest there is very little relief, and the land is either almost flat over large areas or has only low ridges and wide, shallow valleys.

The upland surface slopes southeast or directly towards the Atlantic coast, but there is also a distinct lowering of the elevation, and more uniform topography, southwestwards towards the Gulf of Maine. This is particularly evident from Queens County to Yarmouth.

The highest points along the northern border are rounded hills that rise gently from the surrounding country. Two granite knolls south of Kentville are typical: one of them, north of Lake George, rises to more than 275 m, and another, southwest of Gaspereau, is around 260 m. Several slate hills in the same general area are only slightly lower, at nearly 245 m. In northern Annapolis County, the highest area, southwest of Bridgetown, is a little over 275 m high, and from there the surface slopes gently down to Brier Island. In eastern Guysborough, along the northern edge of the narrow band of upland, the elevation is about 225 m above sea level. Only occasionally throughout the Atlantic Interior does a hill rise significantly above the surrounding area. One of these is Aspotogan Mountain on the peninsula east of Chester, which reaches a height of 145 m in an area with an average elevation of barely 75 m.

Granite Area

Granite comprises the most extensive areas of the Atlantic Interior and reaches the highest elevations. The rock is massive and seems resistant to chemical change, although post-glacial weathering has affected all exposed surfaces. Low, rounded hills or shapeless ridges generally rise less than 20 m above the mean elevation, with intervening broad, shallow depressions which are too irregular to be called valleys. High knolls occur occasionally, but the slopes are rounded and subdued throughout with no particular pattern or design. The drainage is poor, and sluggish rivers or streams meander from one shallow lake to another. Large boulders line these channels, and dot the lakes.

Greywacke Area

The greywacke topography is somewhat more varied. In eastern Nova Scotia, on the northern border of Halifax and Guysborough counties, the surface is much like a plateau, with long, low ridges running east and west. Large, angular blocks of greywacke cover the ground and the soil is usually thin and acid. The intervening hollows are swampy and have their long axes generally oriented parallel to the strike of the strata; drainage is impeded by deposits of glacial drift. The river channels in the interior are shallow because the streams run down the tilted erosion plain across the fold axes and cut across layers of resistant strata. Near the Atlantic coast, the topography is frequently more uneven and the stream channels are deeper, but even here the land tends to be monotonous and covered with scattered rocks of all sizes. Greywacke is also common in southwestern Nova Scotia, where, again, the topography tends to be flat and monotonous.

Slate Areas and Drumlins

The slate areas present a more interesting and varied topography than the areas of greywacke and granite. Slates weather relatively easily. The surface of the slate areas has been planed off, and the resultant loose material has been carried away to form a deep glacial drift with a high percentage of silt and clay. The advancing glacier moved over the area like a bulldozer, scraped off the weathered material, carried it for a kilometre or so, and then, overloaded by the mass of material, dropped it and sometimes shaped it into drumlins.

Where material is sufficient, drumlins produce a rolling topography. The drumlins may be isolated, may overlap to form irregular hills, or may be joined to make beaded ridges. The slate areas of Lunenburg County represent typical drumlin country, a very distinctive type of topography which can be recognized as soon as one enters it. Small, oval hills are scattered over the landscape, with ponds or lakes in the hollows between them. On land they appear as swarms, which are often quite well defined geographically.

CLIMATE

The Atlantic Interior is a large, contiguous region that includes considerable climatic variation but has basically an inland, lowland climate sheltered from direct marine influences. The climate is characterized by cold winters and warm summers. Variations in temperature and precipitation are, to a certain extent, governed by distance from the Atlantic coast and by latitude.

The mean annual temperature varies from 1°C towards the southwestern tip of the province to 5°C and higher in the more inland areas. In most of the Region, January mean temperatures are below -5°C and are generally warmer towards the coast. Mean temperatures rise above freezing by the end of March, with spring arriving somewhat earlier in the southwest. By July, most of the Region has warmed to a mean temperature in excess of 17.5°C, except in the more northerly areas of the Region in Halifax and Guysborough counties. The area around the LaHave drainage basin and Kejimkujik Lake tends to warm up earlier and has hotter summer temperatures. Freezing temperatures return to the Region by the second week in December, and a little later near the southwestern tip.

The mean total annual precipitation ranges from 1200 to 1600 mm. The drier areas are found near the southwestern tip and towards the interior. Mean total snowfall ranges from 150 cm near the coast to 250 cm or more in higher areas and further inland. The snow-cover season varies from about 110 days in the southwest to more than 130 days further north.

The frost-free period varies from less than 100 days in the interior to more than 140 days in the southwest. The number of accumulated growing degree-days are highest in the southern part of the Region and taper off towards the north.

FRESH WATER

Drainage patterns in Region 400 are typically deranged, and surface water is retained in a disorganized series of streams, lakes, and bogs. Chains of lakes, streams, and stillwaters occur in the interior, with low ridges following the trend of the underlying strata. Many of the streams are slow-flowing and interrupted by shallow, rocky ponds and lakes. In Queens and Shelburne counties the rivers and streams tend to cut across bands of harder rock to form rapids and low waterfalls, as along the Medway and Mersey rivers. In Yarmouth County the folds of the strata bend southward, and consequently the flow of the streams is along the strike of the structures rather than across them. The streams flow slowly through wide, shallow valleys, where lakes and stillwaters also occur. In parts of Shelburne County the land is practically flat as far as the eye can see, as if it had been planed off to a level surface to form broad expanses of poorly drained areas and bogs. Ponds and lakes are common in the hollows between drumlins. The highest elevation is near the northern border of the Region, where the divide between streams draining north and those flowing south makes a great arc, north from near Pubnico almost to the slope of the Annapolis Valley and around to the Waverley lakes near Halifax.

Surface waters are dystrophic throughout this Region. Primary productivity tends to be low and most lakes are oligotrophic. Surface water also tends to be low in dissolved solids, providing little buffering capacity. Combined with the low buffering capacities of the thin soils and tills associated with the quartzite, slate, and granite bedrock, much of the fresh water in this Region is susceptible to acidification. Surface water is less acidic in the drumlin areas.

Groundwater in this Region is stored and transmitted through fractures and joints and along fault and contact zones in the bedrock. It tends to be low in dissolved minerals but, like the surface water, is susceptible to acidification from acidic runoff and to discolouration from contact with naturally occurring minerals such as iron and manganese associated with granite and quartzite. The slates of the Halifax Formation tend to have a good overburden of till that somewhat buffers the natural sulphides that can contaminate ground and surface waters.

SOILS

The major factors affecting soil development in this Region are the resistant granite and quartzite bedrock, the undulating and often poorly drained terrain, and the influence of finer-textured tills transported by glacial action from Carboniferous areas. Over most of the Region, strong scouring has left a thin, bouldery till cover on which humo-ferric podzols predominate, with considerable areas of gleysol, Rockland, and peat. Coarse, bouldery, sandy loams have formed in granitic areas, while on quartzite the stony, sandy loams have slightly finer textures. Where soils developed from till over slates and schists, vigorous vegetative growth is prevalent, in marked contrast to that of the quartzite soils. The soils themselves are usually very permeable, but drainage is often impeded by topography or underlying bedrock. Soils are strongly leached and very acidic. An important feature of the soils of this Region are the drumlin fields. Soils formed on drumlins are often better drained, finer textured, deeper, and somewhat more fertile.

PLANTS

The Atlantic Interior covers three of Loucks' Forest Zones. The largest area falls within the predominantly softwood Red Spruce, Hemlock, Pine Zone. The LaHave basin, between Kejimkujik Lake and the

LaHave River, is in the Sugar Maple–Hemlock, Pine Zone. The hilly areas around the Musquodoboit River fall within the Sugar Maple, Yellow Birch–Fir Zone.

The main influences on regional vegetation are the inland climate with its warm summers; the sandy, acid soils; the mixed drainage; and extensive disturbance by fire and logging. Softwoods dominate, but shade-intolerant hardwoods frequently occur on burnt-over land, and pockets of shade-tolerant hardwoods are found on higher, better-drained sites. Red Spruce and Eastern Hemlock were once abundant throughout much of the Region, but both have been depleted by cutting.

In the southern part of the Region, south and west of a line from Windsor to Halifax, where the soils are generally better drained and summer temperatures are slightly higher, spruce and Eastern Hemlock are found in association with Red Oak and White Pine. Balsam Fir and Red Maple are found on disturbed sites, but the fir usually disappears within 30 years. Beech was once abundant but is now found mostly on drier ridges. Ash is found on seepage slopes throughout the Region, particularly on the sides of drumlins. Bogs and swamps are very common, particularly towards the southwestern tip of the Region.

In the more northerly part, north and east of a line from Windsor to Halifax, where summer temperatures are slightly cooler and drainage is poorer, Red Spruce and Eastern Hemlock are found with Black Spruce and Balsam Fir. Sugar Maple and White Pine are found on rolling hills, particularly inland. Black Spruce swamps and peat bogs are extensive, and Red Maple, aspen, and Wire Birch predominate as post-fire species, rather than Red Oak. On the rolling hills around the Musquodoboit Valley, higher elevations and better drainage favour shade-tolerant hardwoods and mixedwoods.

The southern part of this Region is distinguished by the presence of Southwest Flora, or Coastal Plain Flora. This is a group of plants normally restricted to more southern ranges, but because of the milder climate in Nova Scotia, they are able to establish themselves here.

ANIMALS

Softwood and mixedwood forest habitats predominate in this Region, favouring fauna of a more boreal association. Disturbance is widespread, and there are very few areas of mature forest. Moose and bear are scattered with a concentration in the area of the brush barrens east of Yarmouth. With the exception of these barrens, deer are found throughout the Region. New growth on recently cut-over or burnt areas provides good forage for ungulates. Bogs and inland barrens are common. Small-mammal diversity is low to moderately high, depending upon habitat. Two species, White-footed Mouse and Southern Flying Squirrel, are disjunct in Nova Scotia from other North American populations. The Southern Flying Squirrel has a restricted distribution (Kejimkujik Park), but the White-footed Mouse distribution coincides with the boundaries of the Region. Lakes and streams cover a considerable proportion of the Region, but the very acidic and deeply coloured character of the water supports an impoverished freshwater vertebrate fauna.

CULTURAL ENVIRONMENT

The forests of the Atlantic Interior have been commercially managed since the eighteenth century and have experienced repeated fires. Log drives took the timber from the interior to sawmills on the coast where it was exported as lumber. Many sawmills still operate in this Region.

The vigorous regeneration of Balsam Fir has led to the establishment of the Christmas tree industry, centred in District 430. Small pockets of agricultural land are scattered through the Region, often in association with drumlins (District 430). The Lunenburg Drumlins attracted German settlers, and Loyalist, Irish, and Scottish immigrants farmed the Annapolis, Ponhook, Kejimkujik, and Eastern Shore drumlins. Many marginal farmlands were later abandoned, giving way to oldfield succession.

Metals and minerals mined have included gold, tin, and limestone, as well as sand, gravel, and crushed rock. Peat resources underlie much of this land. At various localities, hydroelectric power has been harnessed.

The southwestern part of Nova Scotia is the most significant archaeological area in the province. Many parts of the Atlantic Interior were important to the Mi'kmaq for hunting and fishing. Shell middens found along St. Margarets Bay (sub-District 460b) and arrowheads found along canoe routes at Kejimkujik Park (Unit 433) give evidence of former aboriginal occupation. When sport hunting developed in the latter half of the nineteenth century, Mi'kmaq guides were employed by American hunters for moose-hunting and fishing expeditions. Thus began the hunting and fishing lodge tradition in the southwestern Atlantic Interior where the Tobeatic Game Sanctuary is found. Hunting and fishing continues in many of these areas today. Other recreational land uses include canoeing, hiking, bird-watching, and camping, particularly at Kejimkujik National Park, which was established in the 1960s.

• • • • • • •

Associated Topics

T2.2 The Avalon and Meguma Zones, T2.3 Granite in Nova Scotia, T3.1 Development of the Ancient Landscape, T3.3 Glaciation, Deglaciation and Sea-level Changes, T3.4 Terrestrial Glacial Deposits and Landscape Features, T4.2 Post-glacial Colonization by Plants, T5.2 Nova Scotia's Climate, T8.1 Freshwater Hydrology, T8.2 Freshwater Environments, T8.3 Freshwater Wetlands, T10.2 Successional Trends in Vegetation, T10.4 Plant Communities in Nova Scotia, T10.6 Trees, T11.13 Freshwater Fishes, T11.16 Land and Freshwater Invertebrates, T12.2 Cultural Landscapes, T12.3 Geology and Resources, T12.10 Plants and Resources, T12.11 Animals and Resources.

Associated Habitats

H3 Freshwater, H4 Freshwater Wetlands, H5.1 Barren, H6.1 Hardwood Forest (Maple, Oak, Birch Association; Sugar Maple, Elm Association), H6.2 Softwood Forest (Spruce, Hemlock, Pine Association; Pine Association).

**400
Atlantic
Interior**

410 QUARTZITE PLAINS

Three Units are distinguished within the Quartzite Plains District on the basis of surficial deposits:

411 Southwest Schists
412 Mersey Meadows
413 Quartzite Barrens

GEOLOGY AND LANDSCAPE DEVELOPMENT

District 410 is underlain predominantly by resistant metamorphic rocks: greywacke and schist. It lies on the lowest part of the tilted planation surface, so elevations are low and there is little relief. The lowest part is in the southwest, where elevations rarely exceed 100 m and average 50 m. In the southeast the average is nearer 100 m, with the highest elevations around 150 m.

The bedrock is blanketed and obscured by a thin, sandy till but is exposed locally where the surface has been scraped clean. Beneath the till, the eroded folded strata produce a topography of low parallel ridges separated by shallow valleys.

FRESH WATER

The drainage is controlled by glacial lineations and deposits, and the pattern that develops reflects the angle between the fold structures and the glacial direction. In the west there is parallel drainage, while in the east drainage patterns are at right angles.

SOILS

Where the soils have not been burned, especially near Lake Rossignol (sub-Unit 412a), organic matter in the soil provides good forest-growing conditions. Where repeated burning has occurred, organic matter is depleted and slow to rebuild. This is the situation in the rest of Unit 412 and throughout much of Unit 413. Greater proportions of fine materials in the soils derived from schists in Unit 411 provide good forest growth.

The following description, written by C.D. Howe in 1912, applies to soils in areas where only local quartzite materials are available. It is most relevant to areas in Halifax and Guysborough counties (Unit 413) but also applies to some southern areas of Unit 412 in Queens, Shelburne, and Yarmouth counties: "[Quartzite], composed entirely of quartz and mica, when decomposed, yields about as much plant food material as glass. Moreover, the quartzite soils, unless increased by ice- or water-deposited materials, are naturally thin, often not over two inches [5cm] deep. They support an abundant growth of heath plants, like the blueberries and laurel [Sheep Laurel], whose leaves in decomposing make a sour soil. The fact that usually these quartzite soils are ill-drained adds to the acidity of the soil. In a sour condition, the vegetable matter does not decay normally but accumulates in a peaty mass called raw humus. A sour soil is no more favourable to the growth of trees than to the ordinary farm crops. While the quartzite areas have been extensively burned and are now semi-barren or barren, it is probable that this is not far removed from their original condition. At all events it may be reasonably inferred they never supported forest trees larger than those of pole-wood size."

SCENIC QUALITY

Although this District comprises extensive tracts throughout the Southern Upland, there are common scenic characteristics. There is very little relief and the forest cover is often poor and stunted, particularly in boggy areas. Owing to the paucity of soils for farming, most areas lack settlement and therefore roads. On the positive side, the many lakes provide interest and beauty and allow extensive back-country areas to be reached by canoe. Landscapes rate from low (where lakes are absent) to moderately high (e.g., around Lake Rossignol, Grand Lake) but are generally in the medium range.

411 SOUTHWEST SCHISTS

GEOLOGY AND LANDSCAPE DEVELOPMENT

Unit 411 covers an area in southwestern Nova Scotia that is southwest and west of the South Mountain Granite (sub-Unit 451a). The greywacke-dominated bedrock contains mica and hornblende schists, interfolded with slate in the central area. As suggested in the regional description, the occurrence of schists and soils developed from them is not clearly documented.

The present landscape, morphology, and drainage reflects several phases of glacial deposition (these are considered in more detail under Unit 421). The low-lying bedrock has been covered and its relief obscured by glacial deposits, but in places a system of west- and southward-trending valleys can be seen. The present drainage has been glacially imprinted and is to the south.

The surface deposits are of quartzite and schist tills with numerous low drumlins, 2–20 m high. Drumlins on the quartzite are lower and less frequent than on the schists.

A few small eskers are present south and east of Wentworth Lake in the centre of the Unit, but generally the most interesting glacial deposits are along the shores of St. Marys Bay, where outwash deposits, raised beaches, and deltas, usually less than 5 m deep, are found (these are considered in detail in the description of District 820).

FRESH WATER

Drainage occurs through a deranged pattern of sluggish streams and, because the drumlins create additional impoundments, numerous lakes are scattered across the surface. The surface-water coverage in the southern part of this Unit is one of the highest in Nova Scotia. Lakes are generally shallow and dystrophic. Wetlands are scattered throughout, and concentrations of peat bogs are found in the southern areas.

Unit 411 contains most of the Tusket River, which is sluggish and meanders from one shallow lake to another. Productivity in this system is relatively high, and it is a favoured recreational area for salmon, trout, and gaspereau.

Conductivity in the lakes averages about 45 micromhos/cm, and pH ranges between 4.3 and 6.5.

SOILS

The soils in this Unit are derived mostly from quartzite and schist and are, with the exception of scattered drumlinoid features, generally shallow and stony sandy loams. The major soils derived from quartzite series are well-drained Halifax Formation and imperfectly drained Danesville, with small areas of poorly drained Aspotogan soil and peat. The schists have developed Yarmouth, Mersey, Liverpool, Deerfield, and Pitman soils. Soil drainage patterns are very complex and are reflected in the varied plant cover (see Figure 13).

PLANTS

This Unit falls within the Wentworth Lake District of Loucks' Red Spruce, Hemlock, Pine Zone. Deeper soils on the tops of drumlins, derived from schists, support the shade-tolerant deciduous trees—Sugar Maple, Yellow Birch, American Beech with Red Oak—and some shade-intolerant hardwoods. More Red Spruce, hemlock, and pine occur on the lower slopes with birches and aspen.

Swamp stands are composed of Black Spruce, Balsam Fir, larch, and, in certain localized areas, White Cedar. Swamps of Red Maple and Black Ash are also a common feature. In oldfields, Red Spruce, White Spruce, and Balsam Fir are the colonizers, with White Pine invading oldfields and pastures on coarser soils.

Coastal-plain plants are found on lake margins, meadows, and bogs. Most common in the Tusket Valley, they include some endangered species such as Pink Coreopsis and Plymouth Gentian. Other rare species include Water-pennywort and Dwarf Chain Fern.

ANIMALS

This Unit provides moderately good wildlife habitat, particularly for wintering Bald Eagles, migratory Woodcock (fall), Snowshoe Hare, and bobcats. The brush barrens in the southern portions provide abundant berries, and Black Bear are common. The Tusket River provides habitat for a diversity of freshwater molluscs and arthropods, some with coastal-plain affinities. Typical fish include Gaspereau, White Perch, Yellow Perch, Brook Trout, White Sucker, Chain

411
Southwest
Schists

Pickerel, Golden Shiner, and Brown Bullhead. The Atlantic Whitefish was once found in this area, but appears to be extirpated.

CULTURAL ENVIRONMENT

Part of this area makes up the French shore of Nova Scotia, where Acadians settled on their return after 1763. Backland forests have experienced repeated cutting and fires. Forest management is economically important here. Hydroelectric power has been harnessed at Weymouth Falls. The Tusket River supports an important Gaspereau fishery. The Tusket Valley runs through this area. A small area on Wilsons Lake has been designated as an ecological reserve to protect the habitat of rare coastal-plain plant species. Tin deposits were mined around Kemptville in the 1980s, but the mine was closed down in the early 1990s because of plummeting tin prices.

• • • • • • • •

Sites of Special Interest
• Hectanooga (IBP Proposed Ecological Site 54)—largest known stand of White Cedar in Nova Scotia
• Belliveau Lake (IBP Proposed Ecological Site 57)—spring-fed lake with diverse aquatic plant communities, only known locality for Sweet Pepperbush

Ecological Reserves
• Tusket River Nature Reserve

Provincial Parks and Park Reserves
• Ogden Lake

Proposed Parks and Protected Areas System includes Natural Landscape 5.

Scenic Viewpoints
• Lake Vaughan

Associated Topics
T2.2 The Avalon and Meguma Zones, T3.4 Terrestrial Glacial Deposits and Landscape Features, T4.1 Postglacial Climatic Change, T10.12 Rare and Endangered Plants, T11.4 Birds of Prey, T11.8 Land Mammals, T12.8 Fresh Water and Resources.

Associated Habitats
H3 Fresh Water, H4.1 Bog, H4.3 Swamp, H5.2 Oldfield, H6.1 Hardwood Forest (Sugar Maple, Yellow Birch, Beech Association), H6.2 Softwood Forest (Spruce, Hemlock, Pine Association; Spruce, Fir Association; Black Spruce, Larch Association).

412 MERSEY MEADOWS

Unit 412 is divided into three sub-Units with similar features:

(a) Lake Rossignol
(b) Millipsigate Lake
(c) Rocky Lake

GEOLOGY AND LANDSCAPE DEVELOPMENT

The three sub-Units of the Mersey Meadows are blanketed with quartzite till but have only a few scattered drumlins of the same material (see Figure 13). Glacial outwash deposits and ice-contact drift (such as collects in crevasses) are found on the upper reaches of the Argyle River. Eskers are common in many river valleys but particularly those of the Argyle, Jordan, and Sable rivers (sub-Unit 412a).

FRESH WATER

The area has a number of lakes, but drainage is relatively unimpeded and the rivers form dendritic patterns. Here the rivers flow perpendicularly to the bands of interfolded quartzite and shale, sometimes forming small waterfalls where resistant quartzite ridges are encountered. Many of Nova Scotia's major rivers flow north-south through this Unit, i.e., the Clyde, Roseway, Jordan, Sable, and Broad rivers. Lake Rossignol is the largest lake, dominating surface-

Plate 4: Region 400. Oblique aerial view of Southwest Cove, Tangier Grand Lake in Unit 453, showing an impermeable landscape with abundant surface water and spruce forest. Photo: O. Maass.

water coverage in the northeast. This Unit has the largest concentration of fens and raised and sloped peat bogs in Nova Scotia (see Figure 11). Surface water is fairly acidic, with pH levels ranging from 4.0 to 6.1. Dissolved solids are limited, and conductivity and primary productivity are low.

SOILS

Lake Rossignol (sub-Unit 412a)

Moderately coarse-textured soils that developed from schistose parent materials include large areas of well-drained Mersey soils, and imperfectly drained and mottled Liverpool soils. Towards the coast, imperfectly drained Danesville soils are common, while inland are large areas of well-drained Halifax and Gibraltar gravelly, sandy loams. Around Greenfield is a large area of well-drained Bridgewater sandy loam. A feature of this sub-Unit is the substantial acreage of barrens, some of it caused by repeated burning, but some underlain by a dense ortstein layer. The effects of repeated burning have been profound for these soils. A band of heavily burned forest extends from the Municipality of Argyle eastwards to the Broad River in Queens County. Organic matter loss to fires has severely reduced the ability of this area to support good forest growth. Lands to the north of this burnt section, extending from the Roseway River to the Medway River, south of Lake Rossignol, are able to support good forest growth, even though their origins are similar, because they have been less severely burned.

Millipsigate Lake (sub-Unit 412b)

Soils in this sub-Unit are predominantly shallow, Bridgewater series. North of Minamkeak Lake, and between Millipsigate and Hebb lakes, Rockland occurs.

Rocky Lake (sub-Unit 412c)

Well-drained but shallow Farmville soils derived from slaty to gravelly tills occur with Farmville and occasional Bridgewater drumlins.

PLANTS

The southwestern part of this Unit has been the most extensively burned, regenerating as a mixed forest (see Plate 4) with pockets of White Pine and Red Oak. The natural vegetation appears to have been White Pine and Red Oak, but now many of the hills support only low shrubs and scattered Black Spruce. Barren and semi-barren areas with depleted soils are now colonized by huckleberry, which appears after cut-

ting and after fires. In deeper soil areas, White Pine with shade-intolerant hardwoods occur, with Red Oak on the ridges. Open peatlands are dominated by low ericaceous shrubs such as Leather-leaf, Sheep Laurel, Rhodora, and Labrador Tea.

Describing the southwestern section of this Unit in 1912, C.D. Howe wrote: "Deep sands to coarse materials covered only with a thin layer of sand may be found spread out in billowy masses. Such sands are very common ... giving rise to extensive areas of white pine forests; while the coarse materials are frequent along the southern border of the granite. ... Being heavy and coarse they never got far from their original source. ... They are barren or semi-barren because of too thorough drainage and natural poverty of plant food materials. ... One frequently finds drained lake beds in the possession of coarse grasses and sedges. ... The lower and middle courses of the rivers ... from the Clyde to the Sable are characterized by low undulating deposits of sand interspersed by rocky or gravelly ridges, bogs and swamps. The two latter are most extensive in the valleys of the Clyde and Sable where they occupy from one-third to one-half of the area. They contain spruce and fir pulpwood in about equal proportions, usually, however, the spruce predominates. One finds in these regions blocks of several thousand acres, not over five percent of which are forested, the rest being barren, open bogs and brushland. Thickets of wire birch, red maple and red oak cover the gravelly and rocky ridges. Along the bases of the ridges the young hardwoods are mixed with spruce and fir."

In the less-severely burned areas south of Lake Rossignol, the undulating terrain supports Eastern Hemlock and Red Spruce, with some shade-tolerant hardwoods on well-drained sites. Very large Yellow Birch are found in these forests. Large expanses of organic soils support mature trees. Deeper organic soils are characterized by Red Maple and Ash, while shallower organic soils support larch. The luxurious understory in these larch swamps contains larger-than-usual Interrupted Fern.

In the lower valleys of the Jordan and Sable rivers, sandy soils are found which are extensively burnt and support White Pine stands with Red Oak. Further inland, the Upper Ohio area, which has not been heavily burned, is characterized by Red Spruce, Eastern Hemlock, and White Pine on the drier ridges, with more Yellow Birch than elsewhere.

Coastal-plain plants are relatively common in this Unit.

ANIMALS

Large areas of barren and bog limit the productive wildlife habitat. Snowshoe Hare and bobcat are relatively abundant, and Black Bear occur, particularly where berry bushes are abundant on the barrens. There are large concentrations of deer. The Common Shrew, Short-tailed Shrew, Red-Backed Vole, and White-footed Mouse are the most common small mammals. Rivers and lakes are acidic and often dystrophic, with low natural productivity. Painted Turtles and endangered Blanding's Turtles are found here. Snakes are unusually common in the larch swamps.

CULTURAL ENVIRONMENT

The barren nature of much of the land has left this area sparsely settled. Repeated fires have contributed to the widespread barrens. However, hunting, fishing, and canoeing have long been popular pursuits in the Mersey Meadows, and the Mersey River was a traditional transport route for the Mi'kmaq and the French. New immigrants cut the forests, especially White Pine, to supply timber to the shipbuilding market. Log drives transported timber down the Mersey River, which connects the hinterland with the port of Liverpool.

Lake Rossignol was flooded in the 1920s for hydro power use by pulp and paper companies. Today, six hydroelectric generating stations are located on the Mersey River. The flooding of Lake Rossignol affected animal wildlife populations and, consequently, Mi'kmaq hunting and fishing guides could no longer fish salmon or hunt moose here for a period of time.

The Tobeatic Wildlife Management Area spans part of the Mersey Meadows and is one of the largest remaining wildland areas in Nova Scotia.

• • • • • • • •

Sites of Special Interest
• Tobeatic Game Sanctuary (provincial) (see also sub-District 440a)
• Burnaby Lake (IBP Proposed Ecological Site 42)—mature Red Spruce stand
• Shelburne River (IBP Proposed Ecological Site 43)—old Eastern Hemlock stand
• Sixth Lake (IBP Proposed Ecological Site 44)—Red Spruce, Eastern Hemlock forest
• Broad River (IBP Proposed Ecological Site 45)—Red Spruce forest
• Silvery Lake (IBP Proposed Ecological Site 47)—old Eastern Hemlock forest

• Quinan Lake (IBP Proposed Ecological Site 50)—an example of old mixed forest
• Lake Rossignol—significant archeological site

Ecological Reserves
• Ponhook Nature Reserve

Provincial Parks and Park Reserves
• Ten Mile Lake
• Welcum

Proposed Parks and Protected Areas System includes Natural Landscape 13, and Candidate Protected Areas 28 Lake Rossignol and 30 Tidney River.

Associated Topics
T2.2 The Avalon and Meguma Zones, T3.4 Terrestrial Glacial Deposits and Landscape Features, T8.2 Freshwater Environments, T8.3 Freshwater Wetlands, T10.1 Vegetation Change, T10.3 Vegetation and the Environment, T11.9 Carnivores, T11.10 Ungulates, T11.15 Amphibians and Reptiles, T12.8 Fresh Water and Resources.

Associated Habitats
H3 Fresh Water, H4.1 Bog, H4.2 Fen, H5.1 Barren, H6.1 Hardwood Forest (Maple, Oak, Birch Association), H6.2 Softwood Forest (Pine Association; Spruce, Hemlock, Pine Association; Black Spruce, Larch Association).

**412
Mersey
Meadows**

413 QUARTZITE BARRENS

The Quartzite Barrens are divided into two sub-Units:

(a) Halifax

(b) Guysborough

GEOLOGY AND LANDSCAPE DEVELOPMENT

The mantle of quartzite till ranges in thickness from 1–10 m in this Unit but averages less than 3 m. There are several large areas of exposed rock where the till has been scraped off by glacial ice. Specific localities are:

- north and west of Mount Uniacke
- around the Halifax International Airport
- around Anderson Lake in Dartmouth
- several areas from the Liscomb Game Sanctuary to Country Harbour River

The bedrock-dominated topography of these extensive barrens is best described as "ridge-swamp-swale" in seemingly endless repetition (see Figure 11). Where greater thicknesses of glacial till have accumulated, drumlins and drumlinoid till features are found.

Welt-shaped drumlins of reddish Lawrencetown Till (sub-Units 435a and 435b) are scattered throughout. This glacial material is derived predominantly from the reddish sandstones and siltstones of the Carboniferous and Triassic areas to the north but also includes material from the Cobequid Hills and Pictou-Antigonish Highlands.

Additional small patches of "unmoulded" red till are found in central Guysborough in association with small glacial outwash deposits. At Indian Harbour River, the valley is filled with thick layers of outwash sand and gravel.

In the Halifax-Guysborough area the many long sub-parallel faults create linear valleys which are followed by rivers and sometimes filled by lakes; for example, Porters Lake, Lake Charlotte, Sheet Harbour River, Indian Harbour, and St. Marys River.

FRESH WATER

The many glacial lakes in this Unit vary in size and tend to be dystrophic. In the more developed areas, eutrophication is common. The scattered wetlands, mainly bogs and swamps, tend to be biologically productive. Bogs are raised and associated with flat fens. The Sackville River has an extensive floodplain.

The pH levels have been recorded as low as 5.0 in Beaver Lake and as high as 7.5 in Lake William (sub-Unit 413a). The average pH tends to be around 6.5. Conductivity ranges between 12 micromhos/cm in Indian Lake (sub-Unit 413b) and 98 micromhos/cm in Micmac Lake (sub-Unit 413a).

SOILS

Halifax (sub-Unit 413a)
Much of this area is covered by Halifax soils—well-drained, stony, sandy loams, developed on till derived principally from quartzite. The poorly drained associate Danesville occurs in areas of low relief, together with Aspotogan soils and peat. Some Bridgewater soil, derived from slates, is also found. Scattered Wolfville drumlins occur, with larger areas of continuous Wolfville soil in the Beaverbank and Dollar Lake areas (see Unit 436).

Guysborough (sub-Unit 413b)
Halifax, Danesville, and Aspotogan soils again predominate. Scattered Wolfville drumlins occur, concentrated in the central part of the sub-Unit (see Unit 435). Hebert, Cumberland, and Chaswood soils have developed on alluvial and outwash material along the St. Marys River.

PLANTS

In this Unit the higher and broader ridges are capped by American Beech, Yellow Birch, Red Maple, and Sugar Maple. On the hardwood hills around Liscomb, big Sugar Maples and Yellow Birch occur. Mixed stands of Red Spruce fringe these hardwood hills with some Balsam Fir, Yellow Birch, Eastern Hemlock, and White Spruce. In the depressions, swamps dominated by Black Spruce and larch alternate with patches of sand with some White Pine. Slow-moving streams are bordered by broad, swampy areas with Balsam Fir, Red Maple, and Black Spruce. Extensive shrub-dominated barrens occur, with Wire Birch, Red Maple, and aspen. Scattered Black Spruce and White Pine are also found on the barrens, depending on soil drainage conditions. Bog vegetation includes various species of grass, bulrushes, and low ericaceous shrubs.

This impoverished forest area was characterized in the early twentieth century by C.D. Howe. Since he wrote, there has been a reduction in the number of fires and a consequent improvement in forest conditions. His description in 1912 was: "In the western portion, the country has the appearance of a plateau, in which the low narrow ridges have nearly vertical strata, bare of soil and bare of trees except in the crevices of the rock. The depressions between the ridges are filled with patches of sand, on which are pine stands alternating with swamps in which balsam fir and black spruce predominate. The broader and higher ridges are capped with hardwoods and mixed stands are found on the lower slopes. Most of these are now in a severely culled or second growth condition. The slow moving streams are bordered by broad, swampy areas in which fir and red maple form two-thirds of the stand, the other third being made up of black spruce, yellow birch and black ash in about equal proportions. ... (To the east) the ridges are farther apart and have more extensive sand deposits and bogs between them. ... The fire barren on the quartzite east and northeast of Halifax harbour is covered to the extent of 80 percent with wire birch, the rest being red maple with scattering yellow birch and beech. Fir prevails along the margins of the numerous lakes and ponds and it frequently covers the tops of low ridges. Overtopping these are scattered mature white pine and an occasional red pine. ... For the most part the surface is strewn with boulders and the soil is sandy, although the greater part of the volume is occupied by pebbles and boulders of various sizes. ... It is evident that such soil does not encourage heavy forest growth, even when not pauperized by frequent fires."

ANIMALS

Extensive forest cutting has provided good browsing habitat for deer and Snowshoe Hare. The abundance of hare also supports a good population of bobcat. Small-mammal diversity is moderately high in well-drained mixed and hardwood forest habitats, especially along rivers and streams; elsewhere it is quite low. St. Marys River is an important salmon river. Typical fish species include White and Yellow Perch, White Sucker, Brown Bullhead, Brook Trout, Banded Killifish, sticklebacks, Golden Shiner, Lake Trout and American Eel.

CULTURAL ENVIRONMENT

The Quartzite Barrens have been the most productive area in Nova Scotia for gold mining during the past century, with mines at Goldboro, Goldenville, Waverley, Moose River, and other sites. Hydroelectric power is harnessed at Malay Falls and Ruth Falls.

Loyalist refugees settled in this area, and communities such as Sheet Harbour became prosperous centres for the lumber industry. Black Loyalists settled in Preston (sub-Unit 413a) on small lots situated in swampy areas or on barren, unproductive soil.

The Shubenacadie Canal attempted to provide a link between the Atlantic Ocean and the Bay of Fundy.

Woodlot management occurs in this Unit, and there are two game sanctuaries: the Waverley Game Sanctuary in the Halifax Quartzite Barrens and the Liscomb Game Sanctuary in the Guysborough Quartzite Barrens. St. Marys River is an important site for salmon and trout fishing and other outdoor recreation.

• • • • • • • •

Sites of Special Interest
- Indian River—fault valley filled with glacial outwash deposits
- Route 101 to Mt. Uniacke from Halifax—bedrock ridges overlain with a veneer of quartzite till; an occasional crosscut drumlin
- Liscomb Game Sanctuary–Abraham Lake (IBP Proposed Ecological Site 31)—mature Red Spruce forest
- Melrose (IBP Proposed Ecological Site 27)—old Eastern Hemlock forest
- St. Marys River
- Sherbrooke Village Restoration—heritage village museum
- Fairbanks Centre, Dartmouth, Shubenacadie Canal interpretation
- Hemlock Ravine—urban park of historic and national significance

Provincial Parks and Park Reserves
- Uniacke Estate Museum Park
- Bell
- Cockscomb Lake
- Rocky Lake
- Portobello
- Lake Echo
- Lawrencetown
- Lake Charlotte

- Salsman
- Sheet Harbour
- Stillwater

Proposed Parks and Protected Areas System includes Natural Landscapes 30a and 35b and Candidate Protected Areas 15 Liscomb River, 16 The Big Bog, and 17 Alder Grounds.

Scenic Viewpoints
- Middle Country Harbour Provincial Park (sub-Unit 413b)

Associated Topics
T2.2 The Avalon and Meguma Zones, T3.4 Terrestrial Glacial Deposits and Landscape Features, T11.9 Carnivores, T11.11 Small Mammals, T11.13 Freshwater Fishes, T12.3 Geology and Resources, T12.10 Plants and Resources, T12.11 Animals and Resources.

Associated Habitats
H3 Freshwater, H4.3 Swamp, H5.1 Barren, H6.1 Hardwood Forest (Sugar Maple, Yellow Birch, Beech Association).

**413
Quartzite
Barrens**

420 SLOPES AND RIDGES

District 420 has been divided into three Units:

- 421 Sissiboo Lowlands
- 422 South Mountain Slope
- 423 Slate Ridges

GEOLOGY AND LANDSCAPE DEVELOPMENT

The geology in this District is dominated by Halifax slate, which occurs in folds within the Goldenville greywacke. In most of the District the slate is overlain by Silurian White Rock volcanics and sometimes also by Early Devonian sandstones.

The Units within this District are distributed around the northern and western margins of the Atlantic Interior. Their topography reflects the somewhat lesser resistance of slate compared to the surrounding strata. The District may be divided into seven sub-Units: in three the slate has been buried by glacial deposits and forms a flat lowland, in two the slate forms valleys on the upland slope, and in two the slate forms ridges.

SCENIC QUALITY

This District contains a variety of landscapes because it is geologically rather than topographically defined. The Sissiboo Lowlands (Unit 421) has much glacial till and as a consequence supports good forest growth and some marginal farming activity. The lack of relief is offset by numerous lakes, giving medium scenic ratings. The two South Mountain Slope sub-Units (422a and b) have deep valleys that cut back from the sedimentary lowlands, notably the valleys of the Bear, Nictaux, and Gaspereau rivers. Though small in scale, these valleys have high scenic value, particularly where there is farming settlement on the valley floor. The slate ridges of Rawdon Hills and Wittenburg Ridge (Unit 423), by contrast, rise above surrounding soft-rock areas. They have moderate relief (the Rawdon Hills being more indented) but lack of settlement and lakes gives them only medium scenic value.

420
Slopes and
Ridges

421 SISSIBOO LOWLANDS

This Unit has three subdivisions:
- (a) Sissiboo Lowlands
- (b) Meteghan Lowland
- (c) Lake George

GEOLOGY AND LANDSCAPE DEVELOPMENT

These areas are underlain by synclines containing Halifax slate with, in the Sissiboo and Lake George areas, thicknesses of Silurian White Rock volcanics.

The three sub-Units lie within the Digby-Yarmouth area and share the same complex glacial history. (See also Unit 411.) Four separate glacial phases have been recognized from the last ice advance. In the first phase the ice came from the east and produced a grey till derived from local material. The second pulse was the major one from New Brunswick, which engulfed the entire province and deposited a red till (Red Head Till) in this area. The third pulse of glacial ice, presumably from an ice sheet in Nova Scotia, flowed parallel to the coastline and deposited the Saulnierville Till. Finally, a weak flow from an ice cap on the Southern Upland deposited the loose material of the Beaver River Till. The Beaver River Till is at the surface of the quartzite and slate tills from which the soils have formed over most of the area. Both this and the Saulnierville Till contain fragments of Meguma Group rocks and White Rock volcanics. The relationship between the four different till layers is best seen along coastal sections, although occasionally inland a lower till is just partly covered and revealed in the centre of younger till deposits, for example, from Cape St. Mary north to Lac de Gruau.

The three areas differ somewhat in the composition of the Beaver River Till exposed on the surface. In the Sissiboo Lowlands and Meteghan Lowland, slate tills and drumlins predominate, whereas at Lake George the till and drumlins are composed predominantly of quartzite.

A few isolated deposits of water-deposited debris are present within this Unit; the best examples can be found along the shore of the Tusket River (Unit 831). There are one or two isolated eskers; one is found on the west side of Gaspereau Lake in the Meteghan Lowland.

Overall, the Sissiboo Lowlands have a low relief and a stony drumlin terrain.

FRESH WATER

Lakes are numerous and are elongated north-south, often forming chains. Scattered wetlands are typically raised bogs associated with fens. Swamps are also typical of the Sissiboo Lowlands. Several large areas of shrub swamp and marsh are found in sub-Units 421b and 421c.

Freshwater is generally dystrophic. Conductivity levels range between 32 and 59 micromhos/cm, and pH levels range between 5.4 and 6.7.

SOILS

Sissiboo Lowlands (sub-Unit 421a)
Well-drained Bridgewater and imperfectly drained Riverport soils, both sandy loams derived from slate, occur in this sub-Unit.

Meteghan Lowland (sub-Unit 421b)
Near the coast, Riverport and Bridgewater soils occur on gentle to undulating terrain. Further inland, well-drained Mersey and imperfectly drained Liverpool soils have developed from schists and quartzite, accompanied by poorly drained, mottled Pitman soils and areas of peat.

Lake George (sub-Unit 421c)
Moderately well-drained Yarmouth soils derived from schist and quartzite occur, with mottled Deerfield soils in areas with less relief. Liverpool and Pitman soils occur on very flat areas. To the north of this sub-Unit some well-drained Medway soils have formed on sands and gravels.

PLANTS

This entire Unit exhibits excellent forest growth on schisty and slaty soils. The Sissiboo Lowlands sub-Unit (421a) has considerably more hardwoods than the other sub-Units. The terrain is rolling and, on better-drained sites, American Beech and Red Oak with Sugar Maple, Yellow Birch, and aspen grow interspersed with shade-intolerant hardwoods. On moderately drained sites, a Red Spruce and Black Spruce mixture occurs. Ash is found with the spruces on Deerfield soils. The shade-intolerant Red Maple and White Birch are also mixed with ash on the

Pitman soils. The Meteghan Lowland (sub-Unit 421b) is predominantly mixed with Red Spruce, Black Spruce, Red Maple and White Birch. The Lake George sub-Unit (421c) has been very heavily disturbed. Pure stands of White Spruce have re-colonized oldfields and pastures, and American Beech, Yellow Birch, and shade-intolerant hardwoods are abundant.

Shorelines of lakes and streams may include coastal-plain plants, some of which are considered rare in Nova Scotia.

ANIMALS

An inland breeding colony of Black-backed Gulls and Double-crested Cormorants occurs at Lake George. Freshwater habitats have a relatively rich aquatic fauna with some coastal-plain species of molluscs and arthropods. Fish species include Smallmouth Bass, Yellow Perch, Brown Bullhead and White Sucker. Creek Chub, Atlantic Salmon, Brown Trout, American Eel, and Gaspereau are also found in sub-Unit 421c.

CULTURAL ENVIRONMENT

Acadians settled parts of this area after the deportation of 1755. Forests supplied lumber for the ship-building industry in the nineteenth century along the shores of St. Marys Bay. Much of the fertile land in this Unit has been cleared for agriculture and many areas are still actively farmed. White Spruce is recolonizing abandoned farmlands. Hydroelectric power was harnessed at Sissiboo Falls. The rivers support sport fishing for Brook Trout, Smallmouth Bass and Atlantic Salmon.

• • • • • • • •

Sites of Special Interest
- Placid Lake in sub-Unit 421a (IBP Proposed Ecological Site 56)—dystrophic lake, flood plains, and old Eastern Hemlock stand
- Cape St. Mary to Lac de Gruau in sub-Unit 421b—older till exposed in centre of younger till

Provincial Parks and Park Reserves
- Ellenwood Lake (sub-Unit 421c)
- Corberrie (sub-Unit 421a)

Proposed Parks and Protected Areas System includes Natural Landscape 5.

Associated Topics
T2.2 The Avalon and Meguma Zones, T3.3 Glaciation, Deglaciation and Sea-level Changes, T3.4 Terrestrial Glacial Deposits and Landscape Features, T11.16 Land and Freshwater Invertebrates.

Associated Habitats
H4.1 Bog, H4.2 Fen, H4.3 Swamp, H4.4 Freshwater Marsh, H5.2 Oldfield, H6.1 Hardwood Forest (Sugar Maple, Yellow Birch, Beech Association), H6.2 Softwood Forest (White Spruce Association; Black Spruce, Larch Association).

**421
Sissiboo
Lowlands**

422 SOUTH MOUNTAIN SLOPE

This Unit has two subdivisions:
(a) Bear River
(b) Gaspereau Valley

GEOLOGY AND LANDSCAPE DEVELOPMENT

The two sub-Units of the South Mountain Slope—Bear River and the Gaspereau Valley—are underlain by Halifax slate (Cambrian-Ordovician) interfolded with White Rock Group volcanics (mostly ash) and sandstone (Silurian); and Torbrook sandstones and siltstone (Early Devonian). The younger White Rock and Torbrook deposits are preserved in synclines.

The volcanic ash deposits are relatively thin in this area compared to the 3,000 m of ash and lava in the Yarmouth area. They contain no volcanic bombs and offer no evidence of a volcanic centre nearby, adding weight to the view that the Silurian volcano was well over 100 km to the south, near Yarmouth.

The slates, sandstones, siltstones, and ash deposits are truncated to the south by contact with the South Mountain Granite (see Figure 25). To the north they are overlain by soft Triassic deposits in the Annapolis Valley. They are therefore intermediate in hardness and form a dissected shoulder to the granite next to the low-lying valley floor. Deep valleys have been cut in these rocks, which are relatively unresistant, compared to the granite outcrops to the south. Bear River has cut a deep valley across the fold axis of the slates to reach the Annapolis Basin, which is cut into even less-resistant sandstones. The Gaspereau, in contrast, follows the fold axis and flows parallel to Annapolis Valley sandstones before emptying into the Minas Basin.

Bear River (sub-Unit 422a)
Bedrock in the Bear River area is overlain by a thick glacial till derived from the Halifax slate. This, in turn, is overlain by a thin, clay till veneer. Along the coast are thick deposits of outwash gravel which form a series of terraces from The Joggins in the west to Cornwallis in the east. These date from the immediate post-glacial period when the sea level rose rapidly as the ice caps melted. The sands and gravels washed down from South Mountain formed terraces, beach deposits, and deltas at sea level. When the land rebounded in response to the removal of the ice, the sea level became relatively lower and deposits were left well above high tide. At the same time, in response to the lowering of the sea level, Bear River and Acadia Brook deepened their valleys.

Gaspereau Valley (sub-Unit 422b)
The western part of this sub-Unit is covered with Rawdon till, a ground moraine derived from a mixture of slate, sandstone, and carbonate rocks. Along Halfway River, north and south of Greenfield, are pockets of glacially derived gravel that may be kames and kame terraces. Eskers are also indicated.

An interesting geographic feature in this area is the classic example of river capture shown by the Gaspereau River. The Gaspereau, with a lower base level, has cut back towards the Black River, which originally flowed directly northwards through Deep Hollow to join the Cornwallis River. The Gaspereau eventually captured the headwaters of the Black River, leaving an undersized stream to flow through the original valley and a wind gap just north of White Rock.

FRESH WATER

Rivers make up most of the surface water in this Unit. Bear River divides sub-Unit 422a and is tidal where it drains into the Annapolis Basin. The pH level has been recorded as low as 4.7. Several large rivers and smaller streams flow down from the South Mountain into the Annapolis Valley in sub-Unit 422b. Levels of pH in the larger rivers range between 5.1 and 5.9; Sunken Lake has a pH of 7.4.

SOILS

Soils derived from shaly loam glacial tills characterize this Unit. Bridgewater soils, derived from slaty till, and its associate Riverport and Middlewood soils dominate the Bear River area (sub-Unit 422a). The proximity of various other rock types and different directions of glacial movement has resulted in various other soils, including Wolfville (red-brown sandy till) and Digby (outwash deposits). In the Gaspereau Valley (sub-Unit 422b), the reddish-brown shaly loams have produced Morristown soils. Very steep slopes along the river valleys throughout the Unit have unstable soils with seepage spots.

PLANTS

The usually deep soils support productive mixed forest with spruce, pine, hemlock, aspen, and maple.

ANIMALS

The Gaspereau Valley provides Bald Eagle wintering habitat. The Gaspereau River supports abundant fish spawning runs of Gaspereau, and Striped Bass are known to feed here.

In the cultivated lowland areas, small mammals are predominantly those species associated with non-forested habitats, for example, the Meadow Vole and Meadow Jumping Mouse. The small-mammal diversity is relatively high in well-drained, mixed, and deciduous forest habitats, especially along rivers and streams; elsewhere it is quite low. This Unit supports disjunct populations of the Southern Flying Squirrel.

CULTURAL ENVIRONMENT

This Unit has been extensively cut over and supports a considerable amount of agricultural activity. Planters, and later Loyalists, settled in various parts of Bear River (sub-Unit 422a) and the Gaspereau Valley (sub-Unit 422b), which were soon cleared for farmlands with relatively fertile soils. The stream now known as Bear River is derived from the name Hebert River, which appeared on a map by Lescarbot published in 1609. Lumbering activities take place in wooded backland areas. Hydroelectric power has been harnessed at Hells Gate. A hiking trail at White Rock in the Gaspereau Valley is a popular recreational spot.

• • • • • • • •

Sites of Special Interest
- Bear River above highway bridge at Roop Point—gravel terrace 27 m above sea level
- Bear River, east of river mouth—gravels 30 m above sea level
- Deep Brook—terrace 42 m above sea level
- Smiths Cove—fine stratified sands 30 m above sea level
- The Joggins—fine sands extending westwards for 4 km
- Gaspereau Valley—river capture, and wind gap at Deep Hollow

Provincial Parks and Park Reserves
Proposed Parks and Protected Areas System includes Natural Landscapes 3 and 5.

Scenic Viewpoints
- Sub-Unit 422a: Bear River village
- Sub-Unit 422b: Nictaux Falls; South Mountain south of Morristown; Hells Gate trail at White Rock; Deep Hollow north of White Rock; South Mountain south of Gaspereau village

Associated Topics
T3.2 Ancient Drainage Patterns, T3.3 Glaciation, Deglaciation and Sea-level Changes, T3.4 Terrestrial Glacial Deposits and Landscape Features, T11.4 Birds of Prey, T11.11 Small Mammals, T11.13 Freshwater Fishes, T11.18 Rare and Endangered Animals, T12.9 Soil and Resources, T12.10 Plants and Resources.

Associated Habitats
H5.2 Oldfield, H6.2 Softwood Forest (Spruce, Hemlock, Pine Association), H6.3 Mixedwood Forest (Spruce, Fir, Pine–Maple, Birch Association).

**422
South
Mountain
Slope**

423 SLATE RIDGES

This Unit has two subdivisions:
- (a) Rawdon Hills
- (b) Wittenburg Ridge

GEOLOGY AND LANDSCAPE DEVELOPMENT

The Rawdon Hills and Wittenburg Ridge are two ridges of slate located at the margins of the Windsor Lowlands (Unit 511). They may both be ancient landscape features dating back to the pre-Carboniferous period. The Wittenburg Ridge may have been an island or peninsula in the Early Carboniferous sea that covered this part of the province, because the Horton deposits wedge out on its flanks. The same does not appear to be true for the Rawdon Hills, which were probably engulfed early in this depositional period.

The two ridges are abutted by Early Carboniferous deposits. Both Horton and Windsor deposits outcrop against the Rawdon Hills; the Wittenburg Ridge is almost surrounded by Windsor Group deposits. Where Halifax slate and Windsor deposits are juxtaposed, the latter are preferentially eroded, leaving the slate as higher land. This situation is in contrast to the more common relationship of slate and greywacke in which the slate, being softer, forms valleys (see Figure 11).

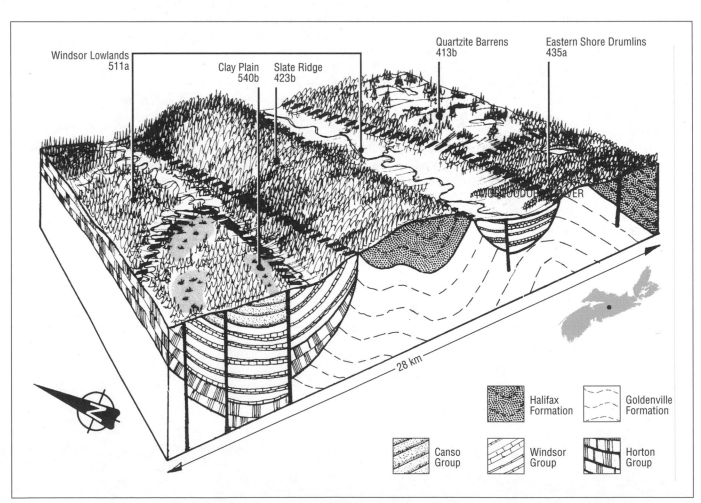

Figure 11: Wittenburg Ridge area. This outlying ridge of slates (Unit 423) is part of an ancient landscape that is still being exhumed from its cover of more recent sedimentary deposits. The south branch of the Stewiacke River flows to the north of the ridge and the Musqodoboit River valley is to the south. Both form parts of the Windsor Lowlands till plain (Unit 511). Parts of the Atlantic Interior are in the background: Quartzite Barrens (Unit 413) and one of the Eastern Shore Drumlin fields (Unit 435). Flat-lying clays derived from Canso Group rocks form the poorly drained clay plain (Unit 540).

Both the Rawdon Hills and Wittenburg Ridge are covered by sheets of the reddish Lawrencetown Till, which is derived from the Carboniferous Lowlands, interspersed with locally derived grey till.

FRESH WATER

Both ridges are drainage divides, but the Rawdon Hills are also crosscut by a number of streams that are tributaries of the Avon River. The Herbert River, Meander River, and Glen Brook all have valleys which lie directly across the ridge and which must have been superimposed by downcutting from a higher level. These three river valleys also contain extensive deposits of outwash gravel on the northern side of the ridge where the slope meets the Windsor Lowlands. The Wittenburg Ridge is the partial headwater for the Musqodoboit River system.

SOILS

Rawdon Hills (sub-Unit 423a)
Soils in this sub-Unit have developed from slates and shales. Soils of the Rawdon catena are most common; they are shaly, sandy loams derived from slates and shales, ranging from rapidly to moderately slowly drained. Elmsdale soils also occur, derived from shales and sandstones, with slate and quartzite cobbles.

Wittenburg Ridge (sub-Unit 423b)
Queens clay loams occur on the slopes, with some imperfectly drained Hantsport soil north of Upper Musquodoboit. On top of the ridge, well-drained Kirkhill shaly loams occur, with small areas of poorly drained Middlewood and Riverport soils, developed from shaly loams.

PLANTS

Although the Rawdon Hills and Wittenburg Ridge are considerably lower than the other areas included in Loucks' Sugar Maple, Yellow Birch–Fir Zone (Maritime Uplands Ecoregion), they are still high enough to produce local climates that encourage shade-tolerant hardwoods. These occur as stands of Sugar Maple, Yellow Birch, and American Beech, but extensive cutting has produced a predominantly mixed forest with Red Spruce, Eastern Hemlock, pine, Balsam Fir, maple, birch, and ash. A vigorous understory of Balsam Fir and Red Spruce under hardwood stands is present throughout the Slate Ridges Unit. Pine is somewhat less common on the Rawdon Hills.

CULTURAL ENVIRONMENT

Both the Rawdon Hills and Wittenburg Ridge have hosted lumbering activity. Farming is marginal in these areas. Gold was once mined at settlements such as Gore. Stibnite, the chief ore of antimony, was mined intermittently at West Gore between 1884 and 1917.

• • • • • • • •

Scenic Viewpoints
*   Sub-Unit 423a—Highway 14, east of Centre Rawdon

Provincial Parks and Park Reserves
Proposed Parks and Protected Areas System includes Natural Landscapes 29a and 29b.

Associated Topics
T2.4 The Carboniferous Basin, T3.1 Development of the Ancient Landscape.

Associated Habitats
H6.1 Hardwood Forest (Sugar Maple, Yellow Birch, Beech Association), H6.3 Mixedwood Forest (Spruce, Fir, Pine–Maple, Birch Association).

**423
Slate
Ridges**

430 DRUMLINS

The Drumlins District has been divided into six units:

431   Annapolis Drumlins
432   Ponhook Drumlins
433   Kejimkujik Drumlins
434   Lunenburg Drumlins
435   Eastern Shore Drumlins
436   Headwater Lakes

GEOLOGY AND LANDSCAPE DEVELOPMENT

Nova Scotia's drumlins are mostly confined to the Atlantic side of the province, where the ice moved across level areas or down a slope, with a free exit to the continental shelf. Most of the drumlins are associated with slate areas. Slate strata are sheared off more readily and to a greater depth than other types of strata, so a large amount of material was available for molding by the ice. Drumlins in Nova Scotia are rare along a band one to five kilometres wide on the northwestern side of a slate area, but to the southeast they may extend for several miles into a greywacke area. Occasional drumlins may be found in a granite area, but generally they quickly disappear once the granitic border is crossed. This restriction to the slate areas is not so well marked in the Halifax-Guysborough area, where drumlins sometimes appear in

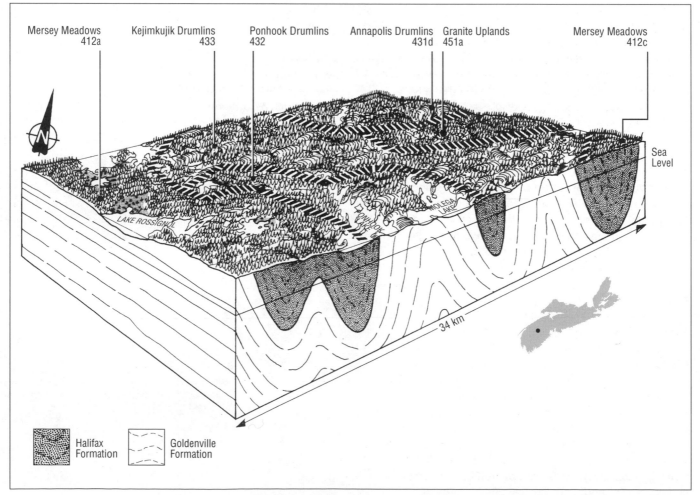

Figure 12: Drumlin field. Lakes and drumlins are major features dominating the peneplain surface of Meguma Group rocks of the Atlantic Interior (Region 400). Three types of drumlins are shown: those derived from slate (Unit 433) which hold moisture throughout the summer, and loose, droughty drumlins derived from granite (Unit 431) or quartzite (Unit 432). Lakes and associated bogs of the otherwise featureless Mersey Meadows (Unit 412) are shown in the left foreground.

a predominantly greywacke area where bands of slate are narrow and widely separated; there, perhaps, more material had been accumulated from areas farther north. Carboniferous materials with a distinct red colour form the eastern sections of the large drumlin field in Lunenburg County (Unit 434), and the drumlins on the Eastern Shore and north of Halifax. Isolated "red" drumlins may occur in any part of the Atlantic Interior. Slate drumlins are "grey," providing an easy field identification of their origins. Almost all drumlins—of any origin, local or distant—seem to exhibit a thin cover of granite pebbles and boulders.

Drumlins were formed with their long axes parallel to the direction in which the ice was moving. Those in southwestern Nova Scotia indicate a nearly southerly ice movement becoming southeasterly in eastern Lunenburg and western Halifax counties. Drumlins around Halifax have about the same size and orientation as those in central Lunenburg County. However, from Sheet Harbour east to beyond the Guysborough County border, the drumlins again have a north-south orientation, as if they were formed by ice that moved directly down from the Gulf of St. Lawrence. The few around Canso are oriented more to the southeast. In general, the ice appears to have moved directly across central and western mainland Nova Scotia from New Brunswick, whereas in eastern Nova Scotia the ice moved southward from Pictou and Antigonish counties and spread out to the east into Chedabucto Bay.

The composition of the drumlins is greatly varied. Most are composed of fine-textured tills derived from underlying or adjacent rocks. In several areas, material from Carboniferous rocks to the north composes the drumlins or drumlin field (see Figure 12):

431 Annapolis Drumlins—granitic materials
432 Ponhook Drumlins—quartzite materials
433 Kejimkujik Drumlins—slate materials
434 Lunenburg Drumlins, 435 Eastern Shore Drumlins, and 436 Headwater Lakes—Carboniferous materials, predominantly "red" drumlins with some slate

SCENIC QUALITY

The drumlins within a single drumlin field or "swarm" have a similar size, shape, and orientation. However, Nova Scotia's drumlin fields provide markedly dissimilar landscapes, depending primarily on their suitability for early farming and settlement. Of the six Districts, only the Lunenburg Drumlins (Unit 434) and Kejimkujik Drumlins (Unit 433) were extensively exploited for their well-drained loam soils.

Here farms still dot the landscape (even though there has been much land abandonment) and provide variety and interest. They cling to the frequent small hills interspersed between lakes and bogs. The dense road network allows easy visual access to the landscape and scenic ratings range from medium to moderately high. The other drumlin Units (431, 432, 435, and 436) have poorer soils and historically have supported very little farming. As a consequence, they have less scenic interest and are also provided with less road access.

**430
Drumlins**

431 ANNAPOLIS DRUMLINS

This Unit has four subdivisions:
  (a) Fisher Lake
  (b) Spectacle Lake
  (c) Alma Lake
  (d) Round Lake

GEOLOGY AND LANDSCAPE DEVELOPMENT

The Annapolis Drumlins are found in four small, isolated localities on the South Mountain Granite. Drumlins do not normally form from granitic material. Those drumlins frequently have a rock core. Occasional granitic drumlins are found in non-granite areas such as on Graves Island, but this is unusual. These drumlins contain large granite boulders, are often well- or excessively well-drained, and have soils with characteristics similar to Gibraltar soils (see Figure 12).

FRESH WATER

Many lakes of various sizes and several chain lake systems are found in sub-Units 431a and 421b. All four sub-Units contain significant wetlands, typically flat bogs associated with fens. This Unit contains the partial headwaters of the Mersey and Medway rivers. The highest recorded conductivity level is 32 micromhos/cm, and pH averages 6.0.

PLANTS

The drumlins provide very productive forest sites. On the better-drained tops and slopes, a mixed forest is most common, with Eastern Hemlock, Red Spruce, White Pine, Sugar Maple, Yellow Birch, and some Red Maple. On the wetter sites between the drumlins, spruce, fir, and pine with shade-intolerant hardwoods predominate. Ash is often found on the steep side slopes where seepage occurs.

ANIMALS

Fish species include White Suckers, Yellow Perch, Banded Killifish, Brown Bullhead, Smallmouth Bass, Creek Chub, and Golden Shiner.

CULTURAL ENVIRONMENT

Drumlins have been used for agriculture in this area, but some of these farms were later abandoned and underwent successional forest regeneration. The woodlands attracted migrants from the timber trade, but it was the fertile drumlins that made them settle. Tourism had its beginnings in this area with the arrival of American sportsmen in the 1870s who came for a hunting and angling experience in the backwoods of Nova Scotia, described by travel books as being "unsurpassed game country." Country lodges and cabins were built to accommodate these first American tourists. Today, tourism and outdoor recreation continue to be an important land use.

• • • • • • • •

Associated Topics
T3.4 Terrestrial Glacial Deposits and Landscape Features, T12.9 Soil and Resources, T12.12 Recreational Resources.

Associated Habitats
H3.2, H3.4, H3.6 Freshwater Lentic; H6.1 Hardwood Forest (Sugar Maple, Yellow Birch, Beech Association); H6.2 Softwood Forest (Spruce, Hemlock, Pine Association).

Provincial Parks and Park Reserves
Proposed Parks and Protected Areas System includes Natural Landscapes 16a and 16b.

432 PONHOOK DRUMLINS

GEOLOGY AND LANDSCAPE DEVELOPMENT

The Ponhook Drumlins lie on a narrow belt of greywacke within the slate-dominated area northeast of Lake Rossignol. The till sheet and drumlins are composed of quartzite till, and their distribution almost exactly coincides with the boundaries of the greywacke from which they were derived (see Figure 12). This illustrates how closely the bedrock geology and the composition of the till are related in this part of the Atlantic Interior. The till cover ranges from 1–10 m, and averages 3 m in thickness. The drumlins are generally low, 2–20 m high, and are strongly aligned northwest-southeast.

These drumlins are very stony, and the matrix containing the rocks is very porous. Drainage is therefore excessively rapid in these Halifax sandy loam soils.

The terrain in this area is very flat, with most of the relief being provided by the drumlins. Overall the landscape is hummocky.

FRESH WATER

Many lakes are found in this Unit, but surface water coverage is dominated by Ponhook and Molega lakes. A few scattered fens and flat bogs are associated with the lake edges.

PLANTS

These dry drumlins support a mixture of White Pine, Red Oak, and aspen with some shade-intolerant species. Burned areas often regenerate in American Beech and aspen. Representatives of Coastal Plain Flora include Buttonbush, Gold-crest, Redroot, Long's Bulrush and Cat Brier. These species are associated with lakeshore wetlands.

CULTURAL ENVIRONMENT

Lumbering and farming attracted settlers to the Ponhook Drumlins. Gold mining took place at Molega in the late 1800s. By the mid-nineteenth century, angling and hunting in wilderness backlands had become a sport for many of the well-to-do, who employed Mi'kmaq guides for moose-hunting expeditions. The sporting reputation of Queens and Annapolis counties brought many Americans to this area by the late nineteenth century. Hunting lodges were built in the 1920s, and by the 1930s tourism had become an important economic factor.

• • • • • • • •

Ecological Reserves
• Ponhook Nature Reserve

Provincial Parks and Park Reserves
Proposed Parks and Protected Areas System includes Natural Landscape 15.

Associated Topics
T2.2 The Avalon and Meguma Zones, T3.4 Terrestrial Glacial Deposits and Landscape Features, T12.10 Plants and Resources, T12.11 Animals and Resources.

Associated Habitats
H3.2, H3.4, H3.6 Freshwater Lentic; H4.1 Bog; H4.2 Fen; H6.2 Softwood Forest (Pine Association).

432
Ponhook
Drumlins

433 KEJIMKUJIK DRUMLINS

GEOLOGY AND LANDSCAPE DEVELOPMENT

The Kejimkujik Drumlins or "grey" drumlins cover an extensive area from Lake Kejimkujik to the drainage basin of the southwestern branch of the LaHave River. The underlying bedrock is entirely composed of Halifax slate, and it is from this that the till sheet is derived. The till ranges in thickness from 1–10 m and has a loose matrix with fragments of bedrock. The drumlins are composed of slaty (Hartlen) till which is compact and clayey (see Figure 12).

The landscape of the Kejimkujik Drumlins is hummocky, with relief provided entirely by the low drumlins, 15–30 m high. The coastal equivalent of Unit 433 is described in Unit 832, LaHave Drumlins.

FRESH WATER

The drainage pattern is deranged with many irregularly shaped lakes and sections of some of the larger rivers. Most runoff in this area is eventually directed to the Medway or LaHave rivers. Scattered small flat fens and bogs are found mainly inland. Kejimkujik is generally considered a clear water lake, as it is low in nutrients. Conductivity in this lake is between 23.8 and 25.8 micromhos/cm, and pH has been recorded as low as 5.0. Other lakes in this Unit have conductivity levels ranging between 24 and 42 micromhos/cm, and pH averages 6.0.

SOILS

Soils in this Unit have been mostly derived from slate. Bridgewater soil, a well-drained sandy loam, mantles both the drumlins and the ground in between. Many of the drumlins have been cleared. In the southwest part of the Unit, Bridgewater drumlins spill over into an area of Halifax soils derived from quartzite. On flat and depressed terrain, pockets of poorly drained Riverport and Middlewood soils occur. There are also a few small areas of coarse-textured LaHave and Torbrook soils, developed on water-deposited materials.

PLANTS

This Unit, together with Unit 434, Lunenburg Drumlins, falls within Loucks' Sugar Maple–Hemlock, Pine Zone, in which shade-tolerant hardwoods are found on a wide range of sites. The bowl-shaped depression occupied by this Unit has a distinct local climate: relatively low rainfall and relatively high summer temperatures. The older forest for much of the Unit is Sugar Maple, Yellow Birch, and American Beech, but extensive disturbance by fire and cutting has resulted in large areas of mixed forest: Red Spruce, Eastern Hemlock, pine, and Balsam Fir with the shade-intolerant maple and birch. In this Unit the coarser, drier soils on some drumlins support more White Pine, and more hardwood stands—particularly American Beech, Trembling Aspen, and Red Oak. Many of the drumlins' tops are cleared for agriculture or have been colonized by a post-fire maple, oak, birch association.

Many coastal-plain flora species can be found in this Unit. The disjunct species Gold-crest has been found in wet areas near Fancy Lake, Lunenburg County.

ANIMALS

A warmer climate permits the survival of a distinct relict fauna, including Blanding's Turtle, the Southern Flying Squirrel and the Northern Ribbon Snake. They also allow greater species diversity and greater numbers of reptiles and amphibians. The hardwood forests provide good Ruffed Grouse habitat. Extensive agricultural settlement provides open-land habitat. There are concentrations of White-tailed deer. Distinctive birds include the Scarlet Tanager, Great-crested Flycatcher, and Wood Thrush. The introduced American Dog Tick is frequently encountered here in early summer. Typical fish species include Brook Trout, Lake Chub, Golden Shiner, Brown Bullhead, perch, Banded Killifish and White Sucker. The Petite-Rivière watershed also contains the only known population of Atlantic Whitefish in the world.

CULTURAL ENVIRONMENT

A portion of Kejimkujik National Park occurs within this Unit. This park was established in 1965, its name taken from the largest lake within its boundaries. Kejimkujik is a Mi'kmaq word which has been given various translations such as "attempting to escape" and "swelled waters." A more credible translation, suggested by Thomas Raddall, is "the stricture passage," given by Mi'kmaq to the outlet of the lake where waters backed up or "swelled" as a result of the placement of weirs. Mi'kmaq artifacts such as arrowheads have been found at former campsites and along canoe routes. Around 1835 the Fairy Lake Indian Reserve was established within the park boundaries at a time when the Mi'kmaq were encouraged by the government to abandon their nomadic life. By the turn of the century, the Mi'kmaq had left this reserve.

A significant number of migrants were attracted by the timber trade in the nineteenth century and then stayed to farm. From the early 1800s to 1940, agriculture was the stable base on which communities in this area were formed. Many farmers were also part-time loggers. By the early years of the twentieth century, log drives often began on the Mersey River above Lake Kejimkujik and continued down waterways to Milton and other points near Liverpool. Water-powered sawmills operated throughout this area. Large sawdust piles and accumulations of slabs at various points in the park and the general area remain as evidence of a vanished industry. Vigorous regeneration of disturbed sites by Balsam Fir has formed the basis for the Christmas tree–growing industry in this Unit and adjacent Unit 434. The Kejimkujik Drumlins area experienced about 20 years of prosperous gold mining, from 1883 to 1905, around Whiteburn and Brookfield. A fish hatchery and culture station is located at McGowan Lake.

• • • • • • • •

Sites of Special Interest
- Part of Kejimkujik National Park
- Big Dam Lake (IBP Proposed Ecological Site 63)—old Eastern Hemlock forest
- LaHave Drumlins—global site for classic drumlin field

Ecological Reserves
- Ponhook Nature Reserve

Provincial Parks and Park Reserves
- Fancy Lake

- Cookville
- Camerons Brook
- Nineveh

Proposed Parks and Protected Areas System includes Natural Landscape 15.

Scenic Viewpoints
- Unit 433: LaHave River, both sides below Bridgewater

Associated Topics
T2.2 The Avalon and Meguma Zones, T3.4 Terrestrial Glacial Deposits and Landscape Features, T11.3 Open-habitat Birds, T11.10 Ungulates, T11.15 Amphibians and Reptiles, T11.18 Rare and Endangered Animals, T12.2 Cultural Landscapes, T12.8 Fresh Water and Resources, T12.10 Plants and Resources.

Associated Habitats
H3.2, H3.4, H3.6 Freshwater Lentic; H5.2 Oldfield; H6.1 Hardwood Forest (Maple, Oak, Birch Association); H6.2 Softwood Forest (Pine Association).

**433
Kejimkujik
Drumlins**

434 LUNENBURG DRUMLINS

GEOLOGY AND LANDSCAPE DEVELOPMENT

These "red" drumlins are composed of materials carried into the area from at least 30 km to the north. In some instances, the reddish Carboniferous rocks have been carried at least 60 km and probably further. These distinctive red tills form prominent drumlins up to 25 m high. Occasional slaty till drumlins derived from local material are found among the red drumlins (see Figure 14).

Two reddish tills have been distinguished: the clayey Hartlen Till and the sandier Lawrencetown Till. Most drumlins have a core of Hartlen Till and a mantle of Lawrencetown Till. This drumlin field reaches the coast in Unit 832.

FRESH WATER

There are many medium to large irregularly shaped lakes in this Unit. Scattered wetlands are associated with the many rapidly flowing shallow watercourses. Swamp and peat areas are more common towards the coast where there is less relief. Conductivity ranges between 23.5 and 33.5 micromhos/cm and pH averages 7.1, although it has been recorded as low as 5.1 in the LaHave River.

SOILS

Drumlins in this Unit are mantled in reddish-brown Wolfville soils, well-drained loams over sandy, clay loams containing Carboniferous material. Soils between the drumlins are mostly Bridgewater sandy loams derived from slate, with poorly drained Riverport soil on flat land.

PLANTS

This Unit, together with Unit 433, Kejimkujik Drumlins, falls within Loucks' Sugar Maple–Hemlock, Pine Zone, in which shade-tolerant hardwoods are found on a wide range of sites. This is due to the Unit's position in a bowl-shaped depression, with a distinct local climate: relatively low rainfall and relatively high summer temperatures. The old forest for much of the Unit is American Beech, Sugar Maple, and Red Oak, but extensive disturbance by fire and cutting has resulted in large areas of mixed forest: Red Spruce, White Pine, Eastern Hemlock, and Balsam Fir. The heavier Wolfville soils on the drumlins result in less White Pine, more Red Spruce, and few pure hardwood stands. Regeneration on drumlin tops is predominantly spruce and Balsam Fir. If left alone, Balsam Fir is replaced by other tree species after about 30 years.

ANIMALS

A distinct relict fauna is supported in this Unit by a warmer climate. Blanding's Turtle, Northern Ribbon Snake and the Southern Flying Squirrel can be found here. Reptiles and amphibians are found in great numbers and exhibit considerable species diversity. Small-mammal diversity within the Atlantic Interior Region is probably highest in this Unit. Deer are common, as are perch, White Sucker, Lake Chub, Brown Bullhead and Golden Shiner.

CULTURAL ENVIRONMENT

This area was settled in the eighteenth century by Germans who quickly cleared forested drumlins to establish prosperous farms. Farmers made use of the woodlands, recognizing the different qualities of specific tree species. Much of the timber cut in the area supplied the shipbuilding industry in Lunenburg. Many of the drumlin tops have been cleared for agriculture and are still farmed today. The vigour of regenerating Balsam Fir on abandoned drumlin farms has resulted in the establishment of the Christmas tree-growing industry in this and adjacent Unit 433.

● ● ● ● ● ● ● ●

Sites of Special Interest
* Ross Farm Museum—the story of pioneer farming traditions

Provincial Parks and Park Reserves
* Pinehurst
* Wentzells Lake
* Maitland

Proposed Parks and Protected Areas System includes Natural Landscape 15.

Associated Topics and Habitats
(See Unit 433.)

434
Lunenburg
Drumlins

435 EASTERN SHORE DRUMLINS

This Unit has two subdivisions:
(a) Tangier River
(b) Moser River

GEOLOGY AND LANDSCAPE DEVELOPMENT

Unit 435 is underlain by interfolded greywacke and slate, which form a series of wide bands oriented east-west. These are overlain by a thin quartzite till (averaging three metres in thickness), and in the Moser River area by a mixture of quartzite and Lawrencetown Tills called Red Till. Above these are drumlins of red, sandy Lawrencetown Till. The latter is derived from the Carboniferous Lowlands to the north and contains fragments of rock from the Cobequid Hills and the Pictou-Antigonish Highlands.

The Moser River watershed contains several deposits of outwash sands and gravels. The largest ones fringe Necum Teuch Bay.

The relief in the Tangier and Moser river areas is low, with most of the visual variety being provided by the drumlins (see Figure 11). The average elevations are different in the two areas, however. At Moser River the hills rarely exceed 80 m, whereas in the Tangier River area the hills average 100–130 m.

FRESH WATER

The drainage in both areas is deranged, with many irregularly shaped small to medium-sized lakes and many streams and brooks. Scattered raised and flat bogs are associated with flat fens. Conductivity is low and pH levels average 6.3 in the lakes and 5.2 in the larger streams.

SOILS

Tangier River (sub-Unit 435a)
The drumlins are mantled in medium-textured Wolfville loam over sandy clay loam till containing Carboniferous material. Between the drumlins, the soil is mostly imperfectly drained Danesville sandy loam, derived from quartzite, with some better-drained Bridgewater soil, derived from slate.

Moser River (sub-Unit 435b)
The drumlins are also covered with Wolfville soil. Between them the soil is mostly Danesville to the east where the topography is flatter, and better-drained Halifax to the west—both are derived from quartzite. Patches of Aspotogan soil and peat occur in depressions.

PLANTS

Shade-intolerant species (Red Maple and White Birch) are found on the better-drained drumlin tops, with Black Spruce, White Spruce, Balsam Fir, and larch growing on the wetter sites in between. Red Spruce occurs on the drumlins more frequently in the Tangier River sub-Unit.

C.D. Howe noted the prominence of these hardwood ridges in his 1912 survey: "One is impressed by the predominance of yellow birch and paper birch on the hills around the lakes. In some places the former makes up four-fifths of the stand and pure stands of the latter are frequent."

ANIMALS

Little information is recorded on the terrestrial fauna of this Unit. Common fish species include White Sucker, Gaspereau, Golden Shiner, sticklebacks, Banded Killifish, Lake Chub, and Brook Trout. The Moser River contains one of the largest populations of sea-run Brook Trout in the province.

CULTURAL ENVIRONMENT

Forest exploitation has characterized land use in this sparsely populated area. Gold was once mined at the Caribou Gold Mines. This Unit contains one of two viable peat-moss sites in Halifax County.

Sites of Special Interest
- Necum Teuch Bay—large outwash deposit of sand and gravel

Provincial Parks and Park Reserves
- Judds Pool

Proposed Parks and Protected Areas System includes Natural Landscape 36b and Candidate Protected Area 18 Boggy Lake.

Associated Topics
T2.2 The Avalon and Meguma Zones, T3.3 Glaciation, Deglaciation and Sea-level Changes, T3.4 Terrestrial Glacial Deposits and Landscape Features, T12.3 Geology and Resources, T12.10 Plants and Resources.

Associated Habitats
H3.1 Freshwater Open-Water Lotic, H3.2 Freshwater Open-Water Lentic, H6.1 Hardwood Forest (Maple, Oak, Birch Association), H6.2 Softwood Forest (Black Spruce, Larch Association; Pine Association).

**435
Eastern
Shore
Drumlins**

436 HEADWATER LAKES

This Unit has two subdivisions:
  (a) Beaverbank
  (b) Dollar Lake

GEOLOGY AND LANDSCAPE DEVELOPMENT

Both sub-Units are underlain by parallel bands of greywacke and slate oriented east-west. These form a low ridge and shallow valley topography which has little variety except where river valleys or lake basins interrupt the rolling surface.

The bedrock is covered by a till sheet dominated by red, sandy Lawrencetown Till. In several locations large areas of rock are exposed. The till sheet changes to a quartzite till composition to the west of Beaverbank Lake, where both Lawrencetown and quartzite tills are overlain by a swarm of drumlins composed of Lawrencetown Tills.

FRESH WATER

In general the drainage in both sub-Units is deranged, with several small irregular lakes connected by wandering streams. The Beaverbank area possesses a long chain of lakes (the Waverley chain), which extends nearly one-third of the way across the province to the head of the Shubenacadie River. These lakes may form part of an ancient river system which rose on the Scotian Shelf and flowed northwards during the Cretaceous. Scattered bogs and fens can be found throughout, but larger wetlands tend to be found in the northern areas. The Sackville River in sub-Unit 436a is on a significant floodplain.

SOILS

Beaverbank (sub-Unit 436a)
Medium textured, red Wolfville loams are dominant in this sub-Unit with some areas of well-drained Halifax and imperfectly drained Danesville sandy loam to the north.

Dollar Lake (sub-Unit 436b)
Fairly deep, red Wolfville soils cover most of this sub-Unit.

PLANTS

Red Spruce and Eastern Hemlock are the characteristic species in this Unit, with White Pine, Balsam Fir, Red Maple, and Yellow Birch. Shade-intolerant birches and aspens occur on shallow soil in burnt areas, and shade-tolerant species grow on well-drained hilltops.

ANIMALS

Shubenacadie Grand Lake supports a landlocked population of Atlantic Salmon as well as unique, freshwater population of striped bass that lives in the lake but spawns in the intertidal portions of the Stewiacke River. Dollar Lake and Pockwock Lake contain relict populations of Lake Trout.

CULTURAL ENVIRONMENT

In earlier times, small-scale farming was a feature of the landscape in this area. Today, primary land uses involve forestry and related industries, such as sawmill operations. The Sackville and Fall River areas have become suburban commuter communities, and the surrounding lakelands are now dotted with cottages.

• • • • • • • •

Sites of Special Interest
• Lake Charles to Shubenacadie Grand Lake—the valley of the Waverley chain of lakes (part of the 19th-century Shubenacadie canal system)

Provincial Parks and Park Reserves
• Dollar Lake
• Oakfield
• Laurie

Proposed Parks and Protected Areas System includes Natural Landscape 30 and Candidate Protected Area 21 Clattenburgh Brook.

Associated Topics
T2.2 The Avalon and Meguma Zones, T3.2 Ancient Drainage Patterns, T3.4 Terrestrial Glacial Deposits and Landscape Features, T12.10 Plants and Resources.

Associated Habitats
H3 Fresh Water, H4.1 Bog, H4.2 Fen, H6.3 Mixedwood Forest (Spruce, Fir, Pine–Maple, Birch Association).

440 GRANITE BARRENS

This District has two subdivisions:
  (a) Flintstone
  (b) Bloody Lake

GEOLOGY AND LANDSCAPE DEVELOPMENT

The Granite Barrens are found in two areas in south-western Nova Scotia. One is at the southwestern extremity of the South Mountain Granite (sub-Unit 451a), and the other lies directly east of the Tusket River near the boundary of Yarmouth and Shelburne counties. As the name indicates, the bedrock in each case is granite. Other areas of granite (District 450) also contain extensive barrens. Unit 452, the Shelburne Granite Plain, has barrens in its western extremity.

Both areas are overlain with a thin cover of loose, stony granite till with no drumlins. The surface is strewn with boulders and is poorly drained (see Figure 13).

The elevations in the two localities are quite different. Flintstone is part of the South Mountain granite body and has undergone extensive erosion. However, owing to its extreme resistance to erosion, the granite is still elevated at over 125 m, higher than the surrounding Meguma strata.

**440
Granite
Barrens**

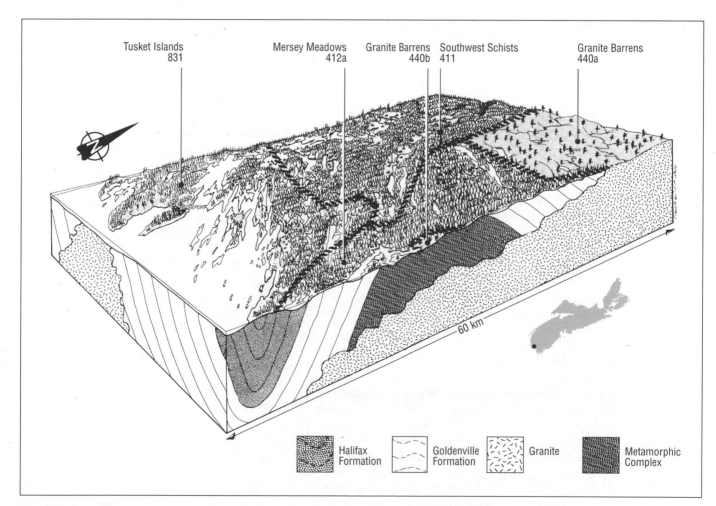

Halifax Formation	Goldenville Formation	Granite	Metamorphic Complex

Figure 13: Tusket Islands area. The planation surface of the southwestern peninsula dips gently into the Atlantic (Unit 911). Inland, extensive barrens are mainly confined to granite outcrops (District 440). Richer soils and more vigorous tree growth are found on the schists in Unit 411 than on the impoverished soils derived from the quartzite tills of Unit 412. At the coast (District 830) the forest grows on a varied landscape of drumlins and tidal marshes which provide habitat for interesting and rich flora and fauna.

Bloody Lake lies over a small granite exposure which is probably a cupola in a large granite body still lying at depth. It has only (geologically) recently been exposed and thus has the same average elevation as the surrounding Meguma terrain, about 30–40 m above sea level.

FRESH WATER

Many streams flow between shallow irregular lakes, and peat bogs are common. Lakes and rivers are yellowish, turbid, and acidic, with considerable amounts of humic matter. Swamps, swales, and bogs occur throughout the Unit. Sub-Unit 440a contains the headwaters of the East Branch Tusket River system. The water in the rivers is highly coloured and very acidic (pH less than 4.6). Large fens occur along the slower rivers such as the Shelburne. Fourth Lake and Fifth Lake flowages dominate sub-Unit 440a and are the headwaters for the Sissiboo River. Sub-Unit 440b contains a few large, sloped, raised bogs, fens and a few medium-sized lakes with peatland borders. Many streams dissect sub-Unit 440b.

SOILS

Flintstone (sub-District 440a)
Soils are basically coarse-textured, well-drained Gibraltar (gravelly, sandy loams derived mostly from granite), with small areas of slowly drained Bayswater and Aspotogan soils on nearly level to depressional topography. All soils are very shallow and stony, and there are large areas of exposed bedrock. Ortstein iron pans are widespread.

Bloody Lake (sub-District 440b)
Gibraltar soils occur to the south of the sub-Unit, with areas of well-drained Halifax sandy loam derived from quartzite, to the north. Patches of Aspotogan soil and peat are also present.

PLANTS

Five factors can lead to the presence of barrens: deep, repeated burns; iron pans; numerous boulders; excessive leaching, causing very low fertility; and the establishment of heath vegetation that prevents the growth of tree seedlings. Because fires are better controlled today than in the early days of forestry, some fire barrens are regenerating in forest species. However, limited planting of Red and Jack pines has resulted in only very slow growth.

Forest vegetation does best in the drainage trenches alongside the deranged drainage system.

Here linear forests of Red Maple, ash, and Wire Birch occur between the slightly higher intervening barren heathlands. The characteristic shrubs on these areas are huckleberries, Sheep Laurel, Wild Raisin, and alder. Also common is a low scrub which may include White Pine, aspen, Black Spruce, Red Maple, Wire Birch, or Red Oak. On boggy sites, Black Spruce, Red Maple, and Larch are common. Several orchids are found in these bogs. They include Grass Pink, Rose Pogonia and Dragon's Mouth Orchid.

ANIMALS

The barrens and semi-barrens are generally unproductive wildlife habitat, except there are some small mammals, which have a low to moderately high diversity, and moose, which have one of the best populations in western Nova Scotia. Although there is some beaver, otter, muskrat, and duck-nesting habitat, aquatic fauna is generally depauperate.

SCENIC QUALITY

Lack of fertile soils and inaccessibility combine to make this Nova Scotia's "empty quarter." It has never been settled and has no roads. Scenically, it presents a bleak landscape of heath and low scrub, relieved by higher trees along shallow drainage trenches. Frequent lakes and bogs add further visual interest, but scenic ratings are generally low to medium. However, these barrens are quite striking in autumn with the changing colours of the vegetation.

CULTURAL ENVIRONMENT

Forestry has characterized land use in some parts of the Granite Barrens. However, much of this area is known for recreational use of waterways and for hunting and fishing. The Tobeatic Game Reserve is part of the Granite Barrens.

● ● ● ● ● ● ● ●

Sites of Special Interest
- Tobeatic Resource Management Area
- Tobeatic Game Sanctuary
- Birch Lake (IBP Proposed Ecological Site 61)— old White Pine forest

Ecological Reserve
- Sporting Lake Nature Reserve

Provincial Parks and Park Reserves
Proposed Parks and Protected Areas System includes Natural Landscapes 8a and 8b and Candidate Protected Area 29 Tobeatic.

Associated Topics
T2.2 The Avalon and Meguma Zones, T2.3 Granite in Nova Scotia, T8.2 Freshwater Environments, T9.1 Soil-forming Factors, T11.9 Carnivores, T11.10 Ungulates, T11.11 Small Mammals.

Associated Habitats
H3 Fresh Water, H4.1 Bog, H4.2 Fen, H4.3 Swamp, H5.1 Barren, H6.2 Softwood Forest (Black Spruce, Larch Association), H6.3 Mixedwood Forest (Spruce, Fir, Pine–Maple, Birch Association).

**440
Granite
Barrens**

450 GRANITE

This District is divided into three Units:

    451   Granite Uplands
    452   Shelburne Granite Plain
    453   Granite Ridge

GEOLOGY AND LANDSCAPE DEVELOPMENT

Granite underlies over 50 per cent of the Atlantic Interior and outcrops in several areas. The largest granite body is the South Mountain Batholith, which stretches in an arc from near the Tusket River across to the Halifax-Dartmouth area. Two other much smaller bodies are the Granite Ridge along the Eastern Shore and the Shelburne Granite Plain. Other smaller outcrops of granite are found throughout the Region.

All of the granite exposed within the Atlantic Interior was intruded during the Acadian Orogeny in the Late Devonian and Early Carboniferous periods. It is quite variable in chemical composition, texture, and colour but has a common origin in the crustal disturbance of the period.

Granite is very resistant to erosion and tends to form the highest ground in an eroded landscape such as the Atlantic Interior. It forms a rounded landscape of shapeless ridges and depressions with occasional knolls.

The drainage across granite is generally severely deranged, with most of the low areas being waterlogged. If the outcrop is narrow, it may form a ridge and thus a drainage divide, as does the Granite Ridge along the Eastern Shore.

SCENIC QUALITY

Granite localities vary in elevation, topography, and vegetation but have common scenic elements. They lack human settlement and their thin soils support a sparse and scrubby second-growth forest. The forest is interspersed with exposed bedrock and barrens, and large glacially deposited boulders are found throughout. The deranged drainage provides many lakes that add much to scenic value and aid recreational access. All areas are plateau-like, but scenic value is greatly enhanced along the steep flank of the South Mountain in Annapolis County, and to a lesser extent on the northern edge of Ten Mile Stream (sub-Unit 451b), overlooking West River St. Marys. With these exceptions, granite areas typically exhibit low to medium scenic ratings.

• • • • • • •

Associated Topics
T2.3 Granite in Nova Scotia, T9.1 Soil-forming Factors.

Associated Habitats
H5.1 Barren, H6.2 Softwood Forest (Pine Association).

451   GRANITE UPLANDS

This Unit has two subdivisions:
- (a)   South Mountain
- (b)   Ten Mile Stream

GEOLOGY AND LANDSCAPE DEVELOPMENT

Despite its size, the South Mountain Granite is a rather uniform topographic feature. It presents a level horizon when viewed from North Mountain, and the surface steadily decreases in elevation down to its southern, eastern, and western boundaries, where fairly steep slopes mark the boundary with Meguma strata (see Figure 25).

Across the surface of the granite are many large boulders that were plucked out and then dumped by the ice. Some were carried beyond the granite boundaries and dropped, as erratics, on unrelated rocks further away. Long, prominent eskers occur in the Kejimkujik area and to the west.

The granite terrain in the Ten Mile Stream sub-Unit is typical. The surface is elevated above the greywacke and slate bands on three sides by about 50 m but forms a rather steeper escarpment on the northern side where it is undercut by the West River St. Marys. Here the drop is nearly 100 m in places.

The surface is thinly covered with coarse granite till with some areas of thicker Lawrencetown Till. Some glacial outwash deposits are found on the northern side.

FRESH WATER

The South Mountain Granite has a typically deranged drainage pattern, but two chains of lakes have maintained a more or less straight line across it. One extends south of Milford in Annapolis County and the other south from Panuke Lake. These may represent old river courses that were superimposed upon the granite as it was exposed.

This Unit contains the headwaters of some of Nova Scotia's largest rivers, such as the Tusket-Silver, Bear, Mersey, Medway, Nictaux, LaHave, and Avon. Except for the tidal rivers, most tend to be shallow and fast flowing.

In the South Mountain sub-Unit (451a), wetlands are scattered along streams and rivers. The occasional lake occurs in Annapolis, Kings, and Digby counties. These counties also contain many raised bogs. Wetlands tend to become more widely scattered and smaller in the eastern portions of sub-Unit 451a. Halifax County has several long north-south oriented lakes running along fault lines.

In the Ten Mile Stream sub-Unit (451b), surface-water coverage is greater in the western portions. Here the numerous, small irregular lakes tend to be oligotrophic and linked by small streams. Raised bogs can be found in the southwestern part of sub-Unit 451b.

Conductivity tends to be below 35 micromhos/cm throughout the Unit and pH ranges between 5.4 and 6.5.

SOILS

The major soil series throughout this large Unit is Gibraltar: a coarse-textured, well-drained gravelly, sandy loam derived from granite—usually shallow, heavily leached, and very acidic. Gibraltar soils are also associated with poorly drained Bayswater and Aspotogan soils, along with many areas of peat. Near the north slope are two large areas of Halifax sandy loam derived from quartzite. Bridgetown soils around Gaspereau Lake and south of Hardwood Lake have developed on tills derived from a mixture of basalt, granite, quartzite, and Carboniferous material. A small number of Wolfville drumlins also occur near these areas. Scattered areas of exposed rock are present throughout the Unit, particularly in Halifax County. Soils in unforested areas have a tendency to form hardpans.

PLANTS

This Unit basically corresponds to the Fisher Lake–Halifax District in Loucks' Red Spruce, Hemlock, Pine Zone. The characteristic species are Red Spruce, Eastern Hemlock, White Pine, Balsam Fir, and Red Maple, with scattered Red Oak. Warm summer temperatures result in high evapotranspiration, which would normally encourage shade-tolerant deciduous trees, but here it appears to favour Red Spruce and Eastern Hemlock. Fire has played a prominent role, but the regeneration of pine and spruce under Red

451
Granite
Uplands

Maple and Red Oak suggests that the area is returning to a mainly coniferous forest. American Beech was formerly abundant, but has been depleted by fire.

White Pine, Red Spruce, and Eastern Hemlock often occur on sites which have not been burned, while fire stands are commonly Red Oak, Red Maple, and White Birch. American Beech, Sugar Maple, and Red Oak are found on exposed slopes and hilltops. Black Spruce and Balsam Fir occupy poorly drained lands. Barrens and semi-barrens are common. Some old Red Spruce and Eastern Hemlock stands can still be found. Coastal-plain plants occur along water courses in this Unit.

Observations made in 1912 by C.D. Howe give some historical insight into the development of present-day forests: "The slopes, facing the Annapolis valley, are abrupt with relatively short streams flowing from them, while the southerly facing slopes are gentle, and their streams have worn rather wide valleys separated by low rounded ridges. In the portion draining northward the forests are of the mixed type with red spruce and hemlock predominating over the hardwoods, but there are frequently hills of pure over-mature and decrepit hardwoods, half composed of beech, 40 per cent hard maple and the rest yellow birch. In going southward, especially between the LaHave and Port Medway rivers, hemlock is of more common occurrence than the red spruce, in some places reaching as high as eighty percent of the stand. Frequent barren and semi-barren areas are scattered through the county, doubtless, in most cases, the result of repeated fires. One type, however, approaches the character of a natural barren, that is, a low rocky ridge, usually ten to fifty feet above its surroundings, covered chiefly with scrubby red oak and red maple. The largest areas of these latter barrens are found east and northeast of the Milford lakes and south of the Molly Upsum and McGill lakes. The very numerous lakes and ponds usually have at their upper ends, extensive peat bogs and black spruce and fir swamps. ... The cut of the mills in the western portion of the county [Kings] consists of approximately 50 per cent hemlock, 40 per cent red spruce and 10 per cent white pine, and these species form from 75 per cent to 80 per cent of the forest. In the eastern portion of the county, the ridges are broader and higher; the hardwoods become more prevalent, and finally dominate. ... Along the basin of the St. Croix lakes the larger percentage of the stands is hemlock. Eastward to the headwaters of Ingram river, red spruce prevails over the hemlock. These areas are near the centre of the granite mass. Both eastward and westward to the limits of the granite in the county, the forest is mixed hardwoods and softwoods, with spruce mostly predominating. ... Southwest of Ingram river and east of Island lake the forest is second growth, paper birch and red spruce being the most common species, with fir and yellow birch next in abundance. Northwest near the Hants County line, hardwood hills compose about one-fifth of the stand, between which red spruce and hemlock prevail, with the spruce in the lead. ... The granite area in the north-western corner of Guysborough county is about one-fourth burned and barren. The soil on the rest is deep, and hardwoods prevail, with frequent patches of pure red spruce and fir."

ANIMALS

The second-growth mixed forests support only sparse wildlife populations. Small-mammal diversity is low to moderate. High concentrations of White-tailed deer occur in sub-Unit 451a. Aquatic environments are acidic and have low productivity, providing poor waterfowl habitat. The area sustains substantial populations of Smallmouth Bass. The south basin of Sherbrooke Lake also supports a relict population of Lake Trout.

CULTURAL ENVIRONMENT

Forestry activities are the dominant land use in this sparsely inhabited area. Mining has also taken place at various localities. Recreational use of the land includes hunting, fishing, hiking, and boating activities.

• • • • • • • •

Sites of Special Interest
- Kejimkujik National Park (part)—eskers and Southern Flying Squirrel (sub-Unit 451a)
- Hollahan Lake (IBP Proposed Ecological Site 41)—Jack Pine forest (sub-Unit 451a)
- Shady Brook (IBP Proposed Ecological site 67)—Red Spruce, Eastern Hemlock forest (sub-Unit 451a)
- Wight Nature Preserve, Hubbards (sub-Unit 451a)

Ecological Reserve
- Panuke Lake Nature Reserve

Provincial Parks and Park Reserves
(All are in sub-Unit 451a, except for Cox Lake.)
- Falls Lake

- Lake George
- Lumsden Pond
- Holden Lake
- Card Lake
- Simms Settlement
- Hollahan Lake
- Halifax Watershed
- Lewis Lake
- Upper Tantallon
- Cox Lake (sub-Unit 451b)

Proposed Parks and Protected Areas System includes Natural Landscape 7a and Candidate Protected Areas 26 Cloud Lake and 27 McGill Lake.

Associated Topics

T2.3 Granite in Nova Scotia, T3.2 Ancient Drainage Patterns, T3.3 Glaciation, Deglaciation and Sea-level Changes, T3.4 Terrestrial Glacial Deposits and Landscape Features, T4.2 Post-glacial Colonization by Plants, T4.3 Post-glacial Colonization by Animals, T8.2 Freshwater Environments, T8.3 Freshwater Wetlands, T10.12 Rare and Endangered Plants, T11.18 Rare and Endangered Animals.

Associated Habitats

H3 Fresh Water, H4.1 Bog, H4.2 Fen, H4.3 Swamp, H5.1 Barren, H6.1 Hardwood Forest (Maple, Oak, Birch Association), H6.2 Softwood Forest (Spruce, Hemlock, Pine Association; Pine Association; Black Spruce, Larch Association), H6.3 Mixedwood Forest (Spruce, Fir, Pine–Maple, Birch Association).

**451
Granite
Uplands**

452 SHELBURNE GRANITE PLAIN

GEOLOGY AND LANDSCAPE DEVELOPMENT

This Unit presents a typical granite terrain, hummocky and covered with large boulders. The elevations are low, in keeping both with its position on the planation surface and with the fact that the granite body is probably not fully exposed.

The surface has a mantle of thin, stony till with no drumlins.

FRESH WATER

Great Pubnico Lake, the largest body of water in this Unit, is the headwater for the Barrington River. Smaller lakes are dispersed throughout and connected by a network of streams and rivers. Scattered medium to large wetlands tend to be associated with the larger watercourses. There are concentrations of sloped and raised bogs. Conductivity averages 35 micromhos/cm, and pH ranges from 4.7 in the Clyde River and Great Pubnico Lake to 6.5 in Alvin Lake.

SOILS

Soils in this Unit have developed from various parent materials—granite, quartzite, and schist. Large areas are poorly drained, either because of topography, shallow depth to bedrock, or the presence of a cemented ortstein layer. Sand plains are common. In the Yarmouth County corner of the Unit, Gibraltar, Bayswater, and Aspotogan soils—all derived from granite—occur with patches of peat. In the rest of the Unit, poorly drained Bayswater and Aspotogan soils, and imperfectly drained Liverpool and Danesville soils, each often gleyed and mottled, are dominant on the largely level topography towards the coast, with some areas of better-drained Medway, Mersey, and Port Hebert soils where the relief is more pronounced.

PLANTS

This Unit is the most southerly portion of Nova Scotia not directly affected by the cold and fog associated with the Atlantic Coast. The growing season is hot and subject to drought on shallow soils. The natural vegetation appears to have been White Pine and Red Oak, but repeated burning has reduced many of the pine sites to a shrub cover of cinquefoil, Bearberry, and Broom-crowberry, with scattered Black Spruce. Black Spruce predominates on ill-drained lands, while Red Oak covers the ridges. Eastern Hemlock and Red Spruce are found in the few unburned areas. The warm climate is indicated by the presence of plants which otherwise occur no further north than southern Maine, for example, Inkberry.

ANIMALS

The barrens do not provide productive wildlife habitat, and this Unit has the lowest small-mammal diversity in the Region, with no more than four species commonly occurring. It does, however, support one of the best moose populations in western Nova Scotia. Typical freshwater fishes include Brook Trout, Yellow Perch, Brown Bullhead, and Golden Shiner.

CULTURAL ENVIRONMENT

Much of this area is barren as a result of repeated fires. Around the turn of the century, meadows in southwestern Nova Scotia were burned annually to promote hay growth, and barrens were burned periodically for production of blueberries. Although there were fewer forest fires than today, they were often unattended unless they threatened settlements and therefore burned much larger areas. From 1900 to 1914, more timber was lost to fire, disease, storms, and old age than was harvested. Barren lands of the Shelburne Granite Plain feature significant moose populations that attract seasonal hunters.

● ● ● ● ● ● ● ●

452
Shelburne
Granite
Plain

Sites of Special Interest
- Many eskers along the shoreline, along Clyde River and north of Clements Pond

Provincial Parks and Park Reserves
Proposed Parks and Protected Areas System includes Natural Landscape 8c.

Associated Topics
T2.3 Granite in Nova Scotia, T3.4 Terrestrial Glacial Deposits and Landscape Features, T9.1 Soil-forming Factors, T10.1 Vegetation Change, T11.10 Ungulates, T12.10 Plants and Resources.

Associated Habitats
H4.1 Bog, H5.1 Barren, H6.2 Softwood Forest (Black Spruce, Larch Association; Spruce, Hemlock, Pine Association).

**452
Shelburne
Granite
Plain**

453 GRANITE RIDGE

GEOLOGY AND LANDSCAPE DEVELOPMENT

The Granite Ridge along the Eastern Shore forms a prominent feature 80 km long and about 8–10 km wide. It rises sharply, sometimes with cliffs, to a narrow plateau 100 m above the Atlantic Coast Region (see Figure 27).

The granite has been cut by faults in two places: along the valley from Spider Lake through Lake Major, and along the Porters Lake valley.

The Musquodoboit River also cuts across it in a narrow gorge and must have been superimposed by downcutting since the Cretaceous.

The surface of the granite has a thin veneer of coarse granite till which, at the eastern end of the ridge, is overlain with a few drumlins of red Lawrencetown Till (Wolfville soils). These have spilled over from the area of the Eastern Shore Drumlins (sub-Unit 435a) to the north.

FRESH WATER

The surface-water coverage in this Unit is very high, with many irregularly shaped lakes and long narrow lakes and rivers following fault lines. A few small, scattered raised bogs and fens are found. Parts of the Musquodoboit River are bordered by large wetlands. Conductivity averages around 42 micromhos/cm, and pH ranges between 4.7 and 6.8.

SOILS

Gibraltar soils (well-drained, gravelly, sandy loams derived from granite) are dominant, with large areas of exposed bedrock and small areas of imperfectly drained Danesville soil and peat bogs.

PLANTS

This Unit is somewhat cooler in summer than Unit 451 and has a climate quite similar to Unit 452. Red Spruce, Balsam Fir, birch, Eastern Hemlock, and White Spruce are common species on well-drained sites. Black Spruce, Balsam Fir, and Larch occur in wetter areas. Parts of the Unit are semi-barren. Scattered Red Oak occurs around the Lake Charlotte area. Shade-intolerant birch and aspen colonize burnt areas.

The ruggedness and effects of repeated burns, which still continue, were well described by C.D. Howe, writing in 1912: "The crests of the granite hills east of Halifax harbour have been deeply eroded by glacial action and have naturally very thin soils; and frequent fires have so exposed the rocks, that from a distance most of the rounded domes appear white. When not burned, they are sparsely covered by a black forest, that is, coniferous, in striking contrast to the lighter green of the hardwoods prevailing on the lower slopes. The higher slopes, especially when facing southward are covered with spruce overtopped by scattered white and red pine. The hardwoods go nearly to the top on the northerly-facing slopes. The low ridges usually support pure hardwoods. Red spruce prevails in the broader flats between the ridges, while hemlock predominates in the ravines and gullies, and at the base of steep slopes along the rivers and smaller lakes."

ANIMALS

There is little recorded information about terrestrial animals in this Unit. Fish species include White Sucker, Brook Trout, White Perch, Gaspereau, Yellow Perch, Brown Bullhead, Banded Killifish, and shiners.

CULTURAL ENVIRONMENT

Forest management predominates in this area. However, farming has also been important in the Musquodoboit Valley. Other resource-based industries here include Christmas tree farms. The Waverley Game Sanctuary spans part of the Granite Ridge. Seasonal hunting is common in this area.

• • • • • • • •

Sites of Special Interest
- Waverley Game Sanctuary

Provincial Parks and Park Reserves
- Paces Lake
- Caribou Lake

Proposed Parks and Protected Areas System includes Natural Landscape 34 and Candidate Protected Areas 19 Tangier Grand Lake, 20 White Lake, and 22 Waverley–Salmon River Long Lake.

Associated Topics
T2.3 Granite in Nova Scotia, T3.2 Ancient Drainage Patterns, T12.11 Animals and Resources.

Associated Habitats
H4.1 Bog, H6.1 Hardwood Forest (Maple, Oak, Birch Association).

**453
Granite
Ridge**

460 BAYS

This District has two subdivisions:
(a) Mahone Bay
(b) St. Margarets Bay

GEOLOGY AND LANDSCAPE DEVELOPMENT

St. Margarets Bay and Mahone Bay are ancient landscape features that were formed during a period of rapid erosion before the Carboniferous. During the Middle Carboniferous, an extension of the Carboniferous sea transgressed this part of the old erosion surface and deposited limestone and evaporites. Most of these strata have now been eroded away, and only a fringe is left around the margins of the two bays. Granite is the dominant rock-type in this District, with slate forming a series of peninsulas on the west side of Mahone Bay.

The slates tend to be covered by fairly deep surficial deposits in the form of glacial tills and drumlins. The drumlin swarms continue into the sea, particularly in Mahone Bay where they form islands called "whalebacks" (see Figure 14). These have been extensively eroded by the sea in recent times to form shoals, spits, and bars. Finer sediment is deposited in small salt-marshes in the low-energy environments at the heads of the bays. Small, sandy pocket beaches

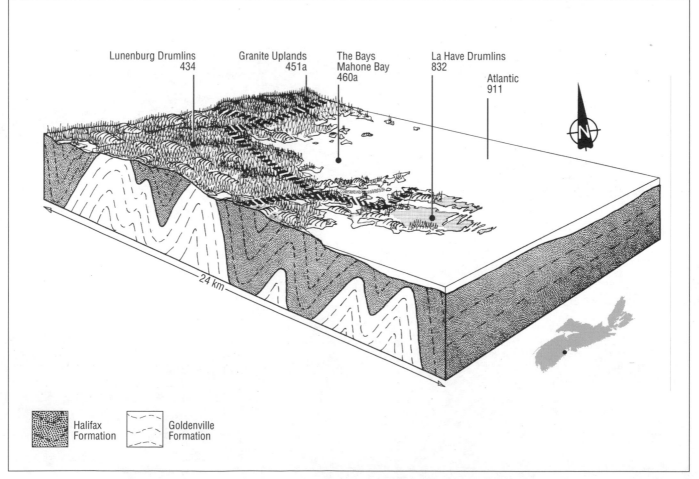

Figure 14: Mahone Bay area. Drumlins cover the surface of the tilted planation surface as it dips beneath the Atlantic (Unit 911). Many of the drumlins are composed of "red" tills (Unit 434) carried by glaciers at least 100 km from the north. Erosion of drumlin islands and headlands has formed many shoals, some beaches, and tidal marshes in Mahone Bay (District 460). Exposed slate headlands with scattered drumlins have a harsher climate, resulting in coastal forest habitat (Unit 832).

are present on exposed coasts at the bay heads, but deep water inland of sills at the bay entrances has prevented the rising sea level from moving nearshore sand deposits onto the present coastline.

A coastal lowland that developed on Carboniferous rocks around the bays is abruptly terminated by the steep-sloping granite inland. On the Aspotogan Peninsula, which separates Mahone Bay from St. Margarets Bay, the till is very thin as a result of the scarcity of softer Carboniferous rocks.

FRESH WATER

Several large rivers drain into this Unit, for example, the Gold River in sub-District 460a and the Ingram River in sub-District 460b. The levels of pH in these rivers ranges between 4.7 and 5.4.

SOILS

Mahone Bay (sub-District 460a)

The soils around Mahone Bay are mostly derived from granite, quartzite, and slate, with some Carboniferous material. Upper Blandford to East Chester is mostly Gibraltar soil with areas of exposed bedrock. Chester Peninsula, including the islands, is mostly Bridgewater soil (sandy loam derived from slate). The remaining soils are a mixture of Bridgewater, imperfectly drained Danesville in flatter areas, well-drained and coarse-textured Farmville (derived from a mixture of granite, quartzite, and slate), and Wolfville loams. A number of drumlins are mantled by either Farmville or Wolfville soils. Most of the islands are Wolfville drumlins.

St. Margarets Bay (sub-District 460b)

St. Margarets Bay shows less variety of soil types than Mahone Bay. Gibraltar predominates, with Rockland areas and a few small patches of Wolfville soil.

PLANTS

The vegetation around both bays has been extensively disturbed and is essentially a modified version of the coastal forest—mainly conifers, with Red Spruce, White Spruce, and Balsam Fir.

ANIMALS

The western shore of Mahone Bay, including the islands, has local importance for waterfowl and shorebirds. Waterfowl found at various times from spring through early winter include Black Duck,

Common Goldeneye, Oldsquaw, Scoter, and Red-necked Grebe. The Osprey is a common nesting bird on islands in this area. Rainbow Smelt and American Eel are common.

SCENIC QUALITY

St. Margarets Bay and Mahone Bay differ visually as a result of bedrock and glacial deposits, but both provide a wealth of beautiful scenes, some panoramic, some intimate. Scenic value is provided partly by the bays themselves, which are visually enclosed or embraced by land, and partly by the many small fishing settlements (supplemented by farming settlements on the drumlins of western Mahone Bay). The whaleback islands of Mahone Bay add much interest, but St. Margarets Bay is more easily comprehended as a whole and impresses by its size. Beauty spots can be found in all localities, but scenic ratings are highest on the northern shore of Mahone Bay and the eastern shore of St. Margarets Bay.

CULTURAL ENVIRONMENT

Shell middens have been found at various sites around St. Margarets Bay and Mahone Bay, indicating the presence of traditional Mi'kmaq camps. In the eighteenth century this area was settled by German and British immigrants who formed fishing villages and towns around the bays. Sheep farming is the major industry in this Unit. Extensive logging operations began in St. Margarets Bay in the 1940s, and forest exploitation today supplies a hardboard plant at East River. In the 1920s the tidewater hydroelectric generating station was built at the Head of St. Margarets Bay on the site of an old sawmill. Other hydro plants in this area include Sandy Lake and Mill Lake. Rocks are quarried in the Bays District by a large crushed-rock producer. Hunting and fishing pursuits first brought tourists to the area in the 1870s, but its attraction as a scenic destination with beaches, inlets, and villages really grew with the advent of the automobile and the development of better roads in the 1920s. Today, although some people living in this area are involved in the fishery or forestry resource industries, many others are commuters who work in Halifax.

• • • • • • • •

**460
Bays**

Sites of Special Interest
- Peggys Cove and Masons Cove are good examples of intertidal zonation on rocky shores

Provincial Parks and Park Reserves
- Graves Island
- East River
- Second Peninsula
- First Peninsula
- Fox Point
- Hubbards
- Cleveland Beach
- Queensland Beach

Proposed Parks and Protected Areas System includes Natural Landscape 14.

Scenic Viewpoints
- Sub-Unit 460a: Graves Island Provincial Park, Chester Harbour, Mahone Bay, Second Peninsula Provincial Park
- Sub-Unit 460b: Queensland Beach, Cleveland Beach

Associated Offshore Unit
911 Atlantic.

Associated Topics
T2.4 The Carboniferous Basin, T3.3 Glaciation, Deglaciation and Sea-level Changes, T3.5 Offshore Bottom Characteristics, T6.1 Ocean Currents, T6.2 Oceanic Environments, T6.3 Coastal Aquatic Environments, T11.6 Shorebirds, T11.7 Seabirds, T12.10 Plants and Resources, T12.11 Animals and Resources.

Associated Habitats
H1.1 Offshore Open Water, H2.1 Rocky Shore, H2.2 Boulder/Cobble Shore, H2.5 Tidal Marsh, H6.3 Mixedwood Forest (White Spruce, Fir–Maple, Birch Association).

500
Carboniferous Lowlands

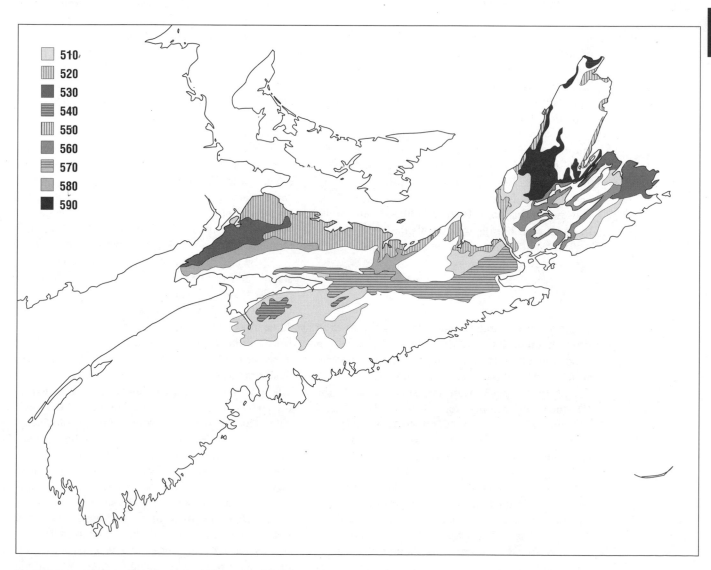

510
520
530
540
550
560
570
580
590

Figure 15: Region 500, Carboniferous Lowlands, and its component Districts.

500 CARBONIFEROUS LOWLANDS

500
Carboniferous
Lowlands

The Region has been divided into nine Districts on the basis of topographic character and soil type:

510 Till Plain
520 Coastal Plain
530 Stony and Wet Plain
540 Clay Plain
550 Coastal Fringe
560 Submerged Lowland
570 Rolling Upland
580 Hills and Valleys
590 Dissected Plateau

REGIONAL CHARACTERISTICS

Lowland Nova Scotia is mainly Carboniferous sedimentary rocks on which deep soils have developed. Many of the rivers flow in valleys eroded from the unresistant Windsor Group rocks, which include gypsum. Horton Group sandstones are more resistant and form higher ground in District 510 in Cape Breton, and on the eastern mainland. Districts 580 and 590 abut the older upland blocks as foothills, while the less-resistant rocks of Districts 520, 550, and 560 form coastal plains, often with heavy soils. Flat-lying sandstones and shales are poorly drained with numerous bogs (Districts 530 and 540), while the relatively infertile sandy soils derived from the resistant sandstones of District 570 cover a large area of central Nova Scotia.

GEOLOGY

The geological character of the area is best portrayed through a description of the paleo-environment in which the sediments accumulated and the processes which affected them after deposition.

The first deposits were coarse sands and grits (Horton Group) washed from the uplifted and folded Meguma Zone and the highland blocks of the Avalon Zone (Pictou-Antigonish and Cape Breton) into basins between mountains. In some areas these deposits were preceded by extrusions of lava as crustal adjustments continued to take place. The first basins were in the Pictou and Mabou-Antigonish areas but, as sediments accumulated, they became increasingly extensive. The early Horton deposits have no fossils and now form resistant bands shouldering the uplands. Later came deposits of silts and fine sandstones which contained abundant fish and plant remains. Towards the end of this period in the Early Carboniferous a marine incursion took place; the basins became enlarged and interconnected, and an inland sea formed with a shoreline on mainland Nova Scotia which closely approximates the present boundary of the Carboniferous deposits. Within this sea was an archipelago of islands including the Wittenburg Ridge, Mount Aspotogan, the Pictou-Antigonish Highlands, the elongated blocks of the Avalon Zone in Cape Breton, and the Cape Breton highlands.

In the marine basin a laminated limestone formed, followed by deposits of evaporites (mostly gypsum) and red and green shales. Near the islands, shelly reefs developed, for example, at Gays River, Aspotogan, and East River (Mahone Bay). In the initial incursion of seawater, the intermontane basins and much of the surrounding area was flooded. The limestone deposited at that time lies on the Horton deposits and, where formerly dry land was covered, directly on the underlying topography. As the basin enlarged, later deposits of Windsor rocks were laid directly onto the older rocks of the basin margin, as can be seen in Mahone Bay, St. Margarets Bay, and on the eastern side of the Cape Breton highlands. Windsor deposits attain a thickness of 450 m in the Shubenacadie area and up to 750 m in Cape Breton.

At the end of the Windsor period, the land rose slightly and the sea withdrew to the east. Red and purple siltstones, shales, and sandstones (Canso Group) were deposited in streams and lakes. The strata may once have been very extensive across Nova Scotia but are now found in only a few major areas: around St. Georges Bay, the Strait of Canso, Stellarton–Mount Thom, and the Stewiacke Valley. They give red or purplish soils and, when exposed on the coast (e.g., Janvrin Island), bright red-coloured cliffs. This period was relatively quiet geologically; there were no tectonic upheavals, and the topography was subdued. The Early Carboniferous deposits were by this time very thick and had buried the lower elevations of the terrain. Rivers developed wide valleys with broad floodplains and estuaries. Sediments deposited in the environment had been compacted to fine sandstones, black shales, and thin coal seams (Riversdale Group). These strata also may once have been very extensive, but deep erosion has confined existing deposits to a few areas: a fringe around the Cobequid Hills, Pomquet, Port Hood, Broad Cove to Margaree Harbour, and Port Hawkesbury to St. Peters.

About this time, conditions became suitable for the proliferation of fern-like swamp plants, which flourished in extensive wetlands across the flat landscape. Great thicknesses of organic deposits accumulated and were compressed (Cumberland, Pictou, and Morien groups). These Late Carboniferous strata, which are predominantly thick sandstones and shales, cover almost the entire area north of the Cobequids and about half of Cape Breton County. The major coalfields of Springhill, New Glasgow-Stellarton, and the Sydney area are all in this group.

Carboniferous strata are relatively unmetamorphosed because, on a geological scale, they were never deeply buried. However, they were affected by compressive crustal movements during the Permian and Jurassic periods. The most intensely affected area was a band across the northern part of the province from Chignecto Bay, through the Pictou coalfield, and up through the Aspy Valley in northern Cape Breton. Resistant strata such as the Late Carboniferous sandstones and the Horton grits were thrown into open folds, whereas the softer strata in the zone, such as shales and gypsum, were distorted and crushed. There was also movement along the Cobequid-Chedabucto and Aspy faults and related movement along associated parallel and crosscutting faults.

Carboniferous deposits accumulated to a depth of many thousands of metres and engulfed most features of the old landscape. The Early Permian erosion has removed hundreds of metres of Late and Middle Carboniferous strata, exposed the underlying Windsor and Horton group blocks, and revealed ridges and valleys of the old erosion surface upon which these beds were deposited. A wide range of different rock types, with different responses to erosive forces, is now exposed. The topography reflects both this differential resistance, the structural character (folds and faults) of the area, and the relationship between the Carboniferous strata and the underlying rocks.

LANDSCAPE DEVELOPMENT

The geomorphology within the Carboniferous Lowlands is variable. There are lowland plains, rolling uplands, and coastal fringe areas. The lowlands fall into three main areas: the Windsor Lowlands (Unit 511), from the Avon River to the Stewiacke Valley; the Coastal Plain of the North Shore (District 520); and the Bras d'Or Lowlands (District 560) of central Cape Breton. These three areas are dominated by unre-

sistant Windsor Group deposits which have been deeply eroded in some places to well below present sea level. The rolling plains are underlain predominantly by Late Carboniferous sandstones of the Cumberland, Pictou, and Morien groups. They cover northern Antigonish, Pictou, Colchester, and Cumberland counties (Units 521 and 532) and the area between Mira Bay and Great Bras d'Or Channel (Unit 531). The strata are fairly resistant and moderately to strongly folded. In the Cumberland/Pictou area, younger and more easily eroded strata are exposed in the cores of the anticlines; consequently, the landscape has developed a ridge and valley topography with moderate relief.

The upland areas are underlain by resistant Horton deposits. The rolling upland which lies between the Chedabucto and St. Marys faults has been affected by folding and faulting to quite a degree, yet it remains a rather featureless elevated area across the central mainland (District 570). This suggests that the topography reflects the more uniform resistance of the different rocks, and therefore a similar response to the forces of erosion.

The Cape Breton uplands are underlain by Horton strata, interfolded with Windsor deposits. A large area in western Cape Breton exhibits strong relief and is varied and interesting. Windsor Group limestones and gypsum have been eroded to form the deep valleys occupied by the Baddeck, Middle, and Margaree rivers. Coastal fringe deposits skirt the Cape Breton highlands and form narrow coastal plains at the base of steep cliffs (District 550). Resistant Horton sandstones form an upland plateau surface which these valleys dissect.

The intervening hilly areas of the Carboniferous Lowlands have a topographic character transitional between lowland, plain, and upland. Faults transect the basins and often set strata of different resistance against each other. Downfaulted younger strata are set against older strata and are thereby preserved, for example, the Pictou Valleys (Unit 582).

Karst Topography

Throughout the Carboniferous Lowlands, in areas underlain by Windsor Group strata, pockets of gypsum and anhydrite (dehydrated gypsum) occur at the surface and produce a special feature called karst topography.

When anhydrite comes in contact with water, it expands and changes to gypsum. Gypsum is readily dissolved by rainwater and, when it lies above the permanent water table, it crumbles and washes away, leaving behind a small amount of reddish clay. Joints in the gypsum beds are enlarged and often

**500
Carboniferous
Lowlands**

subterranean channels are formed. Streams flow through these channels, sometimes enlarging them into caverns. If the roof of the cavern collapses, a sinkhole forms; if the roof of a channel falls in, a long gully with vertical sides is left.

Often the ground over gypsum is so closely covered by pits that only narrow crumbling ridges exist at the surface. The depressions may be underlain by holes or channels, and the whole area is treacherous to walk across.

A good example of karst topography exists at Amherst Point; another is found behind the King's-Edgehill School in Windsor. Both locations have a number of sinkholes, with the largest ones found at Windsor. Caves are infrequent, but a well-developed one called Hayes Cave occurs near South Maitland. This cave can be penetrated for 400 m and has a maximum width of 60 m and a ceiling reaching 22 m. Sinkholes that become plugged form sinkhole ponds which have alkaline water with characteristic plants, such as Stonewort, and abundant molluscs and amphibians.

FRESH WATER

In general, strata of the Carboniferous Lowlands are moderately to highly permeable. Rivers and their tributaries tend to follow fold axes and joint directions, and often exhibit a rectangular pattern. Most of Nova Scotia's major floodplains and intervales are found on the larger, mature rivers of this Region. These include the Margaree River in Cape Breton, the East River of Pictou, the Stewiacke and Musquodoboit rivers, and those draining north from Cobequid Mountain, such as the Philip. Karst topography has developed on the gypsum with the classic pattern of intermittent streams and sinkholes. The groundwater in gypsum areas is usually heavily mineralized, and the lakes and ponds are often saline. Streams are intermittent, disappearing into holes and channels, only to reappear again some distance away.

Overall there is little surface water, except where glacial deposits have impeded drainage to create the few lakes found in the Region. There are exceptions where drainage is very slow on the flat heavy clays of the Stewiacke Barrens, where extensive peat bogs have formed (District 540), and on the very flat isthmus by which Nova Scotia is joined to New Brunswick (Unit 523).

Conductivity levels, and hence productivity, tend to be highest where surface waters drain areas consisting mostly of limestone and gypsum. The levels of pH range between slightly acidic to very alkaline. In-filtration rates are relatively high in the porous soils of this Region and, consequently, groundwater recharge is high.

CLIMATE

The Carboniferous Lowlands form a large, scattered Region. Within it, the climate shows considerable variation, although it is essentially an inland lowland climate characterized by cold winters and warm summers. The major modifying influences are elevation in Cape Breton, and marine influences from the Gulf of St. Lawrence, Bras d'Or Lake, and Atlantic Ocean.

Winters are cold, though not severe. January mean daily temperatures are less than 6°C. Because of the influence of the Atlantic, fall temperatures in the Sydney area are somewhat higher. Spring comes later to those areas near the coast because of the ice cover and persistent cold water. Mean daily temperatures rise above freezing before the end of March, and the growing season is under way before the end of April. Spring is later at higher elevations. Temperatures warm quickly on the mainland but stay cool in Cape Breton and along the coast of the Gulf of St. Lawrence because of winds off ice-covered waters.

By July the whole Region has warmed to a mean daily temperature of over 17°C. Mean daily temperatures of less than 0°C return in November in the mainland interior, and in early December in the rest of the Region.

The total annual precipitation varies throughout the Region. In general it is drier towards New Brunswick, where parts of the Northumberland Plain (Unit 521) receive less than 1000 mm, and wetter in Cape Breton, which receives 1200 to 1600 mm. Snowfall is heavy in the interior and in the Dissected Plateau (District 590) of Cape Breton, but lighter near the coast. The snow-cover season lasts more than 130 days in all areas, except northern Cape Breton and parts of the mainland interior where it can exceed 140 days.

Early spring fogs are a feature along the Northumberland Strait because of the influence of the cold seawater on warm winds. The frost-free period lasts less than 100 days in the interior but lengthens to 140 days or more along the coast and around Sydney. The number of accumulated growing degree-days is high, particularly along the North Shore, where the warm summer waters of the Northumberland Strait boost summer temperatures.

SOILS

The main factors affecting soil development in this Region are the great variety of rock types and landforms, the generally more erodable nature of the rock, and the varied forest vegetation. Soils vary considerably and form a more intricate soil mosaic than is found in Regions such as the Atlantic Interior. The tills tend to be deep, and the soils that have developed on them are often heavy-textured with impeded drainage. Lowland soils usually have fewer stones and are more readily compacted. As elsewhere in the province, humo-ferric podzols cover major areas, but luvisols, brunisols, and gleysols are well represented. Sandy loams occur on the Horton and Pictou-Morien formations, while shaly loams occur on the Windsor, Riversdale, and Canso formations. Extensive Regosols have developed on alluvial materials, especially in the larger river valleys common in this Region.

Gypsum areas are usually overlain by glacial tills rather than by soils developed *in situ*, and exhibit a variety of soil types. However, because some gypsum has usually mixed into the tills, the local soil is often improved in structure and permeability. For this reason, the soils in gypsum areas are usually well-drained, even when otherwise fine-textured. The soils are also less acidic because of the influence of the gypsum. One type of soil commonly associated with gypsum is the Falmouth series, developed from a clay loam till deposited over gypsum. Falmouth soils can be important for agriculture, but when they occur over gypsum, their use is often limited by the sinkhole (karst) topography.

PLANTS

The Carboniferous Lowlands spread over three of Loucks' Forest Zones. One zone is dominated by softwoods, while in the other two, more northerly, semi-upland zones, hardwoods are more prominent. The Windsor Lowlands and the Northumberland Plain fall within the Red Spruce, Hemlock, Pine Zone. The Antigonish, Guysborough, and Bras d'Or areas are in the Sugar Maple–Eastern Hemlock, Pine Zone, and the higher Dissected Plateau District of Cape Breton is in the Sugar Maple, Yellow Birch–Fir Zone.

The main influences on the regional vegetation are the warm summers and cold winters, the heavier soils, and extensive disturbance through logging, fires, and farming. The Windsor Lowlands near Windsor and Truro grow mostly softwoods—Red Spruce, Black Spruce, Balsam Fir, Red Maple, and Eastern Hemlock. On the Northumberland Plain, where landforms are level and drainage is often poor, Black Spruce, Red Spruce, and Balsam Fir are the most common species, sometimes mixing with pine, Red Maple, or shade-tolerant hardwoods. In Cape Breton, White Spruce and Balsam Fir dominate the lowlands, while Red Maple, White Birch, and Yellow Birch are more common on the hilly lands. On the higher ground near Lake Ainslie, better drainage and cooler summers result in larger numbers of shade-tolerant hardwoods.

Bogs are generally not as prominent a feature here as in areas of more impermeable bedrock, but they are still common in the Windsor Lowlands, Bras d'Or, and Sydney areas. Salt marshes and freshwater marshes are abundant. Rich intervale lands in central mainland areas and on Cape Breton Island often provide habitat for rare or unusual Alleghanian plant species.

The vegetation of gypsum areas is influenced by the calcareous nature and dryness of the soils and by a karst topography that limits disturbance through forestry and agriculture. The main form of disturbance associated with gypsum is mining, but this is now mostly confined to deep, unweathered deposits; gypsum outcrops and cliffs are more likely to be left untouched. Mixed forest (often including Eastern Hemlock, Red Spruce, and Red Oak) is interspersed with bare or scrubby areas where the soil is too thin and dry to support tree growth.

Botanical interest is provided by a number of rare or unusual plants that survive in gypsum areas because of the comparative lack of competition. The flowers are best in the early spring, before the soil becomes parched. Fleabane can be found growing on the crumbling cliff faces, and above it on the cliff tops, Gypsum Ragwort grows. Trout Lily and Yellow Lady's-slipper can be found beneath trees on the plateau. Several hardy shrubs exist here, including Round-leaved Dogwood, Buffalo Berry and Shrubby Cinquefoil. Some of these plants require basic soils, while others (cinquefoil and Yellow Lady's-slipper) can also be found in acidic bogs, where the mechanisms to reduce evaporation, which are so necessary on the dry gypsum, help to prevent the plant from being poisoned by excessive take-up of acid water. Rarities occasionally found in gypsum areas include Leatherwood and the Ram's-head Lady's-slipper.

**500
Carboniferous
Lowlands**

500
Carboniferous
Lowlands

ANIMALS

This Region provides a diverse mix of open-land, oldfield, and forest habitats. There are few lakes of much size, but many wide and slow-moving rivers. Deeper soils and level terrain result in numerous productive freshwater marshes. Along the North Shore, the gentle slope of the shoreline provides important intertidal habitat, even though the tidal range is small.

Small-mammal diversity ranges from low (coastal marshes) to high (Ainslie Uplands), depending upon habitat. In agricultural areas an open-land mammal fauna is found: fox, raccoon, and skunk. In the wilder, less-accessible parts of the Region, moose, deer, and some bear can be found. Muskrat and mink are plentiful along streams and rivers. The gypsum provides calcareous soils, which support the greatest diversity of land snails found in Nova Scotia. The caves in gypsum provide hibernating sites for bats. Productive aquatic habitats support a more diverse freshwater fauna than is found elsewhere in the province.

In the Gulf of St. Lawrence the warm summer water temperatures permit the existence of disjunct populations of Virginian marine fauna. The Bras d'Or Lake has an impoverished marine fauna.

This Region provides important freshwater and coastal habitats for waterfowl.

CULTURAL ENVIRONMENT

Many areas of the Carboniferous Lowlands were significant Mi'kmaq hunting and fishing grounds. In the seventeenth century, Acadians settled in marshland areas around the Minas Basin and its river tributaries, choosing to dyke the tidal marshes to create fertile farmland rather than clear the forests. This engineering feat dramatically transformed the coastal landscape. After the Acadian deportation, eighteenth-century Planters and Loyalists claimed these lands. Scottish and Irish immigrants farmed other areas of the Carboniferous Lowlands. Today, parts of the Carboniferous Lowlands comprise some of the most productive and prosperous farms in Nova Scotia.

In the past, hydro power was harnessed by gristmill waterwheels. Now hydroelectric stations operate on various waterways which have been significantly altered to harness maximum hydro energy. Forest management has been intensive in this Region and has supplied diverse industries, including shipbuilding.

Mineral deposits have been exploited, including manganese, gypsum, anhydrite, barite, clay and shale, copper, salt, limestone, and coal. The mining of coal from the Sydney Coalfield and Pictou Valleys has been a major factor in the industrial and social development of Nova Scotia. There are several coal-fired electricity-generating stations in this Region. Sand and gravel deposits and sandstone quarries have also been important to the construction industry.

Coastline areas of the Carboniferous Lowlands have relied on the economically important fisheries of the Northumberland Strait and around Cape Breton. Many rivers of this Region are good for salmon fishing. Hunting, fishing, and other recreational activities are widespread. Scenic vistas and cultural heritage museums also attract tourism to the Carboniferous Lowlands.

● ● ● ● ● ● ● ●

Associated Topics

T2.4 The Carboniferous Basin, T3.1 Development of the Ancient Landscape, T3.2 Ancient Drainage Patterns, T3.4 Terrestrial Glacial Deposits and Landscape Features, T5.2 Nova Scotia's Climate, T8.1 Freshwater Hydrology, T8.2 Freshwater Environments, T9.1 Soil-forming Factors, T10.2 Successional Trends in Vegetation, T10.4 Plant Communities in Nova Scotia, T10.12 Rare and Endangered Plants, T11.2 Forest and Edge-habitat Birds, T11.5 Freshwater Wetland Birds and Waterfowl, T11.8 Land Mammals, T11.10 Ungulates, T11.16 Land and Freshwater Invertebrates, T11.17 Marine Invertebrates, T12.2 Cultural Landscapes, T12.3 Geology and Resources, T12.11 Animals and Resources.

Associated Habitats

H2.3 Sandy Shore, H2.5 Tidal Marsh, H3.1 Freshwater Open-Water Lotic, H3.3 Freshwater Bottom Lotic, H3.5 Freshwater Water's Edge Lotic, H5.2 Oldfield, H5.5 Cave, H6.1 Hardwood Forest (Sugar Maple, Elm Association), H6.2 Softwood Forest (Spruce, Fir, Pine Association; Spruce, Hemlock, Pine Association).

510 TILL PLAIN

District 510 has been divided into two widely separated Units, each of which has a distinctive topographic character:

511 Windsor Lowlands
512 Salmon River Lowland

GEOLOGY AND LANDSCAPE DEVELOPMENT

Across central mainland Nova Scotia is a large area characterized by the close interrelationship of underlying, resistant Horton Group strata and overlying, less-resistant Windsor Group limestone, salts, and shales.

The large rivers (e.g., the Avon and Shubenacadie) that flow across this area follow fault lines or the courses of ancestral rivers. However, their tributaries tend to flow northeast or southwest in synclinal hollows between anticlinal ridges.

The Carboniferous strata were readily eroded by glacial action during the last ice age, and the District is heavily blanketed with glacial debris. Outwash deposits are common.

SCENIC QUALITY

The common element in these areas is human settlement, originally and still largely related to farming. Although settlers were initially interested primarily in dykelands along the tidal Avon and Shubenacadie river systems, they later fanned out across much of the fertile till plain. The farmscapes of the Region's core farming areas, centred on Windsor, Shubenacadie, Stewiacke, and Middle Musquodoboit, provide open vistas and much of scenic interest. A dairy industry offers distinctive landscape elements (grazing cattle, silos, large barns) in areas close to the metropolitan market. Wide tidal rivers add much to the beauty of a scene, as does the steep fault-scarp of Martock Mountain, southeast of Windsor. The Windsor vicinity achieves the highest scenic ratings, largely owing to stronger relief, and the Shubenacadie and Upper Musquodoboit areas rate as medium to moderately high.

**500
Till Plain**

511 WINDSOR LOWLANDS

The Windsor Lowlands Unit is divided into two sub–Units:

(a) Shubenacadie River

(b) East Mountain

The Windsor Lowlands cover a very large area south of the Minas Basin, from the Avon River east to the Shubenacadie and Stewiacke river valleys (sub-Unit 511a), and a small area north of Truro (sub-Unit 511b). These two areas are part of the same depositional area and have the same characteristics.

GEOLOGY AND LANDSCAPE DEVELOPMENT

The southern boundary of sub-Unit 511a against the Atlantic Interior is essentially identical to the shoreline of the Carboniferous depositional basin in this part of Nova Scotia. The Horton deposits range in thickness from zero at the margins to nearly 1,000 m near North Mountain. The Wittenburg Ridge was an upland at the time of deposition, and the Horton deposits thin out on its flanks. It is evident that the Rawdon Hills were not uplands because the same thinning does not occur. Good exposures of Horton strata are found at Victoria Park in Truro, and at Horton Bluff, where fossiliferous middle Horton sandstone and shales outcrop. During the period in which deposition was taking place from the Windsor sea, reefs formed near the shoreline. One of these, north of Wittenburg Ridge, is at Gays River; others are found on the Atlantic Coast at East River and

Plate 5: Region 500. View looking south across the upper branch of East St. Mary's River (Unit 572) to a landscape of rolling hills partly cleared for agriculture that is typical of much of the Carboniferous Lowlands. Photo: R. Merrick.

Aspotogan, where they developed in another arm of the sea which extended to Sable Island.

The Windsor Group deposits are about 425 m thick and overall consist of about 50 per cent shales and 25 per cent each of limestone and gypsum. From Windsor to Brooklyn, white cliffs of gypsum can be seen from the road. A wide area of gypsum is preserved in the Cheverie syncline.

The mantle of glacial till attains a thickness of 75 m near Stewiacke. Under the glacial till at Dutch Settlement, spruce branches have been found dating back to the Wisconsinan glaciation 18,000 years ago. The East Milford gypsum quarry has provided much information on glacial tills and the character of interglacial life. There have been many finds of plants and freshwater animals in ancient sinkholes. Remains of mastodon and other animals were discovered in 1991–93 and provisionally dated as 70,000 years old. Sands and gravels are seen in many locations, including the Stewiacke River and its South Branch, and at Hilden, south of Truro.

FRESH WATER

The landscape generally has low elevations and little relief, and the river system has a rectangular pattern. The rivers tend to be slow-moving mature floodplain rivers with associated intervales (see Plate 5). The Kennetcook, Avon, and Shubenacadie are influenced by the tidal actions of the Bay of Fundy. Water flow in the river valleys fluctuates greatly, sometimes flooding extensively. Small lakes are scattered throughout the Unit, including oxbow and solution lakes. An excavated lake occurs at the East Milford quarry in sub-Unit 511a.

Most of sub-Unit 511a falls within two secondary watersheds draining north into Cobequid Bay. The Avon River (see Figure 16) cuts across low ridges whose intervening valleys are occupied by its tributaries. The Halfway and Cogmagun rivers flow into the Avon estuary from the west and east sides, respectively. The Upper Avon, Kennetcook, and St. Croix rivers lie parallel on either side of the estuary. The lower part of the Avon River valley has been drowned, forming a wide estuary which extends into the tributary rivers. The red silt that forms the wide mud banks within the river is derived from erosion of the Triassic deposits and is carried in from the Minas Basin. The upper courses of these rivers meander widely across a lowland bordered by tidal marshes and meadows. The Avon River may occupy a course similar to its ancestral river, which, it is hypothesized, flowed northwards from the southern uplands during the Cretaceous.

The Shubenacadie River, like the Avon, cuts across the fold axes and bands of hard and soft strata, reaching Cobequid Bay west of Truro. At its mouth a narrow band of Horton rocks overlain by Windsor limestone can be seen at Black Rock. For the next five kilometres inland, it cuts through soft red sandstone containing bands of fibrous gypsum (see Figure 11). North of the South Maitland bridge the river cuts a narrow channel through a faulted block of coarse Horton grits. To the south, a cliff of gypsum is exposed at Big Plaster Rock. Further up the river, passing more grits and red sandstone, a fossiliferous limestone containing corals and shells is exposed at Anthonys Nose.

The Stewiacke River, a major tributary of the Shubenacadie River, flows parallel to the fold axes. The relief and altitude in this area are so low that neighbouring streams flow for long distances in opposite directions. For example, the South Branch follows a narrow bed of Windsor Group rocks northeast, while the Stewiacke flows southwest. Many oxbow lakes are associated with the Stewiacke.

The southeastern portion of sub-Unit 511a falls within the Atlantic coast drainage area, and many first- and second-order streams feed into the Musquodoboit River as it meanders towards Musquodoboit Harbour.

Wetlands include flat bogs and fens and large freshwater marshes. Tidal marshes are scattered along the St. Croix, Avon, and Kennetcook rivers.

Surface-water productivity and diversity are generally high, and pH averages 7.5. Groundwater is high in dissolved minerals, particularly around Windsor and in areas associated with karst topography. There are several aquifers along the Stewiacke River.

SOILS

Shubenacadie River (sub-Unit 511a)
A considerable variety of soils is found in this area, but the dominant series is Queens, an imperfectly drained, sandy clay loam developed on clay loam till derived from shale and sandstones. Well-drained Hansford sandy loams have developed on Horton sandstone in the Hantsport-Walton area. Mottled Hantsport soils, also from shales and sandstones, are found in low-lying areas and close to the coast. Drumlinoid features are common from Brookfield to Enfield, and lacustrine deposits often occur on the till plain. Alluvial soils such as Stewiacke, Cumberland, and Chaswood often occur along stream and river valleys. These range in texture from gravelly sandy loams to silty clay loams.

East Mountain (sub-Unit 511b)

The main soil series in this sub-Unit is Diligence, an imperfectly drained clay loam over clay till derived from grey shales. Along North River, Cumberland gravelly sandy loams occur.

PLANTS

The main factors influencing the vegetation of this Unit are the gentle relief, poor drainage, and the repeated cutting and burning of the forests. The spruces, fir, White Birch, Red Maple, Eastern Hemlock, and White Pine are the major species, with scattered Sugar Maple, American Beech, and Yellow Birch occurring on better-drained low ridges. Abandoned farmlands are common and have usually been recolonized by White Spruce, Red Spruce, and Balsam Fir. In other areas, repeated burning has encouraged Wire Birch, White Pine, Red Pine, and Black Spruce. Repeated disturbance sometimes leads to the development of semi-permanent shrub cover. American Elm, Black Ash, the occasional Sugar Maple and American Beech may be found along the rivers.

C.D. Howe made the following observations on the soil-forest relationships of this area in 1912: "Along the coast, the ridges are capped with hardwoods and the depressions support a mixed forest in which either red spruce or hemlock prevails; and frequently, the conifers occur in pure stands. The mixed forest is very luxuriant on the broad gentle slopes where the composition is from one-half to three-fourths red spruce and usually about 15 percent is yellow birch and five percent beech. The soil is deep and consists mostly of silt and fine sand. When the top of the ridges are narrow, they are crowned with hardwoods, otherwise the mixed type extends over them."

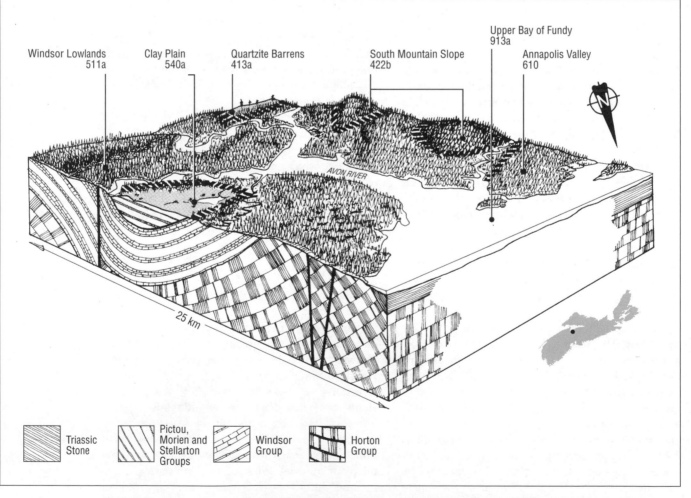

Figure 16: Avon River area. A rising sea level has drowned the Avon River estuary which drains the Windsor Lowlands (Unit 511). The river cuts through resistant Horton sandstones between high banks. Wherever the less-resistant Windsor rocks are encountered, wide valleys have been excavated. The extensive karst topography that developed on the gypsum (part of the Windsor Group) is prominent. Uplands of the Atlantic Interior (Region 400) define the Avon River's drainage basin.

ANIMALS

This Unit offers a mix of lowland, disturbed forest habitats, scattered farmlands, some dykelands, tidal marshes, and fertile river valleys. The mix of land types and fertility provides habitat for a great variety of Nova Scotia wildlife. Deer, which are creatures of edge habitat, thrive in the Windsor Lowlands. Some deer are concentrated in the upper basin of the Stewiacke, but because of the low topography throughout this Unit, there are no huge winter concentrations like those which occur at the foot of the Cobequid Hills (Unit 311). Moose are occasionally seen, but for the most part are absent.

There are few lakes, but the rivers and streams are comparatively productive and the freshwater fauna is diverse. The Unit provides good habitat for raccoon, muskrat, and mink, and diverse breeding habitats for waterfowl. Significant wetland habitats occur at South Branch and Otter Brook. Wood Turtles are abundant in the Musquodoboit Valley and in the Kennetcook and Five Mile Rivers. River Otter find good habitat associated with the major rivers, and beaver are common. Beaver dams do not persist and lodges are often built into riverbanks. Shallow, eutrophic Lake Egmont and its associated freshwater marsh provide one of the richest freshwater plant and animal localities in the province.

The tidal waters of the Shubcnacadie and Stewiacke rivers allow anadromous fish species to reach fresh water for spawning, and allow their offspring access to the ocean, where they mature. Striped Bass occur in both rivers, and many thousands of American Shad spawn in the Stewiacke. Faster-flowing streams that feed the Stewiacke River are important spawning and nursery areas for Atlantic Salmon. Brown Trout, which is an introduced species, and Brook Trout also inhabit the Stewiacke River.

The anadromous Atlantic Tomcod spawns in the Shubcnacadie River in January, attracting concentrations of 50–100 Bald Eagles. The greatest concentrations of eagles occur in the Riverside area. Besides winter visitors, Bald Eagles are seen around roughly 10 or more nesting sites in this Unit in summer. Common Mergansers and Black Ducks overwinter here.

Ospreys have recently become more numerous, and Canada Geese also nest in this Unit. Ring-necked Pheasant can be found here, but in much smaller numbers than in the Triassic Lowlands (Region 600).

A cave near South Maitland is a significant bat hibernation site.

CULTURAL ENVIRONMENT

Many parts of the Windsor Lowlands were favourite spots of the Mi'kmaq for hunting and fishing, and many place names in this area are of Mi'kmaq origin. The name Shubenacadie is derived from the Mi'kmaq word meaning "place where groundnuts grow." It has long been a Mi'kmaq settlement and today features one of the largest Mi'kmaq communities in the province. The name Stewiacke is also derived from Mi'kmaq and means "flowing out in small streams" and "whimpering or whining as it goes."

In the seventeenth century the Acadians settled in the Windsor Lowlands, including along the St. Croix River, the Avon River (which the Acadians called the Pisiquid), and the Kennetcook River (known to the Acadians as the Quenetcou). Dyking significantly altered the coastal and estuarine landscape.

After 1760, New England Planters settled on vacant dykelands and employed remaining Acadians to maintain them. Soon Germans, Yorkshiremen, and a huge influx of Loyalists came to the Windsor Lowlands to farm its fertile soils. Parts of the Windsor Lowlands are today some of the most productive farming areas in Nova Scotia. Much of this area has also been logged for its timber, and many lumbering and sawmill operations are found here.

The mineral resources of the Windsor Lowlands have long attracted mining operations. In 1876, manganese was first mined in Tennycape and the mineral was produced intermittently for the next three decades. Mining operations at Milford, Miller Creek, and Wentworth Creek, among others, exploit the large deposits of gypsum and anhydrite. At Dutch Settlement (Hants County) the gypsum beds are 60 m thick. One billion tonnes have been blocked out and another four billion are in reserve. A large barite deposit near Walton was mined for 30 years, but the mine closed in 1971. Clay and shale deposits at Lantz, Milford, and Shubenacadie are exploited to produce virtually all the province's supplies of brick. Dolomite is quarried for agricultural purposes at Upper Musquodoboit.

A large outwash deposit known as the Hardwoodlands Aquifer is found south of the Shubenacadie Indian Reserve. It is a significant freshwater resource in an area of saline groundwater.

● ● ● ● ● ● ● ●

**511
Windsor
Lowlands**

Sites of Special Interest
Avon River Area

- Horton Bluff (north of Hantsport)—fossil plants, invertebrates, fish, amphibian bones, and tracks (including the largest footprints of Horton Group age ever reported)
- Blue Beach, Hants County—Early Carboniferous strata with bones and footprints of early amphibians and reptiles
- Newport Landing (northeast of wharf)—good exposure of early Windsor Group fossiliferous limestone containing brachiopods, gastropods, bryozoans, cephalopods, and pelecypods; this is underlain by gypsum, limestone, shale, sandstone; fossil corals outcrop on the shore
- Cheverie (near Mutton Cove)—late Horton-age tree stumps 10–20 cm high and 10–30 cm in diameter, karst topography
- Cheverie Point to Summerville—Horton-age soil beds with rootlets
- Wolfville to Windsor (along Highway 101)—road runs along the Wolfville Ridge anticline with the Gaspereau syncline to the south
- Hantsport—road descends into the syncline of Halfway River and up the slope of the next anticline (Grey Mountain)
- Brooklyn—in a gypsum area to the west, Yellow Lady's-slipper, *Shepherdia*, and *Carex flacca* are found
- Gypsum areas (karst topography)—Cheverie, Walton through Goshen to Lower Burlington, Mount Denson to Windsor Forks to Newport Corner; gypsum cliffs along the St. Croix River; sinkhole behind King's-Edgehill School
- St. Croix River (IBP Proposed Ecological Site 66)—mixed forest on karst topography harbouring rare orchids
- Shand House Museum, Windsor—products of the former Windsor Furniture Company

Shubenacadie River Area

- Black Rock (mouth of Shubenacadie)—Horton strata overlain by Windsor limestone
- Eagles Nest (Shubenacadie River)—Horton sandstone
- Big Plaster (Whites) Rock—gypsum cliff
- Anthonys Nose (Shubenacadie River)—fossiliferous limestone, 15 m thick, containing shells and corals
- Victoria Park (Truro)—steeply inclined Horton sandstone and siltstone
- Gypsum areas (karst topography)—Urbania (south of Maitland), South Maitland (Hayes Cave), East Milford (large working gypsum quarry, site of mastodon finds), Dutch Settlement
- East Milford quarry, Halifax County—removal of the overburden of glacial till as part of gypsum mining operations frequently uncovers fossiliferous interglacial deposits. Fossils of plants, insects, molluscs, and vertebrates, including mastodon remains, are found, particularly in deposits in sinkholes
- Lantz—clay for brickmaking
- Shubenacadie (IBP Proposed Ecological Site 68)—clearcut in mixedwoods, regenerated with Leatherwood; *Carex aurea*; *Milium effusum*, var. *cisatlanticum*; Bulblet Fern; and Alder-leaved Buckthorn
- South Maitland (IBP Proposed Ecological Site 69)—river intervale, gypsum cliffs, mixed forest, and cave system
- Lawrence House Museum, Maitland—shipbuilding history
- Creighton Forest Environment Centre, entrance of Shubenacadie Wildlife Park—documents historical aspects of forestry and wildlife in Nova Scotia
- Lake Egmont—diverse freshwater community

Provincial Parks and Park Reserves
- Shubenacadie Wildlife Park
- Smiley's
- Musquodoboit Valley
- St. Croix
- Cheverie
- South Maitland

Proposed Parks and Protected Areas System includes Natural Landscape 28.

Scenic Viewpoints
- Avon area—Highway 101 near exit 4 (view of St. Croix floodplain, gypsum cliffs); Highway 101 south of Hantsport, looking north (view of Minas Basin)
- Shubenacadie area—Highway 102 north of exit 9, looking east (view of large dairy farms); Highway 102 north of exit 11 (view of tidal Stewiacke River)
- Caddell Rapids—lookoff

Associated Topics
T2.4 The Carboniferous Basin, T3.2 Ancient Drainage Patterns, T3.4 Terrestrial Glacial Deposits and Landscape Features, T7.3 Coastal Landforms, T8.1 Freshwater Hydrology, T8.2 Freshwater Environments, T10.12 Rare and Endangered Plants, T11.4 Birds of

**511
Windsor
Lowlands**

Prey, T11.10 Ungulates, T11.13 Freshwater Fishes, T11.15 Amphibians and Reptiles, T12.1 Cultural Landscapes, T12.3 Geology and Resources, T12.10 Plants and Resources.

Associated Habitats

H2.4 Mud Flat, H2.5 Tidal Marsh, H3 Freshwater, H5.2 Oldfield, H5.3 Cliff and Bank, H5.5 Cave, H6.1 Hardwood Forest (Sugar Maple, Elm Association), H6.2 Softwood Forest (White Spruce Association; Pine Association), H6.3 Mixedwood Forest (Spruce, Fir, Pine–Maple, Birch Association).

511
Windsor
Lowlands

512 SALMON RIVER LOWLAND

GEOLOGY AND LANDSCAPE DEVELOPMENT

South of the East Bay Hills, a large wedge of Late Carboniferous sandstone has been downfaulted between blocks of ancient Avalon Zone strata. This is the Salmon River Lowland. The elevations are low in this part of Cape Breton, being on the low side of the tilted planation surface, and the area has been thickly covered by glacial deposits.

The Salmon River has been impounded by ridges of glacial debris to form Loch Lomond, Lake Uist, and Enon Lake, which lie just to the south of the area. Another deposit, oriented north-south, divides a small lake into two at the northern end of the lowland. In general the terrain is low and rolling, with few elevations greater than 100 m.

FRESH WATER

Drainage is dendritic, and many tributaries feed the Salmon and Gaspereaux rivers in the northeastern areas. The headwaters of the Grand River are located in Cape Breton County. Southwestern portions in Richmond County are dominated by the Lake Uist and Loch Lomond system. A drainage divide separates the northeastern and southwestern areas. Surface-water pH levels range between 6.3 and 7.0. Concentrations of raised bogs can be found in the southwestern areas, and wetlands are associated with lake edges throughout.

SOILS

Shulie soils (well-drained sandy loams) cover much of this Unit. Around Rock Elm, to the north of the Unit, is a small area with complex soils—clay loams such as Millbrook and Kingsville, and alluvial soils such as Cumberland and Millar. Near Gaspereaux Lake, in an area known as the Big Barren, poorly drained Arichat and imperfectly drained Debert soils occur, with better-drained Woodbourne soils derived from a gravelly clay loam till. Around the Loch Lomond lakes, the soils are mostly imperfectly to poorly drained, usually sandy or silt loams over compact clay tills such as Millbrook, Woodbourne, Masstown, Debert, and Kingsville soils.

PLANTS

This Unit is transitional between Loucks' Coastal Forest Zone and Sugar Maple–Hemlock, Pine Zone. Shade-intolerant hardwoods also occur with scattered shade-tolerant species. The compact clay soils support mostly Balsam Fir, with lesser amounts of White Spruce. Shade-intolerant Red Maple and White Birch with aspen and a few American Beech grow on the better-drained slopes.

CULTURAL ENVIRONMENT

Farming and forestry characterize land use in this area. Lead ore was mined in the Salmon River area from 1946 to 1966, and a small amount of by-product silver was also recovered. The Mi'kmaq traditionally fished the Salmon River. Today, recreational anglers fish Atlantic Salmon and Brook Trout in these waters.

● ● ● ● ● ● ●

Provincial Parks and Park Reserves
• Two Rivers

Proposed Parks and Protected Areas System includes Natural Landscape 54.

Associated Topics
T2.4 The Carboniferous Basin, T3.1 Development of the Ancient Landscape, T3.4 Terrestrial Glacial Deposits and Landscape Features, T12.3 Geology and Resources, T12.11 Animals and Resources.

Associated Habitats
H3 Fresh Water, H4.1 Bog, H6.1 Hardwood Forest (Maple, Oak, Birch Association), H6.3 Mixedwood Forest (White Spruce, Fir–Maple, Birch Association).

520 COASTAL PLAIN

The Coastal Plain District is divided into three Units:

521 Northumberland Plain
522 Judique Coastal Lowland
523 Tantramar Marshes

GEOLOGY

District 520 of the Carboniferous Lowlands is one of the three true lowland areas of Nova Scotia; the other two are the Windsor Lowlands (Unit 511) and the Submerged (Bras d'Or) Lowland (District 560). This District borders the Northumberland Strait (with one interruption) from Tidnish to Port Hood. It is underlain by Middle and Late Carboniferous strata (Windsor to Pictou groups) which are all unresistant. Consequently the relief is low, and the topography is flat and undulating. This area is also submergent, and many long inlets and estuaries extend inland from sheltered harbours.

SCENIC QUALITY

The most scenic feature of this region is the coast, for two reasons: the water and the farming landscapes. Scenic potential tends to be higher around enclosed bays and along drowned estuaries, particularly Wallace Harbour, Amet Sound, Pictou Harbour, and Antigonish Harbour. The juxtaposition of land and sea in these inlets provides greater visual interest than straighter stretches of coast. Farming tends to be more extensive in the same areas, providing greater visibility and more road access. Scenic ratings are thus very high in coastal embayments, moderately high elsewhere on the coast, and at medium levels inland. Where settlement and farming are absent inland, as around Amherst Head (Route 6), the forested plain has low scenic value. Although not beautiful to every eye, the flat and treeless dykelands near Amherst deserve special mention: their expanses of open prairie may either exhilarate or intimidate.

521 NORTHUMBERLAND PLAIN

The Northumberland Plain is divided into two sub-Units:

(a) Northumberland Strait
(b) St. Georges Bay

GEOLOGY AND LANDSCAPE DEVELOPMENT

Northumberland Strait (sub-Unit 521a)

This coastal plain stretches from the Cumberland Basin to Pictou and Merigomish Island and is underlain by fine red sandstones of the Late Carboniferous Pictou Group (from Merigomish to Knoydart, Canso strata predominate). These sandstones have been thrown into broad folds. In Cumberland County there are two main anticlines: one runs from Pugwash Harbour west to Nappan, Amherst Point, and the area south of Minudie; the other runs from Malagash Point past Oxford and then plunges downward east of Springhill. The crests of these anticlines have been partially eroded away, exposing underlying Windsor evaporites or Canso Group strata. Gypsum outcrops in many places.

In addition to the two main anticlines, there are many minor folds which run east-west before plunging downwards. Differential erosion has created ridges and valleys parallel to the fold axes, creating an undulating landscape. In central Cumberland County, they rise to 120 m or more, for example, Streets Ridge east of Oxford.

Alternating low ridges and valleys determine the outline of the coast along Northumberland Strait (see Figure 17). The ridges run out to sea as headlands at Pugwash and Wallace, and nearly enclose Tatamagouche Bay and Amet Sound. Smith Point, Malagash Point, and Cape John are prominent projections; Caribou Island is a continuation eastwards of the Pictou County shore; and Pictou Island is a remnant of a ridge that existed in the centre of the Northumberland Strait.

Valleys form inlets and harbours along the coast where estuaries of the river were drowned by a rise in sea level.

At the eastern end of the Cobequid Hills the strata have been domed up as the once-underlying crustal block of the Cobequids rose upwards. Consequently, due west from Pictou, progressively older rocks are exposed—Early Carboniferous to Late Devonian to Middle Devonian. These strata become progressively more resistant and form a hilly upland projection at the eastern end of the Cobequids in District 320 (see Figure 9).

From Merigomish to Knoydart, the Northumberland Plain continues as a submerged rolling coastal lowland.

St. Georges Bay (sub-Unit 521b)

Middle Carboniferous strata (Windsor, Canso, and Riversdale) underlie a lowland on the south side of St. Georges Bay. Elevations rarely exceed 50 m. Fine red Canso and grey-brown Riversdale sandstones and siltstones predominate, with a faulted block of Windsor evaporites exposed east of Antigonish. This band of Windsor strata has been eroded and drowned to form Antigonish Harbour. In places where gypsum outcrops, karst topography has developed. At Crystal Cliffs to the north, a 75-m high cliff with bands of white and pink gypsum faces the bay.

On the south side of St. Georges Bay, drowned river valleys that cut through Carboniferous rocks have created several harbours: Pomquet, Tracadie, Little Tracadie, and Havre Boucher.

A variable but ubiquitous cover of glacial till is found throughout the area. Eskers and outwash material are found along River John and elsewhere where rivers carried meltwater from the ice cap over the Cobequids.

FRESHWATER ENVIRONMENTS AND COASTAL WETLANDS

The streams flowing over the lowlands east of Amherst lie in an area of gentle topography and branch irregularly to form dendritic drainage patterns. Most of sub-Unit 521a lies north of the primary watershed boundary that dissects the Cobequids (Unit 311). Five secondary and numerous tertiary watersheds drain north in this part of the Unit. Streams flowing northwards from the Cobequids have been superimposed on bands of alternating weak and resistant strata. The Wallace River, for example, flows directly north from Folly Lake into the Northumberland Strait; its tributaries are adjusted to bands of weaker rocks and join it at right angles to form a trellised drainage pattern. River Philip and River Hebert also have tributaries that have adjusted to the strike of the strata. A small area in the southwest that includes the Nappan River drains west into Cumberland Basin. Flat bogs and swamps are widely scattered in the northwestern areas, and beaver-influenced wetlands are common throughout. Inactive beaver flowages become wet meadows and shrub swamps. Wide floodplains occur along some of the slow-moving mature rivers, such as the Pictou, West, Middle, and Merigomish rivers (see Figure 19).

Lakes on this coastal plain are infrequent, and those that occur tend to be elongated and shallow. Stratified lakes, such as Layton Lake in sub-Unit 521a, are meromictic. Surface-water pH levels are generally alkaline, ranging from 6.5 to 8.0.

The Northumberland Strait sub-Unit (521b) also drains north. It is bisected north-south by a secondary watershed boundary, and numerous tertiary and coastal watersheds drain into St. Georges Bay. A few small, scattered bogs are found in the western areas.

There are brackish lakes at Oxford and salt springs between River Philip and Springhill. The coast is characterized by extensive intertidal marshes and subtidal Eelgrass beds. Barachois ponds and tidal marshes occur in the harbours and inlets.

SOILS

The sandstones and shales that underlie the entire area have produced glacial tills of a sandy loam to sandy clay loam texture. One common characteristic is the tight, impermeable nature of the subsoil. This effectively prevents rapid vertical movement of water, which must therefore be removed laterally, or through evapotranspiration. The most common soils are Debert, an imperfectly drained sandy loam, often with fragipan development; and Queens, a fine-textured, imperfectly drained sandy clay loam. Well-drained soils include Pugwash and Tormentine series on rolling topography. Kingsville and Masstown series occupy most of the poorly drained sites. Hebert soils on outwash materials, and Cumberland and finer-textured Chaswood soils on alluvial materials, are common along streams and rivers.

PLANTS

This Unit falls within the Maritime Lowlands Ecoregion of Loucks' Red Spruce, Hemlock, Pine Zone. The forests are heterogeneous mixtures of early to mid-successional stages dominated by hardwoods and much influenced by site characteristics and disturbances. Black Spruce, Jack Pine, White Spruce, Red Spruce, and Red Maple are the most abundant species, although Eastern Hemlock and White Pine are not uncommon. Eastern Hemlock may occur in pure stands and can be among the first species to colonize disturbed areas. Larch and Black Spruce occur in the extensive boggy areas. American Beech and Sugar Maple are found on a few slopes near the larger streams. Repeated fires have encouraged Jack Pine, especially around Oxford. Although large numbers of poplar remain in the area, they are gradually being replaced by conifers. Much of the area is farmed, and oldfields generally recolonize in alders followed by White Spruce. Larch more commonly colonizes wet fields underlain by fragipan along the coast.

Winds from the Northumberland Strait, often recorded at twice the speed of winds inland, are a strong influence. Trees often lean away from the wind, have one-sided crowns, and do not attain full height. Extensive salt marshes and Eelgrass beds occur in bays.

ANIMALS

This Unit provides mostly oldfield, agricultural, and mixed forest habitats. The amount of abandoned farmland is significant. Relatively flat topography and imperfectly drained soils have resulted in an abundance of beaver-influenced wetlands. The coyote is common, especially in areas associated with agriculture. This is an excellent area for muskrat, mink, and raccoon and provides average habitat for Red Fox. River Otter occur but are not numerous. Freshwater habitats are relatively productive and support an enriched fauna, including Atlantic Salmon, Gaspereau, Brown Trout, and Brook Trout. The rare Brook Stickleback is found in this Unit, as is the threatened Wood Turtle, which can be seen along the abundant river habitat.

Many water birds breed mainly in coastal habitats, and many other species breed in freshwater marshes, which mostly arise near the coast. Given the steep rocky shores and extreme tidal range around the Fundy coast, most species in these bird groups breed in Cumberland County, where the extensive intertidal areas formed by the very shallow slope of the sea bottom provide appropriate waterfowl breeding and staging areas. This occurs mainly in sub-Unit 521a and Unit 523. These species include most ducks and marsh birds, Osprey, Bald Eagle, Semipalmated Plover, and Common Tern. Another group of birds, including Red-breasted Merganser, Willet, Herring Gull, Great Black-backed Gull, and Sharp-tailed Sparrow, breed in suitable situations on both low-lying and steeper coasts, appearing only in sub-Unit 521a and Unit 710.

**521
Northumberland
Plain**

The most significant bird habitats are around Fox Harbour, Wallace Harbour, Tatamagouche Bay, Brule Harbour, and John Bay, where large numbers of ducks and geese congregate in late March and April, and again in September until ice forms in December. Other important areas include Coldspring Head and the mouth of the Shinimicas River; Pugwash Harbour and River Philip; Caribou Harbour; Pictou Harbour, East River, Middle River, and West River; and Little Harbour and Merigomish Harbour. Freshwater impoundments are breeding areas for Pied-billed Grebe, American Bittern, Northern Harrier, Virginia Rail, Sora Rail, and many ducks.

Various bird species, such as Spruce Grouse, Northern Waterthrush, and Mourning Warbler, that are more characteristic of cooler areas are scarce in sub-Unit 521a. However, a few forest birds, such as Broad-winged Hawk and Brown Creeper, are widespread in this sub-Unit but scarce or absent in Units immediately to the south. Rough-legged Hawk, Snowy Owl, and Snow Bunting occur in winter on fields in the more upland areas of sub-Unit 521a.

The Northumberland Strait is a very distinct marine area in which warmer-water species such as oysters and quahogs are found.

CULTURAL ENVIRONMENT

Coastal areas of the Northumberland Plain had traditionally been the summer camps of the Mi'kmaq, and many place names in this area are derived from Mi'kmaq words. Antigonish meant "the place where branches are torn off the trees by bears gathering beechnuts" and Tatamagouche, situated at the mouth of the French and Waughs rivers, meant "the meeting of the waters." Settlers of largely English and Scottish descent cleared much of the land for agriculture, which continues to be an important economic activity. This area once supported many grist mills.

Farming, forestry, and fishing serve as the economic base for most communities here. Agricultural land in the Northumberland Plain is multi-cropped. The largest concentration of small fruit growers in the province has earned Cumberland County the title of "Blueberry-Growing Capital of the World." Vineyards at Malagash produce good quality grapes for wines. The marine life from the Northumberland Strait has been extremely important to the economies of coastal communities on the Northumberland Plain, with lobster, scallop, and oyster fishing predominating. Important seaweed beds of Irish Moss and *Furcellaria* are also harvested commercially.

This area features significant mineral deposits and mining operations. The earliest recorded exploration for copper in the province was near Caribou in 1828, and a small amount of copper production was achieved from mining chalcocite along the Wallace River. In 1946 a huge deposit of salt was discovered at Nappan and, since then, salt mines have operated both there and in Pugwash. Salt deposits at Malagash were mined for 40 years, and deposits up to 450 m thick have been drilled in this area. Today, limestone is mined at Southside Antigonish Harbour to supply the Scott Maritimes paper mill at Abercrombie, which processes pulpwood from surrounding areas. Red and grey sandstones at Amherst and Wallace were quarried to provide building stone for Province House and Government House in Halifax, as well as many other buildings of the early nineteenth century.

Various wildlife management areas (Wallace, Abercrombie) and the Brule Point Game Sanctuary are also found on the Northumberland Plain. Ducks Unlimited has converted many old, inactive beaver flowages back to shallow marshes. Cottages occur along stretches of the coastline. These are the warmest waters for swimming on the Nova Scotia coastline.

● ● ● ● ● ● ● ●

Sites of Special Interest
- Crystal Cliffs—75-m cliff with bands of pink and white gypsum
- Antigonish Harbour—drowned estuary, karst topography
- Pugwash—salt mines
- River John—outwash deposits and eskers
- Oxford—round, water-filled sinkholes make small lakes
- Streets Ridge (120 m high)—brackish lakes
- Amherst Point—sinkholes
- Laytons Lake—a flooded gypsum sinkhole that is permanently stratified
- Pomquet Beach—best example of a prograding dune system in the province
- Amet Island—the only offshore islet with breeding seabirds (gulls and cormorants) in sub-Unit 521a
- Smith Point/Oak Island flats—the most significant area in sub-Unit 521a for shorebirds, with up to 12 species present in late summer, including concentrations of the rare Hudsonian Godwit
- Linden Bay—often significant for Canada Geese and currently the most regular stopover site for migrating Brant in spring

- Tidnish Dock—a useful vantage point for viewing water birds on the extensive shoal waters of Baie Verte and the most regular location in sub-Unit 521a for Red-necked Grebes in autumn
- National Wildlife Areas—Wallace Bay, Chignecto (includes Lusby Marsh and Amherst Point Bird Sanctuary)
- Provincial Wildlife Management Area—Antigonish Harbour, Federal Migratory Bird Sanctuary
- Black River Road (IPB Proposed Ecological Site 6)—Jack Pine forest
- Balmoral Grist Mill—example of early agricultural technology
- Sutherlands Steam Mill, Denmark—once manufactured carriages, sleighs, sleds, and doors from local timber
- McCulloch House Museum, Pictou—home of Thomas McCulloch, one of Nova Scotia's great naturalists and educators
- Northumberland Fisheries Museum, Pictou

Provincial Parks and Park Reserves
- Tidnish Dock (also an historic site of the Chignecto Ship Railway)
- Northport Beach
- Heather Beach
- Gulf Shore
- Fox Harbour
- Tatamagouche
- Barachois Harbour
- Balmoral Mills
- Shinimicas
- Rushton Beach
- Cape John Beach
- Waterside Beach
- Mackenzie Beach
- Doctors Island
- Caribou
- Lyons Brook
- Boat Harbour
- Powells Point
- Melmerby Beach
- Merigomish Harbour
- Big Island
- The Ponds
- Mahoneys Beach
- Pomquet
- Bayfield
- Barrios Beach
- Cape Jack Beach
- Malagash—Beatty Marsh Park Reserve

Proposed Parks and Protected Areas System includes Natural Landscape 22.

Scenic Viewpoint
- Unit 521a: Hardwood Hill, looking east over Pictou Harbour

Associated Offshore Unit
914 Northumberland Strait.

Associated Topics
T2.4 The Carboniferous Basin, T3.2 Ancient Drainage Patterns, T3.3 Glaciation, Deglaciation and Sea-level Changes, T3.4 Terrestrial Glacial Deposits and Landscape Features, T6.2 Oceanic Environments, T8.2 Freshwater Environments, T9.3 Biological Environment, T11.5 Freshwater Wetland Birds and Waterfowl, T11.13 Freshwater Fishes, T11.17 Marine Invertebrates, T12.3 Geology and Resources, T12.11 Animals and Resources.

Associated Habitats
H1.1 Offshore Open Water, H1.2 Offshore Benthic, H2 Coastal, H3.1 Freshwater Open-Water Lotic, H3.3 Freshwater Bottom Lotic, H3.5 Freshwater Water's Edge Lotic, H5.2 Oldfield, H6.2 Softwood Forest (Pine Association; Black Spruce, Larch Association).

522 JUDIQUE COASTAL LOWLAND

522
Judique
Coastal
Lowland

GEOLOGY AND LANDSCAPE DEVELOPMENT

The Judique Coastal Lowland forms a very narrow band along the eastern side of St. Georges Bay and is the geological continuation of sub-Unit 521b. It appears likely that the entire bay area was once composed of the same strata as is now exposed around its rim. The bay may have been carved out by an ancestral river flowing from the Scotian Shelf through the Strait of Canso.

At Port Hood a small area of grey Riversdale sandstone and shale contains thin coal seams. These dip under the waters of the bay at an angle of 20°.

FRESH WATER

Several small, isolated tertiary watersheds run parallel to each other and drain first-order streams into the east side of St. Georges Bay. A few small bogs are scattered further inland.

SOILS

The soils in the Unit are predominantly imperfectly drained Queens clay loams, with their poorly drained associate, the Kingsville series, occurring frequently and over substantial acreages. Better-drained soils of the Woodbourne and Shulie series are developed on tills derived from sandstone in small areas throughout the Unit. Around Port Hood, Springhill soils occur. These sandy loams, related to Shulie soils, occupy imperfectly drained sites where water movement is restricted by the topography. Small areas of peat, coarse Hebert soils, and Falmouth and Cumberland soils occur throughout.

PLANTS

Loucks places this unit in the Sugar Maple–Hemlock, Pine Zone. The main influences on the vegetation are the wet clay soils, the late spring, and the effects of agricultural clearing. Conifers are dominant. Many of the oldfields are regenerating in White Spruce and Balsam Fir. Black Spruce and Larch are found in the wetter areas. Shade-tolerant deciduous trees grow on some slopes, while a mixed forest of spruce and fir with some shade-intolerant hardwoods covers much of the area.

CULTURAL ENVIRONMENT

Small-scale farming, fishing, and woodlot exploitation form the economic basis of communities in this area. In former times, coal was mined at Port Hood.

• • • • • • • •

Sites of Special Interest
• Port Hood—coal seams in Riversdale strata

Provincial Parks and Park Reserves
• Craigmore
Proposed Parks and Protected Areas System includes Natural Landscape 59.

Associated Offshore Unit
914 Northumberland Strait.

Associated Topics
T2.4 The Carboniferous Basin, T3.2 Ancient Drainage Patterns.

Associated Habitats
H3.1 Freshwater Open-Water Lotic, H3.5 Freshwater Water's Edge Lotic, H5.2 Oldfield, H6.2 Softwood Forest (White Spruce Association; Black Spruce, Larch Association), H6.3 Mixedwood Forest (Spruce, Fir, Pine–Maple, Birch Association).

523 TANTRAMAR MARSHES

The Tantramar Marshes, also known as the Border Lowland, occupy a large area at the head of the Cumberland Basin where the flat terrain meets the sediment-loaded waters of the Bay of Fundy. Extensive grasslands occupy much of the former salt marshes that have been dyked and are no longer exposed to siltation. The John Lusby portion of the Chignecto National Wildlife Area is the only large tract still subject to siltation processes.

GEOLOGY AND LANDSCAPE DEVELOPMENT

The marshes are built-up silts and clays that were carried from the Bay of Fundy by the spring tides. The amount of sediment deposited by one tide depends upon the depth of water that covers the marsh and the rapidity with which it drains away. Radiocarbon dating has determined that 25 m of sediment was built up at Aulac Station between Amherst and Sackville, New Brunswick, over a period of 3,000–5,000 years.

The marshes built up quickly during a period of land subsidence and rising sea levels. Increasing tidal ranges in the Bay of Fundy during the last 6,000 years have controlled their formation. The marshes have extended further inland during this period but have always been exposed to erosive forces at their outer edges. As the Bay of Fundy enlarges through rising sea levels and the erosion of headlands, continual deposition of sediments in the littoral zone occurs, creating the foundation for future salt marshes outside the present dykelands.

As the marsh erodes, remains of submerged forests and freshwater marshes are uncovered. The best examples are in New Brunswick off Fort Beausejour. Often the stumps and roots are washed away quickly once they have been uncovered, though more are revealed as new areas are exposed. A submerged forest off Fort Lawrence disappeared around 1985. Along the Missaguash River, however, stumps still remain after 150 years of exposure. At previous times the remains of spruce, beech, pine, and Larch have all been seen.

CLIMATE

The Fundy influence in this area creates climatic conditions similar to those of the fog belt of Nova Scotia: lower temperatures and higher humidity.

FRESH WATER

Two tertiary watersheds drain most of the northern portions of this Unit. The Missaguash and La Planche rivers and their tributaries form the main drainage channels flowing into the Cumberland Basin. In New Brunswick, the Tantramar River forms a third finger at the head of the basin. The headwaters of the Missaguash, Tidnish, and La Planche occur here. A small area of this Unit around the mouth of River Hebert in the southern section drains into the Cumberland Basin.

On the flat terrain, fresh water is impeded from flowing into Chignecto Bay (sub-Unit 913b) by the elevated salt marshes. Rising sea levels and siltation have built the marshes higher than the inland areas, forming a low dam behind which extensive freshwater peat bogs have developed. The abundance of freshwater wetlands is one of the most distinctive features of this Unit. Wetlands include dammed reservoirs and waterfowl impoundments.

SOILS

Three soil types dominate this Unit. The reclaimed dyked soils known as Acadia occur at the coast and extend several miles inland. Fresh water impounded inland from these marshland soils has formed extensive peat bogs. Adjacent mineral soils on flat, low-lying terrain are predominantly very poorly drained Masstown soils.

Acadia soils exhibit little horizon development because of the continued deposition of marine sediments. These silty clay loams are either red-brown or grey with an abrupt boundary; the colour is thought to indicate gleying. When reclaimed and drained, these soils are fertile and valuable agricultural soils.

As the peat is mainly formed on low-lying areas inland of the Acadia soils, it is usually no more than one metre thick. Former forests are often buried in the peat.

Masstown soils are poorly drained because of depressional locations or fragipans. A surface layer of organic material has developed up to 15 cm in depth. The underlying "A" horizon is 25 cm thick. This sandy "A" horizon can dry out very quickly when the water table drops, hence the soil tends to be either saturated or dry.

PLANTS

Extensive grasslands cover much of the former salt marshes. In the brackish and saline marsh areas the dominant species are Cord Grasses, with rushes, sedges, Common Reed, and a variety of other halophytes, for example, Sea-blite, Orach, Sea-lavender, Glasswort, Arrowgrass and Seaside Plantain. Extensive mud flats are exposed at low tide beyond the salt marshes.

Lake and bog areas contain a wide variety of aquatic plants. Cattails, bur-reed and sedge associations predominate in emergent areas. Various pondweeds and Yellow Pond-lily occur in open-water areas. Common species include Arrowhead, Waterparsnip, and bulrushes.

A poorly drained lowland forest composed mostly of spruce and fir lies inland from the dyked fields and marshes of the Chignecto Isthmus and forms part of the cool coastal forest around the Cumberland Basin (see also Unit 532).

ANIMALS

Intertidal areas in the Cumberland Basin form extensive mud flats that harbour the marine crustacean *Corophium*. Thousands of shorebirds congregate in July and August to feed on the crustaceans and polychaete worms.

The Maccan marshes provide significant waterfowl breeding areas and are part of the Cumberland Basin area. High tides usually clear the Lusby Marsh of snow, and each year in late March the first northward flights of Canada Geese and ducks land here to feed. As the ice leaves, many species of ducks move into the managed freshwater marshes. These include Black Duck, Green-winged Teal, Pintail, American Wigeon, Blue-winged Teal, and Ring-necked Duck. The managed marshes have attracted rare or uncommon ducks and marsh birds, including the Northern Shoveler, Gadwall, Redhead, and Ruddy Duck, and the Long-billed Marsh Wren, American Coot, Common Moorhen, Black Tern, Virginia Rail, Sora Rail, and Pied-billed Grebe.

Various species of hawks and owls can be observed hunting small mammals on the marshes year-round. The Marsh Hawk is common in summer, and the Rough-legged Hawk is seen in winter. Shallow lakes, such as Long Lake, support large populations of Brown Bullhead and White Perch. This food source, along with Gaspereau, support several nesting Osprey. The Snowy Owl and Snow Bunting occur commonly in winter on the dyked grasslands.

The marshes also provide good habitat for raccoon, muskrat, mink, fox, beaver, and sometimes otter. Generally, small-mammal diversity is low. The rare Arctic Shrew occurs here, far from other known records. This shrew requires marsh or wet meadow habitat and is usually very limited in range, since continuous large expanses of that habitat are rare. In summer and fall, deer frequent the marshland, but in winter they move westward to more-forested areas in the Tidnish watershed.

CULTURAL ENVIRONMENT

The name Tantramar is derived from the French word "tintamarre," meaning "racket" or "hubbub," a term the Acadians used to describe the sound of the great flocks of waterfowl that visit this area on their seasonal migrations. The "Tantramar Marsh" as it is locally known is in New Brunswick, and the collective term is the Nova Scotia–New Brunswick Border Marshes. Locally dyked lands are known as marshes, unlike in the Minas Basin area where they are called dykelands. This landscape has been extensively altered through agricultural and wildlife management.

Early settlers created farmland by cutting channels to the sea through which the sediment-rich waters of the bay flowed to deposit silts above the peat. The dyking controlled the natural siltation. The John Lusby Marsh is the only remaining salt marsh in this Unit still subject to siltation. Acadian farmers dyked and drained the marshland until 1755, and the English and New Englanders later settled the area in 1760. In the early nineteenth century, a system of tide canals and ditches transformed more marshland into fertile pastures. Where dykelands have been maintained for agricultural use, they are covered by a variety of forage, grain, and introduced plants. Many farms on the Tantramar Marshes were later abandoned, allowing the regeneration of the land. Most farms and homes in the Tantramar Marshes Theme Unit are built on dry ridges, which were once heavily forested. Lands closer to the Cumberland Basin have

**523
Tantramar
Marshes**

a deeper accumulation of marine soils and are used for lawn sod cultivation, pasture, or hayland.

The Missaguash and East Amherst freshwater marshes were developed on provincial lands by Ducks Unlimited. The Chignecto National Wildlife Area encompasses the Amherst Point Bird Sanctuary and the John Lusby Salt Marsh. The freshwater impoundments created on the marshes have encouraged a number of new waterfowl and marsh bird species to nest in Nova Scotia. Geese now feed on the dykelands, especially the Amherst sod farm, as much as or more than on the salt marshes.

Today the Tantramar Marshes continue to serve as an important transportation corridor linking Nova Scotia with New Brunswick. The nature of the marshlands and their position to magnetic north resulted in this area being chosen by CBC Radio as a site for short-wave transmission radio towers that span the marshes. This Unit is used extensively for bird-watching. Muskrat are harvested here.

● ● ● ● ● ● ● ●

Sites of Special Interest
- Amherst Point Bird Sanctuary—interpetive trail
- Chignecto National Wildlife Area: Amherst Point—the salt-marsh spit is a unique vantage point to observe the tidal bore in the Maccan/ Hebert River estuary; John Lusby Marsh (IBP Proposed Ecological Site 4)—salt marsh
- Missaguash Marsh
- East Amherst Marsh
- Eddy Marsh, LaPlanche Marsh, Maccan Marsh— areas impounded for waterfowl; Eddy Marsh is also used for the production of wild rice
- Elysian Marsh—largest dyked grassland in Nova Scotia and the least disturbed of the large dykelands

Provincial Parks and Park Reserves
Proposed Parks and Protected Areas System includes Natural Landscape 21.

Associated Offshore Sub-Unit
913b Chignecto Bay.

Associated Topics
T2.4 The Carboniferous Basin, T3.3 Glaciation, Deglaciation and Sea-level Changes, T6.1 Ocean Currents, T6.4 Estuaries, T7.1 Modifying Forces, T8.3 Freshwater Wetlands, T11.5 Freshwater Wetland Birds and Waterfowl, T11.6 Shorebirds and Other Birds of Coastal Wetlands, T11.13 Freshwater Fishes,

T11.17 Marine Invertebrates, T12.10 Plants and Resources, T12.11 Animals and Resources.

Associated Habitats
H2.4 Mud Flat, H2.5 Tidal Marsh, H4.1 Bog, H6.2 Softwood Forest (Black Spruce, Larch Association), H6.3 Mixedwood Forest (White Spruce, Fir–Maple, Birch Association).

**523
Tantramar
Marshes**

530 STONY AND WET PLAIN

District 530 is divided into two Units:
531 Sydney Coalfield
532 Chignecto Plains

GEOLOGY AND LANDSCAPE DEVELOPMENT

District 530 is underlain by thick deposits of Late Carboniferous sandstone and siltstone, which are either flat-lying or gently folded. The strata contain numerous seams of coal, which provide evidence of the environments of deposition.

During the Late Carboniferous the landscape in this area was low, with little relief. Much of the area was covered with shallow lakes, swamps, and coastal floodplains. In some places (Unit 532) rhythmic variations occurred in the overall rate of subsidence of the basin. Periodic subsidence enabled thick layers of organic material to accumulate before being engulfed with sediments. In other places (Unit 531) the layers of organic material were separated by alluvial material deposited as the rivers meandered across floodplains.

The sandstones were deposited under continental conditions on river floodplains and contain few fossils of aquatic life. Coal seams and shales, however, provide imprints of leaves and delicate parts of plants. Fossil trees are also common and can usually be seen in present-day coastal sections.

Overall, the terrain varies from flat to rolling and is evenly covered with sandy to stony glacial till. This till is thin, and bedrock is frequently exposed at the crests of minor ridges. A complex landscape of bedrock sandstone ridges and poorly drained depressions with organic deposits characterizes these nearly flat landscapes.

SCENIC QUALITY

These areas are generally flat and featureless inland, although the Chignecto Plains (Unit 532) exhibit somewhat greater relief. Scenic values are typically low to medium, but much higher values occur where there is farming settlement (e.g., along River Hebert and on Boularderie Island) and wherever bays and estuaries extend water views inland (e.g., Sydney Harbour and the coastal lagoons of Sydney South Side). Coal mining has produced distinctive landscape elements both at Joggins and on the Sydney field. Although there are now few active mines, coal and steel have created a highly urbanized landscape on the coastal stretch between Little Bras d'Or and Port Morien. The mining settlements are not pretty, but as planned company towns they exhibit strong architectural unity and an almost palpable sense of community.

531 SYDNEY COALFIELD

GEOLOGY AND LANDSCAPE DEVELOPMENT

The Sydney Coalfield lies within an area of Pictou-Morien Group sandstones and siltstones which cover an area of about 1300 km². Within 1,500–2,000 m of strata, about 1,300 m contain coal seams. The strata have been relatively undisturbed and lie in open folds that dip gently seawards at angles of 4–15°.

The area is mantled with sandy to stony till, and the coast offers the best geological exposures, although only a few layers can be seen at any one location. From Point Aconi to Port Morien, including the drowned estuary of Sydney River, exposures of sandstone with coal seams are found. One section northwest along the coast from Cranberry Point, which represents a 560-m vertical section, contains 34 coal seams, and fossil trees. A seam of coal one metre thick is exposed in the cliff at Point Aconi, and abundant plant fossils can be found in the shales on the beach. The shales are rich in leaves and other plant parts, but some beds contain only one species, for example, *Sphenophyllum* in the dark shales at Point Aconi.

The 12 productive seams in the Morien Group average 1–2 m in thickness. They are paralic in character; that is, they tend to be extensive laterally and end abruptly against rock benches rather than merge into shales. The seams also tend to divide laterally. These characteristics reflect their origins on a river floodplain.

CLIMATE

Although rainfall is highest in November and snowfall is highest in January, total precipitation is highest in December when snow and rain occur interchangeably. The annual average fog occurrence is 80 days, with four days per month from December through February, and 11 days per month from May to July. Prevailing winds in fall and winter are from the west or north, and southwest or south-southwest in spring and summer.

FRESH WATER

There are no major rivers in this Unit. Many short streams and brooks form a modified trellis drainage pattern connecting numerous small lakes and ponds. There are four complete tertiary watersheds, parts of two others, and direct shoreline drainage. Streams have pH levels between 6.4 and 7.1, while lakes tend to average between 6.0 and 6.6. Ponds around Point Aconi are soft with shallow anaerobic bottoms. Extensive peat bogs are found in the depressions. Aquifers are confined by the low permeability of the overlying hills.

SOILS

The topography in this Unit is fairly level. On the gently undulating areas away from the coast, well-drained Shulie soils have developed on stony, sandy loam tills. Towards the coast where the terrain is flatter, imperfectly drained Springhill and poorly drained Economy soils have developed from the same material.

Over much of the area the bedrock closely approaches the surface and can be readily observed as slabby sandstone outcrops along roadcuts and shorelines. Around Boularderie Island, imperfectly drained Diligence silt clay loams occur, with small areas of well-drained Falmouth soils formed over gypsum (see Unit 511), and some Hebert soils formed on outwash sands and gravels.

PLANTS

This Unit has a somewhat milder climate than much of the Carboniferous Lowlands, although cold strong winds from the northeast retard springtime warming. A second major factor has been the high degree of disturbance. The Unit lies within Loucks' Sugar Maple–Hemlock, Pine Zone, but repeated disturbance has resulted in a forest dominated by conifers—White Spruce, Black Spruce, Balsam Fir, and Larch. Shade-intolerant species occur on ridges in the coniferous forests, while the maple, aspen, and birch fire association is found on extensive burnt areas.

There are a few salt marsh areas with Eelgrass beds in Lingan Basin, Glace Bay, and Port Morien. Scouring by sea ice in winter limits the growth of marine algae.

531
Sydney
Coalfield

ANIMALS

A large proportion of this Unit is taken up by urban land uses and mammals include those typically found in proximity to developed areas such as deer, coyote, Red Squirrel, Snowshoe Hare, and Red-backed Vole. Elsewhere, mostly scrub or early successional forest habitats are provided. Some Bald Eagle nesting habitat occurs. A significant faunal component exists along the coast, which includes vertical cliffs that provide seabird nesting sites, and sheltered bays cut off from the open sea by barrier beaches. There are few islands, but two of them, Ciboux and Hertford (Bird Islands), are nationally important nesting areas for Razorbill, Atlantic Puffin, Leach's Storm-petrel, and Black-legged Kittiwakes. Big Glace Bay Lake and Morien Bay provide stopover areas for modest numbers of migratory waterfowl but are of particular interest because a wide variety of species are included. The Piping Plover nests at the Glace Bay Sanctuary. Cormorant breeding colonies occur along the coast.

CULTURAL ENVIRONMENT

This Unit has been extensively clearcut for forestry and for transmission-line development. Spruce Budworm infestations have been notable.

Sydney boomed at the turn of the century with the building of the Dominion Steel and Coal Company steel plant at Whitney Pier. Coal was also excavated privately, and in a few areas around Glace Bay the land is unstable due to underground mine tunnels which have caused houses to shift and heave. Sydney Steel and Coal Company (Sysco) is primarily responsible for the creation of the Sydney Tar Ponds, the largest chemical waste site in the country. In 1986, a 10-year Tar Sands Clean Up program was launched—the largest toxic excavation project ever undertaken in Canada. At present, mines extend 8 km from shore under the Cabot Strait, and within the present 10-km economically mineable limit there are 1,000 million tonnes of recoverable coal.

At Coxheath near Sydney, copper occurrences were reported in 1825, with mining production taking place intermittently until 1896. Numerous sand and gravel deposits are commercially exploited in this area. Coal-generated steam turbine power plants at Glace Bay, Lingan, and Point Aconi supply electrical power to the province. Small-scale farming has taken place along the Mira River, and stretches along the river are now cottage country. Outdoor recreational attractions in this area include the Bird Islands,

famous for their breeding colonies of Razorbill, Atlantic Puffin, and other seabirds.

• • • • • • • •

Sites of Special Interest
- Coastline northeast of Cranberry Head—34 coal seams and fossil trees
- New Waterford to Morien Bay—Coastal exposure of the Upper Carboniferous sediments of the Cape Breton coalfield, with plant and animal fossils, including species found nowhere else in North America
- Point Aconi—coastal exposure of Upper Carboniferous sediments with upright tree fossils; plant imprints and fossils in the shales along the beach
- Bird Islands (IBP Proposed Ecological Site 24)— bird nesting site, with rare arctic-alpine plants, one island owned by the Nova Scotia Bird Society, the other by the Department of Natural Resources
- Big Glace Bay Lake Migratory Bird Sanctuary
- Miner's Museum, Glace Bay—outlines aspects of the area's mining history and portrays the life of miners who work the Sydney coalfields in tunnels that stretch miles under the ocean floor

Provincial Parks and Park Reserves
- Groves Point
- Big Bras d'Or
- Dalem Lake
- Dominion Beach
- Lingan

Proposed Parks and Protected Areas System includes Natural Landscape 56.

Scenic Viewpoints
- Dominion cemetery—view over Indian Bay to Lingan power station
- New Waterford, eastern edge—operating coal mine (Lingan) and Lingan power station
- Point Aconi (north end of Highway 162)— operating Prince coal mine and power station

Associated Offshore Unit
915 Sydney Bight.

Associated Topics
T2.4 The Carboniferous Basin, T4.2 Post-glacial Colonization by Plants, T6.2 Oceanic Environments, T7.3 Coastal Landforms, T8.3 Freshwater Wetlands, T9.3

Biological Environment, T10.1 Vegetation Change, T11.6 Shorebirds and Other Birds of Coastal Wetlands, T11.7 Seabirds and Birds of Marine Habitats, T12.3 Geology and Resources, T12.12 Recreational Resources.

Associated Habitats
H5.3 Cliff and Bank, H4.1 Bog, H6.1 Hardwood Forest (Maple, Oak, Birch Association), H6.3 Mixedwood Forest (White Spruce, Fir–Maple, Birch Association).

**531
Sydney
Coalfield**

532 CHIGNECTO PLAINS

GEOLOGY AND LANDSCAPE DEVELOPMENT

The geology varies in this Unit. The northern part is more like Unit 581. However, most of the area is underlain by Cumberland Group strata made up of grey sandstones, siltstones, and shales. In places the sandstone is coarse; in others it is fine-grained and has been used for millstones and building stone. The strata have been thrown into open folds, which become tighter close to the Cobequids (Unit 581). Some of the anticlines in the east of Unit 532 have been eroded, exposing the underlying Early Carboniferous or Mississippian Windsor Group deposits. In these places the folding is accentuated by the movement of salt, which has risen through the strata to form domes.

Glacial deposits mask most of the Chignecto Plains, and the strata can best be seen along the shore of Chignecto Bay. The most important section lies in the 15 km between Minudie and Shulie, where a vertical section of 4,444 m of Cumberland Group strata is exposed. These strata form part of a shallow basin that extends from Minudie to the Cobequids (Unit 311). Towards Shulie the younger strata begin to slope upwards towards the base of the Cobequids.

From the Joggins area to Maccan and Springhill, the luxuriant growth of *Lepidodendron*, *Sigillaria*, *Calamites*, *Chordaites*, tree ferns, and seed ferns resulted in the formation of many coal seams. Up to 70 seams have been found in this basin, with the thickest ones near Joggins (from Joggins to Ragged Reef). The main seam at Joggins is 1.25 m thick.

The seams can be traced inland for 30 km but gradually coalesce towards Springhill. Four outcrop at River Hebert, two each at Maccan and Chignecto. At Springhill the section of coal-bearing strata is 800 m thick and contains 31 coal seams.

The coal seams in the Cumberland Basin formed in an unstable environment characterized by subsidence, plant growth, inundation, and burial by mud and sand, more growth, and so on in a cyclic pattern. The coal seams tend to grade into shaly coal and coaly shale, vertically and laterally. They are structurally weak and dangerous to work at depth.

At a well-known locality near Joggins is a classic coastal section of Late Carboniferous strata. Between Coal Mine Point and Lower Cove, fossilized tree stumps of *Lepidodendron* and *Sigillaria* can be seen in their original growth positions. Siltstones rich in plant debris occur, as well as limestones containing the shells of freshwater and brackish water pelecypods and ostracods. Amphibian and reptile bones and the tracks of giant arthropods have also been found. Sedimentary structures in the strata include ripple marks, wave ripples, current bedding, mud cracks, rain prints, and channel deposits.

Outcrops of sandstone bedrock create a bedrock-dominated landscape west of River Hebert. To the east of the river, extensive sandy tills mask the bedrock, particularly in the Chignecto Game Sanctuary and in the Sand River area, creating a distinct landscape.

FRESHWATER ENVIRONMENTS AND COASTAL WETLANDS

The watershed predominantly consists of numerous second- and first-order rivers and streams, flowing in a modified trellis pattern. The Unit is dissected by a secondary watershed boundary. To the south, the Shulie River and East Apple River fall within separate tertiary watersheds. River Hebert and its tributaries dominate the landscape to the north. Numerous short streams have direct shoreline drainage. There are extensive bog systems, and numerous tidal marshes occur along the coast.

SOILS

Grey and brown sandstones and reddish brown conglomerates have provided the parent materials for the dominant soils of this Unit. Shulie, imperfectly drained Springhill, and poorly drained Economy soils have developed from sandstones. For the most part they are relatively shallow, stony loams. West of the River Hebert are large areas of very shallow soils. The haphazard interference of bedrock with soil drainage creates an intricate pattern of imperfectly and poorly drained depressions.

PLANTS

This Unit falls within the Maritime Lowlands Ecoregion of Loucks' Red Spruce, Hemlock, Pine Zone and has been heavily disturbed by repeated cutting and burning and by scattered agricultural settlements. Sandy areas have a coniferous forest dominated by Jack Pine, Red Spruce, and Black Spruce. Scattered pure stands of Yellow Birch occur on side slopes and ridges near Chignecto Bay. Jack Pine, aspen, spruces, and Grey Birch are abundant after fire. Heathland has formed on some of the old burns, while others are reverting to Red Spruce, Black Spruce, and Balsam Fir. A marked band of coastal forest a few kilometres wide borders the Bay of Fundy. The so-called Chignecto Barrens are now regenerating in Red Spruce and Black Spruce; some have been planted with Red Pine. Well-drained hills are covered with mixed deciduous forest and some shade-tolerant hardwoods. Some cedar is found in this Unit and the adjacent areas. Other areas in Nova Scotia with native cedar include the southern part of Digby County.

In 1912, C.D. Howe made the following observations on soil-forest relationships in this fire-devastated area: "The sandy plain is covered with small sandy knolls from one to two feet above the little depressions which are from a yard to five yards in diameter. The bedrock is a hard, fine-grained sandstone which, in general, is apparently not more than two feet below the surface. The vegetation is composed of wire birch and scattering jack pine, which escaped the fire, with an undergrowth of blueberry, sheep laurel and hair cap moss. The damp pockets contain purple laurel (rhodora), Labrador tea and sometimes spruce seedlings. Jack pine seedlings are frequent on the knolls."

ANIMALS

This Unit is mostly a mix of forest habitats, with few agricultural areas. Cliffs and intertidal sands and muds occur along the coast.

Moose have responded to the regenerating forest following Spruce Budworm infestation by developing one of the more vigorous populations in mainland Nova Scotia. Deer do not winter along Chignecto Bay, which is exposed to westerly winds. In hard winters, deer are absent from the Chignecto Game Sanctuary, preferring to migrate south.

There are few lakes or wetlands, and beaver and otter densities are low. Bobcat, coyotes, and Red Fox are common. Raccoons are found near the scattered agricultural settlements. Black Bear occur in moderate numbers. American Shad, Gaspereau, Sea Lamprey, and Atlantic Salmon enter River Hebert to spawn in fresh water. Gaspereau are known to travel as far as Welton Lake, where they spawn along the lake shore. Salmon also enter Apple River. The edges of River Hebert, Shulie River, Kelly River, and Atkinson Brook provide interesting habitat for a variety of wildlife.

Mud flats towards Minudie are important feeding areas for shorebirds that roost on the New Brunswick shore at high tide. Smaller numbers roost at Mill Creek and at West Apple River during high tides. Approximately 100 Black Ducks winter at Apple River estuary.

The Northern Ringneck Snake has been seen at Chignecto Game Sanctuary.

CULTURAL ENVIRONMENT

The first record of mining in the Cumberland Basin dates to the early eighteenth century, when the "old French Workings" were mined at Joggins. Acadians had once extracted coal from the cliffs here. The Joggins mine was completely closed in the 1960s, and the River Hebert coal mine closed in 1980. A coal-fired steam turbine plant was operated at Maccan. Good harbours are not found on the shores of the Cumberland Basin, so fishing activity is limited. In the 1970s, when the harnessing of the Fundy tides was under serious consideration, the Cumberland Basin was designated as a candidate site for a tidal power generating station. The forest cover in this Unit is variable as a result of past disturbances. Pines may average higher than in other areas, but the Red Pines planted on the sandy areas (after major fires early in the twentieth century) are more prominent than naturally regenerated stands. Forests facing Chignecto Bay were severely affected by Spruce Budworm in the late 1970s and 1980s. The extensive forest harvest areas where infected forest stands were salvaged provide good moose habitat.

• • • • • • • •

Sites of Special Interest
- Joggins (Coal Mine Point to Lower Cove)— coastal exposure of Upper Carboniferous (Pennsylvanian) sediments and coal seams of the Cumberland Basin coalfield; these cliffs are famous for their fossils, which include trees, reptiles, and amphibians; features include sedimentary structure, a classic Late Carboniferous section, coal seams outcropping along the shoreline of Chignecto Bay, and two district tills, different in colour, containing boulders of granite and limestone; this is a protected site, under consideration as a world heritage site because of its scientific interest
- Chignecto Game Sanctuary

**532
Chignecto
Plains**

- Shulie River (IBP Proposed Ecological Site 2)—Red Spruce stand
- Chignecto River (IBP Proposed Ecological Site 3)—pure stand of Red Pine
- Parrsboro Geology Museum

Provincial Parks and Park Reserves
Proposed Parks and Protected Areas System includes Natural Landscape 19.

Scenic Viewpoints
- River Hebert, both sides—dyked farmland

Associated Offshore Units
912 Outer Fundy, 913b Chignecto Bay.

Associated Topics
T2.4 The Carboniferous Basin, T3.4 Terrestrial Glacial Deposits and Landscape Features, T7.3 Coastal Landforms, T8.1 Freshwater Hydrology, T10.2 Succesional Trends in Vegetation, T10.6 Trees, T12.3 Geology and Resources.

Associated Habitats
H2.4 Mud Flat, H4.1 Bog, H5.1 Barren, H5.3 Cliff and Bank, H6.1 Hardwood Forest (Sugar Maple, Yellow Birch, Beech Association), H6.2 Softwood Forest (Pine Association; Spruce, Fir Association).

**532
Chignecto
Plains**

540 CLAY PLAIN

District 540 is divided into two sub-Districts:
   (a)   Cogmagun River
   (b)   Stewiacke Barrens

GEOLOGY AND LANDSCAPE DEVELOPMENT

In the two sub-Units within the Clay Plain (District 540) are found Middle to Late Carboniferous deposits of Canso and Pictou strata (see Figure 11). These strata are predominantly fine red or grey-brown sandstones and siltstones, known as the Scotch Village Formation, which lie horizontally on top of the Windsor deposits.

FRESH WATER

Cogmagun River (sub-District 540a)
This area contains the headwaters of the Tomcod, Walton, and Cogmagun rivers. It falls within three tertiary drainage areas, including a portion of the Kennetcook River watershed, and drains into the Minas Basin. The several extensive wetland systems include Collins Bog and McDonald Bog, both of which are larger than 400 hectares.

Stewiacke Barrens (sub-District 540b)
This landscape is within the Shubenacadie River watershed and contains numerous tributaries that feed into the Stewiacke and Shubenacadie systems.

SOILS

The soils in this Unit are mainly of the Kingsville series—poorly drained clay loams, usually strongly mottled, that have formed from till deposits derived from grey sand and siltstones. Large areas of peat have developed in level and depressed areas.

PLANTS

This clay till plain with scattered mounds supports mostly Black Spruce, with some Red Oak and Balsam Fir. On the better-drained gravelly ridges, Red Pine (on burnt sites) and the shade-intolerant Red Maple and White Birch occur.

SCENIC QUALITY

These featureless plains have some of the lowest scenic ratings in the province. With little relief, few lakes, and no human settlement, the only variation is provided by bogs and extensive cutover areas (in District 540a). There is little public access to these areas; the only paved road is south of Middle Stewiacke (District 540b).

CULTURAL ENVIRONMENT

These sub-Districts have a history of forestry. At present, recreational use of the land includes an airfield that was a Commonwealth training field during the Second World War. Peat harvesting potential exists on the Clay Plain.

• • • • • • • •

Sites of Special Interest
• Scotch Village Barrens—extensive peat deposits

Provincial Parks and Park Reserves
Proposed Parks and Protected Areas System includes Natural Landscapes 27a and 27b.

Associated Topics
T2.4 The Carboniferous Basin, T8.1 Freshwater Hydrology, T12.10 Plants and Resources.

Associated Habitats
H4.1 Bog, H3.1 Freshwater Open-Water Lotic, H3.3 Freshwater Bottom Lotic, H5.1 Barren, H6.2 Softwood Forest (Pine Association; Spruce, Larch Association).

**540
Clay Plain**

550 COASTAL FRINGE

District 550 is divided into two Units, primarily on the basis of oceanographic and climatic conditions:

551 Inverness Coastal Plain
552 Victoria Coastal Plain

GEOLOGY AND LANDSCAPE DEVELOPMENT

Around the shoreline of the northern Cape Breton peninsula is a narrow fringe of Carboniferous strata. This forms a usually flat area at the base of the steep, dissected shoulder of coarse Horton deposits and volcanics which flank the highlands massif.

The widest parts of this band of lowland are found between Margaree Harbour and Chéticamp, and in the Aspy Valley. Around St. Anns Bay to Cape Smokey the band is very narrow, with only vestiges of the original deposits. Many of the strata are Windsor Group deposits that are being eroded very rapidly. Where gypsum underlies the surface, karst topography has formed.

On the west side of the peninsula from Margaree Harbour to Chéticamp, the Windsor deposits are overlain by a narrow strip of younger rocks: Riversdale strata (including some coal seams) and, further north near Chéticamp, red Canso strata. All around the coastline, a pre-Wisconsin wave-cut notch can be seen overlain by loose glacial material. Glacial sands and gravels washed down from the highlands are common throughout the District.

SCENIC QUALITY

Lying between mountains and ocean, these narrow lowlands display scenery that ranges from pleasant to spectacular. Where the mountain plateau is set further inland or rises less abruptly (as at Inverness, Belle Côte, and Cape Egmont), the dramatic effect is somewhat reduced. However, the settled Acadian farmlands between Belle Côte and Chéticamp have much interest and allow unrestricted vistas. Particularly noteworthy are the long-lot field patterns. Vestiges of farming settlement remain in the Aspy Valley, where the embracing effect of surrounding mountains provides a sense of shelter and seclusion.

550
Coastal
Fringe

551 INVERNESS COASTAL PLAIN

The Inverness Coastal Plain is divided geographically into two sub-Units:
(a) Inverness/St. Rose Coalfield
(b) Chéticamp Coast

GEOLOGY AND LANDSCAPE DEVELOPMENT

Inverness/St. Rose Coalfield (sub-Unit 551a)
From Inverness northwards towards Margaree Harbour lies a hilly, faulted, and narrow belt of Late Carboniferous strata. They form two small basins, one centred at Inverness and the other at Chimney Corner. At Inverness they are in Pictou strata and at Chimney Corner in Riversdale strata. Both basins contain coal seams which dip steeply under the Northumberland Strait.

Chéticamp Coast (sub-Unit 551b)
Beyond Margaree Harbour, a thin strip of Windsor strata, overlain by red Canso Group sandstones and siltstones and greyish Riversdale sandstones, form a narrow coastal plain (see Figure 21). The Windsor strata form a valley at the base of the highland slope and, where gypsum is present, karst topography occurs. Crystalline gypsum (selenite) is common.

Chéticamp Island is composed of red Riversdale sandstones and is undergoing rapid erosion. At present it is connected to the mainland by a long sand and gravel bar. Just to the north, coastal erosion has reduced a deposit of red Carboniferous sandstone to stacks which lie at the mouth of Trout Brook. The sandstone generally forms low cliffs along the shore.

North of Chéticamp Village is a terrace of glacial outwash material. A bar has formed across the mouth of the Chéticamp River, and an esker projects out to the bar, dividing the lagoon into two.

FRESH WATER

The short, straight streams in this Unit drain directly into the Northumberland Strait. In sub-Unit 551a, streams flow from ravines and also from Lake Ainslie (Unit 584). The mouth of the Margaree occurs in sub-Unit 551b, and several small tidal marshes occur near Chéticamp. Freshwater systems are productive and generally alkaline. Conductivity in Grand Lac has been recorded at 200 micromhos/cm. Sinkholes and small solution lakes associated with karst topography are common.

SOILS

The soils in this Unit form a complex mix, ranging from sands to clay loams. The dominant soil is Shulie, which has developed from glacial tills derived from coarse grey and brown sandstones of the Riversdale group. They range from stony loam to stony, sandy loam in texture.

Inverness/St. Rose Coalfield (sub-Unit 551a)
The outlet of Lake Ainslie is marked by a large sand plug, with outwash sands and gravels, on which well-drained Canning loamy sands have developed. These soils are on level to rolling terrain and tend to be droughty. Elsewhere, imperfectly drained Queens and poorly drained Kingsville clay loams have developed. Well-drained Shulie soils occur on higher ground north of Broad Cove.

Chéticamp Coast (sub-Unit 551b)
Small areas of sandy Canning soils occur around Margaree Harbour. Further north along the coast, Queens, Kingsville, and Shulie soils occur with some well-drained Pugwash sandy loam and its poorly drained associate Masstown. Digby soils (excessively drained sandy loams) have developed on beach deposits. Near Chéticamp, Hebert soils are found on outwash sands and gravels. Chéticamp Island is a mix of Shulie, Debert, Masstown, and Kingsville soils.

PLANTS

The vegetation in this Unit is heavily influenced by the prevailing westerly winds off the Gulf of St. Lawrence. White Spruce is the most common species, but shade-tolerant hardwoods are found on the better-drained and more sheltered sites. Black Spruce and larch grow in wet depressional areas. Elsewhere, a mixed forest of spruce, fir, and pine with maple and birch is common. Marsh Marigold is scattered along the low lands in wet places.

**551
Inverness
Coastal Plain**

ANIMALS

Margaree Island provides some breeding habitat for seabirds, including a moderate population of Black Guillemot.

CULTURAL ENVIRONMENT

Coal has been mined at Inverness and Chimney Corner in sub-Unit 551a, but the seams dip steeply out under the Northumberland Strait and much of the coal is inaccessible. Near Chéticamp, where the plain broadens (sub-Unit 551b), extensive gypsum deposits have been mined down to the underlying rock.

Acadians settled the Chéticamp area after the deportation, turning to fishing as well as subsistence farming for a living. Protected from Atlantic fogs by the Cape Breton highlands, the fishing stations along the gulf shore of Cape Breton, particularly Chéticamp, were the best places for drying fish. In the eighteenth and nineteenth centuries, Chéticamp fishermen traded dried cod to the Channel Islands (United Kingdom) merchants who controlled the Cape Breton fishing industry and exported dried cod to world markets. Today the lobster and crab fisheries are particularly important in Chéticamp.

In the nineteenth century, Scots settled the Inverness area (sub-Unit 551a), and fishing, farming, and forestry have provided a means of livelihood from the land. Coal continues to be mined at St. Rose, Inverness County. The beaches and scenic coastal views of the Inverness Coastal Plain attract tourism and recreational activities such as whale-watching excursions out of Chéticamp.

• • • • • • • •

Sites of Special Interest
• Petit Étang (IBP Proposed Ecological Site 16)—eutrophic marsh with uncommon plants such as Canada Anemone and Shrubby Cinquefoil
• Chimney Corner, Chéticamp, Cape North, and St. Anns Bay—a pre-glacial wave-cut notch in the side of the cliffs
• Chéticamp—selenite in an old gypsum quarry; karst topography
• Chimney Corner and Inverness—thin coal seams in the sandstone and siltstone along the shore
• Trout Brook (north of Chéticamp)—stacks of red sandstone
• Inverness Miners' Museum—coal mining history
• Chéticamp—exhibition centre for the Cape Breton Highlands National Park

Provincial Parks and Park Reserves
• Broad Cove Marsh
• Friars Head
• St. Joseph du Moine

Proposed Parks and Protected Areas System includes Natural Landscape 61.

Scenic Viewpoints
• Sub-Unit 551b: Margaree Harbour (estuary of Margaree River); north of Chéticamp on the Cabot Trail (view of Jerome Mountain to the north)

Associated Offshore Unit
914 Northumberland Strait.

Associated Topics
T2.4 The Carboniferous Basin, T3.3 Glaciation, Deglaciation and Sea-level Changes, T3.4 Terrestrial Glacial Deposits and Landscape Features, T6.1 Ocean Currents, T7.3 Coastal Landforms, T11.7 Seabirds and Birds of Marine Habitats, T12.3 Geology and Resources, T12.11 Animals and Resources.

Associated Habitats
H6.3 Mixedwood Forest (White Spruce, Fir–Maple, Birch Association).

552 VICTORIA COASTAL PLAIN

The Victoria Coastal Plain Unit is divided into three sub–Units:

(a) Aspy River
(b) Ingonish River
(c) St. Anns Bay

GEOLOGY AND LANDSCAPE DEVELOPMENT

Aspy River (sub-Unit 552a)

The Aspy Valley lies south of the escarpment of the Aspy Fault. From the bars across the harbour south to Sunrise, the valley is underlain by Windsor strata which form a broad level lowland (see Figure 5). Where gypsum underlies the surface, karst topography with sinkholes has formed. South of Sunrise, the Aspy Valley contains Horton strata which form hills below the escarpment.

Ingonish River (sub-Unit 552b)

At Ingonish, Windsor strata lie directly on top of basement rocks with no Horton strata present. They form a narrow lowland on the north side of Ingonish Bay.

St. Anns Bay (sub-Unit 552c)

The coastal margin from Cape Smokey to Indian Brook consists of a narrow band of Windsor and related strata. On the west side of St. Anns Bay are resistant Horton strata. At the southern end of St. Anns Harbour, a strip of Windsor strata lies between the plateau to the west and the parallel upland block to the east known as Kellys Mountain.

The extent of coastal erosion is indicated by the location of the Carboniferous deposits, which once covered a much wider area on the coastline.

FRESHWATER AND COASTAL AQUATIC ENVIRONMENTS

Aspy River (sub-Unit 552a)

The North, Middle, and South Aspy rivers flow parallel to each other, draining into Aspy Bay. A tertiary watershed boundary separates the North Aspy channel from the other two. Tidal marshes and barachois ponds occur in the backwaters.

Ingonish Beach (sub-Unit 552b) and St. Anns Bay (sub-Unit 552c)

Numerous parallel tertiary watersheds drain first-order streams from river valleys in District 220 into North and South Bay Ingonish in sub-Unit 552b, and into St. Anns Bay in sub-Unit 552c. There are large tidal marshes at the back of Ingonish Harbour in Unit 552, and scattered barachois ponds in sub-Unit 552c. Freshwater Lake, located behind a barrier in sub-Unit 552b, has a neutral pH.

SOILS

This Unit is notable for its outwash deposits, on which gravelly sandy loams of the Hebert series have developed. On upland slopes, the soils are derived principally from granite and are mapped as well-drained Gibraltar and imperfectly drained Bayswater sandy loams. Along St. Anns Bay, Thom soils are also found on the slopes. The Aspy River has cut terraces in alluvial deposits. These successive terraces present an ideal opportunity for measuring the time and intensity of soil development processes.

PLANTS

On the floodplains, willow, aspen, Sugar Maple, and Yellow Birch are found. On better-drained gravels, White Birch and beech occur. On granitic slopes, White Spruce is common, with scattered Yellow Birch and Sugar Maple. Along the coast, winter ice scour restricts marine algae.

ANIMALS

Scattered eagle-breeding habitat occurs in this Unit. A moderate-sized heron colony exists in Aspy Bay, which is also visited by a wide variety of waterfowl from spring through fall, though not in large numbers. Barachois ponds occur behind barrier beaches and support a diverse aquatic fauna.

552
Victoria
Coastal Plain

CULTURAL ENVIRONMENT

The fisheries (lobster, mackerel, and others) have been the economic focus of communities in much of this area, along with some subsistence farming. Gypsum was once mined at Dingwall in sub-Unit 552a. Harnessing water power from the Cape Breton highlands, the Wreck Cove hydro station supplies electricity to the province. A wind-turbine electric plant also operates at Wreck Cove. The scenery of the Cabot Trail and the hiking trails of the Cape Breton Highlands National Park attract tourism and encourage the use of this land for recreation.

• • • • • • • •

**552
Victoria
Coastal Plain**

Sites of Special Interest
• Dingwall—gypsum and karst topography

Provincial Parks and Park Reserves
• Cabots Lánding
• Ingonish
• Birch Plain
• Breton Cove
• Plaster

Proposed Parks and Protected Areas System includes Natural Landscapes 73 and 76.

Scenic Viewpoints
• Sub-Unit 522a: White Point Road (south side of Aspy Bay)
• Sub-Unit 522b: Ingonish Bay (views from Keltic Lodge golf course)

Associated Offshore Unit
915 Sydney Bight.

Associated Topics
T2.4 The Carboniferous Basin, T3.4 Terrestrial Glacial Deposits and Landscape Features, T6.2 Oceanic Environments, T6.3 Coastal Aquatic Environments, T7.1 Modifying Forces, T7.3 Coastal Landforms, T10.9 Algae, T11.4 Birds of Prey, T12.8 Fresh Water and Resources, T12.11 Animals and Resources, T12.12 Recreational Resources.

Associated Habitats
H2.1 Rocky Shore, H2.2 Boulder/Cobble Shore, H5.3 Cliff and Bank, H6.1 Hardwood Forest (Sugar Maple, Elm Association).

560 SUBMERGED LOWLAND

GEOLOGY AND LANDSCAPE DEVELOPMENT

The Submerged (Bras d'Or) Lowland forms a fringe around the upland areas of central and eastern Cape Breton (see Figures 8 and 19). The lowlands are underlain by Windsor Group strata containing siltstone, shale, reddish sandstone, limestone, gypsum, anhydrite, and salt. These strata once ranged in thickness from 650–1,200 m. They were often laid down in cyclical deposition patterns under a variety of conditions: in shallow offshore environments, in restricted basins where there was greater evaporation, and in open basins. The depositional basins lay around and between the upland blocks of the Creignish Hills, North Mountain, Sporting Mountain, East Bay Hills, and Boisdale Hills (see Figure 29).

During the Tertiary period a dramatic drop in sea level, probably caused by crustal uplift after the formation of the Cretaceous planation surface, allowed deep erosion to take place. At that time, major features such as the Gulf of St. Lawrence were carved out, and in central Cape Breton the lowlands were eroded to well below present sea level. When the land subsided, the sea was able to enter through two channels, the Great Bras d'Or and Lennox Passage, forming a deep lake 180 m deep in a few places, with access to the sea. Now the Windsor strata form an eroding broken fringe at sea level around the base of the uplands. The landscape consists of steep slopes with some cliffs, dropping to a coastal plain where there are white gypsum deposits and red sedimentary strata. The uplands, lowlands, and channels are oriented in a northeast-southwest direction in accordance with the structural trend in Cape Breton.

FRESH WATER

Most of the streams in this District are short, fast-flowing first- or second-order streams that drain directly into the Bras d'Or Lake down steep banks. The exception occurs in the area around Denys Basin and St. Patricks Channel, where larger systems include the River Denys and River Inhabitants. Tributaries feed into these systems from the Creignish Hills (sub-Unit 313a) to the northwest. The River Denys is also fed by streams flowing from North Mountain to the south in sub-Unit 313b.

The water at the head of St. Patricks Channel is stratified as a result of the restriction of tidal influences at Little Narrows. This creates an interesting marine benthic and freshwater pelagic community.

The largest wetland complex, Big Marsh, a productive wildlife habitat, is associated with the River Denys and contains elements of shallow freshwater marsh, shrub swamp, and grassy meadow.

SOILS

Shales and mudstones have produced most of the soils in this area. Gypsum occurrences are very frequent and produce improved drainage in soils immediately above them. Well-drained Falmouth, imperfectly drained Queens, and poorly drained Kingsville soils predominate. These are loams and clay loams derived from clay loam tills. Areas of coarser-textured Thom and Westbrook soils also occur. Millar soils have developed on outwash deposits. Although these are coarse-textured sandy loams, they are poorly drained because of the depressional topography.

PLANTS

This Unit is part of Loucks' Sugar Maple–Hemlock, Pine Zone, but the heavy soils and repeated disturbances have resulted in a largely coniferous forest, with White Spruce, Balsam Fir, and scattered Eastern Hemlock. Shade-tolerant deciduous trees are found on some of the better-drained slopes. Red Maple and White Birch occur in mixed stands. Oldfields and former pasture have regenerated in pure stands of White Spruce, or in spruce and fir. Black Spruce and larch grow in the wetter areas. The salt marsh vegetation is influenced by fresh water and includes Sweet Grass.

ANIMALS

The Submerged Lowland District includes a mix of flat or rolling softwood or mixed forest habitats, oldfields, open brackish water, sheltered marshy inlets, and exposed rocky shoreline. The Bras d'Or Lake supports a distinct warm-water marine community that is impoverished compared with other estuaries or coastal waters in Nova Scotia. Polychaete and bivalve communities are found in the mud and gravel bottom. The Unit provides very important Bald Eagle nesting habitat, particularly in the vicinity of Boom Island. Great Blue Heron and Double-crested Cormorant colonies are also present. River Denys and the upper Denys Basin are important areas for waterfowl production and act as a staging area for migrating Teal, Black Duck, and Ring-necked Duck; this is also known as a wintering area for Bald Eagles. The estuaries and streams provide good muskrat and mink habitat. Snowshoe Hare and bobcat also use habitats in this Unit.

SCENIC QUALITY

Fine scenery is found along all shores of the Bras d'Or Lake and its associated channels. Where the lowland is squeezed between lake and mountains (e.g., Whycocomagh, north side of West Bay, and south side of East Bay), very high scenic ratings are attained. This District's scenic resources, however, lie mostly offshore and are only fully available to those with boat access to the lake. The inland area between North Mountain and the Creignish Hills is less attractive than the lakeshore, though scattered farms add interest.

CULTURAL ENVIRONMENT

The shores of Bras d'Or Lake have long been an important area for the Mi'kmaq, and today several Mi'kmaq reserves are located around the lake, including Eskasoni, the largest in the province. Since the 1970s, various aquaculture operations for oysters, trout, and salmon have been started in Bras d'Or waters with varying degrees of success. People of Scottish descent settled the fertile tracts of land around Bras d'Or Lake in the first quarter of the nineteenth century, clearing large tracts of forests for farming and often selling timber for export or shipbuilding. Many of these farms have since been abandoned and regenerated into forests. Since Bras d'Or Lake is accessible from the sea, the import-export trade thrived here in the nineteenth century. Visual clues to this former activity are the many remnants of wharves around the lake. Baddeck alone had three major wharves and numerous cargo sheds, principally shipping produce from surrounding farms to the Newfoundland market. Nineteenth-century records indicate that fishing activity took place here, with catches of cod, herring, and mackerel. Significant mineral deposits exist in this area, with gypsum mining at River Denys and Little Narrows, and lime-stone quarried at Irish Cove. Boating and sailing have become popular activities on the Bras d'Or Lake.

• • • • • • • •

Sites of Special Interest
• Spectacle Island Game Sanctuary—nesting cormorants
• Alexander Graham Bell Museum—aspects of the area's history, focusing on the inventions of Bell at his summer home in Baddeck
• Island Point—spectacular example of karst topography

Provincial Parks and Park Reserves
• Big Harbour Beach
• Ross Ferry
• Baddeck Inlet
• Battery
• Orangedale
• Hay Cove
• Irish Cove
• Castle Bay
• Blacketts Lake
• Dundee

Scenic Viewpoints
• Whycocomagh Bay
• Baddeck
• Marble Mountain
• Irish Cove

Associated Offshore Unit
916 Bras d'Or Lake.

Associated Topics
T2.4 The Carboniferous Basin, T3.1 Development of the Ancient Landscape, T6.1 Ocean Currents, T6.4 Estuaries, T8.1 Freshwater Hydrology, T11.4 Birds of Prey, T11.8 Land Mammals, T11.17 Marine Invertebrates, T12.2 Cultural Landscapes, T12.3 Geology and Resources, T12.11 Animals and Resources.

Associated Habitats
H1.1 Offshore Open Water, H1.2 Offshore Benthic, H2.1 Rocky Shore, H2.5 Tidal Marsh, H3.1 Freshwater Open-Water Lotic, H3.3 Freshwater Bottom Lotic, H5.2 Oldfield, H6.2 Softwood Forest (Spruce, Fir Association; White Spruce Association).

570 ROLLING UPLAND

District 570 is divided geologically and topo-graphically into two Units:

571 Mulgrave Plateau
572 St. Marys Fault Block

GEOLOGY AND LANDSCAPE DEVELOPMENT

From the Strait of Canso across the southern side of the Pictou-Antigonish Highlands to the southern border of the Cobequid Hills, Devonian and Carboniferous strata form a rather featureless central axis to Nova Scotia. South and west of the Salmon River in Guysborough County, the boundaries of this block are the major faults that cross the province from east to west. To the north is the Chedabucto Fault, which extends from Cooks Cove across southern Pictou County, merging with the Cobequid Fault along the southern border of the Cobequid Hills. To the south, the St. Marys Fault extends from eastern Guysborough County across to the Stewiacke Valley. The southern district boundary continues along the Cobequids as the Portapique Fault. The area from Salmon River northward to the Strait of Canso is the extension of this band of rocks on the northern side of the escarpment of the Chedabucto Fault.

SCENIC QUALITY

This District is generally of medium scenic quality, being undistinguished in terms of relief, lacking extensive agricultural settlement, and with few lakes (except for the area east of Highway 7, and the lakes inland from the Strait of Canso). There is stronger relief along the Canso Strait shoreline, Milford Haven–Roman Valley, portions of the Chedabucto and St. Marys faults, and in the upper Stewiacke valley. Settlement tends to occur along these same relief lines, which further increases their attractiveness. Milford Haven and the Canso Strait shore are particularly scenic.

• • • • • • • •

Associated Topics
T2.1 Introduction to the Geological History of Nova Scotia.

570
Rolling
Upland

571 MULGRAVE PLATEAU

GEOLOGY AND LANDSCAPE DEVELOPMENT

The Mulgrave Plateau lies within the Avalon Zone of Nova Scotia. The Avalon basement strata are overlain by resistant Middle and Late Devonian rocks, including coarse sandstones and conglomerates with basalts, other volcanic deposits, and a dyke. These strata were deposited at about the time of the Acadian Orogeny when the Avalon and Meguma zone rocks joined together, and it is reasonable to expect that they would reflect these crustal disturbances.

The elevation on the Mulgrave Plateau reaches over 200 m on the west side, falling to below 130 m near the Strait of Canso. At Cape Argos and Chedabucto Bay it is about 50 m. The scarp along the Chedabucto Fault separates these Devonian rocks from younger Horton strata and is an important physiographic feature.

Apart from this regional slope to the east, there is little variation in relief on the plateau (see Figure 17). The upland surface is uniformly covered in a stony till, and there are few features of interest. One rather beautiful area lies along the Roman Valley where the river has exploited a fault line, producing a steep-sided valley which cuts into the plateau. The river flows into a large drowned estuary to Milford Haven and Guysborough.

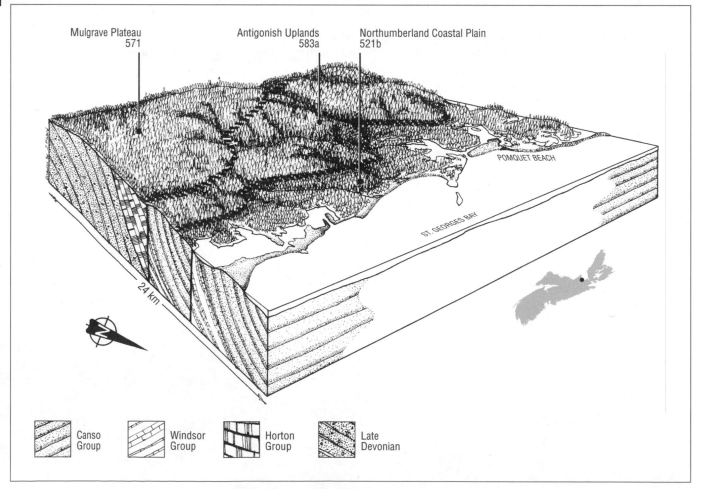

Figure legend:
- Canso Group
- Windsor Group
- Horton Group
- Late Devonian

Labels on figure: Mulgrave Plateau 571 · Antigonish Uplands 583a · Northumberland Coastal Plain 521b · POMQUET BEACH · ST. GEORGES BAY · 24 km

Figure 17: St. Georges Bay area. Slabby sandstones of the Horton Group and Late Devonian underlie the featureless upland called the Mulgrave Plateau (Unit 571). Drainage from this upland dissects the Antigonish Uplands (Unit 583) before entering the Northumberland Plain (Unit 521), with its sandy barrier beaches and extensive coastal lagoons.

FRESH WATER

A primary watershed division bisects this Unit horizontally in the northern portion. The east side is drained by several tertiary watersheds into Chedabucto Bay. The western area falls within a secondary watershed draining the Salmon River system. There are many small, irregularly shaped glacial lakes. Surface water pH levels range between 6.2 and 6.8.

SOILS

Soils in this Unit are derived mainly from shales and tend to be heavy and comparatively shallow (see Figure 28). Millbrook clay loams occur north of Chedabucto Bay. Elsewhere the soils are mainly Riverport and Kirkhill shaly loams, with some blocks of Thom sandy loams, associated with upland areas.

PLANTS

This Unit includes a wide variety of forest associations. On the deeper soils west of Mulgrave, mixedwoods predominate, with Balsam Fir, Black Spruce, Eastern Hemlock, Sugar Maple, and American Beech. On the wetter sites, Black Spruce, Balsam Fir, and larch occur, with White Spruce, Yellow Birch, and aspen appearing on better-drained sites. On shallow soils, such as those around Lincolnville, fir, Black Spruce, and White Spruce grow with larch, shade-intolerant Red Maples, birches, and aspen.

West of Middle Melford, where the clay soils have been waterworked, the better drainage encourages a mixed forest. The changing nature of the forest can be gauged from the following observations on soil-forest relationships made by C.D. Howe in 1912: "The forestal nature of the [western] portion may be characterized very briefly: barrens and semi-barrens interspersed with bogs and low hardwood ridges. The forest on the broad belt of Lake Lochaber is of the mixed type with hardwoods, chiefly yellow birch, forming one-half of the stand, the rest being red spruce and fir in about equal proportions. The crests of the hills and ridges are pure hardwood, 90 percent of which is often yellow birch, the remaining being beech, hard maple [Sugar Maple] and paper birch. East of the Cross Lake region to the Guysborough river, practically pure hardwoods prevail. As one approaches the coast from the interior, fir and spruce form a large proportion of the forest." This "forest" is the coastal forest (Region 800).

CULTURAL ENVIRONMENT

This area is sparsely settled, and forestry is the dominant resource activity. Farming takes place in river valleys. Communities on the Mulgrave Plateau are largely of Scottish descent. Black Loyalists settled the town of Lincolnville.

• • • • • • • •

Sites of Special Interest
- Goshen—view southwards across the St. Marys Fault Block to the escarpment of the St. Marys Fault
- Roman Valley—steep-sided, V-shaped valley leading to a wide estuary near Milford Haven

Provincial Parks and Park Reserves
- Lochaber
- Giants Lake
- Port Shoreham
- Wharf
- Guysborough Railway (part)

Proposed Parks and Protected Areas System includes Natural Landscape 46 and Candidate Protected Area 12 Ogden Round Lake.

Scenic Viewpoints
- Pirate Harbour, on the Strait of Canso
- Roman Valley to Milford Haven
- Roachvale (Salmon River)

Associated Topics
T2.2 The Avalon and Meguma Zones, T3.2 Ancient Drainage Patterns, T3.4 Terrestrial Glacial Deposits and Landscape Features, T8.1 Freshwater Hydrology.

Associated Habitats
H3 Fresh Water, H6.1 Hardwood Forest (Sugar Maple, Yellow Birch, Beech Association), H6.2 Softwood Forest (Spruce, Hemlock, Pine Association; Black Spruce, Larch Association), H6.3 Mixedwood Forest (White Spruce, Fir–Maple, Birch Association).

**571
Mulgrave
Plateau**

572 ST. MARYS FAULT BLOCK

GEOLOGY AND LANDSCAPE DEVELOPMENT

South of the Cobequid-Chedabucto Fault is a band of Horton rocks lying in a graben (a downfaulted block lying between two parallel faults). Across central Nova Scotia it is about 15 km wide and has an escarpment on the south that becomes increasingly prominent from the Eden Lake–Caledonia line eastwards.

Within the graben the elevations decrease gradually to the south and west. In Pictou County the elevation is 225–240 m, falling to 175 m at the Southern Uplands and 120 m near Melrose. From Trafalgar westwards the drainage is all towards the St. Marys

River confluence at Melrose (see Figure 18). The East River St. Marys drains along the Chedabucto Fault in southern Pictou County, eroding crushed material from the fault zone before heading southwards to Melrose. West River St. Marys has extended its headwaters along the line of the St. Marys Fault and has captured all the drainage flowing south across the graben in that area. Erosion by the river has exposed the fault scarp, which becomes increasingly prominent towards Melrose. The drainage pattern in the watershed of West River St. Marys and its tributaries is rectangular. The north-south and east-west directions probably reflect the joint pattern in the coarse Horton sandstones.

**572
St. Marys
Fault Block**

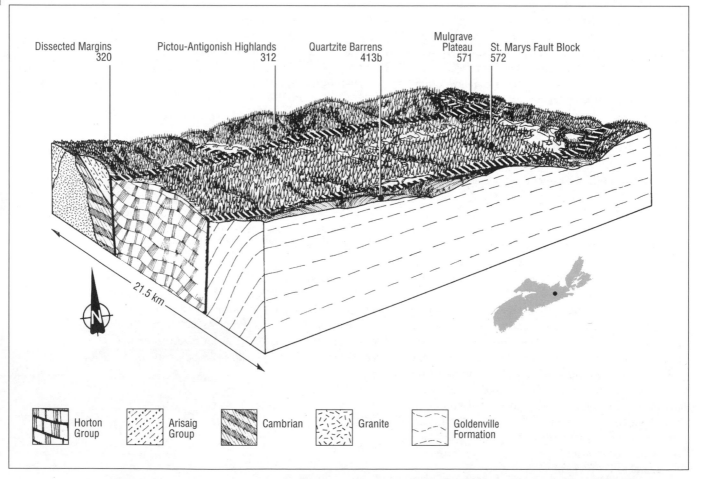

Figure 18: St. Marys River area. A massive downfaulted block (graben) of Horton sandstone (Unit 572) is bounded on the south by Goldenville Formation quartzite (Unit 413) and to the north by Avalon Zone rocks of the Pictou-Antigonish Highlands (Unit 312) and its Dissected Margins (District 320). The more-resistant rocks form prominent dissected scarp slopes. The St. Marys Fault has been excavated by the St. Marys River, while the Chedabucto Fault is followed by the East River of Pictou.

The western half of the St. Marys Fault Block is a uniform upland which runs along the southern side of the Cobequid Hills between the Cobequid Fault and the Portapique Fault. The Cobequid Fault forms the dividing line between the Avalon basement rocks of the Cobequid fault block to the north and the Carboniferous strata (Pictou and Riversdale) to the south. The Portapique Fault sets the Carboniferous rocks against the Triassic deposits which surround Cobequid Bay (see Figure 23).

FRESH WATER

Unit 572 falls within three main watersheds. The headwaters of the East, West, and Middle rivers occur in the middle northern portions and drain into the Northumberland Strait. Along the southern margin of the Cobequids the relief becomes hilly as the fault blocks become narrow and are crosscut by fast-flowing streams draining into Cobequid Bay. The headwaters of the Calvary River occur in the western portion where the North, Salmon, Folly, Debert, and Chiganois rivers flow down from the Cobequids into the head and north side of Cobequid Bay (Unit 913a). The southern middle portion is part of the large watershed that drains the Stewiacke River into Cobequid Bay, and the headwaters of the Stewiacke are located in this part of Unit 572. Drainage is typically trellised with many first-, second-, and third order streams. Freshwater productivity and diversity are high, and pH is generally between 6.0 and 7.5. Conductivity is low.

SOILS

The tills derived from the hard grey sandstones of the Horton Group are midway between those derived from Halifax quartzites and those from the softer Shulie sandstones. Consequently, soils usually associated with both these bedrocks are found in this Unit. Halifax soils (well-drained sandy loams) occur with small areas of Aspotogan soil and peat. Shulie soils (gravelly silt loams to sandy loams) are more prevalent, with Springhill sandy loams and Millbrook gravelly clay loams. The western extension of this Unit south of the Cobequids has a complex mix of soils of all textures from gravels to clays.

PLANTS

The relatively flat, poorly drained topography and the extensive cutting in this Unit have favoured conifers such as Balsam Fir, White Spruce, White Pine, Red Spruce, and Eastern Hemlock. Scattered Red Oak is found throughout. Mixed hardwood stands occur on some better-drained sites. The more gently undulating areas with shallow soils are dominated by spruce and fir. Extensive barren lands, apparently originating from repeated burning, are dominated by Sheep Laurel and Bracken with scattered pine, maple, and Black Spruce. A recent extensive burn near Trafalgar is now being replanted. C.D. Howe made the following observations on soil-forest relationships in 1912: "South of the railway to the height-of-land ... the country is made up of low rounded ridges and depressions. The higher points are covered with hardwoods, while the bases of the slopes and the forested depressions support mixed stands in which the conifers are in the majority. As a whole, one-half of the forested areas is composed of red spruce, fir and hemlock."

Two small floodplains in this Unit, one at Kemptown (Salmon River) and one at Glencoe (East River of Pictou), are of particular botanical interest because they support a rich and rare intervale flora.

CULTURAL ENVIRONMENT

Forestry is the main land use for much of this area. On bottomland river intervales, small farms are established, with pastureland sometimes climbing the base of surrounding hills. Former mining activity included the extraction of manganese in small quantities from Manganese Mines near Truro. Between 1849 and 1906, iron ore was mined almost continuously at Londonderry.

• • • • • • • •

Sites of Special Interest
- Kemptown intervale (IBP Proposed Ecological Site 9)—Carolinian flora such as Wild Leek, Canada Lily and Blue Cohosh
- Glencoe intervale (IBP Proposed Ecological Site 10)—Carolinian flora such as Bloodroot and Horse-gentian
- Economy River (IBP Proposed Ecological Site 8)—old Red Spruce forest

Ecological Reserves
- Indian Man Lake

Provincial Parks and Park Reserves
- Two Mile Lake
- Guysborough Railway (part)

Proposed Parks and Protected Areas System includes Natural Landscapes 24, 26, 40, and 41.

Scenic Viewpoints
- Eden Lake (Highway 347)

Associated Topics
T2.4 The Carboniferous Basin, T8.1 Freshwater Hydrology.

Associated Habitats
H3 Fresh Water, H5.1 Barren, H6.1 Hardwood Forest (Sugar Maple, Elm Association).

**572
St. Marys
Fault Block**

580 HILLS AND VALLEYS

The Units within this District are:
- 581 Cumberland Hills
- 582 Pictou Valleys
- 583 Antigonish Uplands
- 584 Ainslie Uplands
- 585 Iona Uplands

GEOLOGY AND LANDSCAPE DEVELOPMENT

This District includes two areas of Carboniferous strata that have the characteristics of foothills. They are adjacent to faulted upland blocks which have moved vertically upwards in the landscape. The close interrelationship of resistant Horton Group strata and the overlying, less-resistant Windsor Group limestone, salts, and shales is strongly reflected in the eastern sections of this District (Units 583, 584, and 585).

Some areas are lowland, others are upland, reflecting both the position of these strata on the tilted planation surface and the relative proportions of Horton and Windsor deposits. Except in the Pictou Valleys Unit, these strata have been compressed into folds which lie parallel to the axis of the province. Typically, erosion has removed Horton strata in the centre of anticlines (upfolds) and left the Windsor strata in the synclinal hollows in between. In some locations Windsor strata have also been protected from erosion by downfaulting, as in the Pictou Valleys. Where resistant Horton grits are exposed, they stand as ridges and as shoulders on the flanks of highland blocks. The Windsor deposits form low areas and valleys in which salt springs and brackish lakes are common.

SCENIC QUALITY

These landscapes generally lie below 200 m but, owing to river erosion, exhibit varied relief. The exception is the southern portion of the Ainslie Uplands (Unit 584), which tends to be both higher and less dissected. The latter area also possesses less settlement than the norm; elsewhere there are lines of sparse settlement along the valley floors. The dendritic drainage patterns preclude lakes, so water features are seldom present. Lake Ainslie and the shorelines of the Grand Narrows (Unit 585a) are the major exceptions. Scenic value is high to very high around the lakes, on the edge of the Mabou highland, and at Mabou Harbour. Elsewhere it is typically in the medium range. The Pictou and Springhill coalfields possess urban-industrial landscapes which, though hardly attractive, have much of human interest.

581 CUMBERLAND HILLS

GEOLOGY AND LANDSCAPE DEVELOPMENT

North of the Cobequid Hills, between Wentworth and West Apple River, lies a hilly, dissected terrain underlain by Cumberland Group sandstones and conglomerates (see Figure 5). The strata dip northwards away from the Cobequid Hills and proceed through folds of increasing wavelength down to the Northumberland Plain (Unit 521).

Following the retreat of ice across the Cobequids at the end of the ice age, permafrost conditions may have existed, because associated soil structures are found in this area.

FRESH WATER

This Unit is dissected by a primary watershed boundary. The Black River is the major river in the eastern portion and drains north into the Northumberland Strait (Unit 914). In most of the western portion, many second- and third-order streams feed into the Maccan River, which drains into Cumberland Basin. Tributaries in the most western tip feed into the Apple River, which drains into Chignecto Bay (sub-Unit 913b).

Bogs and marginal fens are associated with the stream systems. There is a large concentration of meromictic freshwater marsh on the north side of the Maccan River inlet (associated with Unit 523) and up the Nappan River.

Conductivity is relatively low, and pH levels average 6.5.

SOILS

Soils in this Unit are either relatively coarse-textured, well-drained, and derived from sandstones and conglomerates, or finer textured clay loams developed from shale and mudstone. In the former category are the gravelly sandy loams of the Rodney and Westbrook series. In the latter category are Queens, Kingsville, Joggins, and Diligence soils. In the river valleys, Hebert soils have developed on outwash deposits. Throughout the Unit, small areas of Economy soils, which are strongly acid and saturated for much of the year, occur on poorly drained or gently sloping sites. Commenting on the slow recovery of forests after fire on the conglomerate areas, C.D. Howe wrote

in 1912: "To the westward the conglomerate belt has been severely burnt. From the effects of burning, the conglomerate recovers nearly as slowly as does the quartzite. On the conglomerate at the headwaters of Apple river, there is a fairly good forest in which spruce prevails, although interrupted by frequent barrens and bogs."

PLANTS

Conifers and mixed stands predominate, with Red Spruce, Balsam Fir, Red Maple, and birch being abundant. On the well-drained upper slopes of the high rolling hills, Sugar Maple, Yellow Birch, and American Beech are common. White Pine and Jack Pine are common on old burns.

ANIMALS

Moose occur, particularly near Shulie Lake and the Little Forks watershed. There are some deer, and various locations are important for deer wintering, such as the Thundering Hill–West Brook area. Bird breeding distributions group either with sub-Unit 521a or Unit 311. One apparent exception is the Vesper Sparrow, which is more widespread in Unit 581, where more of its habitat is present than anywhere else in Nova Scotia. Wetlands near Newville Lake are significant for waterfowl. Freshwater fishes include White Sucker, White Perch, Yellow Perch, and Banded Killifish.

CULTURAL ENVIRONMENT

Coal mining at Springhill took place from the mid-nineteenth century until 1970, when the mine was closed. Now the heat from former mining tunnels is harnessed to generate geothermal energy for the town of Springhill. Areas of coal-mine tailings near Chignecto and Springhill are sparsely vegetated decades after the mines were abandoned.

The deeper, less sandy soils and less extensive fires of the past combine with the greater distance from Fundy influence to make this Unit more productive for forestry and agriculture than most other Units in Region 500. Farmland replaced former floodplain forests along the Maccan River, West Brook, and River Phillip valleys. Not all the small farms higher up the slopes have been abandoned, and much of the farmland in this Unit is cultivated for lowbush blueberry. Sand and gravel deposits are found throughout this area, and sites of former quarry operations are used recreationally at Wentworth Station.

● ● ● ● ● ● ● ●

Sites of Special Interest
- Fenwick (IBP Proposed Ecological Site 5)— deciduous forest, primarily Sugar Maple, with a Sugar Maple camp

Provincial Parks and Park Reserves
- Fenwick
- Newville Lake

Proposed Parks and Protected Areas System includes Natural Landscapes 18 and 20.

Scenic Viewpoints
- Newville Lake (Highway 2)

Associated Topics
T2.4 The Carboniferous Basin, T8.1 Freshwater Hydrology, T9.1 Soil-forming Factors, T10.1 Vegetation Change, T11.13 Freshwater Fishes, T12.3 Geology and Resources, T12.10 Plants and Resources, T12.11 Animals and Resources.

Associated Habitats
H3.1, H3.3, H3.5 Freshwater Lotic, H4.1 Bog, H4.4 Freshwater Marsh, H5.1 Barren, H6.1 Hardwood Forest (Sugar Maple, Yellow Birch, Beech Association), H6.2 Softwood Forest (Pine Association).

**581
Cumberland
Hills**

582 PICTOU VALLEYS

Unit 582 is divided into two sub-Units:

(a)   Pictou Rivers
(b)   McArras Brook

GEOLOGY AND LANDSCAPE DEVELOPMENT

This hilly area between the Cobequid Hills and the Pictou-Antigonish Highlands is underlain by Late Carboniferous Canso and Pictou strata, which are interrupted on the southeastern margin by triangular upfaulted blocks of Windsor strata. A separate part of this Unit (sub-Unit 582b) lies east of central Pictou between McArras Brook and Doctors Brook.

The Windsor Group strata are predominantly composed of sandstone and siltstone with minor amounts of gypsum and anhydrite. The landscape reflects the dominance of these relatively more-resistant rocks, and although it is well dissected by streams, elevations exceed 200 m in places and reach 225 m at Hopewell and Lorne.

Part of the East River north of Sunnybrae is a fossil valley that became filled with Windsor deposits and is now being re-exposed. In the central part of the Unit is the Pictou coalfield. The basin in which the coalfield sits developed as a physiographic feature during the Acadian Orogeny when it was downfaulted. Since then it has acted as a sedimentary sink, and during the Late Carboniferous it provided a suitable environment for the development of coal seams.

The coalfield underlies an area about 5 km by 16 km beneath New Glasgow, Stellarton, and Trenton.

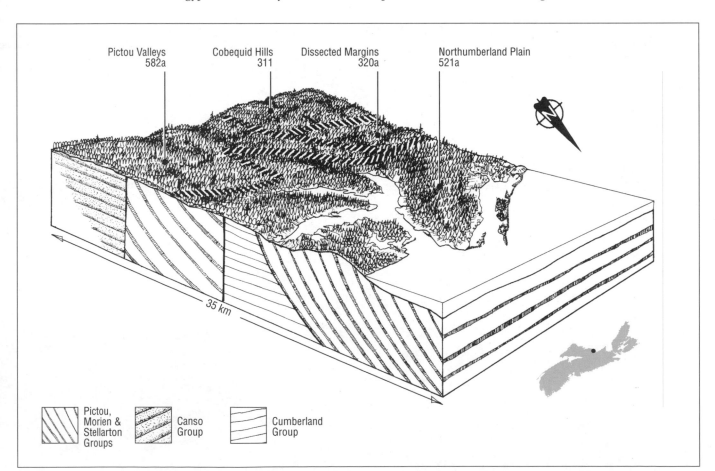

Figure 19: Pictou Basin area. The three rivers (West, East, and Middle) of Pictou drain the Northumberland Plain (Unit 521) through the drowned estuary of Pictou Harbour. The three valleys are deeply eroded into the Carboniferous rocks (Unit 582) which are bounded to the west by the Cobequid Hills (Unit 311) and their Dissected Margins (District 320).

The coal seams lie in grey shales, which are open folds dipping to the east. The total thickness of the coalfield is about 2,600 m and bears up to 45 seams, 11 of which have been mined. The coal seams were formed in a tectonically unstable area in which periods of quiet plant growth were separated by subsidence and inundation by muds. The seams, therefore, grade vertically and laterally into shaly coal and coaly shale.

FRESH WATER

Most of the Pictou Rivers sub-Unit (582a) falls within three tertiary watersheds, draining the East River, Middle River, and West River north into Pictou Harbour (see Figure 19). Drainage patterns are rectangular, and surface water is slightly acidic to neutral. Extensive floodplains occur along the East River in sub-Unit 582a.

SOILS

The soils in this Unit have been derived from shales and sandstones.

Pictou Rivers (sub-Unit 582a)
Well-drained Woodbourne soils (gravelly clay loams) are found associated with imperfectly drained Millbrook clay loams, with small amounts of gravelly Hebert soils formed on glaciofluvial deposits. Clay soils of the Queens and Joggins series are found around Stellarton.

McArras Brook (sub-Unit 582b)
Woodbourne soils also occur together with Barney soils south of Arisaig (well-drained shaly loams).

PLANTS

White Spruce and Balsam Fir grow on old fields and pastures. Sugar Maple, Yellow Birch, and American Beech grow on slopes, with shade-intolerant birches, Red Maple and aspen. Some remnants of intervale old growth forest remain along the West Branch of the East River of Pictou.

ANIMALS

The East, Middle and West Rivers support significant salmonid habitat.

CULTURAL ENVIRONMENT

Soils in this Unit are productive, and much of the area is farmed. For the Scottish settlers coming to this area in the late 1700s, the Pictou Valleys provided reasonably good farmlands once the trees were cleared. Forestry exploitation in this area was very extensive in the 1800s, supplying timber exports to Britain. The forestry industry continues to be important here, as is mining around the Pictou Rivers (sub-Unit 582a).

Coal was discovered in the Pictou coalfield in 1798 on McCullochs Brook and was worked in the early 1800s; mining continued sporadically into the 1900s, with most operations ceasing by 1960. The three main coal-producing districts are Thorburn, Albion, and Westville. Most recently, coal mining took place at Westville. The coal from these mines was a major factor in the industrial development of this area. At McArras Brook (sub-Unit 582b) the economies of small communities are based on fishing, farming, and lumbering. Arisaig has a prosperous fishery.

• • • • • • • •

Sites of Special Interest
• Arisaig (sub-Unit 582b)—a 5-km-long section of the shoreline has the best continuous exposure of Silurian and Devonian sediments in North America; a wide variety of tropical marine fossils occurs, including graptolites, brachiopods, bryozoa, trilobites, crinoids, and cephalopods
• Hopewell—intervale forest with rare plants

Provincial Parks and Park Reserves
• Salt Springs
• Green Hill
• Guysborough Railway (part)
• Arisaig

Proposed Parks and Protected Areas System includes Natural Landscape 42.

Associated Offshore Unit
Sub-Unit 582b: 914 Northumberland Strait.

Associated Topics
T2.1 Introduction to the Geological History of Nova Scotia, T2.4 The Carboniferous Basin, T8.1 Freshwater Hydrology, T10.1 Vegetation Change, T12.3 Geology and Resources, T12.10 Plants and Resources.

Associated Habitats
H5.2 Oldfield, H6.1 Hardwood Forest (Sugar Maple, Yellow Birch, Beech Association).

**582
Pictou
Valleys**

583 ANTIGONISH UPLANDS

Unit 530 is divided into two sub-Units:
(a) South River
(b) Lakevale

GEOLOGY AND LANDSCAPE DEVELOPMENT

South and north of the town of Antigonish are two areas of upland underlain by Devonian to Middle Carboniferous strata of varying character. They include resistant Horton strata, easily eroded Windsor deposits, and slightly more resistant Canso and Riversdale strata. Some volcanic rocks also occur. The areas are cut by faults and are elevated and dissected. They represent a transitional zone between the coastal lowland and the uplands to the west and south.

In the South River area, a valley extends southwards through Lochaber Lake across the southern uplands to the St. Marys River estuary. This may have been the course of an ancestral river that flowed northwards from the Scotian Shelf and was superimposed upon the resistant rocks that the valley now crosscuts.

FRESH WATER

This Unit is divided into a number of tertiary watersheds, most of which drain into St. Georges Bay (see Figure 17). Surface water is dominated by tributaries that flow in a modified trellis pattern into first-order streams draining either into the harbours or directly into the bay. Floodplains occur along many of the Antigonish area streams and rivers in sub-Unit 583a.

SOILS

South River (sub-Unit 583a)
To the west of this sub-Unit, Millbrook soils predominate. These soils have developed from gravelly clay loam tills of mixed origin—sandstones, shales, and metamorphic rocks. In the centre, well-drained Woodbourne soils have developed from shales and sandstones of the Windsor Formation. Woodbourne soils are stony to shaly loams. Stewiacke and Hebert soils are common on water-deposited materials along stream and river valleys, the former having developed from alluvium and the latter from glacio-fluvial deposits.

Lakevale (sub-Unit 583b)
The soils in this sub-Unit tend to be imperfectly drained, either because of fine-textured impermeable subsoil, or because they are underlain by flat-lying bedrock. The finest textured soils are Queens (sandy clay loam) and Millbrook (gravelly clay loam). Hansford soils are coarser but also imperfectly drained. The better-drained Thom soils are derived from a mixture of sandstones and metamorphic rocks. Westbrook soils are found on tills derived from conglomerate.

PLANTS

This Unit falls within Loucks' Sugar Maple–Hemlock, Pine Zone, at the boundary between two ecoregions: a northerly one in which conifers predominate among scattered deciduous stands, and a more southerly one in which shade-tolerant species are found on a wider range of sites. In the western part of the Unit, Sugar Maple, Yellow Birch, and American Beech are common, with spruce, Eastern Hemlock, pine, Red Maple, and birch on less well-drained sites. Oldfields regenerating in White Spruce are common. As one approaches Cape Breton, softwoods became more prevalent.

ANIMALS

This Unit provides mainly forested habitats, with cliffs along St. Georges Bay. There is virtually no information on small mammals in this Unit, but diversity is probably moderately high. Typical freshwater fish species include White Suckers, perch, shiners, Brown Bullhead, Brook Trout, American Eel and Gaspereau. Three isolated populations of Yellow Perch exist in Lochaber Lake.

CULTURAL ENVIRONMENT

Forestry exploitation and small farming in valley intervales characterize much of the land use in this area. In the South River area (sub-Unit 583a), limestone is quarried at Antigonish. The Fraser Mills Fish Hatchery raises small fish for lake stocking programs throughout the province and an exhibition centre at the operation provides information on the hatchery and local angling. At Lakevale (sub-Unit 583b), commercial fishing provides an economic base.

• • • • • • •

Provincial Parks and Park Reserves
• Linwood

Proposed Parks and Protected Areas System includes Natural Landscape 45.

Associated Offshore Unit
Sub-Unit 583b: 914 Northumberland Strait.

Associated Topics
T2.4 The Carboniferous Basin, T3.2 Ancient Drainage Patterns, T8.1 Freshwater Hydrology, T9.1 Soil-forming Factors, T11.13 Freshwater Fishes, T12.11 Animals and Resources.

Associated Habitats
H3.1 Freshwater Open-Water Lotic, H3.3 Freshwater Bottom Lotic, H3.5 Freshwater Water's Edge Lotic, H5.2 Oldfield, H6.1 Hardwood Forest (Sugar Maple, Yellow Birch, Beech Association), H6.2 Softwood Forest (White Spruce Association), H6.3 Mixedwood Forest (Spruce, Fir, Pine–Maple, Birch Association).

**583
Antigonish
Uplands**

584 AINSLIE UPLANDS

GEOLOGY AND LANDSCAPE DEVELOPMENT

The Ainslie Uplands cover a large area of southwestern Cape Breton from St. Georges Bay to Lake Ainslie. The geology is dominated by Horton Group deposits which have been thrown into broad folds trending northeast to southwest.

The area is on the uptilted side of the planation surface and has been deeply eroded. Almost all strata younger than Windsor age have been stripped off. The remaining Windsor Group strata, which still attain a total thickness of 750 m, are preserved in long synclines and fault blocks southwest of Lake Ainslie and east of the Mabou Highlands (Unit 314). In this area, on the southern end of the highlands, volcanic rocks of Devonian to Carboniferous age are found.

The Ainslie Uplands are hilly and fairly rugged, with the hills forming a visual continuum from the Creignish Hills to Lake Ainslie. All the major rivers—the Mabou, Southwest Mabou, Mull, and Black—exploit the bands of Windsor strata lying between the long ridges of Horton rocks and form a roughly rectangular drainage pattern. The Mabou River flows in a faulted block of Windsor strata and reaches the Northumberland Strait through a drowned estuary.

Glacial deposits brought down from the Cape Breton highlands by glaciers and glacial streams mantle the area. Lake Ainslie has been dammed by glacial gravels, which can be seen as ridges near Strathlorne. The westward extension of the lake, Loch Ban, is shallow and bordered with peat deposits, which can be found far up Black River along a flat, low belt of Windsor strata. Coarse glacial gravels can be seen on the lower slopes of the Mabou Hills. Inland, fine sandy deposits in a valley between Loch Ban and the sea ascend to more than 150 m above sea level.

FRESH WATER

The northeastern portion of this Unit is dominated by Lake Ainslie, the largest lake in Cape Breton, draining north through the Margaree into the Northumberland Strait. The southern portions are dominated by the trellised drainage patterns of the Mabou River and its many tributaries. The headwaters of the Skye River occur in this Unit. Most of the streams are shallow and fast-flowing, with pH levels averaging 6.0. Lake Ainslie has a pH of 7.8, and conductivity is 105 micromhos/cm.

SOILS

On the higher elevations—up to 200 m—Diligence, Woodbourne, and Westbrook soils predominate. Diligence soils have developed from grey shales, and Woodbourne soils have developed from reddish-brown sandstones and conglomerates. Falmouth and Queens soils are chiefly found on low-lying areas below 30 m and overlying or adjacent to gypsum deposits. All of these soils, with the exception of Westbrook, are imperfectly drained loams or clay loams over relatively impermeable clay loam tills. The large area of sand between Lake Ainslie and the sea is an interesting feature. Coarse, well-drained Canning soils have developed on this sand plug.

PLANTS

As the highest and one of the most northerly units in the Carboniferous Lowlands Region, the Ainslie Uplands are part of the Sugar Maple, Yellow Birch–Fir Zone which encompasses many of the uplands in Nova Scotia (Region 300). This zone is distinguished by predominantly hardwood forest, in which Sugar Maple, American Beech, Yellow Birch, and Mountain Maple occupy the upper slopes and high ridges. Balsam Fir and White Spruce cover the upland flats and valley slopes. Black Spruce and Larch are found on the extensive clay soils throughout this area. Oldfields regenerating in White Spruce are common.

ANIMALS

Small-mammal diversity is relatively high. Brook Trout and White Perch are typical freshwater species. Lake Ainslie has a rich and diverse aquatic fauna. Snails carry the larvae of the trematode parasites that affect people as "swimmers' itch."

CULTURAL ENVIRONMENT

Farming and forestry characterize land use. Coal was once mined at Mabou Mines. Barite was formerly mined at Lake Ainslie and continues to be extracted at other sites in this area.

• • • • • • • •

Sites of Special Interest

- Strathlorne (Route 19)—a hummocky ridge of sand that dammed a river formerly flowing to Inverness and thus created Lake Ainslie; the lake now drains northward into the Margaree River
- Mabou Harbour mouth to West Mabou Harbour—gypsum area
- Black River (IBP Proposed Ecological Site 12)—alkaline sphagnum bog, including a number of rare plants such as *Rhynchospora capillacea*; *Carex gynocrates*; *Eleocharis pauciflora*, var. *fernaldii*; *Salix candida*; and *Galium tinctorium*

Ecological Reserves

- McFarlane Woods—old deciduous forest

Provincial Parks and Park Reserves

- North Ainslie
- Long Point
- Mabou
- Ainslie Point

Proposed Parks and Protected Areas System includes Natural Landscape 58.

Scenic Viewpoints

- Highway 395 (east shore of Lake Ainslie)
- Skye River valley (Highway 252)

Associated Offshore Unit

914 Northumberland Strait.

Associated Topics

T2.4 The Carboniferous Basin, T3.1 Development of the Ancient Landscape, T3.3 Glaciation, Deglaciation and Sea-level Changes, T3.4 Terrestrial Glacial Deposits and Landscape Features, T8.1 Freshwater Hydrology, T11.11 Small Mammals, T12.3 Geology and Resources.

Associated Habitats

H3.1 Freshwater Open-Water Lotic, H3.3 Freshwater Bottom Lotic, H5.2 Oldfield, H6.1 Hardwood Forest (Sugar Maple, Yellow Birch, Beech Association), H6.2 Softwood Forest (Spruce, Fir Association; Black Spruce, Larch Association).

**584
Ainslie
Uplands**

585 IONA UPLANDS

Unit 585 is divided into two sub-Units:
- (a) Grand Narrows
- (b) Sydney River

GEOLOGY AND LANDSCAPE DEVELOPMENT

In Cape Breton, Horton strata are not found east of the Great Bras d'Or Channel. In eastern Cape Breton the earliest Carboniferous deposits are represented by the Grantmire Formation. These strata are probably the same age as the Horton Group but are made up of coarser materials: conglomerates, grit, and coarse sandstone. The Iona Uplands are predominantly underlain by Grantmire strata deposited as alluvial fans directly onto the ancient granites and schists of the Boisdale Hills when they stood on the side of the intermontane basin (see Figure 20).

The Iona Uplands Unit is divided into Grand Narrows (sub-Unit 585a) and Sydney River (sub-Unit 585b). In both areas the Grantmire rocks form resistant shoulders on the upland block of the Boisdale Hills and give steep slopes rising directly from the

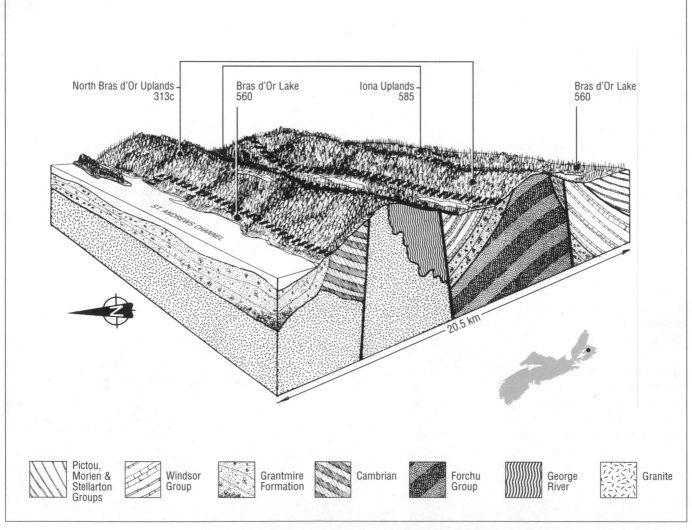

Figure 20: St. Andrews Channel area. The Iona Uplands (Unit 585) are a transitional, hilly area of Carboniferous rocks between the upland fault blocks of ancient metamorphic rocks (Unit 313) and the easily eroded Windsor Group rocks which fringe the Bras d'Or Lake Submerged Lowland (District 560).

Bras d'Or lowland. The elevations reach a maximum of 200 m, in keeping with the location of this area on the tilted planation surface.

Grand Narrows (sub-Unit 585a)

This area includes a section of upland between St. Patricks Channel and the Great Bras d'Or made up of Horton and Grantmire strata. This upland is extensively crosscut by faults and stands as a hill with a fault scarp on the east and a more gradual descent to the Submerged (Bras d'Or) Lowland on the west.

Sydney River (sub-Unit 585b)

This area is mantled by thick glacial deposits, kames, eskers, and outwash gravels which partly fill the river valley and create a series of shallow lakes connected by narrow channels. These deposits are evidence of an ancient lobe of ice in East Bay which extended from the Submerged Lowland during the late stages of the Wisconsinan glaciation. As the ice melted, streams carried outwash material towards the Cabot Strait.

FRESH WATER

There is very little surface-water coverage in sub-Unit 585a. In sub-Unit 585b, several isolated brooks drain into Sydney Harbour, and a few lakes are found in the northern portions. The water is alkaline, with pH levels averaging 7.5.

SOILS

Grand Narrows (sub-Unit 585a)

In this area, soils are mostly well-drained Westbrook sandy loams developed from conglomerates, with imperfectly drained Millbrook clay loams. Small areas of Woodbourne silt loams also occur.

Sydney River (sub-Unit 585b)

Westbrook soils are dominant, with areas of imperfectly drained Debert silt loam (often with a cemented layer). Queens soils, a clay loam, are found at Point Edward. Some areas of coarse Hebert soils occur on outwash sands and gravels.

PLANTS

(See District 560, Submerged Lowland.)

CULTURAL ENVIRONMENT

The Sydney coal mines provide the foundation of much of the industrial base in the Sydney River area (sub-Unit 585b). In certain areas of the Iona Uplands, small farming occurs.

• • • • • • • •

Sites of Special Interest
- Blacketts Lake to Sydney River—kames, eskers, and outwash gravels along the river valley; rare aquatic fauna
- Nova Scotia Highland Village Museum, Iona—Scottish heritage of Cape Breton

Provincial Parks and Park Reserves
- Barra Forest
- Iona

Proposed Parks and Protected Areas System includes Natural Landscape 48.

Scenic Viewpoints
- Unit 585a: Barra Strait (Iona–Grand Narrows)

Associated Offshore Units
915 Sydney Bight, 916 Bras d'Or Lake.

Associated Topics
T2.4 The Carboniferous Basin, T3.1 Development of the Ancient Landscape, T3.4 Terrestrial Glacial Deposits and Landscape Features, T9.1 Soil-forming Factors, T11.16 Land and Freshwater Invertebrates, T12.3 Geology and Resources.

Associated Habitats
(See District 560, Submerged Lowland.)

**585
Iona
Uplands**

590 DISSECTED PLATEAU

The District is divided into two Units on the basis of morphology:

591 Margaree Plateau
592 St. Lawrence Slopes

GEOLOGY

District 590 is underlain by resistant early Carboniferous strata that flank the Highlands Region in Cape Breton. The rocks are predominantly coarse early Horton deposits, but in many places along the western side of the Highlands, Early Carboniferous lava flows are found; some reach 300 m in thickness.

These Early Carboniferous deposits are in some places in fault contact with the Highlands Region and in others have been deposited directly onto the surface. Immediately at the contact, the Carboniferous strata are often tilted up or domed, indicating that the highland block moved up vertically through them. In some places away from the contact, domed hills of Early Carboniferous strata occur. These domed hills may conceal blocks of the ancient rocks underneath them. Examples of these hills are Hunters Mountain and Salt Mountain. Elsewhere, these resistant strata form shoulders high on the slopes of the Highlands. The Highlands may once have been covered by many thousands of feet of Carboniferous rocks, which have been stripped away, leaving these resistant remnants. Occasionally pockets of Middle Carboniferous strata remain, such as those of the Riversdale Group around Chimney Corner, but these have generally been preserved in downfaulted blocks. Similarly, the Windsor strata that are found here and there around the margins of the Highlands lie almost entirely in faulted valleys.

LANDSCAPE DEVELOPMENT

The District is dissected by faults which lie predominantly northeast to southwest, parallel to the fold direction typical of the Carboniferous Basin, and parallel to the general structural trend in Cape Breton. These faults are usually followed by river valleys. The terrain is generally elevated and rugged, reaching 300–350 m in places along the slopes of the Highlands.

The District is heavily mantled with glacial deposits that were washed down during deglaciation of the Highlands. These are thickest close to the Highlands slopes, particularly where the ice followed fault valleys, such as those of the Margaree and Middle rivers.

A wave-cut notch 6–10 m above the high tide mark is prominent around Cape St. Lawrence from Chéticamp to Cape North and beyond to Cape Smokey. In places it is overlain by peat of early Wisconsinan age.

SCENIC QUALITY

Because much of this plateau flanks the Highlands Region and is deeply dissected, there is considerable relative relief, with many fine views from the valley floors. Indeed, a considerable stretch of the scenic Cabot Trail traverses Unit 591, following the broad valleys of the Middle River and the Margaree River system. Other valleys of high scenic quality have been cut by the Baddeck and North rivers. In all cases, the flat river valley floors are enhanced by livestock farms and contain ocean inlets at their mouths. The northern areas (sub-Units 592b and 592c) exhibit fine coastal scenery.

• • • • • • • •

Associated Topics
T2.1 Introduction to the Geological History of Nova Scotia, T3.3 Glaciation, Deglaciation and Sea-level Changes.

591 MARGAREE PLATEAU

GEOLOGY AND LANDSCAPE DEVELOPMENT

The Margaree Plateau is dissected upland that sweeps southward from the Highlands to Lake Ainslie in the southwest and to the Submerged Lowland (District 560) in the southeast (see Figure 21).

Downfaulted blocks of Windsor Group rocks are found within the folds of resistant Horton strata in several areas. The valleys of the Northeast Margaree, Middle, and Baddeck rivers have all been eroded from Windsor strata (see Figure 8).

The escarpment on the west side of the Northeast Margaree valley is straight for more than 15 km. It is in line with other valleys across the Highlands and with the Aspy Fault valley at Cape North.

When it reaches the Windsor strata, the Northeast Margaree valley widens out, flowing between high hills. The floor of the valley is covered with glacial sands and gravels, and a floodplain with oxbow ponds and terraces has developed. At Emerald the river turns 90° to the west, cuts through a band of Horton strata, and flows to Margaree Forks. Originally it probably flowed southwards to the Middle River and St. Patricks Channel, but this exit was blocked by glacial drift. The old river valley is now occupied by a string of lakes: Harvard Lake, First

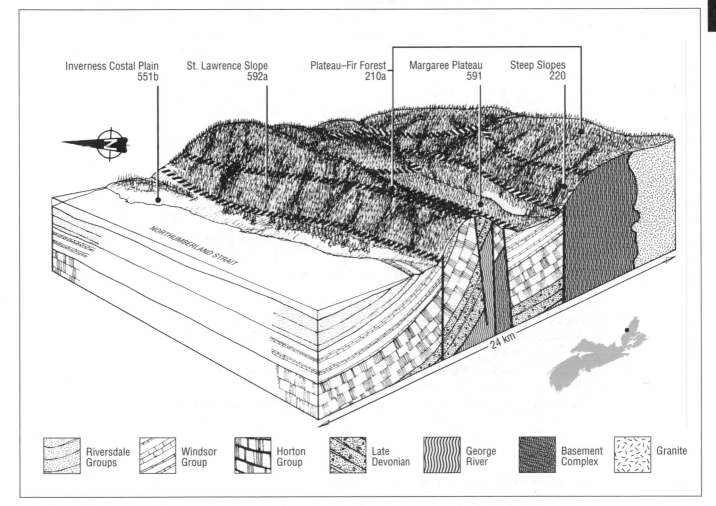

Figure 21: Margaree Valley area. Windsor Group rocks, including gypsum, are preserved in downfaulted sections now occupied by the Margaree River and the Inverness Coastal Plain (Unit 551). Horton conglomerate and sandstone compose the deeply dissected Margaree Plateau (Unit 591) and the St. Lawrence Slopes (Unit 592), which form a shoulder to the Plateau–Fir Forest (District 210). These slopes are the soft rock equivalent of the hard rock of the Steep Slopes (District 220).

Lake O'Law, and Second Lake O'Law. Beyond Margaree Forks the river flows through another strip of Windsor strata before entering its drowned estuary at Margaree Harbour.

The hilly terrain continues to the Baddeck area. There it is intersected by the Windsor lowland through which the Baddeck River flows to its drowned estuary at Nyanza Bay. Glacial deposits are found along most of the major rivers. At Middle River and Skye River (further south) the gravels contain mastodon teeth and bones.

FRESH WATER

Much of this Unit falls within a secondary watershed that drains Lake Ainslie into the Margaree Harbour. The Southwest Margaree River dissects the northern portions and is fed by many smaller-order tributaries. There are large grassy fens and wet meadows along the Margaree where it broadens out north of Margaree Forks. Solution lakes occur in the broader areas of the Margaree Valley. This valley also has several large aquifers in the Carboniferous formations.

SOILS

Soils are mapped only as Rough Mountainland. However, the soils are, for the most part, surprisingly deep, with some smooth, compressed silts, supporting the theory that the area was not extensively glaciated. The soils probably share at least some of the characteristics of those described in Unit 584, Ainslie Uplands.

PLANTS

This Unit forms part of Loucks' Sugar Maple, Yellow Birch–Fir Zone. However, while the Ainslie Uplands have a rolling, hilly terrain, the Margaree Plateau is more level. White Spruce is common in old fields and pastures which have been recolonized. On the flatter upland areas, Balsam Fir and Black Spruce are mixed with shade-intolerant species. Better-drained rolling areas have more shade-tolerant hardwoods: Sugar Maple, Yellow Birch, and American Beech, with a mixture of Balsam Fir.

ANIMALS

This Unit provides eagle-nesting habitat and an important post-breeding concentration area. Atlantic Salmon and American Eel are found in the Margaree River. Freshwater fish such as White Sucker, sticklebacks, and Brook Trout are found in streams further inland. The Middle River supports four species of salmonids.

CULTURAL ENVIRONMENT

Along the Margaree River valley, small mixed farming is the predominant land use. Forestry occurs on the Margaree Plateau. The Margaree is designated as a heritage river and has long been important for salmon fishing. Wildlife and angling attract tourism and recreational use of the area.

• • • • • • • •

Sites of Special Interest
- Northeast Margaree Valley—fault scarp on the west side of the valley, sinkholes in areas of karst topography, river terraces, intervale plants
- Baddeck River (west side, north of Melford)—fossil valley containing Windsor strata
- St. Anns Harbour—gravel and sand bars nearly block the harbour entrance; the narrow gap is crossed by a cable ferry; from Kellys Mountain lookoff (District 220) the old positions of the sand bar can be seen as ridges
- Piper Glen (IBP Proposed Ecological Site 13)—spectacular waterfall, mature mixed forest
- Lake O'Law (IBP Proposed Ecological Site 14)—old growth mixed deciduous forest habitats

Provincial Parks and Park Reserves
- St. Anns
- Whycocomagh
- Scotsville
- South West Margaree
- Doyles Bridge
- Lake O'Law

Proposed Parks and Protected Areas System includes Natural Landscape 63 and Candidate Protected Area 8 Trout Brook.

Scenic Viewpoints
- Cabot Trail (all sections)
- Northeast Margaree valley
- Southwest Margaree valley
- summit of Salt Mountain (views over St. Patricks Channel)

Associated Topics
T2.4 The Carboniferous Basin, T3.2 Ancient Drainage Patterns, T8.2 Freshwater Environments, T11.4 Birds of Prey, T11.13 Freshwater Fishes, T12.11 Animals and Resources.

Associated Habitats
H3.1 Freshwater Open-Water Lotic, H3.2 Freshwater Open-Water Lentic, H3.4 Freshwater Bottom Lentic, H3.6 Freshwater Water's Edge Lentic, H4.2 Fen, H6.1 Hardwood Forest (Sugar Maple, Yellow Birch, Beech Association), H6.2 Softwood Forest (Balsam Fir Association).

591
Margaree
Plateau

592 ST. LAWRENCE SLOPES

The St. Lawrence Slopes is physically separated into three sub-Units:
(a) Squirrel Mountain
(b) Polletts Cove
(c) Meat Cove

GEOLOGY AND LANDSCAPE DEVELOPMENT

St. Lawrence Slopes is a narrow band of resistant Early Carboniferous rocks which shoulder the Highlands Region massif along its west side from Margaree Harbour to Cape North (see Figure 21).

Squirrel Mountain (sub-Unit 592a)
In the Squirrel Mountain area the strata are dominated by Early Carboniferous volcanic lavas. These are very resistant, and the slope from the Highlands plateau drops steeply to the coast where it meets a narrow coastal plain (sub-Unit 551b). At Corney Brook, all the main rock groups in this part of Cape Breton are exposed within a short distance of one another. The Horton strata contain angular pieces of the basement rock.

Polletts Cove (sub-Unit 592b)
The Polletts Cove area lies beside Pleasant Bay and presents unremittingly steep slopes which form a continuum with the underlying Highlands block. Pleasant River flows along a fault and across a small triangle of Windsor Group rocks before reaching the Northumberland Strait.

Meat Cove (sub-Unit 592c)
A larger area of Early Carboniferous strata is found at Meat Cove, but because these rocks are almost as resistant as the granites and gneisses, the landscape remains steep and rugged, with high cliffs bordering Bay St. Lawrence.

FRESHWATER AND COASTAL AQUATIC ENVIRONMENTS

Surface water in all three sub-Units consists mainly of steep, straight streams that originate in the surrounding highlands and drain into the Northumberland and Cabot straits. Many of the streams in sub-Units 592a and 592c are isolated first-order streams that drain in a parallel pattern.

Fresh water is alkaline; for example, Grand Lake in sub-Unit 592a has a pH of 8.0 and a conductivity reading of 200 micromhos/cm. There are colluvial deposits in stream ravines in sub-Units 592b and 592c, as well as several seep and spring zones. A number of barachois ponds and several small salt marshes are found along the coast.

PLANTS

Softwoods predominate: spruce, hemlock, pine, and fir, with maple and birch. Pure stands of White Spruce occur on oldfields, with better stands of shade-tolerant Sugar Maple, Yellow Birch and American Beech on better-drained slopes and rich intervale soils.

ANIMALS

Freshwater habitats support a diverse aquatic fauna. The unit also provides some scattered eagle-breeding habitat. A moderate number of Black Guillemot are believed to breed in part of Bay St. Lawrence.

CULTURAL ENVIRONMENT

A Snow Crab fishery predominates at Pleasant Bay (sub-Unit 592b). Meat Cove was so named because of the smell of the rotting flesh of hundreds of moose slaughtered by a nineteenth-century hunting expedition.

• • • • • • • •

Sites of Special Interest
• Corney Brook—a complete section of local Carboniferous strata
• North Aspy River (IBP Proposed Ecological Site 21)—old deciduous forest

Provincial Parks and Park Reserves
Proposed Parks and Protected Areas System includes Natural Landscapes 75a and 75b and Candidate Protected Area 1 Pollet Cove–Aspy Fault.

Scenic Viewpoints
- Sub-Unit 592b: Pleasant Bay (viewed from Cabot Trail on west side)
- Sub-Unit 592c: North of Capstick (view towards Cape North)

Associated Offshore Unit
914 Northumberland Strait.

Associated Topic
T2.4 The Carboniferous Basin, T7.3 Coastal Landforms, T11.7 Seabirds and Other Birds of Marine Habitats, T12.11 Animals and Resources.

Associated Habitats
H2.1 Rocky Shore, H5.3 Cliff and Bank, H3.1 Freshwater Open-Water Lotic, H6.1 Hardwood Forest (Sugar Maple, Yellow Birch, Beech Association), H6.2 Softwood Forest (White Spruce Association; Spruce, Hemlock, Pine Association), H6.3 Mixedwood Forest (Spruce, Fir, Pine–Maple, Birch Association).

**592
St. Lawrence
Slopes**

600
Triassic Lowlands

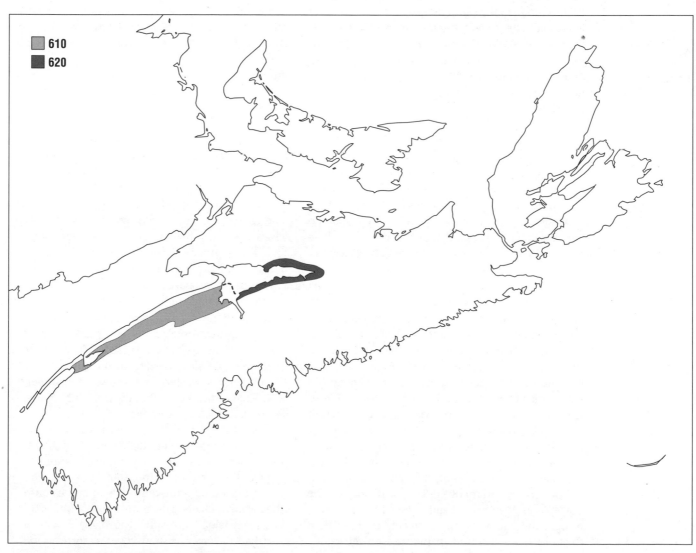

Figure 22: Region 600, Triassic Lowlands, and its component Districts.

610
620

600 TRIASSIC LOWLANDS

Two Districts are recognized within the Triassic Lowlands Region are:

610 Valley
620 Tidal Bay

REGIONAL CHARACTERISTICS

Soft Triassic sandstones have been eroded to form an open-ended valley. Material from the parent rock and glacial and post-glacial deposits provide a mixture of soil types. Shelter by North and South Mountains provides the most favoured climate in the province, with a growing season of 195 days. Where the valley is open to the sea at its east and west ends, the inland climate is moderated by marine influences. Natural vegetation includes Red Spruce, Eastern Hemlock, pine forests, oak and maple forests, bogs, and salt marshes (often turned to dykeland). Mud flats are rich in life and support large flocks of migratory shorebirds.

GEOLOGY AND LANDSCAPE DEVELOPMENT

The distinctive red beds that fringe the Minas Basin and Cobequid Bay, and extend underneath the Annapolis-Cornwallis Valley belong to the Triassic Lowlands. They are made up of weakly cemented and easily eroded sandstones and sandy shale overlain by glacial deposits of varying character.

The red beds were deposited under arid conditions in a narrow, hill-fringed basin while Nova Scotia was still part of Pangaea. The early deposits washed down from South Mountain and the Cobequids were coarse sands that were later consolidated into a crumbly sandstone (Wolfville Formation). Much of the basin was then flooded with lava as volcanoes became active in the Fundy region. Later faulting and subsidence created a spoon-shaped depression or trough in which the sandstones, shales, and basalt dip at 5–10° towards the centre line of the Minas Basin. This trough is now largely occupied by the sea.

The northern side of the trough is downfaulted. The master fault is probably the Cobequid Fault, but the present boundary of the Triassic deposits is the Portapique Mountain Fault. Along this northern margin the strata are more steeply inclined than those to the south and in places are even gently folded.

During the long period of erosion up to and including the Cretaceous, much of the basalt was removed. Some still remains as a protective cap on the sandstones, but to the north, east, and south, wide bands of soft sandstone became uncovered. Rapid erosion then ensued as a river system developed in the trough followed by glacial scouring and finally marine invasion. Much of the Triassic Lowlands Region is now covered by water. The largest area still above sea level is the eastern part of the Annapolis-Cornwallis Valley, which, though undergoing rapid erosion, is protected somewhat by its flanks of resistant rock: the North Mountain basalt and South Mountain granite (see Figure 25). The western end of the valley underlies St. Marys Bay. Elsewhere the Triassic deposits fringe the Minas Basin and Cobequid Bay, forming low, rapidly retreating sea cliffs fronted by wide, wave-cut platforms and mud flats.

CLIMATE

The climate of the Triassic Lowlands is inland in character because of the shelter provided by North and South Mountains, but is modified at the Digby and the Minas Basin ends by marine influences. The main climatic features in this region are a warm early spring, hot summers with less precipitation than elsewhere, and a higher frequency of clear skies.

Winters are cold but not severe. The January mean daily temperature is –6°C, compared to –8°C in northern Nova Scotia, and –5°C in southern Nova Scotia. Mean daily temperatures rise above freezing in late March, with the warming trend moving west to east. Spring temperatures are warm, and by July the mean daily temperature is 18°C. Mean daily temperatures fall below freezing during the first week of December. The western end of the Region, under the influence of the Bay of Fundy, is slightly milder in winter and cooler in summer.

Total annual precipitation at the eastern end and extreme western end of the Region is less than 1200 mm. Towards the centre of the valley it is somewhat higher: between 1200 and 1400 mm. Snowfall is moderate, being more than 250 cm in the centre of the Region and along the north shore of Minas Basin, and decreasing westwards. The Digby area receives less than 150 cm. The snow-cover season lasts longer at the eastern end than at the western end by approximately thirty days.

Most of the Region is relatively protected by North Mountain from seasonal fog, mist, and low cloud of marine origin, making clear sunny days more frequent than in coastal areas.

This is the most favoured bioclimate in the province. The frost-free period and the growing season (145 and 195 days, respectively) are fairly long, with an accumulation of more than 2,400 growing-degree days. Summer precipitation at the eastern end of the Region is lower than elsewhere, and this, combined with the prevalence of coarse sandy soils, can lead to droughty conditions in some years. The warm temperatures and low elevations create a high potential for evapotranspiration and a mesothermal climate. Poor air drainage on the valley floor creates frost pockets.

FRESH WATER

Many streams and very few lakes are found in this Region. Numerous steep and shallow second- and third-order streams drain the surrounding higher elevations. Where they reach the lowlands, productivity is relatively high. Drainage in the Region is dendritic and parallel.

SOILS

The soil map reveals a complex mix of soil types in this Region. This is attributable to the variety of parent materials and to a range of glacial outwash and post-glacial marine deposition processes. The soft, red Triassic sandstones are easily eroded and have formed deep, coarse soils. Along the footslope of North Mountain the parent material often includes a mixture of basaltic rock. Along South Mountain the till is modified at the eastern end by grey and black slates and shales, and at the western end by granite. Most of the soils are well or excessively drained sands and sandy loams. Some limited areas of imperfectly drained soils have developed on finer water-deposited materials. At either end of the Annapolis Valley, and at the head of Cobequid Bay, extensive areas of salt marsh have been dyked. Small areas of organic soils are found scattered all along the valley floor and along the south shore of Minas Basin, but not along the north shore.

PLANTS

The Triassic Lowlands are part of Loucks' Red Spruce, Hemlock, Pine Zone in which Red Spruce and East-

ern Hemlock, now heavily cut, once attained their greatest prominence. This zone is in turn divided into two forest ecoregions. The Annapolis Valley is part of the ecoregion covering the western interior, in which coarse soils predominate and Red Oak is a common species. To the east, slightly heavier soils occur, and Red Maple replaces Red Oak as the successional species after fire.

The main factors influencing regional vegetation are the warm summers, well-drained soils, and extensive disturbances by cutting and fire. The remaining stands are mostly coniferous, but there were probably more deciduous trees on the valley floor before lumbering. The climate suits shade-tolerant species, but the precipitation is just high enough to give spruce and hemlock the advantage. The main species are Red Spruce, Eastern Hemlock, White Pine, Balsam Fir, with Red Oak in the western portion, and Black Spruce and Red Maple to the east. Extensive areas are cleared for agriculture, and oldfields are common, usually regenerating in White Spruce. Extensive Red and White pine stands grow on the sand plains in the centre of the Annapolis Valley, often in association with heath barrens. Dykeland and salt-marsh plant communities are found along the coast.

ANIMALS

This Region provides a wide range of terrestrial and aquatic habitats, including productive intertidal habitats. Terrestrial habitats include a diverse mix of open land and forested areas. The fauna of this Region includes a number of more southerly and opportunistic species often associated with agricultural areas (e.g., fox and skunk). The mud flats, salt marshes, dykelands, and estuaries are important breeding and staging areas for waterfowl and migratory shorebirds such as Semipalmated Sandpiper. Together with wet meadows, the salt marshes and dykelands are among the largest areas of suitable habitat in Nova Scotia for Arctic Shrew. Typical freshwater fishes include Atlantic Salmon, Brook Trout, and Creek Chub.

CULTURAL LANDSCAPES

The Triassic Lowlands attracted the first European settlement in Nova Scotia as the French were lured by fur trade with the Mi'kmaq, the exploitable fisheries, and imperial territorial claims. Acadians chose to dyke tidal marshes to create fertile farmlands rather than clear the forests. Thus the coastal landscape was dramatically transformed. The largest Acadian com-

**600
Triassic
Lowlands**

munity was located on the higher elevations near Grand Pré, and descendants of willow trees planted by the Acadians still stand. Both Mi'kmaq and Acadians weir-fished the river tributaries of Minas Basin and hunted the abundant waterfowl. After the 1755 Acadian deportation, successive waves of immigrants settled these fertile lands, continued to use the dykelands, and cleared valley forests to create prosperous farmlands.

Tidal-powered grist mills were established at Canning and Walton, but most grist mills were powered by river waterwheels. Numerous hydroelectric generating stations now harness waterways in this area. Today, the fertile soils of the Triassic Lowlands support the most productive farms in Nova Scotia. The advent of steamships in the nineteenth century facilitated the transport of produce overseas. The Annapolis valley's apple industry thrived during this period as produce was more likely to reach Britain in marketable condition. Railways and, later, truck transport increased other apple markets. Timber cut from forests of the Triassic Lowlands supplied local shipbuilding, furniture manufacturers, and export markets. In these primarily agricultural lands, forestry exploitation has always been economically important, and today, as in the past, many sawmills operate. Nova Scotia's first tourism ventures took place in the Annapolis Valley, attracting American tourists to the land of Longfellow's fictional "Evangeline" and her Grand Pré home. Today the Triassic Lowlands support many tourism and recreational activities, including bird-watching along the Fundy shores, where migrating flocks may be seen.

• • • • • • • •

**600
Triassic
Lowlands**

Associated Topics

T2.5 The Nova Scotian Desert, T2.6 The Triassic Basalts and Continental Rifting, T3.2 Ancient Drainage Patterns, T3.3 Glaciation, Deglaciation and Sea-level Changes, T5.2 Nova Scotia's Climate, T7.3 Coastal Landforms, T8.1 Freshwater Hydrology, T8.2 Freshwater Environments, T9.3 Biological Environment, T10.4 Plant Communities in Nova Scotia, T11.1 Factors Influencing Birds, T11.3 Open-habitat Birds, T11.5 Freshwater Wetland Birds and Waterfowl, T11.6 Shorebirds, T11.13 Freshwater Fishes.

Associated Habitats

H2.4 Mud Flat, H2.5 Tidal Marsh, H3.1 Freshwater Open-Water Lotic, H3.3 Freshwater Bottom Lotic, H3.5 Freshwater Water's Edge Lotic, H5.2 Oldfield, H5.3 Cliff and Bank, H6.2 Softwood Forest (Spruce, Hemlock, Pine Association; Pine Association).

610 VALLEY

GEOLOGY

The Annapolis Valley extends from the eastern end of St. Marys Bay in the west to the mouth of the Cornwallis River in the east. It is approximately 128 km long and 3–11 km wide.

Early Fluvian Erosion

The Valley has been carved out by river action and deepened by glacial scouring. When the sandstones were first exposed as the basalt wore away, rivers flowed at right angles across the valley. These rivers rose on South Mountain and flowed north across the present valley and North Mountain before discharging into the centre of a river which flowed down the Bay of Fundy. The sandstone wore away more quickly than the basalt, and when the ends of the Valley became open to the sea, the drainage was diverted to the west and east, leaving "wind" gaps across North Mountain, for example, the gap north of Melvern Square.

Sandstone is infrequently exposed within the Valley because it breaks down so readily to form a sandy soil. However, some sandstone can be seen on the slopes of South Mountain in the beds of rivers and resting upon older rocks. Outcrops of the overlying, younger Blomidon Formation that are adjacent to the basalt on the north side of the valley are covered by glacial deposits or scree slopes. At the ends of the valley, where marine erosion has removed the overburden, red cliffs can be seen: along the face of Cape Blomidon (where the lower slope exposes the Blomidon Formation); on the north shore of the Annapolis Basin at Thorne Cove and near Port Wade; and in the bluffs at Rossway. At Kingsport on the Minas Basin, excellent exposures of Triassic Wolfville sandstone occur. These contain fossil plant roots and occasional reptile bones. Because the sandstones lie underneath the basalt and dip northwards, no outcrops are found on the north shore of North Mountain.

Glacial Deposits

As the ice retreated after the last glaciation, the sea level rose and the land surface rebounded from its depressed position. In western Nova Scotia and the Bay of Fundy area, sea levels rose faster and encroached inland. The beaches, marine deltas, elevated shorelines, sand spits, and bars which formed at that time can now be seen raised well above sea level in many places along the Annapolis-Cornwallis Valley. The average elevation is 15–30 m above present sea level, but beaches are often found at different heights in the same vicinity. These, perhaps, have different ages or represent features established along a temporary shoreline as glacial water was impounded against the coast or in a basin. Raised beaches and terraces are best seen in Digby County at the mouths of rivers and around the lower part of the Annapolis Basin.

Glacial outwash deposits are also preserved in this area and near Kentville. Windblown sand, dunes, and loess, possibly from glacial outwash deposits, are found between Kingston and Greenwood. Kentville lies on the edge of the sand area.

Rising sea levels, during the past 4,000 years or so, drowned the lower reaches of the Annapolis and Cornwallis rivers. During this period, St. Marys Bay formed and the Annapolis Basin was flooded as the sea broke through the river-cut gap at Digby Gut.

FRESHWATER AND COASTAL AQUATIC ENVIRONMENTS

The Annapolis-Cornwallis Valley is drained by two main rivers separated by a secondary watershed divide. The Annapolis flows west and the Cornwallis flows east. Many first- and second-order streams drain in parallel and dentritic patterns off North and South Mountains to feed the Annapolis and Cornwallis. In the lower reaches of both systems, drainage becomes more complex with several tertiary watershed divides. Where the tide influences the rivers, large meanders form at high tide. The water can trickle down to a mere stream at low tide when tidal flats and muddy banks prevail, but these streams can resemble rushing torrents when a tidal bore enters the channels.

Large productive freshwater wetlands occur along both the Annapolis and Cornwallis rivers in their headwater areas between Kingston and Kentville. There are many bogs, swamps, and marshes, and many small areas of wet meadow.

The Annapolis and Cornwallis rivers have developed extensive tidal marshes in their lower reaches. The wide, fertile valley north and east of Kentville

610
Valley

that opens onto the Minas Basin was created by five rivers: the Gaspereau, Cornwallis, Canard, Habitant, and Pereaux. The floodplains of these meandering rivers are separated by low ridges and protected from tidal incursions only by the system of dykes originally built by the Acadian farmers, for example, near Port Williams. Grand Pré was probably once a meander in the Cornwallis River, with Long Island Head and Boot Island forming part of the northern bank of the floodplain. At some time, the river swung northwards to form a new meander between Starrs Point and Long Island Head, and the old meander silted up. Rising sea levels have now drowned the lower reaches of this river, forming a wide estuary west of Grand Pré.

SOILS

The soils in this Unit have formed on parent materials from various exposed geological strata, and on water-deposited materials. The finest textured strata are uppermost, and on this soft Triassic shale, well-drained soils of the Pelton series have developed on the footslopes of North Mountain. Coarser sandstones from the middle strata exposed on the Valley floor have produced the deep Woodville and Berwick sandy loams. The lowest strata exposed are a fine-grained conglomerate from which the Somerset series (a well-drained loamy sand) has developed. In the centre of the Valley is a complex, water-deposited series of sand flats. Associated well-drained soils are Canning, Cornwallis, and Nictaux, while Debert, Kingsport, and Lawrencetown soils are imperfectly to poorly drained. Alluvial Cumberland soils have developed beside streams and rivers, and imperfectly drained Fash soils have developed on lacustrine or marine clays in the central part of the Annapolis River drainage basin. Along the south slope are numerous beach terraces of slaty gravel origin from which Torbrook and Nictaux soils have developed. On the lower slopes, well-drained Morristown soils have formed from slaty parent materials, while Bridgetown soils have developed from a mixture of Carboniferous sandy loam till brought from the north, and locally weathered granite and quartzite. Organic soils are scattered through the Valley, the most notable example being the large Caribou peat bog located on the watershed divide between the Annapolis and Cornwallis river systems at Aylesford. Some of the Valley floor is wet because of effluent water. In these areas, water-loving vegetation such as alders and larch prevail.

PLANTS

The Annapolis Valley is most obviously an agricultural region. By the late nineteenth century, extensive clearing had restricted forests to more marginal sites. Now, however, large areas are reverting to forest growth. Apple orchards were originally located on the richer tills of the Valley slopes. Sugar Maple, American Beech, Red Spruce, and Eastern Hemlock are typical in later successional stands (H6.3); White Spruce, fir, and pine, with the shade-intolerant hardwoods maple and birch, are found on more recently disturbed sites. On the dry, sandy soils of the Valley floor, which are more prone to drought and frost, the maple, oak, birch association is common. Red Pine, White Pine, and Red Oak are found on the valley-bottom sand plain. Wire Birch, Red Maple, Red Oak, White Birch, and poplar are common post-fire species. Oldfields usually regenerate in White Spruce, except where wetter conditions favour alder and Black Spruce. Black Spruce and larch are the species found in depressional areas or on poorly drained soils.

Non-forest plant communities are very conspicuous in this Unit and include those found in dykelands, oldfields, tidal marshes, and floodplains. Scattered Alleghanian floral habitat is found throughout the Valley.

ANIMALS

Wildlife habitats in this Unit are diverse and include agricultural lands, orchards, oldfields, woodlands, and heathlands. Freshwater habitats include only a few lakes but many slow, meandering streams and rivers. Because of the high Fundy tides, coastal habitats consist mainly of extensive intertidal areas—salt marshes and mud flats—and associated dykelands.

Mammals often associated with agricultural areas include a large raccoon population, Red Fox, woodchuck, and increasing numbers of skunk. Muskrat and mink are common. The avifauna also reflects the agricultural character, which provides good habitat for pheasant, snipe, woodcock, and hawks. The crow population is high, and the Valley provides wintering habitat for the Bald Eagle. The dykelands provide good habitat for Gray Partridge (declining) and Short-eared Owl.

The west end of the Minas Basin and the Avon River estuary are nationally important because they support high numbers of shorebirds and waterfowl. Shorebird numbers peak in late summer and early fall, and important sites include Kingsport, Pereaux, and Evangeline beaches. Waterfowl include Black

Duck, Canada Goose, Brant, and teal. Boot Island provides nesting areas for gulls, herons, and cormorants and is a crow roost in winter.

At the other end of the Valley, the Annapolis Basin and the Annapolis River are important because they provide migration habitat for concentrations of waterfowl in spring and fall, and because a moderate number of duck remain through the winter. At the head of St. Marys Bay, high numbers of shorebirds occur, primarily in August. Anadromous fish such as American Shad and Atlantic Salmon pass through the Annapolis River estuary to spawn in fresh water further upstream. Striped Bass are also present but do not manage to spawn upstream.

SCENIC QUALITY

Inland portions of the Annapolis-Cornwallis Valley have moderately high scenic value. The most striking scenic feature is the prominent North Mountain escarpment, which provides a uniform and die-straight edge to the Valley. The South Mountain, though rising to a similar elevation, is much less dramatic and often not visible from the Valley floor. The District rates well in terms of landcover, since most sections have an aesthetically favourable mix of farmland and woodland. At the extremities of the Valley, the Annapolis and Minas basins add interest and even splendour to the visual scene. The Annapolis Basin fills the Valley's trough and is connected to the Bay of Fundy by the faultline cleft of Digby Gut. The Minas Basin has distinctive expanses of red mud at low tide,

Plate 6: Region 600. View from Blomidon Look-off at the east end of the Annapolis Valley (District 610) showing an agricultural landscape of cleared forest land and reclaimed tidal marsh. Photo: A. Wilson.

set against the red cliffs of Cape Blomidon, and its shores have been fashioned into rich dykelands by both Acadians and Planters. Panoramic views of the area are provided from the adjacent hills (see Plate 6).

CULTURAL LANDSCAPES

The resource potential of the Valley's land and wildlife have long shaped human settlement patterns here. In 1604 the French established a post at Port Royal, laying territorial claims to the New World, with the fur trade and fishery serving as economic catalysts for their interest in Acadia. Good relations between the Mi'kmaq and the French secured trade relations and political alliances. Acadians soon migrated to other areas outside the vicinity of Port Royal and began dyking tidal marshlands along the Minas Basin, with the largest Acadian settlement at Grand Pré. Thus the coastline underwent radical change as dyke building transformed these estuarine salt-marshes into fertile agricultural lands. With their own food needs met, Acadians traded surplus grain to the Boston States before their own deportation by the British in 1755—an act which a century later would serve as subject matter for one of America's most celebrated poets. Longfellow's poem "Evangeline," published in 1847, was immensely popular for a hundred years. Many Americans travelled here in search of Evangeline's mythical Acadian paradise, attracted in part by the promotion of the Dominion Atlantic Railway, which transported tourists from the Yarmouth Steamship to Grand Pré on its "Land of Evangeline" route, one of the first tourism ventures in the province. Today the Grand Pré National Historic Site commemorates Acadian history. As well, the Annapolis Royal Historical Gardens features a replica of an eighteenth-century Acadian house and garden, and a stand of Elephant Grass, a circumboreal plant species that the Acadians grew in Nova Scotia for use as roof-thatching material.

The first apple trees in Nova Scotia were planted by the French at the beginning of the seventeenth century. By 1698 a French census showed 1,584 apple trees distributed among 54 Acadian families at Port Royal alone. The fertile Acadian farmlands and orchards vacated by the deportation were inherited by successive waves of settlers. First came the New England Planters, then the Loyalists, and others followed. Tidal mills to grind grain or saw lumber were established at various points around the Minas Basin; an 1845 record indicates a tidal mill around Canning. Today, the Annapolis Tidal Power Station on the Annapolis River is one of the first such plants in the world and generates 20 MW of electricity for 12,500

homes. However, it has also changed river currents, caused river erosion upstream, and detrimentally affected some fish populations. Hydroelectric generating stations have harnessed the power of waterways at Lequille, Paradise, Nictaux, Hells Gate, Lumsden Lake, Hollow Bridge, and Methals. Mixed farming characterizes much of Valley land use, including the highest production of hay, tree fruits, vegetables, beef cattle, hogs, and chickens in the province. As a consequence, many secondary industries related to agriculture, such as processing and packing, are established here. In Aylesford, a peat-harvesting operation marks the first commercial exploitation of peat in the province. Several sand and gravel deposits in the valley are exploited by large commercial producers. In some areas, such as Del haven, fishing takes place. Bay of Fundy stopovers during annual bird migrations attract bird-watchers to many areas, particularly Evangeline Beach, Wolfville Sewage Ponds and Canard Pond.

• • • • • • • •

Sites of Special Interest

- North of Melvern Square—wind gap
- Cape Blomidon—red sandstone underneath basalt
- Thorne Cove, Port Wade, Rossway—red cliffs and bluffs
- Annapolis Basin—gravel terraces at river mouths; for example, east of the mouth of Bear River are sands (Torbrook soils) 30 m above sea level
- Smiths Cove—point covered with fine sand, 30 m above sea level
- North of Digby—obscure beach deposit 27–30 m above sea level
- Deep Cove—gravel deposits 42 m above sea level
- Upper Granville—U-shaped sand bar
- North of Wolfville—raised beaches
- Woodside—series of sandy mounds extend for 4 km near Pereau River, 25 m above sea level; the easterly ones are curved like a spit
- West end of Kentville—small lake amongst sand hills is a kettle hole surrounded by kames
- Kingston to Greenwood—kames and esker-like ridges
- Avonport Mountain—view from highway across valley
- Kingsport—excellent exposures of Triassic sandstone with fossil plant roots and rare dinosaur bones and tracks

- Kentville Ravine (IBP Proposed Ecological Site 64)—old-growth hemlock stand, and river floodplain with rich herbaceous flora
- National Wildlife Area—Boot Island
- Provincial Wildlife Management Areas—Dewey Creek, Minas Basin
- Kentville Migratory Bird Sanctuary
- Aylesford Bog (Caribou Bog)
- Near Kingston—sand barrens

Provincial Parks and Park Reserves
- Upper Clements
- Upper Clements West
- Clairmont
- Coldbrook
- Joggins Bridge

Scenic Viewpoints
- The Lookoff (panoramic view looking south over District 610)
- Grand Pré National Historic Park (views over dykeland towards Cape Blomidon)
- Kentville Agricultural Research Station (Elderkin Brook trail)
- Fort Anne National Historic Park, Annapolis Royal
- Digby (views of Annapolis Basin)
- Smiths Cove (views of Annapolis Basin)

Associated Offshore Units
912 Outer Fundy, 913a Minas Basin.

Associated Topics
T2.6 The Triassic Basalts and Continental Rifting, T3.4 Terrestrial Glacial Deposits and Landscape Features, T4.2 Post-glacial Colonization by Plants, T6.4 Estuaries, T8.1 Freshwater Hydrology, T9.2 Soil Classification, T10.2 Successional Trends in Vegetation, T11.2 Forest and Edge-habitat Birds, T11.3 Open-habitat Birds, T11.4 Birds of Prey, T11.13 Freshwater Fishes.

Associated Habitats
H2.3 Sandy Shore, H2.4 Mud Flat, H2.5 Tidal Marsh, H3.1 Open-Water Lotic, H3.3 Bottom Lotic, H3.5 Water's Edge Lotic, H4.1 Bog, H4.3 Swamp, H4.4 Freshwater Marsh, H5.2 Oldfield, H6.1 Hardwood Forest (Maple, Oak, Birch Association), H6.2 Softwood Forest (White Spruce Association).

610
Valley

620 TIDAL BAY

GEOLOGY AND LANDSCAPE DEVELOPMENT

Minas Basin and Cobequid Bay were carved out by rivers which eroded eastwards from the Bay of Fundy, cutting a channel along the Minas Passage Fault between Cape Split and Cape Sharp. The shape and profile of the entire Bay of Fundy was greatly affected by repeated glaciations during the Pleistocene. The floor is smooth and striated like a glacial pavement and covered by a mantle of loose material up to 10 m thick, some of which is glacial till. At the entrance to Cobequid Bay is a glacially scoured trough.

Around Cobequid Bay the Triassic red beds are nearly horizontal and form a low area with gentle undulations (see Figure 23). On the north side of Cobequid Bay, they attain their greatest width but then end abruptly at the Portapique Mountain Fault. The Triassic block has dropped down on the south side of this fault and now lies against older Carboniferous strata. West and east of Truro, Triassic deposits lie unconformably against Carboniferous Horton strata. In both areas the Carboniferous strata are harder and form low rolling hills. The boundary with the flat red beds is generally very distinct.

The Shubenacadie and Salmon rivers, which flow into Cobequid Bay, have drowned estuaries and buried river channels beneath the riverbed deposits. In the Truro area the incised channels of North River

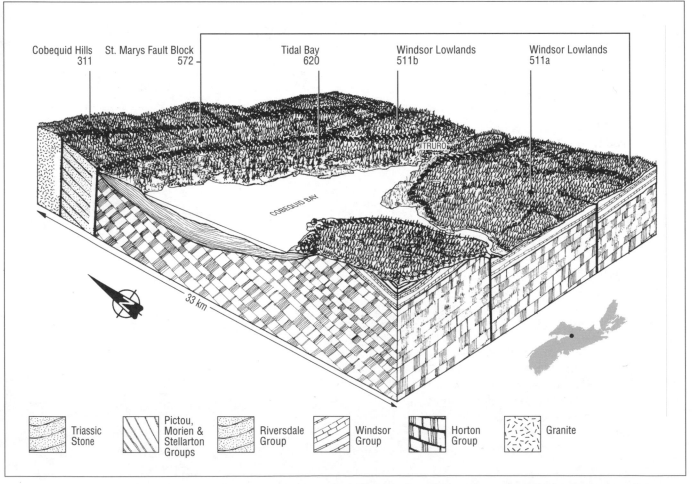

Figure 23: Cobequid Bay area. Very soft, red Triassic sandstones fringing Cobequid Bay (District 620) are surrounded by the somewhat more elevated and resistant Carboniferous rocks of the Windsor Lowlands (Unit 511). A westerly extension of the St. Marys Fault Block (Unit 572) forms a dissected shoulder to the Cobequid Hills (Unit 311), from which short, steep rivers drain into the bay.

and Salmon River can be traced for 6 km and 8 km, respectively. They merge under the town and continue out to the Cobequid Bay, deepening to 40 m and narrowing to one kilometre, following the same course as the present river. These channels, cut in the sandstone bedrock, are filled with fluvioglacial outwash sands and gravels from the end of the last glacial period, about 10,000 years ago.

Much of the Triassic Lowlands from Truro to the north side of Cobequid Bay are covered by glacial deposits. The Truro sub-basin is filled with outwash sands and gravels carried from the north and east that form a plain elevated to 18 m above sea level; this plain is now dissected by streams. On the north side of Cobequid Bay, outwash deposits can be seen in the terraces of rivers. At Glenholme the underlying Triassic sandstone is exposed where the gravels have been washed away.

As sea levels continue to rise, the soft coastal red beds are being eroded rapidly, adding enormous volumes of sediment to the waters of the bay. This sediment is washed up and down the rivers with the tide, and some is deposited in the estuaries as sand bars; for example, in the Avon and Shubenacadie river estuaries.

As the coastline retreats, coastal marshes are also being eroded. In some cases the remains of fossil forests of beech, pine, Black Spruce, and larch are exposed. These trees were buried by bluish marine clay when the combined effects of rising sea levels and increasing tidal ranges brought salt water further up low-lying river valleys and over coastal lowlands. Once exposed to tidal action, the fossil stumps are quickly destroyed; however, new ones are continuously being exhumed. The rapid coastal erosion has created a wave-cut platform 100–300 m wide that borders the shore. This platform is commonly backed by low cliffs.

FRESH WATER

The drainage pattern across the Triassic Lowlands in the Cobequid Bay area is broadly dendritic, with the rivers reaching the bay through drowned estuaries. The District is dissected by four secondary drainage divides. Along the north shore the streams flow steeply down off the Cobequids (Unit 311), forming numerous parallel tertiary watersheds, and are second- or third-order streams by the time they reach the lower elevation of District 620. Short, isolated first-order streams flow directly into Cobequid Bay along the south shore. Major rivers (such as the Shubenacadie, Salmon, Chiganois, and North) and several smaller streams influence seawater chemistry in the estuary at the head of Cobequid Bay.

There are many tidal marshes in the estuary and scattered along the coastline, concentrated in inlets and the mouths of rivers.

SOILS

Hantsport clay loams occur along the narrow strip on the south shore of the Minas Basin. On the western side they are well drained but have imperfectly to poorly drained associates to the east. Around the town of Truro, well-drained Truro soils have developed from the red sandstone, with poorly drained associates covering approximately one-third of the area. Gravelly sandy loams of the Harmony series have also formed in this area over gravelly, sandy clay loams. Coarse Hebert soils on outwash sands, and finer-textured Cumberland and Stewiacke soils on alluvial materials, are found along streams and rivers. Large areas of Acadia soils have formed on dykelands at the head of Cobequid Bay.

PLANTS

This Unit is extensively farmed but differs from District 610 mainly in the presence of heavier soils. Pine is therefore not as dominant a feature of the vegetation. Scattered Sugar Maple, American Beech, and Yellow Birch occur locally on low ridges, but spruce, fir, White Birch, Red Maple, Eastern Hemlock, and White Pine form relatively stable forests on other sites. Red Maple and Wire Birch replace Red Oak as post-fire species. White Spruce, Red Spruce, and Balsam Fir are the usual invaders of oldfields. Heathlands with Jack Pine are found in the Debert area, and the Minas Basin is fringed with areas of salt marsh. Rich intervale sites in the Truro area support Alleghanian floral species.

ANIMALS

This District provides a mix of forested and open land and intertidal habitats occupied by a fauna similar to that described in District 610. The south coast of Minas Basin and Cobequid Bay is regionally important because of the significant concentrations of shorebirds in late summer and early fall, and the moderate numbers of waterfowl. The north shore of Cobequid Bay is also visited by several thousand shorebirds in August and September, and by waterfowl in spring and fall—mostly Black Duck with some Canada Geese. The provincial waterfowl sanctuary near Debert has a unique population of American Wigeon and several hundred geese use this wetland in the fall. A small population of Gray

620
Tidal
Bay

Partridge occurs in open dykeland and coastal farmland. Freshwater fishes include Creek Chub and Brook Trout. Anadromous species, such as Atlantic Salmon, Atlantic Sturgeon, American Shad, Striped Bass, and Rainbow Smelt, occur in Cobequid Bay. In order to spawn, many thousands of shad enter the Shubenacadie River, and Atlantic Salmon enter most Cobequid Bay rivers.

SCENIC QUALITY

This area shares many of the Valley's scenic characteristics: it is a narrow and elongated farming region based originally on dyking of tidal marshlands. The water element, however, is more visually prominent (as the District forms a narrow fringe around Cobequid Bay) and relief is more muted. With the exception of the stretch west of Economy, there is no dramatic escarpment to mark the northern edge of the District; rather the land rises gently to the slightly more elevated Carboniferous Lowlands. From the southern side of Cobequid Bay, however, the Cobequid Hills provide a distant backdrop to a northward view.

CULTURAL LANDSCAPES

An excavation at Debert uncovered an important Paleo-Indian campsite estimated to be 11,000 years old. Artifacts indicated that these early peoples hunted Woodland Caribou that had migrated northward after the retreat of the glaciers. In the seventeenth century, Acadians first settled in tidal-bay marshland areas that could be dyked to create fertile farmlands. After their 1755 deportation, Planters, Loyalists, and others settled much of this land, with an important farming area established around Truro. Today, farmlands here support the highest concentration of dairy cows in Nova Scotia. Timber supplied a thriving shipbuilding industry in the late 1800s, aspects of which are documented at Maitland's Lawrence House Museum, the home of shipbuilder and designer W.D. Lawrence. Hardwoods from the Cobequid Hills supply lumber to the Bass River Furniture Company. A large barite deposit near Walton was mined for 30 years, closing in 1971. Walton was also the site of an early tidal mill, where water power was used to grind grain or saw lumber. In the 1970s the tidal bay was seen as a candidate site for a large tidal power project. Peat is now exploited in the tidal bay area for the horticulture market.

- - - - - - - -

Sites of Special Interest

- Walton (Whale Cove)—Triassic sandstones (Wolfville Formation) unconformably overlie the vertical Horton red siltstones exposed at low tide
- Route 215 between Maitland and Cambridge—road follows the boundary between the low Triassic coastal fringe and the adjacent rolling Carboniferous hills
- Inner Minas Basin shoreline—coastal sections of Triassic sandstone with plant fossils and bones of early dinosaurs
- Salter Head, Maitland—low sandstone cliffs fronted by a wave-cut platform and large sand bars in the estuary of the Shubenacadie River
- Selma—large sand bar
- Victoria Park, Truro—a river gorge carved during Triassic times in the Carboniferous Horton Group and now being exhumed by Lepper Brook; under the bridge in the park is an angular unconformity between the Horton Group and the younger Wolfville Formation
- Glenholme—glacial gravel overlying Triassic sandstone in the river terrace
- Debert Wildlife Management Area

Provincial Parks and Park Reserves

- McElmons Pond
- Anthony

Scenic Viewpoints

- Highway 215, east of Selma (view over Cobequid Bay)
- Burntcoat loop
- Highway 2, Economy to Lower Economy

Associated Offshore Unit

913a Minas Basin.

Associated Topics

T2.6 The Triassic Basalts and Continental Rifting, T3.3 Glaciation, Deglaciation and Sea-level Changes, T6.4 Estuaries, T7.1 Modifying Forces, T11.5 Freshwater Wetland Birds and Waterfowl, T11.6 Shorebirds, T11.13 Freshwater Fishes.

Associated Habitats

H2.4 Mud Flat, H2.5 Tidal Marsh, H6.1 Hardwood Forest (Sugar Maple, Yellow Birch, Beech Association), H6.3 Mixedwood Forest (Spruce, Fir, Pine–Maple, Birch Association).

700
Fundy Coast

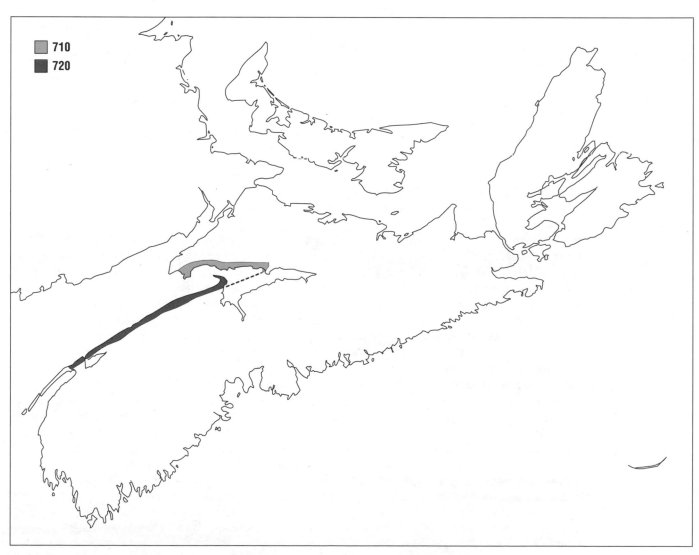

710
720

Figure 24: Region 700, Fundy Coast, and its component Districts.

700 FUNDY COAST

The Fundy Coast Region has two Districts:
710 Basalt Headlands
720 Basalt Ridge

REGIONAL CHARACTERISTICS

In the central sections of the Bay of Fundy, the coastal zone is protected from the extreme climatic conditions of the Atlantic Coast. Cape Blomidon on the south coast and Economy Mountain on the north mark the inland limits of this oceanic influence. The Fundy Coast is a climatic and vegetation transition zone dominated by basaltic rocks. Coastal sediments are locally abundant, forming small areas of salt marsh, gravel beaches, and mud flats. Wide intertidal platforms have been eroded in both basaltic and sedimentary rocks, giving a wide variety of coastal habitats.

GEOLOGY AND LANDSCAPE DEVELOPMENT

About 200 million years ago the Atlantic Ocean began to form as the continents drifted apart. The gently sloping, sandy arid plain between the Cobequid Hills and South Mountain sank down as the spreading continued. Tensions created by this movement opened rifts in the plain from which basaltic lavas welled up to spread over the sands and gravels. Faulting continued after the lavas had cooled, causing fractures, tilting, and offsets in the basalt.

Basalt occurred as far east as Portapique and is still preserved in four downfaulted blocks inland of Economy Point. From Gerrish Mountain west, on the north side of Minas Basin, a series of faulted basalt blocks form headlands with vertical cliffs. Inland, sandstone cliffs have been protected by basalt caps. South of Minas Channel, the basalt lava flows have formed the continuous ridge of North Mountain. High, continuous vertical cliffs are found on the outer side of this escarpment, on the coast from Cape Split to Cape Blomidon, and inland from Cape Blomidon to the Annapolis Basin.

Vertical or columnar jointing in the basalt makes it susceptible to erosion. Wide intertidal platforms have been cut at the base of the basalt, and even wider platforms have been cut in the sandstone bays of the northern shore. Erosion around the margins of the Bay of Fundy is still proceeding very rapidly.

During the glacial period the Bay of Fundy was deeply scoured by ice and then thickly covered by glacial debris. From 12,000 to 6,000 years ago the sea was probably excluded from the Bay. Before this time the sea had covered the Bay and adjacent land areas up to the ice front, forming beach deposits. These old beaches are the "raised beaches" found throughout this Region, up to 40 m above present sea level. Then, as the ice load was removed, the land began to rebound more rapidly than sea level rose and the Bay floor was exposed. During this period (12,000 to 6,000 years ago) the rivers flowing into the Bay incised their valleys down to the new base level.

When the last inundation by the sea began 6,000 years ago, the conditions for increased tidal amplitude were created by the shape of the Bay. Subsidence of the land and a slowly rising sea level worldwide have caused recently measured sea-level increases of 40 cm per century in the outer reaches of the Fundy coast. Rapid erosion of the soft rocks has been accelerated by this rise of relative sea level. Wide intertidal platforms, salt marshes, submerged forests, and freshwater marshes have formed, and large intertidal sand bodies have built up.

CLIMATE

Waters in the Bay of Fundy profoundly affect the climate of the adjacent coasts. Extreme tidal-induced turbulence prevents the coastal waters from freezing and, more important, prevents warming of the surface layers in summer. By late summer, surface coastal water in the Bay of Fundy is cooler than any other surface water off Nova Scotia's coasts, never exceeding about 12°C. This same water, after crossing sun-exposed intertidal sands, may reach 20°C or more.

Moist summer air masses result in thick fogs over the Bay of Fundy. These fogs commonly extend to the crest of North Mountain before being dissipated by the heat of the land. Although the climate is similar to that of the Atlantic Coast in temperature (moderated with low ranges of temperature) there is less exposure to winds (except on some cliffed headlands) and salt spray from ocean swells.

East of the Minas Channel, surface waters are considerably warmer, summer fogs are much less frequent, and coastal climates resemble a modified

Annapolis Valley temperature and precipitation regime. The climatic boundary is closely approximated by the eastward limit of basaltic rocks.

FRESH WATER

There are very few lakes, but many shallow, fast-flowing streams drain into the Minas Channel and Bay of Fundy.

SOILS

Coarse-textured soils, somewhat richer in nutrients than is usual among Nova Scotia's podzols and luvisols, are found on the basaltic rocks of the Fundy Coast. Glenmont and Rossway soils are better supplied with calcium and magnesium than other soils but are low in available phosphorous. This simple pattern of soil formation on the North Mountain Basalt Ridge (District 720) is complicated only by patches of reddish glacial till, carried south from the floor of the Bay of Fundy, on which fine-textured Wolfville soils have developed.

By contrast, the Basalt Headlands (District 710) on the north Fundy Coast has a great variety of soils developed from basalt, sandstone, shale, and extensive glacial outwash sands and gravels reworked by higher post-glacial sea levels.

PLANTS

The Fundy Coast Region shows evidence of being a climatic transition zone between a more-inland type of regional vegetation and the true coastal forest, although the coastal influence is still strong. Red Spruce is abundant here (but is not found in the Atlantic Coast Region). American Beech and Sugar Maple are found here at higher elevations.

On exposed basalt cliffs, arctic-alpine plant communities are found, containing some plants with a boreal distribution. Cliff-top forests are of the true dense coastal-forest type but change within a few metres to a more open hardwood forest with a rich herbaceous understory.

Coastal waters support sometimes dense growths of marine algae where sediment content is low. Where sedimentary rocks outcrop at the coast, turbidity is high and species diversity is severely restricted.

ANIMALS

Deer populations are large, particularly in the Basalt Headlands District where they spend their winters.

Richer soils in the basaltic rock areas support diverse woodland soil fauna. At the coast, marine algae and nutrient-rich waters support a variety of marine animals.

CULTURAL ENVIRONMENT

Mi'kmaq legends surround areas of the Fundy Coast, explaining the origins of geographical features such as the Five Islands. Bay of Fundy fisheries provide an economic base for many communities. Weir-fishing and commercial clamdigging are particularly distinctive to this Region. Since the nineteenth century, small-scale farming and forest exploitation have been characteristic land uses. During the nineteenth century, several tidal-powered grist mills were in operation. Timber continues to supply sawmills. Fossil-bearing cliffs, where dinosaur remains have been excavated, are sites of immense interest to scientists and fossil enthusiasts. Rockhounds are also attracted by the presence of agates and amethyst in coastal cliffs of this Region. Impressive coastal scenery, hiking trails, and parks attract recreation and tourism to the Fundy Coast.

• • • • • • • •

Associated Topics
T2.2 The Avalon and Meguma Zones, T2.6 The Triassic Basalts and Continental Rifting, T3.3 Glaciation, Deglaciation and Sea-level Changes, T7.1 Modifying Forces, T9.1 Soil-forming Factors, T10.4 Plant Communities in Nova Scotia, T11.10 Ungulates, T11.16 Land and Freshwater Invertebrates.

Associated Habitats
H2 Coastal, H6.3 Mixedwood Forest (Spruce, Fir, Pine–Maple, Birch Association; White Spruce, Fir–Maple, Birch Association).

**700
Fundy
Coast**

710 BASALT HEADLANDS

GEOLOGY AND LANDSCAPE DEVELOPMENT

This District extends from Economy to Cape Chignecto along the northern shore of the Minas Basin. The geology and landscape are varied and interesting. Parallel faults and juxtaposed resistant basalts and erodable sandstones create a varied landscape of hills and lowlands, bays, cliffs, and headlands (see Figure 5).

The area has been cut by three major faults into a series of slices which have minor faults within them. At the base of the Cobequids, the east-west trending Cobequid Fault forms the northern boundary of the District and sets Carboniferous strata against the ridge of the Cobequid Hills (Unit 311). Here they form a line of hills from Cape Spencer to the eastern border of the District and beyond. Cliffs have formed along Greville Bay where these strata reach the coast. Further south, the Portapique Mountain Fault (which extends eastwards from Partridge Island) has brought younger erodable Triassic sandstone and resistant basalt into contact with Carboniferous deposits. Within this block, a smaller east-west fault, the Gerrish Mountain Fault, and other small crosscutting faults further divide the bedrock into small blocks. These have shifted vertically and in some cases have tilted.

From Economy to Partridge Island the hilly landscape reflects the contrasting resistance to erosion of basalt and Triassic sandstones. The sandstone is very soft and normally forms lowlands. However, where it is capped by basalt, it forms high, steep-sided hills, for example, Portapique Mountain (150 m), an unnamed hill north of Lower Economy (180 m), Economy Mountain (245 m), and Spencers Island (150 m). The high sandstone cliffs at Five Islands Park and on the islands themselves result from the protective effect of basalt. Some of the high basalt-capped blocks have cliffs with columnar jointing; for example, Partridge Island, Cape Sharp, and Spencers Island. Semiprecious stones are found in the amygdaloidal basalts at Partridge Island.

Exposed Triassic sandstone is easily eroded. At Lower Economy a tidal platform more than one mile wide has been cut by wave attack on the coastal exposures of these rocks. The low Triassic area immediately north of Cape d'Or will presumably eventually be removed completely, leaving the basalt-capped sediments as stacks, similar to Five Islands and Isle Haute (in Unit 810).

Near the village of Parrsboro, younger Jurassic sediments which lie on top of the basalt are known to contain dinosaur bones and footprints.

Large glacial outwash deposits are common along the Parrsboro shore. The town of Advocate is built upon an outwash plain. The harbour is enclosed by a bar and cobble beaches derived from gravels eroded from the outwash deposits. In immediate post-glacial time, about 13,000 years ago, a higher sea level created beaches on the hillside north of the present village. These raised beaches are remarkably similar to those in the present Advocate Harbour. At Parrsboro and throughout the District a nearly horizontal wave-cut surface can be seen on the glacial outwash gravels. This surface, eroded at the same time as the Advocate raised beach was being formed, gradually descends eastwards. The sloping nature of the former shoreline is conclusive evidence of differential recovery of the coast since the last glaciation and, hence, of differential crustal loading during the glaciation.

FRESH WATER

District 710 falls within two secondary watersheds that divide into numerous tertiary drainage areas and direct shoreline drainage into the Minas Channel and Basin. Streams draining this District tend to be straight and fast-flowing, with narrow, steep-sided valleys. There are many waterfalls. The mouths of the Parrsboro and Diligent rivers occur here. Many small bogs and shrub swamps are scattered throughout.

SOILS

The principal soils in this area are the Kirkhill and Diligence series. Both are developed on tills from shale of the Riversdale Group. However, Diligence shales are softer and produce clay loam soils, while Kirkhill shales produce shale loam soils. Other soils in the area have formed from extensive deposits of gravel laid down as glacial and post-glacial outwash plains. These soils are mapped as Hebert gravelly loams.

PLANTS

The coastal forest is somewhat modified because the climate moves through a transition from maritime to continental. Spruce, Eastern Hemlock, and pine forests with shade-intolerant birches, maple and aspen are found here, together with the more common spruce, fir and pine forest. Pure stands of pioneer White Spruce are found on oldfields. Blueberry fields are scattered on former farmlands in lowlands and sometimes far up the slopes. The exposed cliffs at Cape d'Or provide habitat for locally rare arctic-alpine plant species.

Some small salt marshes are found along the shore, but there is generally no Eelgrass. As turbidity of coastal waters diminishes westwards, seaweeds increase, for example Laverbread.

ANIMALS

The shore provides wintering habitat for deer coming down from the Cobequid Hills. Deer winter in softwood areas and in spring are often seen in fields. In winter the coastal waters remain open and there is less accumulation of broken ice than is found further up the Bay of Fundy. Black Duck winter at Advocate Harbour and Parrsboro Harbour, and small numbers of other waterfowl species such as Common Goldeneye and Bufflehead are sighted along this coast during the winter.

Pinnacle Island at Five Islands and Spencers Island provide breeding areas for Double-crested Cormorant, Common Eider, Great Blue Heron, Herring Gull, and Black-backed Gull. Black Guillemot nest at Spencers Island. There are a few other breeding sites for gulls and cormorants.

In summer, large flocks of mostly male Common Eider are observed along the coast. Scoters and second-year loons are also seen. Cape d'Or and Five Islands have been release sites for a Peregrine Falcon reintroduction program. Blomidon is another release site (District 720). Bald Eagle nest near Five Islands.

The tidal flats and salt marshes at Advocate Harbour attract some migratory shorebirds, but not the

Plate 7: Region 700. View of the coastal landscape from Cape d'Or lighthouse (District 710) showing basalt cliffs topped by coastal spruce forest. Photo: R. Lloyd.

huge numbers found in the larger mud-flat areas of the Bay of Fundy. Smaller numbers of varied species are seen, for example, Ruddy Turnstone and Black-bellied Plover. Willet and Sharp-tailed Sparrow are also seen, and Vesper Sparrow occurs in blueberry fields.

The shoreline is mostly gravel with considerable silt. The marine fauna is characteristic of rocky, cobbly, and muddy shores but with limited diversity because of the silty water. Shells of Slipper Limpets, sponges, and Hornwrack are commonly found washed ashore.

SCENIC QUALITY

The varied relief of this District allows a frequently changing scene. Basalt-capped hills jut out into the bay as cliff-lined headlands (and sometimes as islands). Behind them, a band of lowland is backed inland by the fault scarp of the Cobequid Hills. Panoramas across the bay are seen at some points (see Plate 7), while at others one finds intimate scenes along small inland valleys (e.g., along the Diligent and Parrsboro rivers). Settlement is light, but sufficient to create interest. Overall, this small District is one of the most scenic in mainland Nova Scotia.

CULTURAL LANDSCAPES

At the beginning of the seventeenth century, Champlain reported the presence of native copper on this shoreline. As a result he called this site "Cap des Mines," referring to an attempt to mine copper. Later it became known by the French as Cape d'Or (Golden Cape), even though copper is the principal mineral found here. Many interesting legends surround the great cliffs, beaches, and masses of rocks at Five Islands. According to one, these islands were great pieces of earth which Kluskap (Glooscap), the divine warrior, threw in a rage at his ancient enemy, the beaver. Fishing has always been economically important to communities on the Basalt Headlands. In the distinctive weir-fishing methods of this area, fish are trapped in walled nets with the rise and fall of the Fundy tide. A fleet of small boats works out of Advocate Harbour mainly for scallop, lobster, and Winter Flounder. Clamdigging has been commercially important here, but overexploitation led to the development of clamdigging regulations in 1993. Kelp is picked at extreme low tide near Cape d'Or. In the nineteenth century, communities on the Basalt Headlands were well known for shipbuilding, using local timber. Forestry and farming have been characteristic land uses. Fossil-bearing cliffs are distinctive

in this area, and fossil finds on the Basalt Headlands include some of the earliest dinosaurs.

• • • • • • • •

Sites of Special Interest

- Parrsboro Shore, Five Islands to West Bay—long coastal section of basalt lavas and sediments across the Triassic-Jurassic boundary, fossils include fishes, and bones and trackways of dinosaurs and other reptiles; the site is protected under the Special Places Protection Act
- Cape d'Or (IBP Proposed Ecological Site 1)— windswept headland providing arctic-alpine habitat; plants include two species of Milk-vetch
- Moose River (IBP Proposed Ecological Site 7)— mature Red Spruce forest
- Economy Mountain Lookoff—to north and west, the steep escarpment of Cobequid Fault; in the foreground, low-lying Carboniferous and Triassic sediments
- Moose Island—agate and basalt sea stacks
- Partridge Island—semiprecious minerals
- West Bay—angular unconformity; fossil rain prints, ripple marks, mud cracks, channel
- Advocate—raised beaches 35 m above high water; spit across harbour
- Isle Haute—an island of Jurrasic basalt is clearly visible from Cape d'Or; included in Unit 810 because of its open coastal character, with White Spruce forests, even though the main part of the Unit is some distance away on Digby Neck; the fauna is poorly known but includes nesting Common Eider and Black Guillemot
- Wasson Bluff—important exposed Triassic-Jurassic boundary with trackways and fossils, including those of early dinosaurs and other reptiles; site protected under the Special Places Protection Act; information available at the Fundy Geological Museum at Parrsboro

Provincial Parks and Park Reserves

- Five Islands Provincial Park—dinosaur bones and footprints below park; geological and estuary interpretation trails

Scenic Viewpoints

- Economy Mountain Lookoff (view northwards)
- Five Islands Provincial Park (view west to Five Islands)
- Clarke Head Trail
- Highway 209, Greville Bay shore
- Cape d'Or Trail

Associated Offshore Units
912 Outer Fundy, 913a Minas Basin.

Associated Topics
T2.6 The Triassic Basalts and Contintental Rifting, T3.4 Terrestrial Glacial Deposits and Landscape Features, T4.2 Post-glacial Colonization by Plants, T11.6 Shorebirds.

Associated Habitats
H2 Coastal, H5.3 Cliff and Bank, H6.2 Softwood Forest (Spruce, Hemlock, Pine Association).

**710
Basalt
Headlands**

720 BASALT RIDGE

Jurassic basalt lava flows above soft sedimentary rocks form a ridge with a steep south-facing escarpment and a shallower north-facing dip-slope (see Figure 25). Cliffs of columnar basalt rise from wide wave-cut platforms along the Fundy shore. Semiprecious minerals occur within the basalt. The coastal forest gives way to hardwoods at higher elevations. Diverse and interesting rocky shore fauna are present on the Fundy coast, and relict arctic-alpine flora are found at Cape Split.

GEOLOGY AND LANDSCAPE DEVELOPMENT

On the southern side of the Bay of Fundy lies a steep-sided ridge (cuesta) which rises to more than 225 m at its eastern end and slopes to near sea level in the west. The ridge is composed of several basaltic lava flows which dip northwest towards the Bay of Fundy at a shallow angle. They form the southern rim of a tilted spoon-shaped trough which underlies the bay. The rounded up-tilted eastern side of the trough can be seen in the curve of Scots Bay. The basalt in the lower western part eventually disappears under the water beyond Brier Island (District 810).

The highest elevations and most dramatic scenery are found on North Mountain, particularly at Cape Blomidon where Cape Split sweeps around into the Minas Basin. The steep southern escarpment of the ridge may represent a fault line; the shallower northern side is a dip slope. The shore from St. Croix Cove

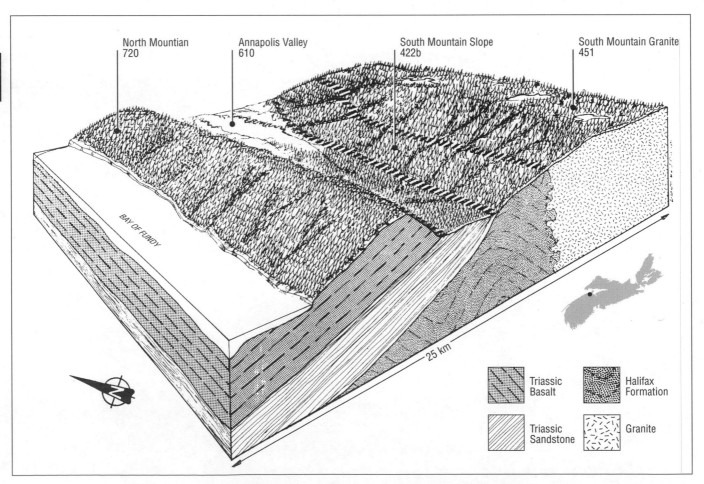

Figure 25: Annapolis Valley and North Mountain area. Basaltic lava flows of the North Mountain (District 720) effectively insulate the Annapolis Valley (District 610) from the climatic effects of the Bay of Fundy. The south side of the valley is composed of a dissected slope with deep, well-drained soils (Unit 422) and with thin, droughty soils derived from the enormous granite batholith which dominates South Mountain (Unit 451).

to Cape Split provides a rich ground for mineral collecting because fresh rock is exposed each year after the winter storms.

Wind gaps through the ridge are found at Parkers Cove and Delaps Cove. These represent the abandoned lower valleys of rivers that flowed northwards from central Nova Scotia into the present Bay of Fundy and were captured by the Annapolis River. Digby Gut is the drowned lower valley of Bear River.

The emergent shoreline is smooth, exposed, and rocky with little coastal sediment.

Lava Flows

The number of flows varies along the length of the ridge. Up to seventeen have been counted at Digby Gut, but only two can be seen along Digby Neck. The total thickness has been estimated at 300 m. Layers of green grit are found between the flows. These represent the weathered surface of the underlying flow and are easier targets for erosion than the massive flows; thus the basalt pile appears banded. Basalt lava flows exhibit interesting features that reflect their volcanic origins:

- Amygdules: Gas bubbles trapped in the lava are filled with minerals over time, for example, agate, amethyst, jasper and zeolite minerals such as stilbite and heulandite.

Erosion

Coastal erosion has cut tidal platforms 100–300 m wide along the Fundy shore, above which rise vertical sea cliffs. The columnar jointing can best be seen along this shoreline. Overlying the basalt is the Jurassic Scots Bay formation in which fossil fish and dinosaur footprints can be found. These sediments are present in six small inlets in Scots Bay.

Glaciation

Glacial ice moved across the Basalt Ridge both southwards and northwards at different times. The best evidence of south flow are pebbles of basalt found up to 200 km away along the South Shore. Basalt pebbles are very common in stony areas of the Annapolis Valley. Evidence of northward movement of glacial ice is provided by occasional boulders of granite, presumably from the South Mountain, which are scattered across the top of the Basalt Ridge. These were deposited late in the last glacial period when the South Mountain acted as a local ice centre (Unit 451). Deposits of glacial gravel are found along the Basalt Ridge at various points. The post-glacial emergence of this area is recorded in the raised beaches found at 40 m above present high tide near Digby and at 30 m on Brier Island.

The Basalt Ridge owes its prominence not only to the resistant nature of basalt but to the fact that it overlies soft, erodable sediments. The southern side of North Mountain has a steep scarp slope where these softer rocks have been carved out to form the Annapolis Valley. Along Digby Neck these same sediments have been removed to below sea level to form St. Marys Bay. Erosion is actively narrowing the Basalt Ridge on the Fundy side, although the energy of wave attack is diminished by wave-cut platforms. St. Marys Bay is more sheltered.

FRESH WATER

The southern boundary of District 720 follows a tertiary watershed divide across the top of North Mountain. Streams drain in a parallel pattern, directly into the Minas Channel. Gene pools of first- and second-order streams are isolated. Productivity is greatest where they originate on the higher elevations. The streams flow down the slopes quickly, but they are straight and small and have little erosive power. The area is heavily wooded and surface water is cool.

SOILS

Soils in this District are fairly shallow when developed from the underlying basalt. Rock outcrops as ridges parallel to the coast. The main soil derived from basalt is Rossway, a shallow, well-drained silt loam; this soil is associated with Roxville, a poorly drained sandy loam found in depressions. On the plateau along the crest of the Basalt Ridge a fine sandy loam appears. This soil, called Glenmont, developed from a mixture of basalt and red Wolfville Till, which originated north of the Basalt Ridge. Finer-textured Wolfville soils (not drumlinized) occur between Harbourville and Victoria Harbour. A large area of Middleton soil (moderately well-drained, sandy clay loam) is found between Mount Hanley and Arlington West. Small patches of Kingsport and Nictaux soils, developed from water-deposited sands and gravels, are also found in this area. Along the Fundy Shore some areas of excessively drained loamy sand (Gulliver series) have formed on wave-washed gravels.

The District is unusual because earthworms are found in large numbers in the woodlands and their activity has incorporated the surface "mull" into the mineral soil.

720
Basalt
Ridge

720
Basalt
Ridge

PLANTS

A much-disturbed version of the coastal forest is found at lower elevations in this District. Shade-tolerant hardwoods occur at higher elevations, where they may be above the cold air from the Bay of Fundy. Red Spruce is more common here than along the Atlantic coast, and White Spruce is also found throughout, often seeding in abandoned fields. Away from coasts, the spruce, fir, pine forest with maple and birch gradually turns into Sugar Maple, Yellow Birch, and American Beech at higher elevations.

Rare arctic-alpine and uncommon Alleghanian plant species are found in the Cape Split/Blomidon area. Seaweed growth (e.g. Laverbread) is extensive at the west end of the District but decreases eastwards as the silt content of coastal waters increases. Almost no salt marsh is found along this part of the coast.

ANIMALS

The Basalt Ridge provides mostly forest habitats with few lakes or wetlands. It supports a dense population of deer, but few bear or bobcat. Small-mammal diversity is moderate. The Basalt Ridge funnels the movements of migratory birds, particularly hawks and owls, as they head towards Brier Island in the fall. This funnelling may also occur with migratory bats which cross the Bay of Fundy or Gulf of Maine en route to their wintering areas. The exposed basalt along the shoreline provides good intertidal habitat with well-marked zones and large tidepools. Shells of subtidal molluscs and crustaceans are often found near wharves where lobster traps have been emptied. Some weir fishing is done.

SCENIC QUALITY

The North Mountain provides spectacular views of the Annapolis-Cornwallis Valley and the Minas Basin at lookoffs along its southern escarpment. On the north-facing dip slope, lack of relief and paucity of settlement often yield landscapes of indifferent quality. However, where higher-quality soils (CLI classes 3 and 4) have encouraged larger blocks of cleared farmland (e.g., West Glenmount, Burlington, Mount Hanley, Mount Rose), north-facing routes present impressive yet curious panoramic views, as if the traveller were being tipped gently but inexorably into the wide Bay of Fundy. The opposing shores of the Chignecto peninsula and New Brunswick's Caledonian highlands, which seem to float on the bay, add to the illusion. The vertically cliffed coastline is punctuated by "hollows" or "vaults" of eroding stream-valleys. Squeezed in at the mouths of larger brooks are delightful fishing hamlets such as Baxters Harbour, Halls Harbour, and Harbourville.

CULTURAL LANDSCAPES

Many of the coastal communities along the Basalt Ridge focus on fishing as an economic base, concentrating on lobsters and weir-fishing. The latter requires very large net walls to catch fish trapped by ebbing Fundy tides. Small farms are a feature of parts of this landscape, as is forest exploitation. In the nineteenth century, tide-powered grist mills operated at Moose River and Parrsboro. The agates, amethyst, and zeolites found on cliff faces are world famous and every summer attract visitors who come to collect. Cape Split and Cape Blomidon feature dramatic landscapes with hiking trails, impressive scenery, and a provincial park that attracts recreation and tourism. Mi'kmaq Kluscap (Glooscap) legends are associated with this area.

● ● ● ● ● ● ● ●

Sites of Special Interest
- Cape Split (IBP Proposed Ecological Site 65)—primarily deciduous woodlands with rich herbaceous flora; rare minerals and semiprecious minerals found in amygdaloidal basalt
- Cape Blomidon—steep sea cliffs
- Cape Blomidon to St. Croix Cove—good mineral localities
- Digby—raised beach 40 m above high tide; Digby Gut; drowned lower valley of Bear River
- Point Prim—wide, wave-cut platform
- Scots Bay—limited occurrence of the Scots Bay Formation in a few small coves in the only accessible portion of Jurassic sediments that underlie the Bay of Fundy; fossils include algal stromatolites, plants, fish, and dinosaur footprints and bones

Provincial Parks and Park Reserves
- Valley View
- Cottage Cove
- Blomidon Lookoff
- Baxter Harbour

Scenic Viewpoints
- Cape Split
- Cape Blomidon beach
- The Lookoff
- Route 360 south of Garland (view of the Valley)
- Valley View Provincial Park
- Point Prim

Associated Offshore Units
912 Outer Fundy, 913a Minas Basin.

Associated Topics
T3.2 Ancient Drainage Patterns, T3.4 Terrestrial Glacial Deposits and Landscape Features, T9.3 Biological Environment, T10.12 Rare and Endangered Plants.

Associated Habitats
H2 Coastal, H5.3 Cliff and Bank, H6.1 Hardwood Forest (Sugar Maple, Yellow Birch, Beech Association), H6.3 Mixedwood Forest (Spruce, Fir, Pine–Maple, Birch Association).

**720
Basalt
Ridge**

800
Atlantic Coast

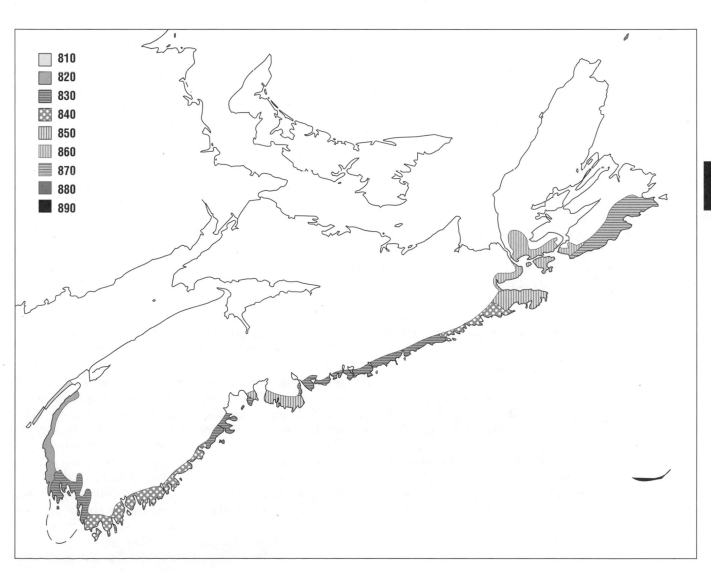

Figure 26: Region 800, Atlantic Coast, and its component Districts.

800 ATLANTIC COAST

The Atlantic Coast Region is divided into nine Districts based upon major geomorphological characteristics:

810 Basalt Peninsula
820 Cliffs and Beaches
830 Beaches and Islands
840 Quartzite Headlands
850 Granite Barrens
860 Sedimentary Lowland
870 Till Plain
880 Cliffed Island
890 Sandy Island

Districts 830, 840, and 850 are further divided into Units based upon geomorphological, soil, and vegetation characteristics.

REGIONAL CHARACTERISTICS

Exposure to winds from the Atlantic Ocean dominates coastal environments from Digby Neck to Scatarie Island. The Region includes Isle Haute and St. Paul Island. The coastal forest is found throughout, and its inland extension marks the regional boundary. Headlands, especially in granite and quartzite areas, are frequently barren. Almost every major rock type in Nova Scotia is found in this region, but the soils are often dominated by hardpans that result from excessive moisture. Coastal erosion is rapidly reshaping coastal areas containing drumlins; there beaches, marshes, and waterfowl habitat are found. Seabird nesting colonies and marine mammals are common on coastal islands.

The Atlantic Coast Region is much influenced by the adjacent Offshore/Continental Shelf (Region 900). There is a transition zone where the marine and terrestrial conditions interact, and it is sometimes difficult to make a distinction between coastal and offshore waters. In general, Region 800 extends to the low tide mark, and marine conditions are described in Region 900. However, in some bays, such as St. Margarets and Mahone bays (District 460), the marine characteristics are more typically coastal and the District encompasses subtidal waters.

GEOLOGY

The Atlantic Coast Region of Nova Scotia cuts across a great variety of rock types.

The Western Shore, South Shore, and Eastern Shore (Districts 820, 830, and 840) are dominated by the old and generally very hard rocks of the Meguma Group. These are interfolded slates and greywackes, with local outcroppings of metamorphosed volcanic ash and lava (Yarmouth area). Areas of very resistant granite (District 850) also occur. In contrast, Chedabucto Bay has been eroded from weakly metamorphosed Carboniferous sandstones (District 860). Southeastern Cape Breton (District 870) is underlain by metamorphosed Precambrian volcanic ash deposits, sandstone, and granite.

At the entrance to the Bay of Fundy, Digby Neck (District 810) is a low-lying basalt ridge. St. Paul Island (District 880) consists of very ancient Precambrian rocks similar to those found in the Cape Breton massif.

The coastal bedrock is low-lying and exhibits low relief. Elevations rarely exceed 100 m, except on the granite promontories and knolls at Pennant Barrens (Unit 851) and Canso Barrens (Unit 852), where the maximum elevation is 250 m.

LANDSCAPE DEVELOPMENT

The coastline can be divided into two sections based upon classic features of emergence and submergence. Post-glacial readjustment north of a pivot line that lies parallel to the length of the province from Yarmouth to Truro resulted in the emergence of Bay of Fundy coasts. From Yarmouth to Scatarie Island, the Atlantic coast has been continuously submerged as sea levels have risen. The emergent shore has raised beaches, raised wave-cut platforms, and a smooth shoreline. The submerged shore is highly irregular, with drowned estuaries and headlands producing an indented coast fringed by islands. The post-glacial rise in sea levels recorded over the past 10,000 years or so has affected all coastal areas. Drowned forests, eroding headlands, tidal marshes, and beaches driven inland are all evidence of the continuing transgression of the sea.

The shape of the coastline is also strongly influenced by faults, especially along the Eastern Shore and the southern boundary of Chedabucto Bay. Many of the long inlets in Guysborough County have formed along fault lines. The straight shore west of Cape Canso marks the position of the Chedabucto Fault. The smooth eastern shoreline of the Louisbourg lowlands (and Gabarus Bay) may also be fault-controlled. The orientation of St. Marys Bay, North Mountain, and the Parrsboro shore also owe much to fault movements within the Bay of Fundy area.

GLACIAL DEPOSITS

The last major flood of ice across Nova Scotia during the Wisconsin Period left a predominantly north-south to northwest-southeast imprint upon the landscape. Pre-existing drainage channels and any faults lying parallel to the flow were deepened. Interfolded strata oriented parallel to the direction of ice flow were differentially eroded, leaving ridges and valleys (Tusket area); ridges perpendicular to the ice flow were smoothed off. The whole area was then blanketed with glacial till derived mainly from local sources but also carried from one geological district to another and deposited as drumlins.

Along the coast the amount of sediment available for redistribution depends largely upon the nature of the glacial deposits. Areas with drumlin headlands and islands tend to have adequate sediment supply derived from coastal erosion. Another very limited source of coastal sediment, quartz sand, is washed from the surface of coastal granite bodies by sub-aerial erosion. A more important source of coastal sediment is silt and sand that was carried landward from glacial deposits on the Scotian Shelf by the sea as it rose during the post-glacial period. Many of the present sand beaches owe their origins to material driven landward in this manner.

CLIMATE

Although the Atlantic Coast Region is generally an exposed, high-energy environment, the many indentations along the coast provide sheltered bays and estuaries. The average tidal range is small: at Guysborough Harbour it is 1.4 m, at Halifax 1.4 m, at Lunenburg 1.6 m, and at Barrington Passage 1.9 m. In the Gulf of Maine, however, the tidal range increases sharply. At Woods Harbour, 10 km west of Barrington Passage, the average tidal range is 2.6 m, which becomes 3.7 m at Yarmouth and 4.7 m in St. Marys Bay. Ocean swells move in from the south and east, though their erosive power is somewhat reduced by refraction and by northerly offshore winds, particularly in winter.

The median extent of sea ice just reaches the eastern limit of this region. In heavier-than-average ice years, ice fields may extend as far southwest as Halifax County.

The background features of the ocean climate are controlled by the southwest-flowing Nova Scotia Current, which is relatively low in salinity; superimposed upon this are meteorological events which can bring large runoffs of fresh water or upwellings of saltier deeper waters. In general, the Region is a cool-water coast. In summer the coldest temperatures are found around Cape Sable and in the Bay of Fundy, as a result of a strong mixing of surface waters by tidal currents.

The ocean is the dominant influence on the Region's climate. The main features are moderated seasonal and daily temperatures, high precipitation and humidity, strong winds, fog, and salt spray.

The winters are comparatively mild, and the summers are short and cool. The mean annual temperature range is 15–20°C and is least in the southwest, increasing towards Cape Breton. This can be contrasted to a mean annual temperature range of 20–25°C throughout the rest of the province. Along the coast, spring starts early but is long and cool. Mean daily temperatures rise above the freezing point about the second week of March in the south, and about two to three weeks later along the Eastern Shore and in Cape Breton. Because of frequent fogs, and the cooling influence of ocean waters, the mean daily temperature in July stays below 15°C near the coast, increasing somewhat inland. Mean daily freezing temperatures return to northern inland areas before the end of November, but in the Atlantic Coast Region this does not usually happen until after the second week in December, or even as late as the end of December in the southwest. Mean daily January temperatures stay above –5°C and, in some areas, remain above 0°C.

Like most of the province, the Atlantic Coast Region receives fairly high total precipitation, generally between 1200 and 1400 mm, but between 1400 and 1600 mm in Queens and Lunenburg counties and in the northern half of Halifax County. Only about 15 per cent falls as snow because of the mild winter temperatures. Most of the Region receives less than 200 cm of snow annually, and Guysborough County and Cape Breton receive less than 150 cm. The snow-cover season starts late and finishes early, ranging from less than 100 days near Cape Sable to more than 130 days in Cape Breton. Snow accumulations are usually low.

Fog and high humidities are common along the Atlantic coast. Summer and fall are the main seasons for fog, when warm, moist air moving in from the south comes into contact with cool Atlantic coastal waters. On average, fog occurs 15–25 per cent of the year. The southwestern section of the coast is the foggiest, with Yarmouth registering an average of 120 days in which fog occurs.

The main features of the bioclimate of the Atlantic coastal forest are the long frost-free period and long growing period, combined with cool summer temperatures, low evapotranspiration rates, and exposure to wind.

FRESH WATER

The Atlantic coast is dissected by many fault-controlled river and lake systems that drain into the ocean. At the mouths of most rivers, wetlands receive both tidal and freshwater influences. Surface waters tend to be soft and acidic. The brownwater lakes are shallow and often associated with bogs.

SOILS

The important factors that influence soil development in this Region are the high precipitation and shorter winters, which result in strong leaching action over a greater part of the year, resistant igneous or metamorphic bedrock, low relief, and slow decomposition of leaf and needle litter. In general, the soils are shallow, coarse podzols, usually sandy loams, acidic and strongly leached, alternating with areas of exposed bedrock and organic deposits. Gleyed podzols and gleysols are also common, particularly in southwestern Nova Scotia. Small areas of coarse soils that developed on glacial outwash sands and gravels are found throughout the Region. Mixtures of finer-textured Carboniferous material show up in drumlin areas. In eastern Cape Breton, heavy clays can be found on deeper, flat, poorly drained tills. All along the Atlantic coast extensive pan formations (ortstein) are common; these severely impede soil drainage, causing thick layers of surface humus to accumulate.

PLANTS

The Atlantic Coastal Forest Region lies within and is defined by Louck's Spruce, Fir Coast Zone. The major influences on the regional vegetation are the marine climate and extensive disturbances by fire and cutting. The cool, wet, acidic conditions favour conifers. Deciduous trees are usually restricted to higher, better-drained sites sheltered from coastal winds. On headlands and exposed ridges, trees are usually se-

verely stunted. Continuous high winds increase transpiration, and trees may actually become "desiccated" in spite of high rainfall. Salt spray can kill part or all of a tree, but its effects are limited to a fairly narrow band along the coast. White Spruce, which has a high tolerance to wind and salt spray, is the characteristic species closest to the sea.

In the southwestern part of the Region, White Spruce, Black Spruce, and Balsam Fir are accompanied by White Birch and Red Maple (H6.3). The reappearance of White Pine and Red Oak inland usually indicates less rigorous climatic conditions and can therefore mark an approximate inland boundary. In the northern part of the Region, where the winters are colder, White Spruce continues to be prominent along the shore but is less abundant away from the water. Dense stands of Balsam Fir, Black Spruce, and White Spruce are characteristic, along with a virtual absence of Red Spruce, White Pine, and most hardwood species. Jack Pine sometimes occurs on fire barrens, and larch is common on wetter soils, particularly in Cape Breton. Excessive stand density may be another factor besides wind exposure that limits tree growth in this part of the Region. Throughout the Region, barrens or semi-barrens are common, supporting mostly low, ericaceous (heath) vegetation. Sphagnum bogs are also common in depressions.

C.D. Howe's description of this "black" forest written in 1912 is still true today: "The numerous peninsulas formed by the long re-entrant bays and harbours are covered with an inferior black spruce–fir forest and exhibit abundant bogs. The softer places in the rock have been worn into little hollows and pockets, sometimes only a few feet and usually not many rods apart. These fill with water which cannot drain away freely because of the massive quartzite beneath. The loss by evaporation is replaced by frequent rains, but it is also very much retarded by the natural humidity of the air. The result is a sour soil composed of raw humus, and hence the stunted forest. The trees are about ten to fifteen feet high, and frequently not more than three or four feet high in the more boggy situations. A section of one of these trees, three-eighths of an inch in diameter, when placed under a compound microscope revealed 47 annual rings. On the drier portions where a little real soil is present, one finds sapling thickets and dense polewood stands of fir. Along the streams of normal rapidity the stand is mostly second growth yellow birch and red maple."

ANIMALS

The terrestrial habitats provided by the Atlantic Coast Region are mainly forests (mostly conifers), barrens, and bogs. The main faunal interest is provided by the extensive range of coastal and marine habitats, including rocky shores, sandy beaches, dune systems, mud flats, salt marshes, and islands. These habitats provide breeding and feeding areas for a wide range of resident and migratory birds.

The coastal strip from Halifax around to Meteghan and inland for 10–20 km has the least persistent winter snow cover of any area in the province. This creates severe microclimatic stress for small mammals during cold snaps, and in the case of the Deer Mouse this stress is at the limits of tolerance. Almost certainly because of this, deer mice are very rare there and usually absent from most areas in this zone at most times; White-footed Mouse is the dominant species of *Peromyscus* in the District.

Marine fauna is mostly cold-water boreal in character but is not homogenous along the coast. Sheltered inlets and pockets of warmer water support many species with a more southerly distribution. Productivity is high along the edge of the Scotian Shelf, and marine mammals are quite numerous. The Atlantic coast is often visited by unusual bird and marine species carried by winds and currents from other parts of the Atlantic Ocean.

CULTURAL ENVIRONMENT

Shell middens found in coastal sites give evidence of former Mi'kmaq camps. Before European colonization, the Mi'kmaq frequented various river estuaries along the Atlantic coast, living primarily on abundant fish, clams, and other shellfish. European settlers were attracted to these same areas, drawn by the fisheries and the presence of deep harbours from which timber and fish could be shipped. Some Acadians settled on the French Shore, Germans settled around Lunenburg, and Loyalists along the southwestern coast at Shelburne, Liverpool, and Barrington. The remainder of the Atlantic coast was settled by Scots, Irish, and Loyalists. In the early 1500s, long before European settlement, the Canso area had been an important fisheries post because it was the nearest point of land in Nova Scotia to the great North Atlantic fishing grounds. The fisheries continue to be critical to the survival of many coastal communities, but the collapse of fish stocks in the early 1990s threatened this. Many infrastructure industries depend on the fisheries. Fish processing plants are common along the Atlantic coast, with the largest in North America operating at Lunenburg. The construction of Cape Island boats has long been a shipbuilding tradition in southwestern Nova Scotia. In the 1920s, with the development of roads and car travel, Peggys Cove was made famous by tourists and urban artists and has become one of the central symbols of the Maritimes, representing a quintessential fishing village.

The islands along the Atlantic coast were used as fishing stations and for sheep grazing, and small seasonal fishing communities and flocks of sheep remain on some of them today.

Drumlins found along the Atlantic coast have been cleared and used as productive farmlands. Forestry exploitation occurs at various coastal sites and this wood, along with that from the interior, supplies newsprint and hardboard mills at Brooklyn, East River, and Point Tupper. In the nineteenth century, many Nova Scotian ports on the Atlantic coast shipped immense volumes of timber to Britain. The viability of several of Nova Scotia's resource industries (pulp and paper products, gypsum, aggregates) is closely tied to the accessibility of marine transportation. Deepwater harbours such as Halifax and Port Hawkesbury are an important resource and are among the largest ice-free deepwater ports in the world. Today, as in the past, the shipping industry and transport by water are very important to the provincial economy and ports along the Atlantic coast. Most of the coastline has rocky, shallow, and acidic soils and offers low agricultural capability except for subsistence gardening.

● ● ● ● ● ● ●

Associated Offshore Region
900 Offshore/Continental Shelf.

Associated Topics
T3.1 Development of the Ancient Landscape, T3.2 Ancient Drainage Patterns, T3.3 Glaciation, Deglaciation and Sea-level Changes, T3.4 Terrestrial Glacial Deposits and Landscape Features, T3.5 Offshore Bottom Characteristics, T4.1 Post-glacial Climatic Change, T6.3 Coastal Aquatic Environments, T6.4 Estuaries, T7.1 Modifying Forces, T7.2 Coastal Environments, T7.3 Coastal Landforms, T9.1 Soil-forming Factors, T10.4 Plant Communities in Nova Scotia, T11.5 Freshwater Wetland Birds and Waterfowl, T11.6 Shorebirds, T11.7 Seabirds and Birds of Marine Habitats, T11.12 Marine Mammals, T11.14 Marine Fishes, T11.17 Marine Invertebrates.

Associated Habitats
H1.1 Offshore Open Water, H1.2 Offshore Benthic,
H2.1 Rocky Shore, H2.2 Boulder/Cobble Shore, H2.3
Sandy Shore, H2.5 Tidal Marsh, H2.6 Dune System,
H4.4 Freshwater Marsh, H5.1 Barren, H5.3 Cliff and
Bank, H6.3 Mixedwood Forest (White Spruce, Fir–
Maple, Birch Association).

**800
Atlantic
Coast**

810 BASALT PENINSULA

A westerly extension of the North Mountain basalt ridge forms a double ridge with an intervening drainage catchment. Isle Haute is also part of this District. Topographic elevations decline westwards. The ridge is cut by parallel faults. Brier Island and Peter Island are important staging areas for birds, and Brier Island has rare plants. Offshore upwelling creates a rich plankton with abundant seabirds and whales.

GEOLOGY AND LANDSCAPE DEVELOPMENT

Digby Neck is formed from two thick lava flows with an intervening erodable layer. The flows dip to the northwest, forming twin ridges with a central valley along the spine. The elevation of the Digby Neck decreases westwards, reaching sea level at Brier Island and continuing as rock ledges beyond.

Digby Neck is cut by four parallel faults. Two of these have been eroded to below sea level and form the passages at the northern ends of Long Island and Brier Island. The other two have not been flooded and are manifest as coves and valleys crossing Digby Neck at Mink Cove and Gulliver Cove. Sandy Cove is a wind gap probably cut by an ancient predecessor of the Sissiboo River that flowed northwards before being "captured" by a river that flowed westwards in what is now St. Marys Bay.

FRESHWATER ENVIRONMENTS AND COASTAL WETLANDS

Relatively little surface water covers this District. The main drainage is along the central depression of Digby Neck where long streams interconnect occasional geologically controlled lakes and ponds. Freshwater wetlands in the central depression are associated with Little River and Long Island Brook. Tidal marshes occur in the northeast cove of St. Marys Bay.

SOILS

The soils of Digby Neck are similar to those on the rest of North Mountain (District 720). Rossway, a well-drained sandy loam, covers much of the area. Its imperfectly drained associate, Roxville, occurs in the central depression. Poorly drained Tiddville soils develop where organic material accumulates. Brier Is-

land has large areas of peat. In the coves, coarse Medway soils have developed from stratified quartzite or schist gravel.

PLANTS

Digby Neck is more exposed to marine influences, particularly storms moving in from the south and east, than is the Fundy Coast (Region 700). Therefore its coastal spruce-fir forest (H6.2) is dominant, and hardwoods are not found in pure stands. A series of bogs are found along the central depression. The sedge and sphagnum bogs on Brier Island contain rare and unusual plants such as Eastern Mountain Avens, Dwarf Birch, and Curly-grass Fern. The Brier Island orchid flora is diverse.

The rocky shores and low silt content of coastal waters provide a good substrate for seaweed, including well-developed *Laminaria* beds, and the economically important seaweeds dulse and Irish Moss.

ANIMALS

The fauna of this District is of great interest for two reasons: (1) Brier Island is the final westward staging point for migratory birds, insects, and bats, and (2) an area of upwelling and high productivity occurs just off the coast. In the summer and fall, large flocks of phalaropes gather off Brier Island prior to migration. In spring, Brant and Black Duck are frequently seen. In summer a wide variety of shorebirds collect, but by the fall their numbers will have diminished somewhat. Over the winter, Common Goldeneye and sea ducks will be present but not abundant. Purple Sandpipers winter along the rocky shores of the entire coast. Common and Arctic terns breed on Peter Island between Brier Island and Long Island, and this area also shelters moderate numbers of Black Duck and Common Eider in winter. Small numbers of breeding Turkey Vultures have recently become established on Long Island.

The upwelling off the coast makes Brier Island an important area for observing migratory whales.

Rocky shores show good zonation and have large tidepools, providing diverse fauna. Common Periwinkle grows to the largest size in Nova Scotia here. Subtidal molluscs may be found on the shore as a re-

810
Basalt
Peninsula

sult of the emptying of lobster traps. Weir-fishing is carried out largely for herring.

SCENIC QUALITY

The sea is less apparent on this narrow peninsula than one might expect, because the paved road is mostly confined to the shallow central depression and its scattered abandoned fields. However, the road periodically skirts delightful coves on St. Marys Bay and is interrupted by the narrow passages between the islands. The land is much higher towards the east and faces the sea more steeply on the southern scarp face.

CULTURAL ENVIRONMENT

Various fisheries are important to this area, including shellfish, herring, lobster, and Digby scallops. Seaweeds are also commercially harvested. Brier Island, with its unique flora and bird populations, attracts outdoor enthusiasts for bird-watching and whale-watching trips.

• • • • • • • •

Sites of Special Interest
- Brier Island (IBP Proposed Ecological Site 59)—two bogs with relict, rare plants, and orchid flora, stopover area for migrating birds, and wintering area for Common Eider
- Central Bog (IBP Proposed Ecological Site 60)—sphagnum bog with a nearly neutral humus layer; contains disjunct plants, especially skunk cabbage, and is a possible refugia for coastal-plain flora
- Lake Midway—relict aquatic fauna
- Sandy Cove—glacial gravels, kettle holes, and wind gap
- Brier Island—columnar basalt on south side, raised beach 45 m above high tide
- East Ferry—columnar basalt south of ferry landings
- Isle Haute—further up the Bay of Fundy from the main part of Unit 810 but included because of its geology, coastal climate, and vegetation; fauna poorly known but includes nesting Common Eider (see also Unit 710)
- Long Island—balancing rock—unique geological phenomenon

**810
Basalt
Peninsula**

Provincial Parks and Park Reserves
- Central Grove
- Lake Midway

Proposed Parks and Protected Areas System includes Natural Landscape 1.

Scenic Viewpoints
- Central Grove Provincial Park
- Sandy Cove
- Gullivers Cove

Associated Offshore Unit
912 Outer Fundy.

Associated Topics
T2.6 The Triassic Basalts and Continental Rifting, T10.9 Algae, T10.12 Rare and Endangered Plants, T11.1 Factors Influencing Birds.

Associated Habitats
H1 Offshore, H2 Coastal, H4.1 Bog, H6.3 Mixedwood Forest (White Spruce, Fir–Maple, Birch Association).

820 CLIFFS AND BEACHES

This smooth coastline with raised beaches and wave-cut platforms emerged in the early post-glacial period and is now being submerged. It has many subglacial and glaciofluvial deposits. The cliffed coast has sheltered muddy areas with some salt marshes, sandy beaches, dune systems, and submerged forests. Coastal waters provide important wintering grounds for the Common Eider.

GEOLOGY AND LANDSCAPE DEVELOPMENT

This District encompasses a strip of coastline along the eastern shore of St. Marys Bay. The bedrock consists of metamorphosed, interfolded slates and greywacke of the Meguma Group which are highly eroded and have little relief. Overlying the bedrock is a ground moraine of varying thickness on which are good examples of subglacial and glaciofluvial deposits such as end moraines, deltas, and spits. Evidence of coastal rebound, and tilting following glacial withdrawal, is found in raised beaches and wave-cut platforms. The effects of the more recent coastal submergence are seen in beach erosion, retreating till cliffs, and submerged forests along the shore. Glaciomarine deposits can be found along St. Marys Bay.

Detailed analysis and description of the surficial geology was completed by the Geological Survey of Canada during the 1970s.

FRESHWATER ENVIRONMENTS AND COASTAL WETLANDS

Most surface-water coverage in this District occurs north of Yarmouth where many small to medium-sized irregularly shaped lakes are linked by small rivers and streams. A few freshwater wetlands are associated with Rivière Grosses Coques. Many small tidal marshes and barachois ponds are scattered along the coast in coves. Larger marshes can be found at the mouth of the Chegoggin and Salmon rivers and in Yarmouth Harbour.

SOILS

The soils in the northern part of this District derive from moderately coarse-textured quartzite till and are predominantly imperfectly drained Danesville with poorly drained Aspotogan. South of Meteghan the tills are somewhat finer in texture and derived from slate. The three associated soils are well-drained Bridgewater, imperfectly drained Riverport, and poorly drained Middlewood. In Yarmouth County the soils are developed on drumlinoid mounds of till derived from schistose rocks. On the drumlins the soils are moderately well-drained sandy loams of the Yarmouth series, often cleared and farmed.

Between the drumlins, Deerfield soils are prevalent. Drainage is restricted by a compact, nearly impervious parent material, and seepage spots are common. Areas of peat, and Bridgewater, Mersey, and Halifax soils also occur. Digby soils can be found on raised beaches all along the coast; these are rapidly drained sandy loams over a gravelly till containing many shells of marine origin.

PLANTS

The vegetation of this District has been extensively disturbed by cutting. Poor drainage conditions over much of the area has given rise to large numbers of peat bogs. White Spruce and Balsam Fir are the most common species, together with shade-intolerant birches, maples and aspens. On the wetter areas, Black Spruce and larch are found. In this area, Blue-joint Grass meadows are common. Along the more sheltered, muddy coast, small salt marshes have developed, and unlike the Bay of Fundy, Eelgrass beds can be seen.

ANIMALS

This section of the coast has a mixture of intertidal muds, sandy beaches with some dunes, rocky shores, and some salt marshes. The south shore of St. Marys Bay is considered regionally important because large numbers of Common Eider overwinter there. Waterfowl are also present in moderate numbers in early spring and fall, but not in summer. The salt marshes and mud flats at Cape Cove also provide attractive habitat for Black Duck and shorebirds, although their numbers are not large. Because of the ample sediment, marine infauna is richer than the epifauna. Unusual offshore species are often washed up on the sandy beaches, which offer good shell collecting. In the warm, sheltered waters towards the head of the bay, relict marine fauna may be found, for example, Quahog shells and marsh snails at Gilbert Cove. Typical freshwater fish species include White Sucker, Brown Bullhead, and White Perch.

SCENIC QUALITY

The coast north of Pointe à Tom differs from that to the south. The area to the north is a level till plain, while to the south is found a drumlinized landscape of rounded hills interspersed with marshes and lakes. The human element also differs; the northern plain has uninterrupted farmland, while the southern area has discontinuous farmland on drumlin tops. Both areas have moderately high scenic value, but the Acadian settlements of Clare district have certain unique features, for example, unusually large churches (e.g., St. Bernard, Church Point) and characteristic long-lot field patterns.

CULTURAL ENVIRONMENT

This area, known as the French Shore, was where the Acadians came to settle after making their way back to Nova Scotia following the 1755 deportation. Small-scale farming, hunting, and waterfowling were commonly practised along the French Shore. Today, fishing is an important economic base, particularly the lobster, clam, scallop, and herring fisheries. The village of Grosses Coques is so named because of the big clams common there. Fish scraps are used to feed the significant mink ranching operations. Forestry in backwoods areas provided timber for the extensive shipbuilding which took place here in the nineteenth century. A shipyard in Meteghan continues to build wooden boats. Acadian settlement patterns have shaped the human landscape along the French Shore, with homes stretching along a cleared, open coastal landscape in a linear fashion as one community blends into another. Yarmouth has a good harbour and is a commercial centre for this area. Speckled Trout is a popular recreational fishing species near Yarmouth.

• • • • • • • •

Sites of Special Interest—Glaciation and Post-glacial Emergence (north to south)

- Bingays Brook (northeast of Barton)—evidence of oysters in interglacial deposits show high sea levels occurred between ice advances
- Church Brook (northeast of Gilbert Cove)—glaciomarine delta 22 m above high tide, now a gravel pit
- Belliveau Cove to Meteghan River—end-moraine complex forms prominent ridge fronting the coast for 20 km (best developed at Saulnierville)
- Meteghan—glaciomarine delta upraised 20 m above high tide
- Picnic park to south of Pointe à Tom—perfect fossil wave-cut platform forms a beach at 5 m, also a modern equivalent
- Mavillette—large fossil spit exploited for gravel
- Cape St. Marys—Pleistocene raised beaches and glacial till containing fossils of marine shells; one of several coastal exposures in southwestern Nova Scotia; similar occurrences found in Kings County and Cape Breton
- Cape Cove (south of Cape St. Marys)—complete sequence of glacial tills from last 120,000 years (see T3.4)
- Green Cove (north of Port Maitland)—marine terrace under campground
- Red Head (south of Port Maitland)—raised and tilted wave-cut platform, with a modern example; area provides the most southerly evidence of post-glacial coastal tilting and emergence; the pivot point for coastal rebound and tilting is close to Yarmouth

Recent Submergence (north to south)

- West of Church Point—a submerged forest 5,000 years old, 5 m below high tide
- Pointe des Maréchal—submerged forest, 3 m below high tide
- South of Overton—submerged forest, one metre below high tide
- Yarmouth Bar—eroding tombolo
- Cape St. Marys (IBP Proposed Ecological Site 55)—salt marsh and sand dune system of more than 120 hectares
- Grosses Coques (IBP Proposed Ecological Site 58)—salt marsh system; wintering ground for Common Eider

Provincial Parks and Park Reserves
- Savary
- Smugglers Cove
- Mavillette Beach
- Port Maitland Beach
- Bluff Head
- Pembroke
- Sand Hills Beach
- Cape Fourchu
- Kellys Cove

Proposed Parks and Protected Areas System includes Natural Landscape 4.

Scenic Viewpoints
- Weymouth Harbour
- Smugglers Cove Provincial Park
- Cape St. Marys
- Cape Fourchu

Associated Offshore Unit
911 Atlantic.

Associated Topics
T2.2 The Avalon and Meguma Zones, T3.1 Development of the Ancient Landscape, T3.3 Glaciation, Deglaciation and Sea-level Changes, T7 The Coast.

Associated Habitats
H1 Offshore, H2 Coastal, H4.1 Bog, H5.3 Cliff and Bank, H6.3 Mixedwood Forest (White Spruce, Fir–Maple, Birch Association).

**820
Cliffs and
Beaches**

830 BEACHES AND ISLANDS

District 830 is divided into four Units based upon coastal morphology, soils, and vegetation:

831 Tusket Islands
832 LaHave Drumlins
833 Eastern Shore Beaches
834 Bay of Islands

GEOLOGY AND LANDSCAPE DEVELOPMENT

This District is found in the exposed southeast-facing central portion of the Atlantic Coast Region and the southwest-facing portion south of Yarmouth. It is generally underlain by slate bedrock but also includes outcrops of greywacke/quartzite and granite. The slate and greywacke bands are interfolded and the fold axes are either perpendicular to (Tusket Islands) or, more commonly, parallel to the coast. Differential erosion of softer slate and harder greywacke has created a ridge and valley topography which is distinctive in places. The best example occurs where glacial north-south scouring was parallel to fold axes (Tusket Islands).

The shoreline is submergent and exhibits drowned headlands and estuaries; it is irregular and very indented.

Sediment Sources

The major sediment sources are:

1. offshore deposits—sand carried landward during the post-glacial marine transgression over glacial deposits on the Scotian Shelf; the volume of sand reflects the nature of these deposits, i.e., whether they were unsorted till (less sand) or sorted glaciofluvial deposits (more sand)
2. eroding headlands—thick till deposits that form cliffs on exposed shores
3. drumlin islands—clay, sand, and cobblestone material dumped offshore and directly exposed to wave attack
4. glaciofluvial deposits—sands and gravels in river valleys now being redistributed by fluvial action
5. quartz from granite—white sand of only local significance

Deposition

The pattern of deposition depends upon the size distribution of the material, the morphology of the coastline, and the exposure to and direction of wave attack. Coarse material is found in exposed localities around headlands, where the proportion of sand is small and an oblique wave front carries fine material along the shore. Sand is found in sheltered coves and inlets, on the lee side of headlands and islands, and where a change in direction of the coastline provides a sink for sediment transported along the shore. Depending upon the location, sediments form bay and barrier beaches, spits, bars, tidal marshes, and dune systems.

PLANTS

Coastal forest vegetation is typically White Spruce and Balsam Fir, with Red Maple, birch, and poplar on better soil. Further inland these give way to spruce, fir, and pine. Drier sites have more pine and oak, and wet sites have Black Spruce and larch. The coastline has barren headlands with krummholz White Spruce, salt marshes, sand dunes, and Eelgrass beds. Southwestern (coastal-plain) plant species are found along the edges of streams and lakes and in bogs. Areas of better soil, particularly on drumlins, have been cleared for agriculture. Pure stands of White Spruce are regenerating on oldfields.

ANIMALS

The indented coastlines and abundant sediment supply result in a wide diversity of coastal habitats in this District, including rocky shores, sand and cobble beaches, mud flats, and tidal marshes, resulting in the presence of a large variety, and sometimes large numbers, of waterfowl and shorebirds that shelter in the inlets and estuaries and feed in the mud flats and tidal marshes.

SCENIC QUALITY

Though possessing little relief, all four Units have high scenic value, owing to indented coastlines and many offshore islands. The three more westerly Units are most similar because their coastal drumlin fields produce similar erosional and depositional features (till headlands, egg-shaped islands, tombolos, spits, sandbanks, and salt marshes). The drumlins also allowed scattered farming, the marginal viability of which is reflected by many abandoned fields. The easterly Unit (Bay of Islands) lacks drumlins and farming and has a rocky coast with few beaches. All Units except the Eastern Shore Beaches (Unit 833) provide their best scenery to the offshore boater.

• • • • • • • •

Associated Offshore Unit
911 Atlantic.

Associated Topics
T2.2 The Avalon and Meguma Zones, T7 The Coast.

Associated Habitats
H1 Offshore, H2 Coastal, H5.1 Barren, H5.2 Oldfield, H6.3 Mixedwood Forest (White Spruce, Fir–Maple, Birch Association).

**830
Beaches
and Islands**

831 TUSKET ISLANDS

A submerged coastline with long promontories and inlets characterizes this Unit. The abundant sediment supply allows extensive tidal marsh development. Mild winter conditions permit the survival of relict coastal-plain flora species. Relatively ice-free conditions provide important wintering habitat for waterfowl. Upwelling and tidal mixing create nutrient-rich waters that support a diverse marine fauna.

GEOLOGY AND LANDSCAPE DEVELOPMENT

In this part of southwestern Nova Scotia the geological structures intersect the coastline more or less at right angles. As the glacial ice flowed north-south, more or less parallel to these structures, it exploited weaker bands and left a series of long, parallel ridges and valleys. These have become progressively submerged as sea levels have risen during the last 12,000 years, creating a highly indented coastline with many elongated islands oriented north-south.

Drumlins occur onshore and as offshore islands. Glaciofluvial deposits are common, especially eskers. Glacial deposits provide an ample sediment supply.

FRESHWATER ENVIRONMENTS AND COASTAL WETLANDS

Many medium-sized, elongated lakes are found in the Tusket area. The surface waters tend to be dystrophic and associated with bogs. The mouths of the Tusket and Chebogue rivers occur in this Unit, and many small freshwater wetlands are associated with the streams and rivers. Long Savannah and Spinneys Heath are large wetlands considered significant for wildlife. Large peat areas occur around Pubnico Harbour. The coastal inlets are predominantly lined with salt marshes, which are extensive upriver on the Chebogue and in Little River Harbour and Goose Bay.

SOILS

The dominant feature of this Unit is its extensive areas of salt marsh. These are a uniform silt loam in texture and occupy more than 3,200 ha. Upland soils have generally developed from schistose slate or quartzite on drumlinoid land forms, but the central strip from Dunn Lake to Comeau Hill is an exception, being relatively flat with shallow soils. Better-drained soils are Yarmouth and Mersey, derived from schist and quartzite, and Medway soils derived from outwash sands and gravels. Imperfectly or poorly drained soils (which are often mottled, indicating saturation for considerable periods of time) include Deerfield, Riverport, Liverpool, Danesville, Aspotogan, and Pitman. Large peat areas have developed near Pubnico Harbour. The islands are nearly all either Mersey (drumlins) or Liverpool soils.

PLANTS

Areas of Yarmouth, Deerfield, Medway, and Mersey soils are often cleared for agriculture. Otherwise they normally support good growths of White Spruce and Balsam Fir, with Red Maple, birch, and poplar. Better drained, more sheltered sites may have some pine or oak. Black Spruce and larch swamps are common. Because of the fairly high rate of erosion, the transition from salt marsh to spruce woods is often quite abrupt. A fringe of grey, dead trees is usually found at the rear of the salt marshes, where the rising sea level drowns their root systems. The Southwestern floral element is well represented in this Unit, particularly along river and lake margins and in bogs. Examples include a bladderwort and Curly-grass Fern (see Figure 13).

ANIMALS

The mild winter temperatures, the many islands and sheltered inlets, and the extensive areas of salt marsh and intertidal sands and muds produce a very important wintering area for waterfowl and certain other species such as the Bald Eagle. Present in the greatest numbers are the Black Duck, Canada Goose, scaups, and the Common Goldeneye. Less common birds include the Red-breasted Merganser and Oldsquaw. Shorebird numbers as the birds begin to arrive in spring are small, then peak in early to mid-August, and sharply decline in September. Osprey breed along this shore and Leach's Storm-petrel breeds on the Tusket Islands.

A rich marine fauna is associated with this Unit. The warmer inshore waters support a number of invertebrate species with a more southerly distribution. An area of upwelling offshore, combined with tidal mixing, provides nutrient-rich waters which support abundant algae, crustaceans, and open-sea fish. The Tusket supports a large run of Gaspereau in the spring. The introduced Chain Pickerel has had a major impact on species in this Unit. It is a predator of both migratory and exotic freshwater fish, and is thought to have played a critical role in the extirpation of the Atlantic Whitefish in the Unit. Two anadromous species, Rainbow Smelt and Striped Bass, are also found here.

The more fertile soils derived from schists result in more productive inland waters and a fairly diverse freshwater fauna, particularly molluscs. The fauna also includes a southwestern element, the best known example being the Atlantic Whitefish.

CULTURAL ENVIRONMENT

Acadian settlement in this area was based around the tidal marshes. Pubnico is derived from the Mi'kmaq word "Pogomkook," meaning "cleared land," a landscape favoured by the Acadians. The productive herring, lobster, clam, and scallop fisheries continue to provide an important economic base. Rockweed and Irish Moss are commercially harvested. Hydroelectric power has been harnessed by a generating station at Tusket Falls. Large sand and gravel deposits have been commercially exploited. Mi'kmaq shell middens have been found in the Tusket Islands area. In the early 1990s, exercise of aboriginal hunting and fishing rights led to confrontations over unregulated native fishing practices. The name Tusket is derived from the Mi'kmaq word "Neketaouksit" meaning "the great forked tidal river." Migratory bird populations of Seal Island attract bird-watchers to this Unit. Sheep were left to graze year-round on the Tusket Islands.

• • • • • • • •

Sites of Special Interest
- Spinney Heath (IBP Proposed Ecological Site 52)—large undisturbed bog near Central Argyle
- Chebogue Lake (IBP Proposed Ecological Site 53)—large inland salt lake, also known as Melbourne Lake, with rich beds of Eelgrass, is a provincial sanctuary for waterfowl
- Moses Lake (IBP Proposed Ecological Site 51)—old-growth deciduous forest
- Road from Arcadia to Pinkney Point—follows an esker
- Tusket River shore—water-deposited debris

Provincial Parks and Park Reserves
- Glenwood
- Upper West Pubnico

Proposed Parks and Protected Areas System includes Natural Landscape 10.

Scenic Viewpoints
- Chebogue River
- Surettes Island
- Ste. Anne du Ruisseau
- Pubnico Harbour (various points)

Associated Offshore Unit
911 Atlantic.

Associated Topics
T4.2 Post-glacial Colonization by Plants, T10.12 Rare and Endangered Plants, T11.4 Birds of Prey, T11.7 Seabirds, T11.13 Freshwater Fishes, T11.16 Land and Freshwater Invertebrates.

Associated Habitats
H2.5 Tidal Marsh, H4.1 Bog, H6.2 Softwood Forest (Black Spruce, Larch Association), H6.3 Mixedwood Forest (White Spruce, Fir–Maple, Birch Association).

**831
Tusket
Islands**

832 LAHAVE DRUMLINS

This Unit is dominated by swarms of drumlins on land, in shoals, and on islands offshore. Slate forms promontories and bedrock islands. An ample sediment supply and varied coastline provide a rich diversity of coastal habitats that support a mixture of southern and northern fauna, and significant numbers of waterfowl and seabirds (see Figure 14).

GEOLOGY AND LANDSCAPE DEVELOPMENT

Between Voglers Cove (at the mouth of Voglers Brook) and Aspotogan, the South Shore of Nova Scotia is characterized by the presence of many drumlins with a predominantly northwest-southeast alignment. They occur inland, where they are cleared and farmed, and offshore, where they form wooded islands with rounded profiles. In the southern part of the area, promontories and islands of slate bedrock are found.

The drumlins are the coastal and offshore equivalents of the Kejimkujik Drumlins (Unit 433) and Lunenburg Drumlins (Unit 434). The former are composed of grey-brown clay till derived from local slate, and the latter of red-brown sandy till from Carboniferous and Triassic deposits more than 100 km to the north. The slate-till drumlins are characteristically not found far beyond the slate belts. The red Lunenburg Drumlins commonly form islands, especially north and east of Cape LaHave.

The variable quantity and texture of the coastal sediment supply has built up a range of shoreline deposits which vary from extensive sandy beaches to small shale beaches to cobble beaches. Most of the sediment appears to be of local origin and comes from glacial tills. Crescent Beach is a sand bar connecting some of the Cape LaHave islands to the mainland.

COASTAL WETLANDS

There are few lakes or streams, and most of the wetlands are tidal. The LaHave estuary is very wide when it crosses into this coastal Unit. There are many small, scattered tidal marshes.

SOILS

Drumlin soil parent materials are of two main types. To the west of the LaHave River, drumlins are derived from slate on which shale loam soils of the Bridgewater series have developed. Soils between the drumlins are derived from the same material but are shallow and often poorly drained. To the east the drumlin materials are finer-textured, reddish, sandy clay loams. These Wolfville soils are similar to those found throughout District 430, east of the LaHave River. They may have originated in New Brunswick. Most of the islands have Wolfville soils, the main exception being Cape LaHave Island, which is mostly Rockland.

PLANTS

White Spruce and Balsam Fir are the dominant species along the coast, with some maple and birch intermixed in more sheltered locations. Pure stands of White Spruce are found on some drumlins and on oldfields. Further inland, spruce, fir, and pine forest occurs. Salt marshes and Eelgrass beds are common.

ANIMALS

This Unit provides a diversity of coastal habitats: rocky shores, cobble beaches, extensive sand beaches, tidal flats, and salt marshes. The area around Cape LaHave Island to Rose Bay, and the western shore of Mahone Bay at Blue Rocks, are locally important as waterfowl and shorebird habitat. In spring, fall, and early winter, waterfowl numbers are low. Black Duck, Common Goldeneye, and Oldsquaw may occur, and Scoter are sometimes present in significant numbers. The Red-necked Grebe overwinters in this area. From early August through September, shorebirds congregate at Crescent and Cherry Hill beaches in moderate numbers. Piping Plovers breed at Cherry Hill and Kingsburg beaches, and at East Iron-bound Island. Pearl Island (a provincial wildlife management area) is regionally important because it provides breeding habitat for the Atlantic Puffin, Leach's Storm-petrel, Razorbill, and Black Guillemot. Gulls, cormorants, terns, and the Great Blue Heron breed on other islands along the coast.

Sheltered inlets support a southern mix of marine fauna, while exposed rocky shores support a more northern fauna. The major rivers provide distinct estuarine conditions for brackish water species. Periodic slope-water incursions bring in warm-water species such as seahorses, Blue Crabs, and sharks.

CULTURAL ENVIRONMENT

Small farms are found on many of the LaHave Drumlins. In the early 1600s an Acadian settlement was established at LaHave but was later abandoned. The Lunenburg area was favoured by the Mi'kmaq and there were several confrontations between the Mi'kmaq and the Germans who settled here in the 1750s. Lunenburg was built on a peninsula with a front and back harbour ideal for fishing and seafaring. Fishing dominates most of this coastline, and access to offshore fishing banks results in prosperous fishing industries. Lunenburg has been one of the most important fishing communities in the province, with large offshore fishing fleets and local processing plants. Drumlin forests were exploited to supply timber for the flourishing nineteenth-century shipbuilding industry. Built in Lunenburg, the Bluenose schooner is a symbol of the province's seafaring tradition. A whaling station once operated out of Blandford but closed in the early 1970s when opposition to whaling led to a Canadian ban. The LaHave Drumlins area is a popular tourist and recreational destination. The Fisheries Museum in Lunenburg documents aspects of the area's fishing history.

• • • • • • • •

Sites of Special Interest
• Blue Rocks—blue-grey slates and sandstones of the Halifax Formation
• Ovens Natural Park—gold has been mined from steeply inclined sandstones and slate strata; sea caves have developed through erosion of the softer layers
• Kingsburg—coastal exposures of Goldenville Formation sandstones and siltstones; Piping Plovers
• Pearl Island—provincial wildlife management area
• Tancook Island—metamorphosed Ordovician Meguma slate with rare trilobite fossils; graptolites also occur rarely in the Meguma

Provincial Parks and Park Reserves
• Rissers Beach
• Bush Island
• Feltzen South
• Upper Blandford
• Bayswater Beach

Proposed Parks and Protected Areas System includes Natural Landscape 14.

Scenic Viewpoints
• Crescent Beach
• Ovens Point (private park)
• Lunenburg Harbour (both sides)

Associated Offshore Unit
911 Atlantic.

Associated Topics
T3.3 Glaciation, Deglaciation and Sea-level Changes, T3.4 Terrestrial Glacial Deposits and Landscape Features, T11.4 Birds of Prey, T11.6 Shorebirds, T11.7 Seabirds.

Associated Habitats
H2 Coastal, H5.2 Oldfield, H6.2 Softwood Forest (Spruce, Fir, Pine Association; White Spruce Association).

**832
LaHave
Drumlins**

833 EASTERN SHORE BEACHES

This is an indented drowned coastline with headlands, long inlets, and drumlin islands. An active reworking of ample coastal sediment is building spits and barrier beaches between headlands and islands. The inlets provide migration and overwintering habitat for waterfowl.

GEOLOGY AND LANDSCAPE DEVELOPMENT

This Unit extends from Halifax to Owls Head, near Clam Harbour, along an indented submergent coastline. The bedrock is dominated by greywacke, with bands of slate, folded parallel to the coastline. The coast is divided into headlands separated by long inlets. Most inlets are drowned river estuaries and do

not appear to be fault-controlled. Porters Lake, which stretches inland from Terminal Beach, is an exception, as it occupies a fault zone.

Loose cobbly quartzite till forms the ground moraine and is overlain in two areas by drumlins composed of red-brown Lawrencetown Till. The drumlins are concentrated in the Chezzetcook to Lawrencetown and Clam Bay areas. They rarely form islands but are more usually seen as eroding coastal bluffs, such as Hartlen Point. Three of the islands within Chezzetcook Inlet are drumlins.

The irregular character of a youthful submergent coastline is being smoothed off here as sediment is redistributed (see Figure 27). Sand and gravel are supplied from the erosion of deep glacial tills and

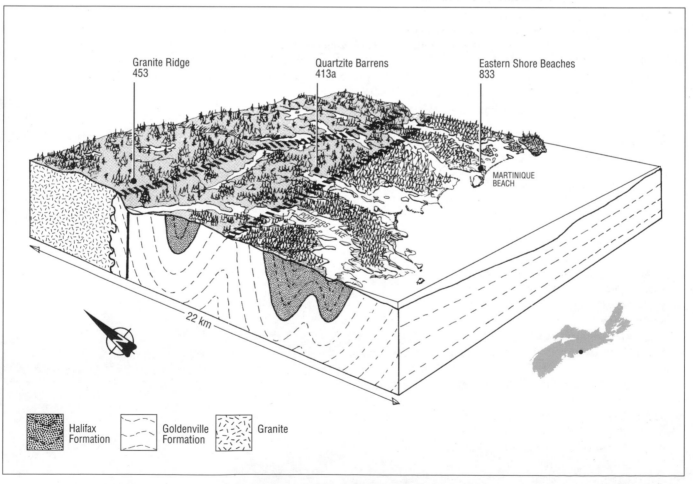

Figure 27: Eastern Shore Beaches area. The severe environment created by Meguma Group rocks is tempered by the presence of drumlins between Cow Bay and Clam Bay. Long, drowned estuaries, tidal marshes, and sand beaches are found in this coastal forest zone (Unit 833). Inland, the Quartzite Barrens (Unit 413) give way to a significantly higher granite upland (Unit 453) on which many lakes are found.

glacial outwash deposits along the coast. Spits and barrier beaches, connecting promontories and islands, protect the large, shallow estuaries from ocean waves, allowing salt marshes to develop.

FRESHWATER ENVIRONMENTS AND COASTAL WETLANDS

The many small and medium-sized lakes in this Unit exhibit pH levels of 5.5–7.3. Several lakes around Dartmouth, including Morris and Bisset lakes, have high levels of turbidity and nutrients. A few scattered freshwater wetlands occur inland, usually associated with lakes or small streams. There are many large areas of tidal marsh in barachois ponds and inlets.

SOILS

Well-drained Halifax gravelly sandy loams derived from quartzite cover much of this Unit. On areas with less relief, imperfectly drained Danesville soil is common, with peat, Rockland, and some small areas of poorly drained, mottled Aspotogan soil. Some areas of shaly loam Bridgewater soil have developed from parent materials derived from slate. Finer textured Hantsport soils (imperfectly drained, sandy clay loam) which have developed from Carboniferous parent materials are found around Eastern Passage. Wolfville drumlin soils are common, especially in Cole Harbour, Three Fathom Harbour, and Clam Harbour. The Halifax peninsula, which is underlain by slate except in the extreme north end, has mostly Bridgewater soils.

PLANTS

The coastal White Spruce and Balsam Fir forest with maple and birch predominates. On old farmlands and drumlins, pure stands of White Spruce are common. Further back from the coast are spruce, fir, and pine stands. Salt-marsh and sand-dune plant communities and large beds of Eelgrass are common.

ANIMALS

The mix of coastal habitats is similar to that found in Unit 832 (LaHave Drumlins), where sheltered inlets favour a more southerly marine fauna; exposed rocky shores support more northerly species. Periodic incursions of warmer slope water bring in warm-water fish and invertebrates in the summer.

Cole Harbour, Chezzetcook Inlet, Petpeswick Inlet, and Musquodoboit Harbour provide important migration and winter habitat for waterfowl. In spring,

particularly mid-March to mid-April, these areas are a stopover for several thousand Black Ducks and Canada Geese. The numbers peak again in October. Black Ducks breed in the coastal barrier beach, estuary, and coastal marsh habitats. More Black Ducks and Canada Geese come here than anywhere else in the province. Other overwintering birds are the Common Goldeneye, which occurs in moderate numbers, and an occasional scaup. Great Blue Heron and Osprey nest on McNabs Island and elsewhere. Piping Plovers nest at Lawrencetown and Clam Bay. This coast also provides feeding areas and some scattered nesting habitat for the Bald Eagle. Freshwater fishes include White Sucker, shiners, sticklebacks, perch, Banded Killifish, and Brook Trout.

CULTURAL ENVIRONMENT

The drumlin fields at Cole Harbour and Lawrencetown caused the British to single out this area in the mid-1700s for farming. Small-scale farming on the Eastern Shore drumlins has taken place since then. After the deportation of 1755, a group of Acadians settled in Chezzetcook. For many people in this area, earning a living from the land necessitated fishing in the summer, subsistence farming, hunting, waterfowling, and winter work in the woods—a pattern prevalent in many areas of the province and in some ways similar to Mi'kmaq subsistence patterns. The commercial centres of Halifax and Dartmouth have affected settlement along the Eastern Shore Beaches, and many inhabitants now commute to work in the cities. Fishing continues to be an important economic activity for some communities along the Eastern Shore, and includes clams, lobsters, cod, and haddock. Some of the recreational uses for the land are bird-watching at important migratory bird stops, hiking, camping, swimming, and enjoying the beach. Government administration, shipping, and the military continue to be economically important to Halifax and Dartmouth. Dartmouth is the Atlantic end of the Shubenacadie Canal. Numerous quarries around the Halifax area supply crushed rock to the construction industry. The Fisherman's Life Museum at Jeddore Oyster Ponds, the Fairbanks Centre, and the Dartmouth Heritage Museum present aspects of this Unit's history.

• • • • • • • •

**833
Eastern Shore
Beaches**

Sites of Special Interest
- Hartlen Point—eroding coastal bluff
- Cole Harbour—migration and overwintering of waterfowl
- Conrods Beach (IBP Proposed Ecological Site 36)—barrier sand dunes
- West Lawrencetown Marsh—Piping Plover
- Three Fathom Harbour—drumlins
- Chezzetcook Inlet—drumlins, waterfowl
- Petpeswick Inlet—waterfowl
- Martinique Game Sanctuary

Provincial Parks and Park Reserves
- South East Passage
- McCormacks Beach
- Cow Bay
- Cole Harbour
- Lawrencetown Beach
- Porters Lake
- East Chezzetcook
- Martinique Beach
- Clam Harbour Beach

Proposed Parks and Protected Areas System includes Natural Landscape 33.

Scenic Viewpoints
- McNabs Island
- Lawrencetown Beach and headlands
- Clam Harbour Beach

**833
Eastern Shore
Beaches**

Associated Offshore Unit
911 Atlantic.

Associated Topics
T2.2 The Avalon and Meguma Zones, T3.4 Terrestrial Glacial Deposits and Landscape Features, T7.1 Modifying Forces, T11.4 Birds of Prey, T11.5 Freshwater Wetland Birds and Waterfowl, T11.6 Shorebirds, T11.7 Seabirds.

Associated Habitats
H2.5 Tidal Marsh, H2.6 Dune System, H6.2 Softwood Forest (Spruce, Fir, Pine Association), H6.3 Mixedwood Forest (White Spruce, Fir–Maple, Birch Association).

834 BAY OF ISLANDS

In this Unit, a submerged, rocky coastline with parallel geological structure gives a series of elongated offshore islands. Variable sediment accumulation produces a variety of coastal habitats, from rocky shore with extensive seaweed growth to salt marsh. The islands provide important breeding habitat for seabirds.

GEOLOGY AND LANDSCAPE DEVELOPMENT

This Unit extends from the headlands of Little Harbour (southwest of Ship Harbour) to Liscomb Harbour and north to the head of major inlets. The axes of folds within the greywacke bedrock are parallel to the coastline, forming a ridge-and-valley topography. This orientation is reflected in the shape and alignment of the offshore islands, which formed as the low, eroded headlands were drowned during recent coastal submergence. The islands tend to be elongated east-west and have average elevations of less than 15 m. They are divided into groups by bays and inlets. Drumlins occur in scattered groups and form headlands all along the Eastern Shore but are rarely found as islands in this area.

Sedimentary structures that illustrate how the Meguma bedrock has been built up from the accumulation of gravity slide deposits are found at Taylors Head.

FRESHWATER ENVIRONMENTS AND COASTAL WETLANDS

Surface-water coverage is relatively low, with small scattered lakes and streams, and small wetlands associated with the streams. Most freshwater wetlands are concentrated east of Sheet Harbour. Levels of pH in the lakes average 6.1. Tidal marshes are small and scattered.

SOILS

On the flatter areas close to the coast around Ecum Secum, Moose Hill, Quoddy, and Sheet Harbour, imperfectly drained Danesville sandy loams have developed from the underlying quartzite. Drainage is impeded by bedrock and topography. Elsewhere the soils are mostly rapidly drained Halifax sandy loams with poorly drained Aspotogan and peat areas. Some

Wolfville drumlins (sandy clay loam) are found around Quoddy, Beaver Harbour, Popes Harbour, and Ship Harbour. Coarse, rapidly drained Hebert soils are found near Moser River. The islands are usually either Rockland or covered by a thin layer of Halifax soils, but a few have Wolfville or Danesville soils. Iron pans are common throughout this Unit.

PLANTS

The coastal White Spruce, Balsam Fir forest predominates, with some maple and birch mixed in on less exposed sites. On the wetter soils, Black Spruce, larch, and Balsam Fir are found.

Barrens cover many of the headlands, and krummholz vegetation is conspicuous. The parallel quartzite ridge topography gives rise to a fairly regular pattern of White Spruce on the ridge top, and Black Spruce and small bog areas in the depressions. Many of the islands have been deforested by the combined effects of exposure and cormorant guano and may not regain a tree cover.

ANIMALS

Coastal habitats in this Unit are mostly low-lying rocky shores with some small beach and salt-marsh areas. The firm substrate and low sediment supply results in excellent seaweed growth, especially along the rocky quartzite shoals that stretch into the water. Of major interest are the islands, which provide important breeding habitats for many kinds of waterfowl and seabirds. Together with Unit 842, this Unit provides a major portion of the Common Eider breeding habitat for Nova Scotia. Other breeding birds include cormorants, gulls, Arctic and Common terns, Black Guillemot, and Leach's Storm-petrel. Considerable numbers of waterfowl migrate through in spring and fall, including scoters, Black Duck, Oldsquaw, and Canada Goose. Some Oldsquaw, Black Duck, and Common Goldeneye remain during the winter. Seals are common on the islands and rocky shoals. Anadromous fishes include Gaspereau and Banded Killifish, and White Sucker is a typical freshwater species.

834
Bay of
Islands

CULTURAL ENVIRONMENT

Fishing provides an economic base for many communities on this part of the Eastern Shore. The forest hinterland is heavily exploited, and the community of Sheet Harbour, with its deep, well-protected harbour, has become a centre for the processing of forest products and the shipment of pulpwood. Distinctive recreational use of the land includes kayaking, with enterprises operating out of Tangier. In the 1860s, when a gold-mining frenzy swept across Nova Scotia, gold was discovered at Tangier, resulting in the development of numerous mining operations, which were exploited until the 1940s.

• • • • • • • •

Sites of Special Interest
- Eastern Shore Islands Wildlife Management Area—extends from Ecum Secum (Little White Island) to Sheet Harbour Passage (Round Island)
- Little White Island (IBP Proposed Ecological Site 30)—dense nesting colonies of cormorant and Common Eider
- Brokenback Island (IBP Proposed Ecological Site 32)—one of the few breeding sites for the Fox Sparrow in Nova Scotia; Osprey nests
- Long Island (IBP Proposed Ecological Site 33)—eider and cormorant nesting site and locality for rare Beach Senecio
- Pumpkin Island (IBP Proposed Ecological Site 34)—important nesting site for Leach's Storm-petrel and Black Guillemot
- Horse Island (IBP Proposed Ecological Site 35)—one of the few islands in the local area not deforested by cormorant nesting
- Taylors Head—sand volcanoes and slump structures

Provincial Parks and Park Reserves
- Taylors Head
- Popes Harbour
- Spry Bay
- Ecum Secum
- Marie Joseph

Proposed Parks and Protected Areas System includes Natural Landscape 37.

Scenic Viewpoints
- Taylors Head trail

Associated Offshore Unit
911 Atlantic.

Associated Topics
T2.2 The Avalon and Meguma Zones, T9.3 Biological Environment.

Associated Habitats
H2 Coastal, H5.1 Barren, H6.2 Softwood Forest (Black Spruce, Larch Association), H6.3 Mixedwood Forest (White Spruce, Fir–Maple, Birch Association).

**834
Bay of
Islands**

840 QUARTZITE HEADLANDS

The District is divided into two Units:
- 841 Capes and Bays
- 842 Guysborough Harbours

GEOLOGY AND LANDSCAPE DEVELOPMENT

This District is dominated by greywacke/quartzite and granite. Till deposits are relatively thin and there are few drumlins. Large areas of exposed bedrock occur.

The coastline is submerged and indented with headlands and long inlets but has few islands. The thin till deposits provide little sediment through coastal erosion, so coastal fringe deposits tend to be limited in volume and composed of coarse material. Sand beaches are found only where the rising sea level has eroded sand from now submerged glacial deposits and carried it shorewards. Very limited amounts of sand collect locally to form occasional white sand beaches.

SOILS

Shallow soils, low relief, extensive burning, and the widespread occurrence of impenetrable ortstein layers have all combined to produce a predominantly bog and barren landscape in this District.

SCENIC QUALITY

Where the ocean is in view, this District has moderately high scenic value. Unit 841 has greater coastal variety, in the form of salt marshes and tidal flats, but suffers from excessive coastal fog. Away from the shore, the low relief and poor forest of both Units is uninviting, but it is relieved in Unit 842 by deeper fault-aligned river valleys (Indian Harbour, Country Harbour, Isaacs Harbour, and New Harbour) which are drowned in their lower reaches. Bogs and barrens are more prevalent in Unit 841.

• • • • • • • •

Associated Offshore Unit
911 Atlantic.

Associated Topics
T2.2 The Avalon and Meguma Zones, T9.3 Biological Environment.

Associated Habitat
H4.1 Bog.

**840
Quartzite
Headlands**

841 CAPES AND BAYS

Granite and greywacke bedrock give a hummocky terrain with little relief. The till cover is variable but often thin. Shallow bedrock and ortstein development impedes drainage, creating bogs. Exposed bedrock and burning has led to the development of barrens. Long, sheltered inlets and relatively mild, ice-free winters provide wintering habitat for waterfowl.

GEOLOGY AND LANDSCAPE DEVELOPMENT

This Unit extends from Lower Woods Harbour in the west to Medway Harbour in the east. The bedrock geology is dominated by greywacke into which several bodies of granite have been intruded. The heat from the largest granite bodies baked the surrounding Meguma sediments and enabled minerals of a high metamorphic grade to form.

Throughout this area, granite and greywacke form a hummocky, rather uninteresting terrain with little relief. The coastline is very indented and divided into well-developed capes and long narrow bays. The bays are drowned river estuaries.

Glacial till deposits are variable in thickness but are generally less than 3 m deep; bedrock is exposed in fairly large areas, especially on the granite. Typically, very few drumlins are found on this granite and greywacke bedrock. Three have been mapped around Lockeport Harbour, but otherwise they are absent. Other glacial deposits include a series of outwash fans along the Medway River and around Medway Harbour.

Little coastal sediment is currently derived from local glacial till deposits. Sand is abundant locally, but since it was carried landward from offshore glacial material during the post-glacial marine transgression, it is now no longer replaced from the same source. The coastal area is a high-energy wave environment and experiences strong winds. Barrier beaches and dune systems are subject to periodic destruction during storms. The sand is carried either seawards into deep water or over the beach into lagoons as overwash. The wide expanse of flat beach created is subject to wind erosion, eventually leading to the re-creation of dunes further inland.

FRESHWATER ENVIRONMENTS AND COASTAL WETLANDS

Many of Nova Scotia's most extensive river and chain-lake systems drain into the Atlantic through the many estuaries and inlets in this Unit. Small and medium-sized lakes and ponds are scattered throughout, and pH levels average 6.0. Concentrations of wetlands are associated with the river and lake systems. The freshwater wetlands are largest in the western areas, with large concentrations in the middle of Cape Sable Island. Tidal marshes are scattered all along the coast in the inlets and barachois ponds.

SOILS

Soils in this area have mostly developed from coarse-textured parent materials: granite, quartzite, and schist. The principal soils are Port Hebert (well-drained sandy loam) and Lydgate, its imperfectly drained associate; both often develop subsurface cemented layers. Well-drained Halifax soils are found between Medway Harbour and Port Mouton, together with imperfectly drained and usually mottled Danesville soils. Lydgate and Port Hebert soils, together with areas of Rockland, are also found on the granite headlands near Port Mouton. South of Port Hebert, Lydgate soils predominate with extensive areas of Roseway (imperfectly drained sandy loam with organic layers of greasy "mor") and large organic deposits. Well-drained Medway soils (gravelly sandy loam) have also developed in a number of areas from quartzite and schist outwash gravel.

PLANTS

The low relief, the effects of fire, and the ready formation of ortstein layers have resulted in large areas of bog and barren. Labrador Tea, Lambkill, and blueberries provide the main vegetative cover on the barrens. Elsewhere the forest is chiefly White Spruce and Balsam Fir with maple, birch, and poplar. Some pine and Red Oak can be found on better-drained sites further inland. In wet, peaty areas, Black Spruce, larch, and alders are found.

ANIMALS

Coastal habitats include many sand beaches, salt marshes, intertidal muds and sands at the heads of the longer inlets, and cobble beaches. Rocky shores are mostly confined to the shoreline between Liverpool and Port Medway. This section of the coast is on the route for migratory waterfowl and shorebirds. The relatively mild winters and ice-free waters also make this Unit a prime wintering area for many species.

Clarks Harbour and Cape Sable are important staging areas for shorebirds, with highest concentrations in August. Barrington Bay has extensive mud flats which also attract many shorebirds. Moderate numbers of waterfowl, including Black Duck, scaups, and Common Goldeneye, are found there between October and March. During January and February, moderate numbers can also be seen at the heads of Jordan Bay and Green Bay. The coast from Lockeport to Port Mouton is very important for wintering waterfowl, particularly Canada Goose and Black Duck. Also present are scaups, Common Goldeneye, Oldsquaw, Common Eider, loons, scoters, and Red-breasted Merganser. Wintering Harlequin Duck is found in the Port Joli area. St. Catherines River Bay (Cadden Bay) also has the densest breeding concentration of Piping Plover in the Maritimes (up to 35 pairs). Birds breeding on the scattered offshore islands include gulls, cormorants, Black Guillemot, Arctic and Common terns, Leach's Storm-petrel, Osprey, and Great Blue Heron.

Offshore, nutrient-rich waters provide food for overwintering pelagic seabirds and whales. In the summer, warm-water incursions from the Gulf Stream often bring exotic tropical species to the beaches and inlets in this area.

The area immediately around Barrington Passage is unique in that its population of Red-backed Vole exhibits an exceptionally high incidence of melanism (an excess of black pigment which is genetically controlled). The incidence has been calculated at 18.4 percent, compared to 0.01 percent elsewhere in Nova Scotia. Brook Trout and Yellow Perch are typical freshwater fish species.

CULTURAL ENVIRONMENT

Land grant settlements in this Unit during the mid-1700s were based on deep harbours at Liverpool, Barrington, and Shelburne. This coastline, primarily settled by Loyalists, has always had a marine orientation and focused on fishing, shipbuilding, and forestry exports. Wood from backland areas supplies the Brooklyn newsprint mill. Sand and gravel deposits are commercially exploited by large producers at several coastal locations. The tradition of building Cape Island boats originated along this shoreline and continues today. Farming operations are small-scale, and sheep-rearing takes place on isolated islands with no predators. Aspects of the wool trade in this area are presented at the Barrington Woollen Mill Museum. Like most mills of its time, the Barrington mill was water powered.

• • • • • • • •

Sites of Special Interest
- Port Joli Federal Migratory Bird Sanctuary—chiefly for protection of Canada Goose habitat
- Carters Beach at South West Port Mouton (IBP Proposed Ecological Site 46)—illustrates a classic sand-dune successional sequence and has the highest dunes in the Atlantic Coast Region; Pearlwort is found in the depressions
- Sandhills Beach in Barrington Bay (IBP Proposed Ecological Site 49)—combines a sand dune with a Cord Grass–Rockweed salt marsh community
- Port l'Hebert Pocket Wilderness Trail—access to forest and coastal habitats
- Kejimkujik National Park has a Seaside Adjunct in the Port Joli area at Mouton Head and Cadden Bay

Provincial Parks and Park Reserves
- Port Joli
- Broad River
- Summerville Beach
- Summerville Centre
- Western Head
- Liverpool

Proposed Parks and Protected Areas System includes Natural Landscape 11.

Scenic Viewpoints
- Shelburne Harbour (both sides)
- Lockeport town (unusual site)
- Port Medway (road and trail to Medway Head)

Associated Offshore Unit
911 Atlantic.

Associated Topics
T2.2 The Avalon and Meguma Zones, T6.4 Estuaries, T7.1 Modifying Forces, T7.3 Coastal Landforms, T9.3 Biological Environment, T10.1 Vegetation Change, T11.5 Freshwater Wetland Birds and Waterfowl, T11.6 Shorebirds, T11.7 Seabirds.

841
Capes
and Bays

Associated Habitats
H2 Coastal, H4.1 Bog, H6.2 Softwood Forest (Black Spruce, Larch Association), H6.3 Mixedwood (White Spruce, Fir–Maple, Birch Association).

**841
Capes
and Bays**

842 GUYSBOROUGH HARBOURS

A submerged coastline with faults perpendicular to the coast gives long, drowned parallel estuaries separated by greywacke headlands. Thick glacial outwash deposits block the upper reaches of some valleys. Shallow soils give extensive bog and barren development. Light winter snowfall results in important wintering habitat for deer. Sheltered inlets and islands provide important habitat for waterfowl, shorebirds, and seabirds. The cold-water coast allows little diversity in marine fauna.

GEOLOGY AND LANDSCAPE DEVELOPMENT

The Guysborough Harbours Unit extends from Marie Joseph to New Harbour Cove.

The bedrock is predominantly greywacke with interfolded slates. The fold axes intersect the coastline at about 45°. Slip movements along the Chedabucto Fault caused a series of parallel faults to develop, dividing the bedrock into a number of blocks. These blocks have moved slightly northwards in a step pattern (en echelon). Weaknesses in the fault zones have been exploited by rivers, producing relatively straight valleys. These have been inundated by the sea and now form very long, narrow inlets. Sheet Harbour, Indian Harbour, Country Harbour, Isaacs Harbour, and New Harbour are examples of these drowned, fault-controlled river valleys. The valleys tend to be narrow and steep-sided, providing interesting variety in an otherwise uniform terrain with little relief.

Liscomb Harbour and Fishermans Harbour (near Port Bickerton) have been formed by erosion of the relatively weak slate bedrock. The east-west orientation of these two harbours contrasts with the northwest–southeast orientation of all other harbours. The only comparable feature in the Atlantic Coast Region is Yarmouth Sound.

The Unit is mantled with a thin quartzite till derived from the underlying greywacke. A single group of drumlins made up of red-brown till from the Carboniferous strata to the north crosses the area parallel to Indian Harbour River. The drumlins reach the coast between Holland Harbour and St. Marys Bay (Guysborough), where they form coastal bluffs.

There are several large areas of exposed bedrock. Glaciofluvial deposits are well developed along the valleys of the Indian Harbour and Country Harbour rivers, and along the shore of New Harbour. Thick sand and gravel deposits choke the valleys and impede drainage. New Harbour Lake is impounded by a gravel barrier across the valley at Port Hilford.

The coastal sediment supply is limited and there are few sand beaches. Coastal fringe deposits tend to be rocky or cobbly.

FRESHWATER ENVIRONMENTS AND COASTAL WETLANDS

Many oligotrophic lakes are scattered throughout this Unit, as are a few small freshwater wetlands and tidal marshes. A classic example of a freshwater tidal marsh occurs in the St. Marys River estuary.

SOILS

Most of the soils have developed from medium to moderately coarse textured tills derived from the underlying quartzite. Because quartzite does not weather easily, there is only a thin mantle of stony soil over bedrock; where the relief is more pronounced, rapidly drained sandy loams of the Halifax series are found. On flatter areas, imperfectly to poorly drained Danesville and Aspotogan soils predominate. This Unit includes large areas of organic deposits and Rockland. On the drumlins scattered between Cape St. Marys and Holland Harbour, finer-textured Wolfville soils (sandy clay loam with moderately slow drainage) have formed. Hebert soils (excessively drained sandy loams) are found along a number of the valleys, formed on glacial outwash sands and gravels.

PLANTS

On better-drained soils the forest is mixed, but predominantly softwood—White Spruce and Balsam Fir with maple and birch. On wetter soils the main species are Black Spruce, larch, and Balsam Fir. Huckleberry is common on the extensive barren and semi-barren areas.

Few tidal marshes occur along this coast because so little sediment is available, but some Eelgrass beds are found.

842
Guysborough
Harbours

ANIMALS

Because snowfall is considerably lower here than elsewhere on the coast, this Unit is an important wintering area for deer. Together with adjacent Units, the highly indented coastline with its many islands provides breeding and feeding habitats for a wide range of waterfowl and shorebirds, both resident and migratory. Like Unit 834, the area is regionally important since it provides a major portion of the breeding and brood-raising habitat for the Common Eider in Nova Scotia. Other breeding species in this area are the Great Black-backed Gull, Herring Gull, Double-crested Cormorant, Black Guillemot, Common Tern, Arctic Tern, and Great Blue Heron.

In the spring, substantial numbers of Black Duck, scoters, Common Goldeneye, Canada Goose, Old-squaw, and Red-breasted Merganser migrate through the area. A number of species are winter residents but are thinly distributed. Oldsquaw, Black Duck, and Common Goldeneye are fairly common.

Along this cold-water coast, marine species diversity diminishes from west to east. Freshwater runoff strongly influences coastal water conditions and the distribution of brackish water species. The Banded Killifish, the Mummichog and their hybrids are found in the St. Marys River.

CULTURAL ENVIRONMENT

This area is more sparsely settled because of its lower resource potential. Limited fishing and forest exploitation occur here. Gold mining once took place at Goldboro. Peat resources in this area are now being exploited.

• • • • • • • •

Sites of Special Interest
- Bickerton Island (IBP Proposed Ecological Site 28)—typical coastal island nesting area for many species
- Tobacco Island (IBP Proposed Ecological Site 29)—one of the few known nesting areas for Fox Sparrow
- Eastern Shore Islands Wildlife Management Area—provincial area extending from Ecum Secum Inlet (Little White Island) to Beaver Point (Round Island), Halifax County
- Goldenville gold mine
- New Harbour Lake—impounded by gravel barrier

Provincial Parks and Park Reserves
- Liscomb Mills

Proposed Parks and Protected Areas System includes Natural Landscape 38.

Scenic Viewpoints
- Indian Harbour Lake
- Country Harbour (ferry)
- Isaacs Harbour (both sides)

Associated Offshore Unit
911 Atlantic.

Associated Topics
T2.2 The Avalon and Meguma Zones, T3.4 Terrestrial Glacial Deposits and Landscape Features, T11.7 Seabirds, T11.10 Ungulates.

Associated Habitats
H2.1 Rocky Shore, H2.2 Boulder/Cobble Shore, H4.1 Bog, H5.1 Barren, H6.2 Softwood Forest (Black Spruce, Larch Association), H6.3 Mixedwood Forest (White Spruce, Fir–Maple, Birch Association).

842
Guysborough
Harbours

850 GRANITE BARRENS

District 850 has two Units:
  851 Pennant Barrens
  852 Canso Barrens

GEOLOGY AND LANDSCAPE DEVELOPMENT

Within this District the bedrock is dominated by granite, which forms headlands and knolls well above the upland surface and provides some of the most significant relief in the Atlantic Coast Region. The hills are rounded and tend to have a very thin till cover with many large boulders. There is much exposed bedrock. Although the thin granite till is a source of quartz grains for occasional white, sandy pocket beaches, in general the sediment supply is very poor. The shallow impermeable bedrock allows little infiltration and consequently the surface is covered by streams, lakes, and bogs.

PLANTS

Thin acidic soils and frequent rock outcrops restrict tree growth even more than the rest of the coastal forest. Barrens with ericaceous and stunted krummholz vegetation are widespread.

SCENIC QUALITY

Some may regard these areas as bleak and forbidding, but others are enchanted by the strange landscapes and seascapes. Along the coast, smooth rock headlands and boulder-strewn barrens provide wide and scenic vistas. Small fishing villages nestling within tiny coves (typified by Peggys Cove) contrast markedly with their raw surroundings and add considerable charm. Relief is strong along the Chedabucto Bay fault-scarp (Dorts Cove to Queensport), but this advantage is offset by the straightness of the coastline. Inland, the variety of barrens, hills, and lakes is interesting but hardly attractive.

● ● ● ● ● ● ●

Associated Offshore Unit
911 Atlantic.

Associated Topics
T2.3 Granite in Nova Scotia, T10.1 Vegetation Change, T10.12 Rare and Endangered Plants.

Associated Habitats
H3 Freshwater, H4.1 Bog, H5.1 Barren, H6.3 Mixedwood Forest (White Spruce, Fir–Maple, Birch Association)

**850
Granite
Barrens**

851 PENNANT BARRENS

This granite promontory, elevated above the surrounding upland surface, with thin rocky tills and exposed bedrock, gives extensive coastal barrens with bogs. Exposed conditions provide habitat for rare arctic-alpine flora. Generally the shoreline is rocky; in places it has been swept clear of all sediment and is bordered by a boulder and cobble shore.

GEOLOGY AND LANDSCAPE DEVELOPMENT

The Pennant Barrens include the promontory between Halifax Harbour and St. Margarets Bay and part of the Aspotogan Peninsula. The area is underlain entirely by granite which forms knolls elevated up to 150 m, well above the planation surface.

Joints within the granite divide it into large blocks. At the shoreline these can be loosened and moved by storms, providing dramatic coastal topography as at Peggys Cove. There are also steep cliffs which were probably formed in the Early Carboniferous and later buried by younger deposits. Now that the sedimentary cover has been eroded away, they are exposed once again, for example, Chebucto Head. Granite islands and shoals formed as the headlands became submerged. Similarly, the lower reaches of rivers have been drowned and form long inlets (e.g., Shad Bay).

The surface of the granite has a patchy, thin covering of granite till. On the many areas of exposed bedrock, glacial striations can be seen. The till contains

Plate 8: Region 800. Typical view of the coastal landscape along the Atlantic shoreline showing exposed rock-weed beds at low tide and coastal spruce forest in the background (Unit 833). Photo: O. Maass.

many boulders of varying size (erratics) which have been dumped randomly across the landscape, giving it a bulldozed appearance. The sediment supply is very limited and only the accumulation of sediment carried inland by the transgressing sea has provided enough sand for beaches such as Crystal Crescent (see Plate 8).

FRESH WATER

The surface of the granite has a deranged drainage pattern, with many lakes interconnected by wandering, slow-moving streams. Many small wetlands are associated with the streams and headwaters. Many wetlands are also found in depressions isolated from other surface-water features. Fresh water tends to be slightly acidic, ranging between 5.0 and 6.5, and conductivity is low.

SOILS

The main soil found in this area is Gibraltar (well-drained sandy loam), with small areas of poorly drained Aspotogan and peat. A strip of Bridgewater soil (well-drained, shaly loam derived principally from slate) is followed by the road through Hatchet Lake. A number of small drumlins with Wolfville soils occur, particularly between Spryfield and Pennant.

PLANTS

Much of the area is covered by coastal barrens, with Reindeer Moss, other lichens, and Broom-Crowberry interspersed with small sphagnum and sedge bogs. Where exposure to wind and spray is most severe, stunted White Spruce is usually found. Black Spruce, larch, and Balsam Fir occur on more sheltered sites with maple and birch. Stands of post-fire maple, oak, and birch occur on well-drained sites further inland. Jack Pine can also be seen. Some arctic-alpine species are present (see T4.2, Post-glacial Colonization by Plants).

Commenting on this enormous fire barren in 1912, C.D. Howe wrote: "The largest fire barren in Halifax county lies between St. Margaret bay and Halifax harbour ... [and] is chiefly barren of commercial trees, the forest being composed ... of wire birch, red maple, alder and poplar, and frequently it has scattered white pine of polewood size reaching up above them. The soil is sandy and is filled with pebbles and boulders. In many places the bare rock is exposed, and the surface strewn with granite boulders. The tops of the sandy knolls where the soil is deep frequently support young red oak. On the more moist, deeper soil of the slopes one finds scattered patches of thrifty hardwoods from twenty to forty years old. In one of these patches the composition of the stand was as follows: fir 24 percent, black spruce 16 percent, yellow birch 21 percent, shad tree seven percent, red maple 19 percent, mountain ash two percent, paper birch one percent."

ANIMALS

The shoreline is mainly rocky with low cliffs, some islands, and a few sand beaches; it does not provide much suitable habitat for shorebirds or waterfowl. Breeding birds include gulls, cormorants, Osprey, and Great Blue Heron. There are a few Bald Eagle breeding sites and Double-crested Cormorant colonies. Slope-water influence often results in productive plankton areas and the presence of whales, particularly in the late summer. Small-mammal diversity in the vegetation on the barrens is low (three or four species). Populations also appear to be low, except in close proximity to fresh water. Brook Trout is a typical freshwater species.

CULTURAL ENVIRONMENT

Writers, artists, and photographers who spent summer vacations at Peggys Cove in the 1920s drew attention to its allure, and Peggys Cove is now famous as a symbol of Nova Scotia and a tourist destination.

• • • • • • • •

Sites of Special Interest
- Bear Cove (IBP Proposed Ecological Site 38)— example of a small coastal bog
- Duncans Cove (IBP Proposed Ecological Site 39)—large area of coastal barrens with rare plants
- West Dover (IBP Proposed Ecological Site 40)— example of a lichen-dominated, virtually treeless barren
- Portuguese Cove—contact between granite and Meguma sediments; loose blocks of country rock can be seen "floating" in the granite
- Chebucto Head—large white crystals of feldspar, showing flow patterns within the granite
- Crystal Crescent—relict white sandy beach

851
Pennant
Barrens

Provincial Parks and Park Reserves
- Hollahan Lake
- West Dover
- Blind Bay
- Terence Bay
- Crystal Crescent Beach
- Herring Cove

Proposed Parks and Protected Areas System includes Natural Landscape 32 and Candidate Protected Area 23 Terence Bay.

Scenic Viewpoints
- Peggys Cove—village and headland
- Crystal Crescent Beach—white beaches
- Herring Cove—cliff-top trail off Highway 253

Associated Topics
T2.3 Granite in Nova Sotia, T3.4 Terrestrial Glacial Deposits and Landscape Features, T4.2 Post-glacial Colonization by Plants, T10.12 Rare and Endangered Plants.

Associated Habitats
H2.1 Rocky Shore, H2.2 Boulder/Cobble Shore, H2.3 Sandy Shore, H3 Freshwater, H4.1 Bog, H5.1 Barren, H6.1 Hardwood Forest (Maple, Oak, Birch Association), H6.2 Softwood Forest (White Spruce Association), H6.3 Mixedwood Forest (White Spruce, Fir–Maple, Birch Association).

851
Pennant
Barrens

852 CANSO BARRENS

Granite knolls rise prominently above the surrounding upland surface. The straight northern coastline is fault-controlled, in contrast to the indented southeastern coastline, which has many bays and bedrock islands. Extensive areas of exposed rock give these barrens the appearance of a moonscape (see Figure 28). Seabirds breed on some islands.

GEOLOGY AND LANDSCAPE DEVELOPMENT

The Canso Barrens extend northeastwards from New Harbour to Cape Canso. The area is composed of rounded bodies of granite intruded into Meguma Group slates and greywacke. The Meguma greywacke and slates have been extensively metamorphosed to form schists. All bedrock components have been affected by shearing movements along the Chedabucto Fault. The granite appears as knolls in the landscape, rising up to 200 m above sea level.

Thin deposits of granite, schist, and slate tills cover about 50 per cent of the surface, but the remainder is exposed bedrock, giving the area a bleak, moonscape appearance. A few drumlins composed of red-brown till derived from Carboniferous deposits are found on the northeast side of Tor Bay and south of Canso Harbour. The supply of coastal sediment is very limited.

The shape of the coastline reflects two influences: the presence of the Chedabucto Fault on the straight northern coast and submergence on the southern shore. New Harbour is a long, narrow inlet formed by the inundation of a fault-controlled river valley. Glacial outwash deposits are found along a 7-km section of the valley and block the drainage at two points, creating two ribbon lakes.

FRESH WATER

The many different-sized lakes and ponds are fed by complex patterns of streams and tributaries. Surface water tends to be slightly acidic, with pH levels generally below 6.0.

SOILS

Over much of the area, soils are very thin or non-existent. Over the granite, where soil cover has developed, is mostly Gibraltar soil (well-drained sandy loam). On flatter areas near the coast, Danesville gleyed podzol (imperfectly drained sandy loam) is common. In the middle of the Canso peninsula, Bridgewater soils (well-drained, shaly silt loams) have developed on the slate, interspersed with many boggy areas. Small, finer-textured Wolfville drumlins are strung out along the road to Canso and near Port Felix. Around Larrys River is an area of excessively drained Nictaux soil on outwash sands and gravel.

PLANTS

Where enough soil is present for trees to become established, the trees are mostly Black Spruce and Balsam Fir in dense stands with some White Spruce, maple, and birch (H6.3). On wetter areas, Black Spruce and larch predominate. The presence of Jack Pine on the Canso peninsula indicates that extensive fires have occurred. Vegetation on the barrens includes Sheep Laurel, Huckleberry, Labrador Tea, scrubby Black Spruce, Bracken Fern, and alders.

C.D. Howe's 1912 comments on the "forests" of this unproductive area are: "The bare rock is largely exposed and is strewn with boulders. The soil cover in the drier portions is not over two inches deep and is composed of raw humus. The deeper soils are of the same nature and both are covered with small herbs and shrubs. The crevices of the rock and the depressions are filled with alder and stunted black spruce and fir."

Rocky shores provide good substrate for rockweed and kelp growth.

ANIMALS

The large areas of barren do not provide productive wildlife habitats. The rocky southeastern coast provides breeding grounds for gulls, the Double-crested Cormorant, Great Blue Heron, Arctic Tern, Common Tern, and Common Eider (see Unit 842). The cobble beaches and cliffs, and the lack of inlets and islands, make the presence of the waterfowl around the Chedabucto Bay coast much less interesting. A cold-water shore with little slope-water influence means that marine productivity is diminished and marine fauna impoverished. An arctic indicator species *Mysis gaspensis*, a crustacean, occurs here. Typical

852
Canso
Barrens

fish include Rainbow Trout, Brook Trout, Banded Killifish, and sticklebacks.

CULTURAL ENVIRONMENT

Since the 1500s, Canso has been a strategically important fishery base. Situated at the entrance of Chedabucto Bay, it is the nearest point on the mainland of North America to the great Atlantic fishing banks. It is said that the harbour of Canso was frequented by European fur traders and fishermen within a dozen years of the arrival of Columbus in America, and an attempt at settlement was made here as early as 1518. The name "Canso" is derived from the Mi'kmaq word "Kamsok," meaning "opposite the lofty cliffs." With the closure of a major fish-processing plant in the early 1990s and the collapse of fish stocks, Canso's long history as an important fishery centre was threatened.

Sites of Special Interest
- Along Highway 16—fault-scarp of Chedabucto Fault
- Grassy Islands National Historic Site—commemorates the role of the Canso fishery in the early eighteenth century

Provincial Parks and Park Reserves
- Cape Ann Island
- St. Andrews Island
- Third Lake
- Harbour Head
- Tor Bay

Proposed Parks and Protected Areas System includes Natural Landscape 39 and Candidate

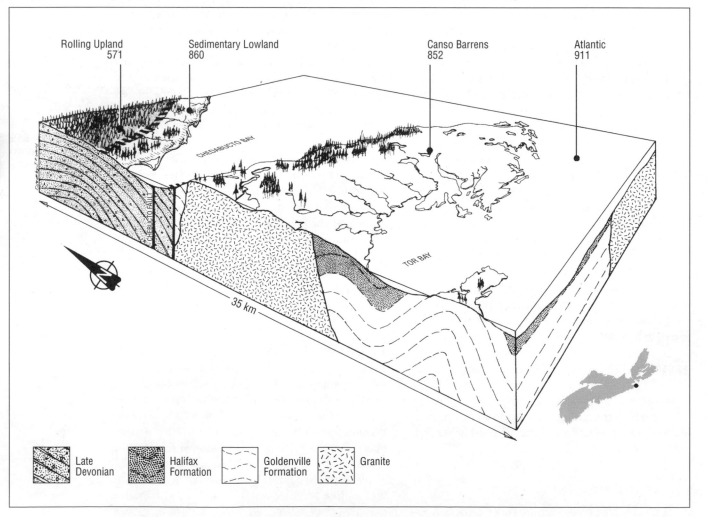

Figure 28: Canso Barrens area. The predominantly granite peninsula (Unit 852) is, for the most part, barren of trees because of its extreme exposure and impoverished soils. Very old sandstones (Unit 571) north of the Chedabucto Fault also support thin soils. The wind- and spray-influenced coastal forest extends to the Sedimentary Lowland (District 860) on the north side of Chedabucto Bay.

Protected Area 13 Bonnet Lake Barrens and 14
Canso Coastal Barrens.

Associated Offshore Unit
911 Atlantic.

Associated Topics
T2.2 The Avalon And Meguma Zones, T2.3 Granite
in Nova Scotia, T3.4 Terrestrial Glacial Deposits and
Landscape Features, T9.1 Soil-forming Factors.

Associated Habitats
H2.1 Rocky Shore, H2.2 Boulder/Cobble Shore, H4.1
Bog, H5.1 Barren, H5.3 Cliff and Bank, H6.2
Softwood Forest (Black Spruce, Larch Association),
H6.3 Mixedwood Forest (White Spruce, Fir–Maple,
Birch Association).

852
Canso
Barrens

860 SEDIMENTARY LOWLAND

Chedabucto Bay is the largest bay on the Atlantic Coast and was formed by the drowning of part of an ancient river system. The river developed on the erodable Carboniferous sediments, which can now be seen on the lowland margins of the bay. Various soils have developed on deep tills and include extensive clay areas. This part of the Atlantic Coast Region is more sheltered, but the coastal forest still dominates. Freshwater habitats are more productive than elsewhere in the Region. Water temperatures are warmer in the summer than on more exposed coasts and support some southern marine fauna species.

GEOLOGY AND LANDSCAPE DEVELOPMENT

Chedabucto Bay lies immediately to the east of the Horton sandstone Rolling Upland (District 570) of the Carboniferous Lowlands. It is dominated by sedimentary rocks deposited during and after the formation of Pangaea in the late Devonian and Carboniferous periods.

Apart from slices of Precambrian Fourchu volcanics, which have been faulted up against younger rocks on Isle Madame, the oldest deposits in the District are coarse conglomerates, including some volcanics. These were deposited during the unsettled period from Late Devonian to Early Carboniferous when major crustal movement and adjustment was taking place in Nova Scotia. These conglomerates and related deposits are extensively exposed in eastern Guysborough County, on Isle Madame, and between L'Ardoise and Loch Lomond.

The succeeding deposits are salts (Windsor Group), reddish siltstones (Canso Group), and fine sandstones (Riversdale Group). All these rocks are relatively soft and erodable, and they have formed a rolling lowland which slopes towards Chedabucto Bay and the Strait of Canso.

LANDSCAPE DEVELOPMENT

Chedabucto Bay owes its origin and shape to a number of factors. Its southern boundary marks the position of the Chedabucto Fault, which extends across central Nova Scotia from the Bay of Fundy to the Canso peninsula. This fault line, the Strait of Canso, and Chedabucto Bay itself were probably part of a major river system which rose on the continental shelf and flowed northwards into the Gulf of St. Lawrence during the Triassic and Cretaceous periods. Later tilting and submergence drowned the valley, creating both the bay and the strait.

Glacial ice moving into Chedabucto Bay from the northwest and from local ice caps deposited a locally derived red-brown sandy till across the Carboniferous rocks. Drumlins are entirely absent on the northwest side of the bay but are common in the eastern part where they have an east-west (Isle Madame) or northwest-southeast orientation. Consequently, rivers rising in the uplands flow southwards across the Carboniferous Lowland into Chedabucto Bay. River Inhabitants, the largest in the District, rises in the Maple Brook area south of the Creignish Hills and empties into the bay through a drowned valley. Marine erosion provides abundant coastal sediment for numerous small gravel beaches. The beaches often enclose small lagoons or salt marshes.

FRESH WATER

Many small to medium-sized lakes are scattered throughout the District, and pH ranges between 6.0 and 7.0. Bogs are particularly common on Isle Madame, and large wetland areas can be found along the Inhabitants River.

SOILS

The soils in this area have developed for the most part from sandstones, slates, and shales, giving tills ranging in texture from sandy loam to shaly clay loam. In Guysborough County, mottled, imperfectly drained clay loam Millbrook soils are common. The better-drained Westbrook sandy loam is found around the town of Guysborough. Riverport (imperfectly drained shaly loam) and Kirkhill (sandy loam) soils have both developed from shales. On Cape Breton Island the western section of this District has more Millbrook soils, imperfectly drained Diligence and Queens clay loams, and poorly drained Kingsville soils. Further east, including much of Isle Madame, soils have developed from stony tills derived from hard sandstones and angular metamorphic rocks. They are the same as those found in the Louisbourg area; i.e., Thom and Arichat soils, with extensive peat deposits.

Along the River Inhabitants the soils are a complex mix of peat; alluvial fine sandy loams known as Kingsville, Cumberland, and Bridgeville soils; and the coarse Hebert series which has developed on outwash gravels.

PLANTS

Although this part of the Atlantic coast is more sheltered, the coastal forest is still manifest, with the predominant forest association being White Spruce and Balsam Fir with maple and birch. On the clay Queens soils of Cape Breton sections of this District, Balsam Fir and Black Spruce are the dominant species, with scattered shade-intolerant hardwoods. Some aspen also occur, especially in disturbed areas. Barren and bog vegetation are common, particularly on Isle Madame. Old farmland is found mainly on the clay soils and is mostly regenerating in pure White Spruce. The low coastal relief and abundance of sediment give areas of salt marsh, but significant local winter ice action restricts the growth of seaweeds.

ANIMALS

Chedabucto Bay is not a productive area for waterfowl or seabirds because there are few undisturbed islands, and winter sea ice restricts feeding from open water. However, salt marsh and estuary areas do provide some wading bird habitat (herons and shorebirds).

Warm water temperatures in summer permit the reproduction and survival of some more southerly marine species. Many of them are also found in the Gulf of St. Lawrence but are no longer able to interact freely with those in Chedabucto Bay because of the presence of the Canso Causeway. The diversity and populations of epifauna are restricted by ice action. Whales are sometimes seen in Chedabucto Bay.

The River Inhabitants provides rich aquatic habitat and is important for nesting Wood Turtles. Freshwater lakes on Isle Madame contain interesting relict fauna with a more continental distribution, including a species of freshwater clam.

SCENIC QUALITY

Scenically, this District is dominated by Chedabucto Bay and its extension into the Strait of Canso. Localities adjacent to both higher relief and the ocean (i.e., around Guysborough Harbour and the eastern end of Canso Strait) are of high scenic quality, particularly where farming adds a human element to the landscape. Isle Madame, though flat, has salt marshes

and much of human interest, with characteristic Acadian village forms. Inland, scenic values are generally low to medium because there is little settlement or relief, and only a few lakes (almost none in Inverness County). There is added scenic value, however, where this lowland abuts the Avalon Uplands (Region 300), notably along the upper reaches of River Inhabitants.

CULTURAL ENVIRONMENT

Nicholas Denys established a fur trading and fishing post at St. Peters in 1636. During the eighteenth century, Isle Madame was an important Acadian settlement in close communication with Louisbourg. In general, small-scale farming, fishing, and forestry have been the resource use of the land and sea in this area. Shipbuilding was once common and, today, shipbuilding and maintenance industries continue. An industrial base established along the Strait of Canso is strategically located to make use of the shipping lane connecting the Gulf of St. Lawrence with the Atlantic Ocean.

Forestry exploitation yields pulpwood, which supplies a sulphite mill and a newsprint mill at Point Tupper. A coal-fired, steam-turbine electrical plant is also located at Point Tupper. St. Peters Canal is an important link to the Bras d'Or Lake, facilitating recreational boating. Prior to the completion of the canal, small vessels were pulled by oxen over the narrow strip of land on skids, and thus the area was referred to on Admiralty charts of the time as "Haulover Isthmus." In 1970 the Greek tanker *Arrow*, carrying 16,200 tons of bunker C oil to a pulp mill at Point Tupper struck Cerberus Rock in Chedabucto Bay, creating a massive oil spill which polluted half of the bay's 600-km coastline. Twenty years later, Bedford Institute of Oceanography scientists studying Chedabucto Bay concluded that little evidence of this oil spill remained.

● ● ● ● ● ● ● ●

860
Sedimentary
Lowland

Sites of Special Interest
- Loch Lomond—exposed conglomerates and deposits
- Janvrin Island—exposed red and purplish strata

Provincial Parks and Park Reserves
- Mast Cove
- Boylston
- Ragged Head
- Dorts Cove
- Kempt Road
- Louisdale
- Lennox Passage
- Cap La Ronde
- Pondville Beach
- Arichat
- Cove Road

Proposed Parks and Protected Areas System includes Natural Landscape 47.

Scenic Viewpoints
- Guysborough Harbour (both sides)
- River Inhabitants (tidal reaches)
- Salt marshes between Isle Madame and Janvrin Island
- Arichat Provincial Park (Arichat Harbour)
- St. Peters Canal

Associated Offshore Units
911 Atlantic, 916 Bras d'Or Lake.

Associated Topics
T2.4 The Carboniferous Basin, T4.3 Post-glacial Colonization by Animals, T11.15 Amphibians and Reptiles, T11.16 Land and Freshwater Invertebrates.

Associated Habitats
H2 Coastal, H4.1 Bog, H3.2 Freshwater Open-Water Lentic, H3.4 Freshwater Bottom Lentic, H3.6 Freshwater Water's Edge Lentic, H5.1 Barren, H5.2 Oldfield, H6.3 Mixed Forest (White Spruce, Fir–Maple, Birch Association).

**860
Sedimentary
Lowland**

870 TILL PLAIN

This is a low-lying, almost flat District with a highly eroded bedrock surface thickly covered with glacial till, sands, and gravel. The poorly drained surface gives numerous bogs, swamps, lakes, and slow-moving, wandering streams. A rocky coastline in the east gives way to a coast dominated by barrier beaches in the west. Balsam Fir is the dominant tree species, with Black Spruce and larch in wetter areas. Limited snow cover provides good wintering habitat for deer. Abundant offshore marine life thrives on plankton-rich, cool, upwelling coastal waters.

GEOLOGY AND LANDSCAPE DEVELOPMENT

The Till Plain lies on the southeastern side of Cape Breton, on the lower part of the tilted planation surface (see Figure 29). The bedrock is dominated by Precambrian Fourchu volcanics with large outcrops of Cambrian granite and metamorphic sediments of varied composition. The bedrock is highly eroded and is presumed to be almost flat under the glacial deposits. This is difficult to verify because the whole District is covered by a thick layer of glacial till, sands, and gravels, with the bedrock exposed only along the coast.

The bedrock is cut by many parallel, northeast-southwest faults along which vertical movement has taken place. Gabarus Bay is believed to be the product of downfaulting along another set of faults oriented northwest to southeast.

Surficial Deposits and
Landscape Development
Glacial ice from the exposed Scotian Shelf flowed onshore and then northeast during the Wisconsin glacial period, depositing a thick mantle of sands and gravels across the entire area. The thickness is variable but commonly achieves 30 m, with 12 m representing an average depth. Drumlins are common. The glacial deposits have completely altered the original drainage pattern. The surface is now covered with irregular lakes and wandering streams.

Inland the terrain is low-lying and rolling, rising across a series of ridges to about 125 m in the northwest. A dominant landscape feature is the Mira River valley, which extends from Framboise Cove northwards to about Marion Bridge and then sweeps eastwards to exit at Mira Bay. Its preglacial flow, which may have been to the south, was redirected by small changes in elevation and blockage of the original exit by glacial deposits. The lower reaches of the river have been dammed by glacial gravels to form a long lake. At Mira Bay the river funnels through a very narrow valley, in places only 50 m wide, with steep banks 20 m high.

The coastline of the Till Plain is relatively even and dips gently into the sea. Gabarus Bay is the only stretch of coast where sea cliffs are found. Sediment supply along the coast is variable. North of Gabarus, rocky shorelines, boulders, and cobble beaches are most common; south of Gabarus, the coast is indented with protected bays. Sand and gravel beaches are numerous. Between Point Michaud and Fourchu Bay an extensive series of cobble barrier beaches enclose large barachois ponds (see Figure 29). These beaches may have originally formed offshore and moved landward as sea levels rose.

FRESH WATER

The many small lakes and freshwater wetlands are associated with streams scattered throughout this District. The pH levels tend to be neutral, ranging between 6.5 and 7.5.

SOILS

The soils in this District illustrate how a strong podzol development associated with the climate along the Atlantic coast can override the effects of different parent materials. The soils have developed from sandstones, quartzites, and shales. The most common soil series is Thom, a well-drained sandy loam podzol usually associated with cooler and wetter highland areas such as the Cobequids. A feature of Thom soils is the accumulation of organic matter on the surface and "B" horizon. Closer to the coast, the imperfectly to poorly drained Mira and Arichat associate soils are more common.

On the granites around Lower St. Esprit, Gibraltar and Aspotogan soils are found. Shulie sandy loams occur between Loch Lomond and the Mira River. These are similar to soils in Unit 532 to the north. To the east of the Mira River, well-drained Kirkhill soils occur; these have a shaly loam texture and are relatively deep and free of stone. Ortstein layers are common in this District, and large areas of peat have built up.

870
Till Plain

PLANTS

The main controlling factors in this District are the cool, wet soils, the marine exposures, widespread disturbance, and insect damage. Along the coast, White Spruce is common, but inland Balsam Fir grows much better and is the dominant species. Some shade-intolerant species with fewer shade-tolerant species are found on better-drained soils inland. Black Spruce and larch are common in wet depressions. Hemlock was once common but is now rare, presumably having been removed through selective logging by early settlers. Spruce Budworm is rampant here.

Large bogs are a prominent feature. Considerable quantities of Bakeapple are found in the bogs on Scatarie Island, exposed headlands, and other coastal bogs and barrens. Heath vegetation, particularly Crowberry, is found on exposed headlands.

Sand-dune and tidal-marsh communities with some beds of Eelgrass are found along the coast. Limited warm-water influence in summer has permitted the penetration of some marine plant species from the Gulf of St. Lawrence, such as Serrated Wrack, but marine flora is restricted by the cold water and ice action.

ANIMALS

Low snowfall provides good deer-wintering habitat in this District. Staging areas for migratory waterfowl and shorebirds are found along this coast between Fourchu Bay and Framboise Cove. The islands provide important breeding habitat for seabirds. Green Island has the most southerly nesting colony of Black-legged Kittiwakes and is the only one known in the Maritimes. Elsewhere breeding populations of gulls, cormorants, Black Guillemot, and Common Ei-

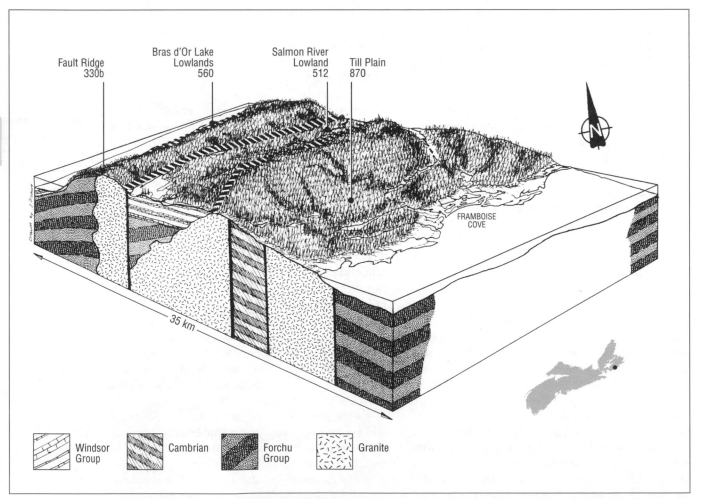

Figure 29: Louisbourg lowland area. Glacial deposits mask the very old rocks of this Till Plain (District 870). At the coast, the reworking of these sediments has created an extensive system of barrier beaches and coastal lagoons. Inland, softer rocks are preserved in the downfaulted Salmon River lowland. Windsor Group rocks are also found on the lowland fringe (District 560) of Bras d'Or Lake abutting the resistant upland known as the East Bay Hills (District 330).

der can be seen. Pelagic seabird concentrations occur off Louisbourg and are probably associated with an area of deepwater upwelling. Ptarmigan and Arctic Hare have been introduced on Scatarie Island.

The Louisbourg lowland is a cold-water coast with extensive sea ice, resulting in an impoverished marine fauna of an exposed boreal character. Harbour Seals are common; Grey Seals used to breed on the Basque Islands.

Typical freshwater fish species include White Perch, Banded Killifish, sticklebacks and Brook Trout. The Mira River supports a unique population of Lake Whitefish.

SCENIC QUALITY

This District contains a variety of landscapes and coastal scenery, the only constant being low relief—the area is almost flat except for Gillis Mountain and the hills around Gabarus Bay. Coastal scenery varies from rocks to cliffs to beaches, with the most impressive views being in Gabarus Bay. Inland, scenic ratings are typically low to medium, though lake sections of Mira River provide many delightful scenes from boats. Despite the presence of drumlins, there is very little settlement, except for a scattering of fishing villages and long lines of summer homes ("bungalows") along the Mira.

CULTURAL ENVIRONMENT

This is a rugged coastline, sparsely populated, with scattered fishing villages. The French were drawn to Louisbourg by its ideal harbour and strategic location on Cape Breton Island. Today the Fortress of Louisbourg National Historic Site is the largest historical reconstruction in North America and presents the fascinating story of the French fort. The first recorded coal mining in the province was undertaken here in 1720. Small farms originally settled by Acadians who planted apple and plum trees can be found along the Mira River. Salmon and trout fishing have a long history on the river, beginning with the Mi'kmaq. Mira shores have yielded harvests of sand and gravel, but this industry has declined. A small coal mine operated at Broughton. Fireclay, found on both sides of the river, was used as early as 1727 by the French to create bricks for the construction of Fort Louisbourg. The French brickyard was later operated by the British for many years. Large quantities of stones have been quarried from the cliffs along the Mira.

• • • • • • • •

Sites of Special Interest
- Point Michaud (IBP Proposed Ecological Site 26)—beach and sand dune system showing succession from bare sand to White Spruce forest
- Scatarie Island—provincial wildlife management area with bogs and barrens
- Little Lorraine to Big Lorraine—barren, rocky headlands with interesting flora
- Gooseberry Cove—a hanging bog, nesting sites
- Baleine—arctic-alpine flora
- South Head—bog contains Grass-pink
- Louisbourg National Historic Park—bogs, barrens, and forest; Precambrian volcanic ash, vent deposits, and dykes
- Green Island—nesting site for Black-legged Kittiwakes
- Main-à-Dieu—exposed cobble beach
- Hilliards Lake, Winging Point Lake, Belfry Lake, Marcoche Lake—barachois ponds enclosed by barrier beaches
- Mira River—a rare outcrop of fossiliferous Cambrian sandstone and shale on the south side of Mira River on the road between Marion Bridge and Albert Bridge

Provincial Parks and Park Reserves
- Point Michaud Beach
- St. Esprit
- Belfry
- Main-à-Dieu

Proposed Parks and Protected Areas System includes Natural Landscapes 51, 52, 53, and 55, and Candidate Protected Areas 9 Middle River Framboise, 10 Gabarus, and 11 Scatarie Island.

Scenic Viewpoints
- Fortress of Louisbourg—restored eighteenth-century fortress
- Louisbourg Harbour (east side)
- Gabarus Bay (Oceanview and Deep Cove)

Associated Offshore Units
911 Atlantic, 915 Sydney Bight.

Associated Topics
T2.2 The Avalon and Meguma Zones, T9.3 Biological Environment, T10.9 Algae, T11.12 Marine Mammals.

Associated Habitats
H2 Coastal, H4.1 Bog, H5.1 Barren, H6.3 Mixed Forest (White Spruce, Fir-Maple, Birch Association).

870
Till Plain

880 CLIFFED ISLAND

GEOLOGY AND LANDSCAPE DEVELOPMENT

St. Paul Island is 25 km northeast of Cape North in Cape Breton. It is 5 km long and peaks at 121 m high on Corgan Mountain. It is accompanied by a much smaller island, The Tickle, which is only 300 m long. Geologically the island is part of the Cape Breton highlands. Most of the gneiss and schist that forms the island belongs to the Precambrian George River Group, although some slightly younger Fourchu Group rocks are found on the northeast coast.

Almost vertical sea cliffs surround St. Paul Island, except on the southwestern side. A sloping plateau surface, reminiscent of the Cape Breton highlands, occupies most of the island; but it has an average elevation of 100 m above sea level, much lower than the highlands' 500 m. There is no sheltered anchorage; the shoreline is scoured by sea ice moving out of the Gulf of St. Lawrence in spring. Storm waves attack the cliffs at all times of year.

FRESH WATER

Two distinct freshwater ponds on the central plateau drain into the Cabot Strait. Several streams and small bogs provide the remaining surface-water coverage.

PLANTS

Despite its lower altitude, the plateau surface is exposed to winds comparable to those in the Plateau-Taiga (Region 100). The response of the vegetation is similar, with stunted spruce-fir coastal forest (H6.2) dominating the island. The barrens, bogs, and exposed cliffs are home to a number of northerly species not normally found in Nova Scotia, as follows:
- barrens: Bearberry Willow and Alpine Whortleberry, both of which have widespread boreal distributions but are rare in Nova Scotia
- bogs: the sedge *Carex gynocrates*, the orchid Grass-pink, and the bog birch are all found in bogs and wet depressions; all are widespread but rarely find the right habitat in Nova Scotia
- cliffs: *Oxytropis johannensis*, one of the pea family of flowering plants, is found here and on other exposed cliffs, particularly around the Bay of Fundy
- shorelines of ponds and streams: Butterwort and Bird's-eye Primrose, although the latter has a more southerly distribution

ANIMALS

Little information is recorded on the terrestrial and aquatic fauna of St. Paul Island. Avifauna records confirm that eight species of birds breed in this Unit: Leach's Storm-petrel, Black Guillemot, Common Raven, Mourning Warbler, Blackpoll Warbler, Tennessee Warbler, Grey-cheeked Thrush, and Bald Eagle.

• • • • • • • •

Scenic Quality
Inaccessible, flat-topped St. Paul Island is visible only from vessels in the Cabot Strait or, distantly, from northern Cape Breton Island.

Cultural Environment
St. Paul Island and its lighthouse have long been used as navigational aids. Shipwrecks found in nearby waters have attracted recreational divers to the island.

Associated Offshore Units
915 Sydney Bight, 923 Valleys and Plains.

Associated Topics
T7 Coast, T10.12 Rare Plants, T11.1 Factors Influencing Birds, T11.3 Open Habitat Birds, T11.4 Birds of Prey.

Associated Habitats
H2 Coastal, H4.1 Bog, H5.1 Barren, H5.3 Cliff and Bank, H6.3 Mixedwood Forest (White Spruce, Fir–Maple, Birch Association).

890 SANDY ISLAND

Sable Island is composed almost entirely of sand. Constant winds, salt spray, and blowing sand limit the growth of trees and shrubs. Climatic winter and summer extremes are modified by the ocean's influence. The island is a breeding ground for seals and is home to Sable Island horses.

GEOLOGY

Sable Island is an elongated sand island which lies 300 km east of Halifax. It is oriented east-west and measures 42 km by 1.4 km at low tide. Shallow bars extending underwater at either end give it an overall length of 80 km. The island is the emergent part of a very large sand deposit on Sable Island Bank which occupies an area measuring 250 km by 115 km on the Scotian Shelf. Beneath the sand is a wedge of Cretaceous and Tertiary sediments which thickens seaward and is being actively surveyed and drilled for hydrocarbon deposits.

The sand was deposited in a sand and gravel mixture as an outwash fan from a late Wisconsinan ice front which approached but never covered Sable Island Bank. As glacial ice melted and sea levels rose, the sand was winnowed out. Tides and wind-driven currents now keep it in continuous motion within a circulating "sand cell." The sand moves around the island, removing and replacing sand on the emergent part of Sable Island.

LANDSCAPE DEVELOPMENT

Sable Island has the shape of a shallow crescent which is concave northwards. It consists of two lines of high dunes which were originally separated by a tidal gap. The southern range has now disappeared, leaving a wide beach area. The form of the island changes constantly as strong winds and frequent storms shift the sand around the island and back and forth from offshore. The beach profile undergoes normal seasonal changes; it is steeply inclined in winter and gently inclined in summer.

Records and maps for the past 200 years or so show that though the island has changed its form, it has more or less maintained the same position and overall size. The eastern half, though more stable than the western half, has decreased in altitude from

50 m to 24 m at its highest elevation. The violent storms which have caused considerable changes in morphology on the island seem to be counterbalanced by a slow rebuilding process during quieter periods when sand is added from offshore.

CLIMATE

The climate of Sable Island is characteristically maritime with a narrow range of temperature and high winds. Sable Island is warmer in winter and cooler in summer than the neighbouring mainland. Fogs are frequent during the summer.

Mean daily temperatures in January hover around 0°C, in April they rise to approximately 4°C, and by July mean daily temperatures are around 15°C. In comparison to the mainland, the temperature regime on Sable Island shows a slightly lower annual mean maximum and a much higher annual mean minimum.

The total annual precipitation is similar to that of Halifax. Only a very small proportion falls as snow because of the mild winter temperatures. The snow that does fall does not linger.

Cloud or fog cover over Sable Island is frequent; the mean number of hours of sunshine is substantially lower than on the mainland. The incidence of foggy days increases between April and August. July is the foggiest month; fog occurs on average 21 days of the month. Average monthly windspeeds are significantly higher, as strong winds blow more of the time and Sable Island is more exposed than the mainland.

The main features of the climate are mild temperatures, constant high winds, and high humidity.

FRESH WATER

Several small freshwater ponds are located within the dunes in the vegetated areas, and some larger brackish ponds and lakes are found on the southern beach. Rainwater filtering through the sand collects to form a freshwater lens which, by displacing seawater, appears as pools in depressions. The pH of most of these freshwater pools varies from 5.0–5.7. Brackish ponds receive seawater during storm surges, and both their size and water chemistry can

890
Sandy
Island

change dramatically. The major brackish pond is Wallace Lake, which can vary in size throughout the year from two or three small ponds to an area up to 14 km long.

The physical and chemical characteristics of pools on Sable Island may be influenced by fluctuating water levels, the grazing and trampling of horses, and nutrient enrichment from colonies of gulls and terns.

SOILS

On the beaches, there is no soil development (i.e., no identifiable soil horizon) because of the constant shifting of the sandy substrate. In more sheltered areas in the central part of the island some peat has formed. But the soil is of poor nutritive quality and contains only small amounts of organic material. Podzolization occurred in the past when the sands were more stable, but only remnants remain.

PLANTS

The main influences on the regional vegetation are the high winds, salt spray, sandblasting, lack of nutrients, and effects of grazing by the Sable Island horses. The variety of plants found on the island has been increased by numerous introductions, both deliberate and accidental. A total of 154 native and 69 introduced vascular plants have been recorded.

Trees cannot survive the effects of wind and salt damage. In 1901, in a massive attempt to stabilize the dunes, over 80,000 trees were transplanted. Almost all died immediately, and by 1981 only one, a maple, could be found. Two pine trees planted in the early 1970s are barely surviving.

In a botanical study completed in 1981, plant communities were divided into several categories: Sandwort, Dense Marram, Sparse Marram, Marram-Fescue, Shrub Heath, Cranberry Heath, and Pond-edge Herbaceous. The first three communities are marked by a relatively low species diversity, which increases through the remaining communities. The greatest diversity is found at the edges of the fresh-water ponds.

In the Sandwort community, nearly all the cover is provided by Sea-beach Sandwort. The most important species in the Dense Marram community are American Beach-grass, Beach-pea, and Yarrow. American Beach-grass is the most important species in the Sparse Marram community, with Beach-pea and Seaside Goldenrod. In the Marram-Fescue community, American Beach-grass is joined by Red Fescue and a number of other species.

In the Shrub Heath community, Black Crowberry, Common Juniper, Bayberry, Wild Rose, blueberry, and Heather (in one area) are common plants. In the Cranberry Heath community, cranberries grow with such plants as Baltic Rush, Bayberry, and aster.

Freshwater pools are usually fringed by a wide variety of plants, such as bulrushes, irises, Spike-rush, Baltic Rush, and Lance-leaved Violet, usually grading into the Cranberry Heath. In the brackish ponds, Ditch-grass and Sago Pondweed grow, surrounded either by bare sandy margins or salt-tolerant plants. The only vascular plant to grow in very brackish water is Eelgrass.

ANIMALS

Sable Island provides sand-beach, sand-dune, and heathland habitats, with a number of fresh and brackish pools. The fact that the island is the only landfall for 160 km also ensures that it receives many migratory and marine visitors. The only terrestrial mammal now found on the island is the horse. The Sable Island horses were probably deliberately introduced in the eighteenth century. The horse population fluctuates and in recent years has varied between 150 and 350. At one time 500 cattle lived on the island, and pigs roamed wild. Both Grey and Harbour seals whelp on the island, and whales and dolphins are quite regularly washed up on the beaches. A number of other mammals have at one time been introduced to the island, including rats, cats, rabbits, and foxes, but all are now extirpated.

A total of 489 species of insects have been recorded on the island. The pattern of their distribution in North America has given rise to theories that Sable Island may have acted as a coastal-plain refugium during the Pleistocene glaciation. Insects have also been introduced with livestock, vegetation, and shipwrecks. A number of rare and unusual insects occur on Sable Island, and numerous moths appear, different enough to warrant the status of sub-species. More than 100 other invertebrates have been recorded, including the freshwater sponge *Heteromyenia macouni*.

Five species of fish—Mummichog, American Eel, Black-spotted Stickleback, Ninespine Stickleback, and Fourspine Stickleback—are found in the freshwater and brackish pools. All five species are capable of crossing salt water to reach the island.

Of the 12 species of birds that regularly breed on Sable Island, the most famous is the Ipswich Sparrow, which is an endemic sub-species of the Savannah Sparrow. Other birds include the European Starling, Great Black Back Gull, Herring Gull, Arctic Tern,

890
Sandy
Island

Common Tern, Roseate Tern, Spotted Sandpiper, Least Sandpiper, Semipalmated Plover, Black Duck, and Red-breasted Merganser. Up to 312 other birds have been recorded as vagrants, strays, or migrants.

SCENIC QUALITY

For those lucky enough to visit, Sable Island presents unique vistas from the higher dunes, which allow the island's shape and size to be seen. Elsewhere the sand beaches and dune systems are notable for their number and size. Sheltered hollows around the interior ponds provide visual relief from the surrounding ocean.

CULTURAL ENVIRONMENT

For years, Sable Island was the bane of sailing ships, and many were wrecked on its shores. A series of stations here, including a lighthouse, have long been lifesaving navigational aids to ships. In 1901 the Canadian government attempted to forest Sable Island to control shifting sands. More than 80,000 trees and shrubs were planted, and 30 pounds of pine seed were scattered over some parts of the island. Several years later, 2,000 willow transplants from sandy soil in France were sent to Sable Island. The first planting was made with no fencing, and the Sable Island horses soon consumed the entire plantation. A second attempt with this willow was made the next year by planting and fencing about a half acre. But these transplants did not survive either, because the wind-driven sand blasted the young trees. By the 1920s, nothing was left of these efforts except for some fence posts.

Most of the ecological damage on Sable Island resulted from disturbances to the vegetation, leaving loose sand exposed to the wind. Small holes in the sand soon blow out to become big holes and gullies. In the 1970s, snow fences were erected at strategic points, causing the wind to drop sand leeward of the fences and marram grass colonized the dunes. Government approval must be gained to visit the island, which is off limits to most people. Oil exploration has been conducted on the island and current production wells are located offshore. Sable Island has considerable scientific value as a unique ecological environment. It is one of the most intensively studied areas in the province (Catling, 1984; Wright, 1989).

• • • • • • • •

Provincial Parks and Park Reserves
Proposed Parks and Protected Areas System includes Natural Landscape 77.

Associated Offshore Unit
931e Sable Island Bank.

Associated Topics
T2.7 Offshore Geology, T3.4 Terrestrial Glacial Deposits and Landscape Features, T3.5 Offshore Bottom Characteristics, T4.1 Post-glacial Climatic Change, T6.1 Ocean Currents, T7.1 Modifying Forces, T7.3 Coastal Landforms, T11.1 Factors Influencing Birds, T11.8 Land Mammals, T11.12 Marine Mammals, T11.14 Marine Fishes, T11.16 Land and Freshwater Invertebrates, T11.18 Rare and Endangered Animals.

Associated Habitats
H1.1 Offshore Open Water, H1.2 Offshore Benthic, H2.3 Sandy Shore, H2.5 Tidal Marsh, H2.6 Dune System.

890
Sandy
Island

900
Offshore/
Continental Shelf

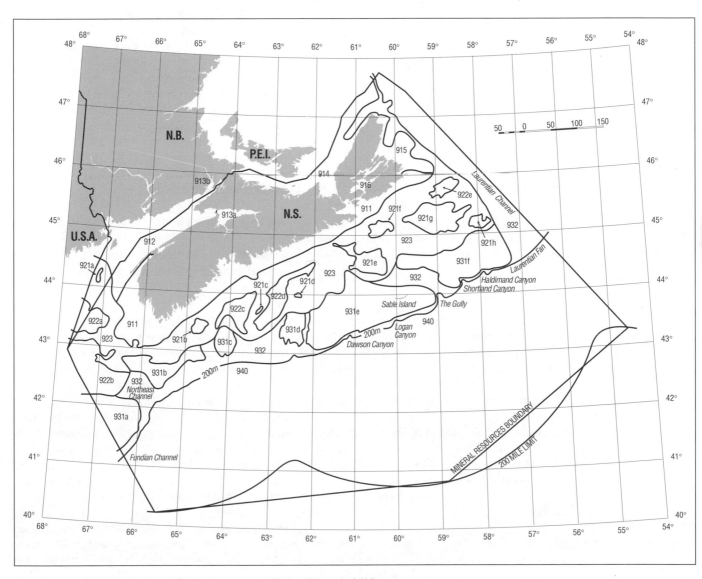

Figure 30: Region 900, Offshore/Continental Shelf, and its component Districts, Units, and sub-Units.

900 OFFSHORE/CONTINENTAL SHELF

The following physiographic features are the basis for the division of the Districts of Region 900:

- District 910, Inner Shelf, is a zone of gradually sloping bottom adjacent to shore and extending to depths of about 110 metres in all areas
- District 920, Middle Shelf, is a zone of fishing banks and deep basins in the mid-portions of the continental shelf and includes the Scotian Shelf and the Gulf of Maine
- District 930, Outer Shelf, is a zone of large offshore banks and intervening channels and saddles on the outer edge of the continental shelf
- District 940, Scotian Slope, is the deep-water area beyond the shelf break and continental slope extending to Canada/Nova Scotia jurisdictional limits

REGIONAL CHARACTERISTICS

The continental shelf extends from 125–230 km offshore to depths of about 200 metres. Major offshore areas that make up the shelf are the Northumberland Strait, southeastern Gulf of St. Lawrence, Sydney Bight, Scotian Shelf, Georges Bank, Gulf of Maine, and Bay of Fundy. The landscape is that of a submerged coastal plain, and the structure reflects long periods of terrestrial erosion, the passage of continental ice sheets, and the influence of the ocean. Features include basins up to 280 m deep on the central shelf; fishing banks; channels; and Sable Island (District 890), on Sable Island Bank, extending 26 m above sea level. Waters from the Gulf of St. Lawrence and from further offshore (the slope water) mainly influence biological processes on the shelf; and the animals and plants, and seasonal cycles of productivity and abundance, follow patterns typical of cool temperate regions.

Beyond the shelf break (200 m) the bottom slopes steeply to a depth of 2,000 metres, reaching a maximum of 5,000 metres at the edge of the Region. The area experiences full oceanic conditions.

GEOLOGY

Various geological or bedrock provinces are represented on the continental shelf (see T3.5). Inshore, the bedrock is usually a seaward extension of rock formations on the adjacent land. Areas of complex geology may have different subtidal bedrock than on the coast. Patterns and variations of bedrock geology are not as easily identified in the offshore but are probably as varied as on land.

Four major geological or bedrock units are represented: (1) the Acadian Basin, an area of Triassic rocks in the Bay of Fundy and northern Gulf of Maine, (2) terrestrial bedrock extending to 25 km offshore along the Atlantic coast of Nova Scotia and into basins on the south side of the Gulf of Maine, (3) an outer area comprising the Middle and Outer Scotian Shelf, consisting of Jurassic, Cretaceous, and Tertiary rocks and including Georges Bank, the outer Gulf of Maine, and the outer part of the Laurentian Channel, and (4) Sydney Basin, an area of Carboniferous rocks northeast of Cape Breton Island. Northumberland Strait is underlain in places by Ordovician to Middle Carboniferous rocks of the Antigonish and Cape Breton highlands, and by horizontal or gently folded Upper Carboniferous and Permian sedimentary rocks.

SEABED MORPHOLOGY

The basic features of the marine "landscape" were formed during long periods of terrestrial erosion of ancient bedrock surfaces. This topography was subsequently modified by the passage of glaciers and, on a smaller scale, by the action of the sea. The large features (e.g., banks and basins) are not unlike uplands, peneplains, and valley systems on the modern mainland surface, sharing their elevation and extent, although the continental shelf lacks prominent geological features like those found on land (e.g., Cape Breton highlands, North Mountain). Where ancient drainage systems reached the edge of the continental shelf, dramatic, steep-sided submarine valleys reach down the continental slope. Glacial features create more localized variations in landscape and include moraines and other features, such as pockmarks and iceberg scours (see T3.4). The surface sediment patterns on the continental shelf result from the action of the ocean and its interaction with retreating Holocene glaciers. The finest surface features are caused by waves and currents, and include sand ridges, waves, and ripples. Sable Island (Region 890) is a unique offshore feature derived from glacial material on top of early bedrock features.

CLIMATE

The climate of the Offshore/Continental Shelf Region follows the general pattern found on land but does not show the same degree of local variation. In addition to atmospheric factors, the temperature of the ocean and distance from land influence climate at sea. The ocean can hold heat and tends to moderate the temperature of the air above it.

In general, wind speeds are higher over the sea than over land because of reduced wind resistance. However, offshore winds are reduced within a few kilometres of the shore because of the shielding effect of the land. Further out to sea, wind is virtually unhindered and assumes a speed which more closely resembles the velocity of the wind tens of metres above the surface.

The temperatures of water masses influence air temperatures, significantly in some cases. In early spring the water is cold and cools the air above it, frequently forming fog. As the season progresses, the surface waters are heated by sunlight and grow gradually warmer. This rise is punctuated by periods when storms bring cold water to the surface and bring temporary declines in temperature. The annual peak water temperature occurs in the fall in the Atlantic (Unit 911) and the Outer Bay of Fundy (Unit 912), but warmer temperatures are observed in late summer in the Northumberland Strait (Unit 914), Minas Basin (sub-Unit 913a), and shallow coastal bays and inlets (District 460) where water is shallower and less influenced by colder, deeper water. The resulting warmer water temperatures make these areas popular for tourists.

Areas where warm and cold water masses meet are also marked by abrupt changes in air temperature. Just beyond the outer edge of the continental shelf, a warmer water mass (slope water) meets the shelf water and results in a sudden temperature change for ships passing across the boundary. Further offshore, the edge of the Gulf Stream heralds a sudden jump in temperatures to near tropical conditions. Even in winter, sailors can work comfortably here in shirt sleeves. In both cases, fog frequently occurs along the boundaries as warmer humid air flows over cooler water and condensation (fog) develops.

The waters of the Outer Bay of Fundy seldom have a chance to warm at the surface because of the significant mixing caused by tidal movements. Consequently, the water is cool most of the year. Just outside the Bay of Fundy, however, the water is more sta-

ble and can warm up more. The contrast in the temperatures of these water masses is one of the causes of the frequent fogs in southwest Nova Scotia, particularly near Yarmouth.

OCEANOGRAPHY

Tides, winds, buoyancy, and remote forcing are important oceanographic factors on the continental shelf (see T6.1). The large ocean currents include the extension of the Gaspé Current in Northumberland Strait, and the Nova Scotia Current along the continental shelf. The Gulf Stream comes closest to the Canadian continental shelf off East Georges Bank (sub-Unit 931a). Other oceanographic features include coastal upwelling, estuarine circulation, tidal fronts, tidal gyres, shelf-break fronts, and warm-core rings.

Temperature and salinity are important components of oceanic climate and influence biological productivity. In February, upper layer temperatures in some areas are at or near freezing, while temperatures on the South Shore of Nova Scotia and in the Bay of Fundy are considerably warmer. August temperatures are highest in Northumberland Strait and become cooler southwestwards from Cape Breton along the Atlantic Coast (Region 800). At the sea surface on the Scotian Shelf, temperature and salinity increase as one moves southeastwards from land.

SEDIMENTS

Most sediments on the continental shelf originated as glacial deposits. Glacial till was deposited in some places, while silt from glacial meltwater extended widely. Following glaciation, glacial till on the shallower parts was exposed to the action of the ocean, which washed and sorted it and spread a layer of clays to the deep basins and a fringe of sand to the offshore banks, resulting in the general pattern observed today. Unlike the land, the ocean bottom has not been modified significantly by the growth of plants and soil formation, and in many cases is being continually altered, at least in surface layers, by ocean processes.

The tops of banks and shallow coastal areas throughout the Region are generally sandy to gravelly in character and occasionally have large boulders like the glacial erratics found on land, thus making bad trawling ground. Below a depth of 100–120 m, the sediments have more sand and finer material but still contain boulders and gravel. These deeper sediments were never reworked by rising sea levels at the end of the last glaciation and consequently have

900
Offshore/
Continental
Shelf

retained more fine sediment components. In contrast, near the Atlantic coast of Nova Scotia and up to 25 km offshore, the bottom is rough and rocky—part of the bedrock of the coastal land mass. The relatively steep slope, in combination with rising sea levels, led to the scouring of most of the surface sediment, leaving only bedrock.

In the deeper basins, clays occur, because water motion is low enough to permit fine particles to settle. Deep channels and submarine canyons frequently have strong currents and usually contain coarse sediments. The bottom of the continental slope has thick surficial sediments of clay and sand.

PLANTS

Beds of kelp and other marine algae grow on the seabed close to shore, and microscopic phytoplankton occur both nearshore and in most other waters. Most anchored marine plants can occur only to a depth of about 30 m and generally fall into two types: those attached to rocks and those in soft bottom. The main attached species of the Nova Scotia coast are the kelps and rockweeds, but more than 300 species of seaweed occur around Nova Scotia coasts.

Marine seaweed growth is most abundant on exposed rocky shores typical of the Atlantic coast, where there are sites for attachment and adequate water movements to supply nutrients. Seaweeds generally grow less and their shapes change in sheltered environments. In areas with ice cover through part of the year, profuse algal growth can develop only beneath the depth of winter ice scour, even on a suitable substrate. These areas—the Northumberland Strait (Unit 914), Inner Bay of Fundy (Unit 913), and Bras d'Or Lake (Unit 916)—have a characteristic intertidal zone scraped clean of algae every year but upon which a carpet of algae can develop seasonally. Irish Moss develops in the subtidal zone beneath the ice in western and northern P.E.I.

Particularly in the Northumberland Strait but also in protected inlets and bays throughout Nova Scotia, soft bottoms, usually just below tide level, are populated by Eelgrass. This flowering plant grows the world over and is important in marine food chains. Eelgrass beds support a diverse invertebrate fauna as well as the young stages of a variety of fish and shellfish species.

Phytoplankton, notably diatom growth, occurs throughout the offshore and creates the main food source for planktonic animals and bottom-dwelling filter feeders. It eventually reaches and supports the extensive offshore fisheries resource. Areas of enhanced phytoplankton growth occur where ocean conditions bring nutrients to the surface, such as along the Atlantic coast, off southwest Nova Scotia, on the northern margin of Georges Bank (upwellings), and in a band stretching along the outer edge of the Scotian Shelf, where shelf and slope water meet and nutrients come to the surface. Water column activity peaks from spring to summer.

Plants in the Nova Scotia offshore are generally typical of the boreal cold-water species which occur throughout much of the North Atlantic. Plant production of both seaweeds and phytoplankton in these areas is typically among the highest in the world. Occasional warmer-water species occur, often introduced by shipping. A suite of warm-water algae occurs in the Gulf of St. Lawrence in estuaries and lagoons where water temperatures are higher.

ANIMALS

Oceanic food chains are based on phytoplankton primary production. Most organisms in the ocean feed on phytoplankton, if only in their juvenile stages. Microscopic phytoplankton is consumed directly by grazing vertebrates, invertebrates and by suspension feeders such as mussels, scallops and oysters. Seaweeds also form the basis for food chains involving grazers such as sea urchins, or a wide variety of detritivores, upon death. Invertebrate communities are much more in evidence in these ecosystems, within the water column, on substrate surfaces as well as within the sediments.

The major commercial fish species are groundfish that live on or near the bottom and include cod, haddock, pollock, halibut, and various species of flatfish. These feed on seabed invertebrates as adults but consume zooplankton as they develop from eggs and larvae.

Principal pelagic fish species on the continental shelf (herring, mackerel, Bluefin Tuna, capelin, and some smaller species) feed on zooplankton or smaller fish all their lives (herring can use gill structures to filter the water). Deep water beyond the shelf break has an oceanic fauna with characteristic zooplankton and mesopelagic fish, cephalopods, and crustaceans. Baleen whales such as the Humpback feed on zooplankton, and toothed whales, including the endangered Northern Right Whale, another common Nova Scotia species, feed on fish and squid. Nova Scotia has a summer population of rare Bottlenose Whales near Misaine Bank that feeds on squid concentrated there.

900
Offshore/
Continental
Shelf

Seabirds include common species associated with land and coastal areas (Herring and Black Back gulls, Great and Double-crested cormorants) and truly oceangoing birds such as shearwaters, terns, jaegers, phalaropes, and Storm-petrels, which migrate seasonally into Nova Scotia waters. Nesting colonies of gannets, puffins, petrels, and kittiwakes use offshore waters as a food source, with certain species sometimes flying daily to outer parts of the continental shelf. Waters off Nova Scotia are resting places for more northerly species and for overwintering waterfowl such as geese and seaducks.

CULTURAL ENVIRONMENT

For thousands of years the waters off Nova Scotia have been important for coastal transportation and their marine resources have been used by aboriginal peoples and later immigrants. The abundance of marine fisheries was noted by early European explorers. Excellent harbours provided sites for European settlement, commerce, and strategic naval and military bases (e.g., Louisbourg 1712 and Halifax 1749). The wide range of seaweed, shellfish, groundfish, pelagic fish, and marine mammal resources are now regulated to compensate for overuse and the effects of coastal pollution. Closure of the ground fisheries in 1992 had a severe economic impact. Hydrocarbon (oil and gas) and other mineral resources of the seabed are under development. Several marine locations have been used as dumping areas, particularly for munitions, and many submarine cables have been laid throughout the Region.

• • • • • • • •

Associated Topics
T2.7 Offshore Geology, T3.5 Offshore Bottom Characteristics, T5.1 The Dynamics of Nova Scotia's Climate, T5.2 Nova Scotia's Climate, T6.1 Ocean Currents, T6.2 Oceanic Environments, T6.3 Coastal Aquatic Environments, T10.9 Algae, T11.7 Seabirds, T11.12 Marine Mammals, T11.14 Marine Fishes, T11.17 Marine Invertebrates, T12.3 Geology and Resources, T12.6 The Ocean and Resources.

Associated Habitats
H1.1 Offshore Open Water, H1.2 Offshore Benthic, H2 Coastal.

**900
Offshore/
Continental
Shelf**

910 INNER SHELF

The Inner Shelf District comprises a large geographic area extending from the Northumberland Strait to the Bay of Fundy. The District has been divided into the following Units:

911 Atlantic
912 Outer Bay of Fundy
913 Inner Bay of Fundy
914 Northumberland Strait
915 Sydney Bight
916 Bras d'Or Lake

GEOLOGY AND SEABED MORPHOLOGY

The Inner Shelf District borders the landmass of Nova Scotia, extending seaward from the coastline to a depth of 100–120 m. In most places the bottom gradually slopes offshore and is generally covered by reworked glacial till containing sand, gravel, and larger material, including boulders. Exposed bedrock occurs in places. Topography follows the ancient bedrock surface, but in some cases ancient features eroded in the bedrock (e.g., the valley of the ancient Sackville River on the continental shelf) have been infilled by later deposits. Inner Shelf banks occur in several areas (German Bank and Lurcher Shoals off southwestern Nova Scotia; St. Anns Bank in Sydney Bight).

On the Atlantic Coast (Region 800), the Inner Shelf is part of the Atlantic Uplands, a geomorphic division of the Appalachian Region. Here the bottom slopes steadily offshore to a distance of about 25 km and has had much of its glacial deposits removed by the sea level advance, leaving significant exposures of bedrock.

In the Bay of Fundy and eastern Gulf of Maine, the Inner Shelf falls in the Fundian Lowlands, a part of the Carboniferous-Triassic lowlands of the Appalachian Region. The bottom contours largely follow the coastline and reflect its origin as a former drainage system originating in the Minas Basin–Truro area.

In Sydney Bight the Inner Shelf is largely underlain by Carboniferous rocks of the Sydney Basin. The topography is relatively flat and slopes gradually out to sea, forming an Inner Shelf bank. Bedrock exposures occur throughout this area.

West of Cape Breton in the southeastern Gulf of St. Lawrence, Ordovician to Middle Carboniferous rocks of the Antigonish and Cape Breton highlands extend under St. Georges Bay to approximately 16 km offshore. The west and central parts of the Northumberland Strait are underlain by horizontal or gently folded Upper Carboniferous and Permian sedimentary rocks.

SEDIMENTS

Coarse sand and gravel mixtures predominate in the Inner Shelf District, though there are significant local variations. Often the sediments vary locally in composition based on the kinds of material derived from local erosion and their degree of exposure to waves and currents. Depressions in the Inner Shelf, as found in Chedabucto Bay and deeper areas of Northumberland Strait, have clay deposits.

PLANTS

Seaweeds grow in a band extending down to 30 m along the coast. Growth is patchy, reflecting the availability of suitable rock substrate and other factors, such as the activity of grazing animals and exposure to sea ice. Stunted and encrusting marine algae can be found attached to rocks throughout most of the Inner Shelf, but growth is most dense near mean low water. Kelps are commonly the most conspicuous species below mean low water along exposed coasts. Rockweed frequently occurs in the intertidal zone in coastal areas. Introduced species occasionally occur. Dead Man's Fingers has been found in dense stands in Prospect and Mahone bays (Unit 911); this species is believed to have been introduced from Japan to Europe, to New England, and then to Nova Scotia.

Algal cover in the Northumberland Strait and the Inner Bay of Fundy tends to be less dense in exposed areas because of the abrasive action of ice. The intertidal zone is scraped clean of algae every year to a depth of several metres below low tide marks and results in the development of a "lawn" of short developing plants in the scraped areas. Ice also lifts off large patches of Eelgrass in some areas, creating many underwater "potholes" and bare areas.

Phytoplankton productivity is high as a result of oceanographic processes which enhance nutrient supply in the coastal zone. Algal "blooms" of dinoflagellates and diatoms occur at peak productive times of the year—the spring and early fall. Dense

concentrations of dinoflagellates can create lumines-
cent displays in coastal inlets and add a glow to the
wake of passing ships, and they can also cause shellfish poisoning.

ANIMALS

Most of the major offshore marine animal groups
can be found in the Inner Shelf. Species that rely on
filtering phytoplankton from the water, and estuarine species concentrate in this District. Suspension
feeders include mussels, oysters, and scallops on appropriate substrates.

Many species of fish and invertebrates such as
lobster live on the Inner Shelf because of its favourable temperatures and feeding conditions. The
young of many fish species find food and protection
in the algal beds and rocky surface features. Many
fish species live in coastal waters and nearby freshwater environments during part of the year.

Migratory fish species such as herring and mackerel move seasonally into these areas; herring frequently spawn in shallows and on some offshore
banks, attaching their eggs to the seabed. Large
schools of adult Mackerel approach the Atlantic
coast in late May and leave again in the fall, accompanied by young-of-the-year. Coastal populations of
Sand Lance and Atlantic Silverside shoal in nearshore
waters. Cod move inshore as the water warms in the
summer. The shelter provided by algal beds, rocks,
and boulders—and an ample food supply—provide
ideal habitat for lobster. Large clam species, particularly the Ocean Quahog, occur in the sediments.

Seals and whales use the Inner Shelf as both a seasonal and year-round food source. Whales, including
the Humpback and Northern Right, move into the
area from more southerly areas to feed on summer
populations of plankton and fish. Many North Atlantic whale species also move through Nova Scotia inshore and offshore waters en route to summering areas further to the north. The small Harbour Porpoise
is characteristic of the coastal zone.

The Inner Shelf supports Harbour and Grey seals
which feed on fish and invertebrates in the nearshore
zone for at least part of the year. Grey Seals from
most Atlantic coastal areas migrate to Sable Island,
where they give birth in the spring.

The Inner Shelf is also home to a host of North Atlantic seabirds, many of which nest on shore and
feed on the rich animal life just offshore; included are
gulls, terns, cormorants, and Storm-petrels. Isolated
colonies of seabirds such as Atlantic Puffin, Razorbill,
Black-legged Kittiwake, and gannets also occur along
the coasts.

OCEANOGRAPHY

Oceanographic features of the Inner Shelf include
coastal upwelling, tidal fronts, tidal gyres, and a residual drift current eastwards through Northumberland Strait, around Cape Breton Island, and southwestwards to Cape Sable. Waters in the Inner Shelf
tend to have higher turbidity owing to suspended
sediments and increased phytoplankton growth at
certain times of the year.

In general, the seasonal range of average water
temperatures is higher in the upper layers than in the
deeper layers, and is higher off Cape Breton than off
Yarmouth. This reflects the reduced stratification and
increased tidal mixing off Yarmouth.

CULTURAL ENVIRONMENT

The Inner Shelf District provides the most accessible
marine resources for Nova Scotians, and several fisheries of high economic importance are found here.
The relative importance of fisheries varies around
the coast depending upon species, seasons, and environmental factors. Included are seaweeds, molluscs (clams, oysters, mussels, scallops, periwinkles,
and squid), crustaceans (crabs, lobsters, and
shrimp), demersal (bottom) fish (cod, pollock, and
flounders), and pelagic fish (mackerel, herring, and
tuna). Coastal waters offer the potential for the culture of various other species that can thrive on the
phytoplankton found there. The inshore fishery for
lobster occurs exclusively in this District. Anadromous fish that enter rivers and estuaries (e.g.,
Gaspereau and Atlantic Salmon) are also important.
A wide range of gear, techniques, and vessels are
used in these fisheries and often have local variations. The coast is divided into management districts,
each of which has particular regulations regarding
season, catch limit, and gear to be used. These resources have been greatly affected in recent years by
pollution and sediment runoff from activities on
land, red tides, and overexploitation. Aquaculture,
particularly for mussels and salmonids, is becoming
important. Other uses of the District include mining
of placer deposits for sand and gravel, coastal recreation, marine transportation, and communications
(submarine cables).

• • • • • • • •

**910
Inner
Shelf**

Associated Topics
T2.4 The Carboniferous Basin, T2.7 Offshore
Geology, T3.5 Offshore Bottom Characteristics, T6.1
Ocean Currents, T6.2 Ocean Environments, T10.9
Algae, T11.7 Seabirds, T11.12 Marine Mammals,
T11.14 Marine Fishes, T11.17 Marine Invertebrates,
T12.3 Geology and Resources, T12.11 Animals and
Resources.

Associated Habitats
H1 Offshore, H2 Coastal.

**910
Inner
Shelf**

911 ATLANTIC

GEOLOGY AND SEABED MORPHOLOGY

The Atlantic Unit extends from Scatarie Bank off eastern Cape Breton Island to Brier Island on the west coast of Nova Scotia and includes German Bank off southwestern Nova Scotia. It is underlain by coastal extensions of Meguma bedrock, part of the Atlantic Uplands formation, and the surface is a combination of sandy/gravelly till, larger rocks and boulders, and exposed bedrock ledges. Most of the Atlantic Unit occurs on the Scotian Shelf, and bedrock slopes gradually offshore for 25 km to depths of approximately 110 m. There are significant surficial features, including gravel waves, bedrock folding, drumlins, and small glacial moraines. An extensive field of sand waves occurs on German Bank (50–100 m long). Most of the exposed coastline is rocky or in sand beaches but contains numerous protected bays and inlets, in many of which finer substrates occur.

SEDIMENTS

Surface sediments are thin and represent the remnants of glacial till which was extensively modified and removed during the recent advance of the sea. What remains of the glacial deposits is coarse gravel and sands (Sable Island Sand and Gravel) confined to depressions on the bedrock surface. The bedrock contains eroded valleys filled with glacial till. These extend from shore at the mouths of many major rivers that once flowed out onto the exposed shelf. Nearshore areas can have a variety of sediments as a result of local formation. A few localized depressions such as Chedabucto Bay contain pockets of clay.

OCEANOGRAPHY

The Unit is exposed to the Atlantic Ocean and, for the most part, the influence of the coastal Nova Scotia Current. Water movement shows a predominant drift southwestwards (the Nova Scotia Current). Coastal upwelling is driven in most of the District by southwesterly summer winds; however, off Cape Sable it is apparently driven by alongshore density variations maintained by tidal mixing (see T6.1).

Conditions in the western portion overlap those in the Bay of Fundy, possibly because of cooler ocean temperatures associated with upwelling induced by tides, but this part of the District differs from the Bay of Fundy by having a reduced tidal regime.

Surface waters are relatively fresh and warm. Underneath is a cold, more saline intermediate layer, and near the bottom a slightly warmer yet more saline layer with a larger slope water component.

PLANTS

The Atlantic Unit has some of the most significant seaweed growth and productivity in the province owing to the availability of suitable rocky bottom and adequate wave energy. Sheltered bays and estuaries have significant Eelgrass beds and tidal marshes.

Seaweeds occur in shallow water near shore, and phytoplankton is important throughout the Unit. The dominant species of kelp are *Laminaria longicruris, L. digitata,* and *Alaria esculenta* in the shallow subtidal; and *Agarum cribrosum* in deeper waters. Encrusting coralline algae cover rock surfaces in the shallower parts. Eelgrass grows in soft substrates in sheltered inlets along the coast.

ANIMALS

Similar species of lower animals (arctic-boreal in exposed areas and Virginian in sheltered situations) can be found throughout the Unit, varying according to local distributions of substrates and plants. The distribution of fish, birds, and marine mammals is more complex, reflecting long-established movement patterns and stock distributions. The spawning, summer, and larval distributions of herring coincide with the upwelling zones in southwestern Nova Scotia. Inshore concentrations of Atlantic Halibut are known off Cape Sable Island.

Bottom invertebrate communities typically include the Horse Mussel; sea cucumbers *Cucumaria frondosa* and *Psolus fabricii*; a sea star *Asterias vulgaris*; the amphipods *Corophium bonelli, Ischyrocerus anguipes, Jassa falcata,* and *Caprella* spp.; the barnacles *Balanus crenatus* and *B. hameri*; the crabs *Cancer borealis* and *C. irroratus*; and lobsters, scallops, quahogs, and sea urchins.

Several species of seabirds occur in offshore waters and Leach's Storm-petrel breeds on coastal islands chiefly in this Unit. Grey and Harbour seals frequent coastal waters, and the small Harbour Porpoise is sparsely distributed along the coast. Several species of whale, including the Humpback, Fin, Minke, Northern Right, Pilot and Sei Whales, move through coastal waters and can be seen near the coast, though significant feeding areas are found only at the mouth of the Bay of Fundy.

Common Eider form large summer moulting concentrations offshore in the Port Mouton to Port l'Hebert area of the South Shore. Dense concentrations of Canada Geese overwinter in inlets in the above area and in the Musquodoboit to Cole Harbour area of the Eastern Shore, feeding on Eelgrass beds there.

CULTURAL ENVIRONMENT

The Atlantic Unit contains valuable resources of seaweed, lobster, herring, and mackerel. These tend to be most abundant in the southwest, but herring are important in Chedabucto Bay during the winter. Many communities have fleets of fishing vessels that make trips to Middle and Outer Shelf Districts 920 and 930 and further. Concentrations of Ocean Quahog are found mainly within a few miles of the shore, but Sea Scallop are fished commercially on the German Bank. Seaweeds, particularly Irish Moss and rockweeds, are harvested and processed in the southwestern part of the Unit. Fisheries are regulated as part of Fishing Zone 4. Productive salt marshes, mud flats, sand beaches, and offshore islands are significant wildlife habitat and provide recreational opportunities for field naturalists and hunters. Waterfowling in the fall is a traditional, regulated hunt for ducks and geese. Several provincial and federal wildlife management areas have been created on the coast (e.g., the Eastern Shore Island Wildlife Management Area). The coast is generally used for commercial shipping and recreational boating, and there are some military training areas (e.g., off Osborne Head).

● ● ● ● ● ● ● ●

Associated Coastal Districts
810 Basalt Peninsula, 820 Cliffs and Beaches, 830 Beaches and Islands, 840 Quartzite Headlands, 850 Granite Barrens, 860 Sedimentary Lowlands, 870 Till Plain.

Associated Topics
T2.2 The Avalon and Meguma Zones, T3.5 Offshore Bottom Characteristics, T6.1 Ocean Currents, T6.2 Oceanic Environments, T10.9 Algae, T11.7 Seabirds, T11.12 Marine Mammals, T11.14 Marine Fishes, T11.17 Marine Invertebrates, T12.6 The Ocean and Resources, T12.10 Plants and Resources, T12.11 Animals and Resources, T12.12 Recreational Resources.

Associated Habitats
H1 Offshore, H2 Coastal.

912 OUTER BAY OF FUNDY

GEOLOGY AND SEABED MORPHOLOGY

The Bay of Fundy is underlain by the Fundian Low-lands formation of Triassic sedimentary rocks. It can be divided into the Inner Bay (Unit 913), consisting of the semi-enclosed Minas Basin and Chignecto Bay, and the Outer Bay (Unit 912), the remaining portion that opens onto the Gulf of Maine. Bottom topography roughly parallels the coastline, sloping gradually away from it.

Tidal currents have formed significant surface features in the Outer Bay of Fundy/Gulf of Maine system, including extensive fields of sand waves, small ripple-like features, and isolated megaripples. The sandwaves are up to 18 m high and 183 m in length. An extensive field of sand waves occurs just east of Grand Manan Island at depths of 60–100 m and in scattered fields to the south and southwest of Lurcher Shoal (60–80 m). Large sand waves (up to 6 m high) with crests perpendicular to the tidal direction occur seaward of Minas Basin in Scots Bay.

SEDIMENTS

Shallower portions of the Outer Bay of Fundy have coarse sands and gravel "lag" formed when fine fractions of sediment are removed by currents. Deeper parts have a sandy bottom with silt and clay mixed in, and glacial till in the fringe areas.

The Outer Bay of Fundy lacks the intertidal mud flats and salt marshes of the inner reaches; the bottom consists of exposed bedrock and a coarse sand and gravel substrate winnowed by tidal currents. Rock formations in the Bay of Fundy are extensions of those that make up the shoreline. This area frequently has a range of wave-like bottom features, but often exposed bedrock occurs.

OCEANOGRAPHY

Tidal circulation predominates in the area. Secondary variations on tidal circulation occur seasonally because of freshwater runoff and the proximity of the slope water front. The ocean environment is determined by the environmental condition of Scotian Slope waters far offshore, tidal and residual currents, slope water incursions, and atmospheric influences (see T6.2). Storm waves can also be significant. The

Outer Bay is cooler because of deeper water being brought to the surface by tidal action.

PLANTS

Seaweeds are distributed on rocky shores on both sides of the Bay of Fundy. The biomass is dominated by a small number of species of seaweed, including the rockweeds *Ascophyllum nodosum, Fucus vesiculosus, F. edentatus*, and *F. spiralis*. The extreme lower littoral and sublittoral zones are dominated by the kelps *Laminaria digitata, L. longicruris, Alaria esculenta*, and *Agarum cribrosum*.

A frontal zone at the south side of the mouth of the Outer Bay leads to high plant productivity, large populations of herbivorous and detritus-feeding animals, and eventually to concentrations of animals of higher trophic levels. The dominant intertidal alga is the rockweed *Ascophyllum nodosum*.

Tidal mixing at the mouth of the Bay of Fundy is important in the growth, during the summer months, of the dinoflagellates that cause paralytic shellfish poisoning.

ANIMALS

Major stocks of scallops (Digby Scallops) are found in nearshore waters off (and to the east and west of) Digby Neck, partially in response to the elevated productivity in the water. The area also supports strong lobster populations. Herring spend the summer feeding in nearshore zones. Witch Flounder are locally abundant in deeper waters at the mouth of the Bay of Fundy, and large spawning populations of Red Hake occur in Passamaquoddy Bay. Inshore concentrations of Atlantic Halibut are known around Grand Manan. Large populations of the euphausiid *Meganyctiphanes norvegica* are present near the mouth of the Bay of Fundy.

Species of bottom animals are similar to those in the Atlantic Unit 911, but the area has several localized concentrations of particular species, probably related to the tidal currents and rock bottom in some places. Dense beds of the Horse Mussel occur across the Outer Bay from inside Digby Neck to inside Saint John Harbour. Horse Mussels are the most important suspension-feeding organisms in the Unit. Concentrations of the brachiopod *Terebratulina septen-*

trionalis occur seaward of those areas in the central axis of the Bay of Fundy. The burrowing polychaete *Sternaspis scutata* and the tube-building amphipod *Haploops fundiensis* are common in silt-clay bottoms towards the outer portion on the New Brunswick side. The deep-sea Red Crab occurs in deeper parts of the area on mud, sand, or hard bottoms.

The Outer Bay of Fundy has been recognized as a feeding ground for Right Whales during the summer and autumn. The vicinity of Grand Manan Island is visited by a population of about 200 Northern Right Whales in summer, and they can be observed in Head Harbour Passage, Grand Manan Channel, and along the edges of Grand Manan Basin.

Southernmost breeding colonies of Atlantic Puffin and Razorbill occur on Machias Seal Island near Grand Manan Island in the Outer Bay of Fundy.

CULTURAL ENVIRONMENT

The highly productive waters of the Outer Bay of Fundy support important fisheries that form the economic basis of many communities. The summer herring fishery, scallops (Digby), and lobsters are most important. Lurcher Shoal is an important area for commercial scallop fishing. Herring are caught from the shore using weirs in some places, adding a distinctive feature to the coastal landscape. Harvesting of dulse, Irish Moss, and the rockweed *Ascophyllum nodosum* is locally important. Shell fisheries are usually closed in summer because of the danger of paralytic shellfish poisoning. The Annapolis Basin is the site of the first permanent European settlement in Canada (1605), and Digby remains a centre for marine fisheries and transportation. Bay of Fundy tides have been harnessed to generate electricity on the Annapolis River at Annapolis Royal. Tidal marshes have mostly been dyked and drained for farmland. The high productivity of the waters of the Bay of Fundy provide food for seabirds and marine mammals, including the Humpback Whale, which are important tourist attractions.

● ● ● ● ● ● ● ●

Sites of Special Interest
- Brier Island—the waters off this island at the mouth of the Bay of Fundy are important feeding areas for seabirds, particularly phalaropes and shearwaters from July to September and murres and kittiwakes in the winter; in fall and winter the Red Phalarope is largely confined to restricted zones such as the tide-rips in the Bay of Fundy; Northern Right Whales are seen in summer
- Digby Neck area—intertidal populations of Common Periwinkle
- "French Shore" of Nova Scotia (St. Marys Bay)—known for coastal fog

Associated Coastal Districts and Units
311 Cobequid Hills, 710 Basalt Headlands, 810 Basalt Peninsula, 820 Cliffs and Beaches.

Associated Topics
T3.5 Offshore Bottom Characteristics, T6.1 Ocean Currents, T6.2 Oceanic Environments, T11.7 Seabirds, T11.12 Marine Mammals, T11.14 Marine Fishes, T11.17 Marine Invertebrates, T12.2 Cultural Landscapes, T12.10 Plants and Resources, T12.11 Animals and Resources.

Associated Habitats
H1 Offshore, H2 Coastal.

**912
Outer
Bay of Fundy**

913 INNER BAY OF FUNDY

GEOLOGY AND SEABED MORPHOLOGY

The Inner Bay of Fundy comprises Cobequid Bay and Minas Basin (sub-Unit 913a) and Chignecto Bay (sub-Unit 913b). This Unit differs in many ways from the Outer Bay, particularly because of the effects of the high tides and the more sheltered environments there. Minas Basin and Cobequid Bay have extensive areas of intertidal mud flats, owing to the high tidal range, coastal erosion, and sediments brought in from several of the major rivers of Nova Scotia—the Salmon, Shubenacadie, Kennetcook, Avon, and Cornwallis rivers which flow into Cobequid Bay or Minas Basin, and the Petitcodiac River of New Brunswick which flows into Chignecto Bay. The coastlines of these basins have extensive salt marshes or dykelands. Beyond the mud flats in the subtidal zone, the bottom is variable in character, consisting in places of exposed bedrock, sand, and gravel and mud. The strong tidal currents create sea-bottom sand waves several metres in height and hundreds of metres in length.

In the intertidal zone of the Minas Basin is a complex series of sand waves, megaripples, and sand bars that reflect the locally strong tidal flows. These occur at Economy Point, Five Islands, and the Avon River estuary, and over wide areas subtidally.

SEDIMENTS

Glacially derived sediments comprise much of the seabed of the Inner Bay, but sediment derived from coastal erosion is important in some cases and accounts for local differences in bottom sediments, especially between Minas Basin and Chignecto Bay. Sediments in Minas Basin are principally sands and gravels, but intertidal and sheltered environments have muddy bottoms. The sand comes from the wave erosion of sandstone cliffs along the shoreline and from glacial outwash deposits. Chignecto Bay has extensive mud flats and the bottom is muddy, derived largely from shales on the nearby coasts.

OCEANOGRAPHY

The tidal force is predominant and, because of resonance, establishes a macro-tidal environment. Tidal mixing tends to minimize seasonal variations in temperature and salinity. Ice occurs in the upper reaches from December to April.

The Inner Bay of Fundy is estuarine in character and generally warmer than the Outer Bay, because of the pronounced warming of water as it moves over the mud flat, restricted circulation, and high turbidity. Suspended sediment levels in the Inner Bay of Fundy are high and significantly higher in Chignecto Bay than in Minas Basin. Phytoplankton productivity may be limited because suspended sediments make the water opaque.

PLANTS

Seaweeds are not generally abundant and occur in isolated patches where suitable hard bottom is present. *Fucus* species and *Ascophyllum nodosum* occur in the upper intertidal, and seaweeds of various kinds occur below extreme low water. A significant bed of the kelp *Laminaria saccharina* containing various seaweeds, including the dulse *Palmaria palmata* and coralline algae *Corallina officinalis,* has been found between Cape Blomidon and Medford Beach in western Minas Basin, and a dulse bed occurs near Parrsboro.

Phytoplankton populations are not generally as productive as in other Inner Shelf areas because light levels are reduced by high sediment loads in the Minas and Cumberland basins. The majority of plant production comes from microscopic algae growing on the surface of mud flats and from salt marsh grasses.

ANIMALS

The Inner Bay of Fundy supports large populations of various coastal fish species. Some migrate into the bay for feeding and reproduction, and others are resident in the area throughout the year. Most of the American Shad from east coast waters spend the summer in the basins of the Inner Bay of Fundy. More than 40 species of fish can be considered regular residents, some of the more common being Atlantic Herring, alewife, Blueback Herring, American Shad, smelt, Atlantic Tomcod, Atlantic Silverside, Windowpane, Smooth and Winter Flounder, Striped Bass, Atlantic Salmon, and American Eel. Waters are productive despite high turbidity and reduced phytoplankton production, be-

913
Inner
Bay of Fundy

cause of the high abundance of zooplankton, which feed on detritus from salt-marsh grasses in suspension in the water. The mud flats are home to invertebrates, including numerous species of polychaete worms; softshell clams; intertidal snails; and crustaceans, including the tube-dwelling amphipod *Corophium volutator* (a small shrimp which is food for migratory shorebirds). Several species of flatfish, which live in the deeper water, come into the tidal flats and streams to reproduce and feed. Inshore concentrations of Atlantic Halibut at one time occurred in Minas Basin. Various seabirds occur, including gulls and cormorants, as well as various birds of prey (Ospreys and Bald Eagles) which use the coastal bluffs and nearby inland areas for nesting. Shorebirds in large numbers visit the mud flats on their passage north in spring and then return late in summer from Arctic breeding areas.

CULTURAL ENVIRONMENT

Both Minas Basin (sub-Unit 913a) and Cumberland Basin (in sub-Unit 913b) have muddy waters with generally poor fisheries, but the extensive tidal marshes are of great economic and cultural significance. Salt marshes are highly productive systems that support the fisheries of the Outer Bay of Fundy. These once-extensive marshes have been progressively dyked and drained since the seventeenth century to provide some of the finest agricultural land in the province. The dykes that protect the marshland from the sea must be constantly maintained, a task of increasing importance as the sea level continues to rise. There are some traditional fisheries of shad, shellfish (clams), and bait (bloodworms). Projects to generate electricity from the tides have been proposed for both Cumberland Basin and Cobequid Bay.

• • • • • • • •

Sites of Special Interest
- Most major rivers entering the Inner Bay of Fundy—tidal "bores"; extensive areas of mud flats and beaches extend out from shore
- Minas Channel between Cape Split and Rams Head near Parrsboro—significant tidal currents flow into the outer reaches of Chignecto Bay; shifting sea ice is a significant winter feature
- Coastal areas—extensive dykelands and salt marsh; concentrations of shorebirds, chiefly Semipalmated Plover, can be observed on mud flats in the spring and late summer

- Grand Pré—extinct oyster bed at extreme low water mark reflects the progressively changing environment of Minas Basin, though several warm-water species, including Lady Crab and Angel Wing Clam, remain as disjunct populations in the area

Associated Coastal Units and Districts
523 Tantramar Marshes, 532 Chignecto Plains, 540 Clay Plain, 610 Valley, 620 Tidal Bay, 710 Basalt Headlands, 720 Basalt Ridge.

Associated Topics
T3.5 Offshore Bottom Characteristics, T6.1 Ocean Currents, T6.2 Oceanic Environments, T6.4 Estuaries, T11.4 Birds of Prey, T11.7 Seabirds, T11.12 Marine Mammals, T11.14 Marine Fishes, T11.17 Marine Invertebrates, T12.10 Plants and Resources.

Associated Habitats
H1 Offshore, H2 Coastal.

913
Inner
Bay of Fundy

914 NORTHUMBERLAND STRAIT

GEOLOGY AND SEABED MORPHOLOGY

This Unit consists of the Northumberland Strait and the southeastern Gulf of St. Lawrence between Prince Edward Island and Cape Breton. The coastlines of the western portion are low and featureless, and the steep terrains of the Antigonish and Cape Breton highlands border the area to the east. Underlying Northumberland Strait is a system of troughs and depressions, including a continuous trough along the axis. At the eastern end, water depth gradually increases in the direction of the Laurentian Channel. Between Wood Islands and Caribou this trough is 3.5 km wide and has a series of depressions to 90 m. The bridge to Prince Edward Island at Cape Tormentine crosses a maximum depth of about 30 m. The trough extends along the Cape Breton coast and reaches a depth of 90 m in the north, adjacent to the Laurentian Channel.

Western parts of the Unit are underlain by horizontal or gently folded sedimentary rock of Upper Carboniferous and Permian age, while folded and faulted Ordovician to Middle Carboniferous rocks of the Antigonish and Cape Breton highlands extend under St. Georges Bay and to about 16 km offshore at the eastern end. Prince Edward Island was separated from the mainland as the result of the drowning of a pre-glacial river valley system that was later enlarged by glacial erosion. The low coastlines of the Unit consist of sandstone cliffs, intertidal platforms with sand and mud deposits, barrier islands, and beaches. This area has a generally sheltered wave environment, small tides (0.5–2 m), and a relative abundance of sediments. The sea bottom in the area is sculpted into a variety of features, including sand waves, megaripples, and sand ridges.

SEDIMENTS

The Gulf of St. Lawrence, including Northumberland Strait, has patches of reworked sand and gravel, glacially derived marine silt, and clays at greater depths. Sediments originated largely during the post-glacial period as the sea transgressed the area and reworked material deposited during the glaciation, but sediments originate locally through erosion of coastal bedrock. Local sand deposits in the littoral zone arise in part from sandstone deposits along the coast. Little sediment is supplied to the coast by rivers owing to the small size of the drainage systems.

OCEANOGRAPHY

The major driving forces for circulation are freshwater runoff, winds, and tides. The surface currents flow from west to east (from Gaspé to the Cabot Strait). Currents are generally weak and shallow depths prevail. The ocean environment exhibits a large temperature range from winter to summer. Ice forms in winter to thicknesses of as much as 120 cm, and water temperatures fall to approximately -1°C. In summer, mixing is constrained by shallow depths and stratification, and open-water temperatures reach 20°C. Erratic tides are diurnal or semi-diurnal, ranging from 1.1–2.9 m.

The Northumberland Strait has warmer water temperatures in summer than other continental shelf regions of Nova Scotia. Temperatures in winter are comparatively colder due to extensive winter ice and low surface salinities in spring. The west- and north-facing coasts of Northumberland Strait are exposed to higher wave energy levels than east-facing shorelines because wave heights increase from west to east. Beaches and intertidal zones are affected by ice from mid-December to April or May of each year.

PLANTS

Seaweeds are diverse and moderately abundant on exposed rock surfaces but not as abundant as in other Inner Shelf areas because of winter ice scouring. However, the red seaweeds *Furcellaria* and Irish Moss are abundant enough to be commercially exploited. Irish Moss occurs throughout Northumberland Strait from the sublittoral to 12 m in depth. The warm coastal waters allow several warm-water species to survive, including *Gracilaria tikvahiae*, *Stilophora* spp., *Dazilea* spp., *Chondria* spp., *Griffithsia globulifera*, and *Lomentaria baileyana*.

Phytoplankton in Northumberland Strait include diatoms (most abundant) and dinoflagellates. Diatoms tend to dominate blooms (typically

914
Northumberland
Strait

in spring and fall), and the other groups dominate at other times of the spring-to-fall period.

Eelgrass beds develop subtidally adjacent to shore and in coastal bays and estuaries in areas having fine substrate. In many areas the Eelgrass is scoured during winter by sea ice. In some embayments, salt marshes occur with other halophytic vascular plants.

ANIMALS

The Northumberland Strait is shallow enough in areas to support species of plants and animals associated with warm, shallow water. Among the nearshore invertebrate fauna is a shallow warm-water fauna which includes a group of benthic invertebrates associated with American Oyster.

The Unit has relatively high levels of primary and secondary productivity and supports a range of species of invertebrates, fish, and algae.

Key fish species include American Plaice, herring, mackerel, cod, Winter Flounder, White Hake, alewife, silversides, smelts, and Atlantic Salmon. Atlantic Salmon occur in many of the rivers, and Capelin spawn in the intertidal-to-immediate subtidal waters in localized areas near Chéticamp and in the St. Georges Bay area. Localized winter fisheries for smelt occur in bays and estuaries along Northumberland Strait. Other species include redfish, Witch Flounder, Yellowtail Flounder, American Eel, and Thorny Skate. Witch Flounder are plentiful on smooth muddy bottoms northeast of Prince Edward Island and just west of Cape Breton Island. Bluefin Tuna can occur in the fall in the southeastern Gulf of St. Lawrence, particularly St. Georges Bay.

Sea Scallop are distributed throughout Northumberland Strait and major concentrations occur in the Caribou/Wood Islands area. The American Oyster is native to coastal areas of Northumberland Strait where it is restricted to the shallow inshore waters of protected bays and estuaries. Oysters can tolerate low winter temperatures and summer temperatures up to 32°C but require warm summer temperatures to reproduce and grow. Lobster are also abundant in the area. Productive soft-shelled clam flats are found in Northumberland Strait, particularly in protected bays and estuaries. Adults live in sediments which range from clean, medium fine sand and anaerobic mud to mud and gravel. Snow Crabs occur on muddy bottoms between Prince Edward Island and Cape Breton and extend through Cabot Strait into Sydney Bight (Unit 915). Other invertebrates

include Rock Crab, Ocean Quahog, and Softshell Clam.

Grey and Harbour seals and Harbour Porpoise are found year-round in nearshore areas. Harp and Hooded seals can be found on ice in the Gulf of St. Lawrence and may drift through the Unit. Grey Seals are known to whelp in the vicinity of Pictou Island, and many can be found on ice in the Northumberland Strait.

Whales and porpoises enter the area in spring, feed through the summer, and leave in winter. A range of species occurs, including Killer Whale, Pilot Whale, Blue Whale, Minke Whale, Fin Whale, Atlantic White-sided Dolphin, and White-beaked Dolphin.

CULTURAL ENVIRONMENT

The warm summer water temperatures of the Northumberland Strait support a warm-water fauna which includes shellfish of commercial importance: lobsters, Snow Crab, Softshell Clam, quahogs, and oysters harvested from natural populations. Offshore are scallop and ground fisheries, seasonal pelagic fisheries (e.g., tuna), and the harvested seaweeds *Furcellaria* and Irish Moss. These are all small boat fisheries from many small harbours (e.g., Toney River and Ballantines Cove). Fisheries are managed as part of Fishing Zone 1. Aquaculture for Blue Mussels is becoming important in the warm bays. Marine life and bird- and whale-watching, particularly based from the Cape Breton Highlands National Park, are important for tourism. There is considerable recreational and commercial vessel traffic in the summer.

• • • • • • • •

Sites of Special Interest

- Eastern Prince Edward Island and St. Georges Bay—Bluefin Tuna migrate into the southern Gulf of St. Lawrence and may be caught here in the fall
- Pictou Causeway between Trenton and Pictou—colony of cormorants on old bridge pilings

Associated Coastal Districts and Units

210 Plateau–Fir Forest, 220 Steep Slopes, 312 Pictou-Antigonish Highlands, 314 Mabou Highlands, 521 Northumberland Plain, 522 Judique Coastal Lowland, 551 Inverness Coastal Plain, 582 Pictou Valleys, 583 Antigonish Uplands, 592 St. Lawrence Slopes.

**914
Northumberland
Strait**

Associated Topics

T2.7 Offshore Geology, T3.5 Offshore Bottom
Characteristics, T6.1 Ocean Currents, T6.2 Oceanic
Environments, T6.4 Estuaries, T10.9 Algae, T11.7
Seabirds, T11.12 Marine Mammals, T11.14 Marine
Fishes, T11.17 Marine Invertebrates, T12.10 Plants
and Resources, T12.11 Animals and Resources.

Associated Habitats

H1 Offshore, H2 Coastal.

**914
Northumberland
Strait**

915 SYDNEY BIGHT

GEOLOGY AND SEABED MORPHOLOGY

This Unit extends from the eastern extension of Cape Breton Island, in the vicinity of Scatarie Island, to Cape North on the northern tip of the island. It is underlain mainly by Carboniferous rocks of the Maritime plain, a continuation of onshore geological formations and part of the Carboniferous-Triassic lowlands. Rocks of the Sydney Basin (which contain the onshore coal formations in the Sydney area) extend northward to Newfoundland, where they emerge in Georges Bay. Nearshore rocks in the northern portions are igneous where the Cape Breton highlands extend under the sea. The relatively flat bottom which slopes only gradually offshore in Sydney Bight forms St. Anns Bank, the only major bank in the Inner Shelf zone.

SEDIMENTS

Sediments at depths of less than 100 m are sand and gravel mixtures, frequently in a thin layer through which bedrock is exposed. Deeper parts fall in the Middle Shelf (Unit 923) and are chiefly sands containing silt and clay (Sambro Sand). Nearshore deposits are formed of material eroded from coastal bedrock, and local hydrographic conditions can lead to the development of deposits of sand, gravel, clay, and other materials in some cases.

OCEANOGRAPHY

Especially in summer this area is influenced by the warmer, fresher waters that flow from the Gulf of St. Lawrence. In winter and spring the area is exposed to sea ice which moves out of the Gulf of St. Lawrence.

PLANTS

Many common seaweed species of the Atlantic coast are represented at shallow depths, including the kelps *Laminaria longicruris, L. digitata, Sacchorhiza dermatodea*, and *Agarum cribrosum*, the rockweed *Fucus* spp. and Irish Moss (*Chondrus crispus*). The latter two occur more frequently and kelps occur less frequently on Sydney Bight coasts than Atlantic coastal areas (Unit 911). The coast from Mira Bay to Great Bras d'Or Channel is sandstone, which is less suitable for attachment of seaweeds.

ANIMALS

Atlantic Cod form dense wintering concentrations in deep water in the area and move into the southern Gulf of St. Lawrence in spring to spawn.

Concentrations of Snow Crab occur on soft bottoms on the Middle Shelf (Unit 923) surrounding Sydney Bight. Populations extend at suitable depths to the west of Cape Breton Island into the Northumberland Strait (Unit 914). Colonial seabirds such as puffins occur on the northern reaches of Cape Breton Island. The offshore waters have seabirds in summer which include puffins, shearwaters, and kittiwakes, and winter distributions of fulmars, kittiwakes, and murres.

CULTURAL ENVIRONMENT

In addition to fishing, considerable industrial and transportational use is made of the waters of Sydney Bight. Fisheries include lobster, Snow Crab, and ground fisheries, and Capelin have recently been coming to the shores to spawn in early summer, providing a small recreational fishery. Industrial plants, electricity-generating stations, and urbanization have created several forms of pollution in the coastal water. Some fine beaches (e.g., Dominion), the scenic east side of the Cape Breton highlands, and wildlife (e.g., Bird Islands) are important tourist attractions. There is heavy marine traffic, including the Newfoundland ferries and vessels en route to and from the St. Lawrence River.

• • • • • • • •

Sites of Interest
- Bird Islands (IBP Proposed Ecological Site 24)— bird nesting sight, with rare arctic-alpine plants
- Point Aconi and area

Associated Coastal Districts and Units
210 Plateau–Fir Forest, 220 Steep Slopes, 552 Victoria Coastal Plain, 531 Sydney Coalfield.

915
Sydney
Bight

Associated Topics
T3.5 Offshore Bottom Characteristics, T6.1 Ocean Currents, T6.2 Oceanic Environments, T6.4 Estuaries, T10.9 Algae, T11.7 Seabirds, T11.12 Marine Mammals, T11.14 Marine Fishes, T12.11 Animals and Resources.

Associated Habitats
H1 Offshore, H2 Coastal.

**915
Sydney
Bight**

916 BRAS D'OR LAKE

The Bras d'Or Lake comprises an irregular brackish body of water covering 260 km². The western part of the lake is generally shallow, with the sheltered bays of West Bay, Denys Basin, and Whycocomagh Bay. Three long narrow arms extend to the east: East Bay, St. Andrews Channel, and Great Bras d'Or Channel. Great Bras d'Or Channel connects to the open sea in the Sydney Bight across a depth of at least 8 m. Little Bras d'Or Channel is a 6-m deep, sinuous estuary that connects St. Andrews Channel with the sea. A narrow isthmus at St. Peters separates the southern part of Bras d'Or Lake from St. Peters Bay.

GEOLOGY AND SEABED MORPHOLOGY

There is no direct information on the bedrock geology beneath the Bras d'Or Lake. Extrapolation of observations along the shoreline and in the adjacent lowlands suggests that the lakes are largely underlain by Carboniferous Windsor Group sedimentary rocks, principally shale, sandstone, gypsum, and salt. A large negative gravity anomaly beneath West Bay suggests the presence of salt.

The Bras d'Or Lake occupies a regional lowland that developed in soft Windsor Group rocks before the Quaternary glacial period. Some deepening of the floor of the lake might have resulted from solution collapse of gypsum, but the main excavation of the very deep channels (280 m in St. Andrews Channel, 81 m in East Bay) appears to be a consequence of glacial erosion, probably over hundreds of thousands of years through the Quaternary. The cliffs bordering the lake are unusual because they preserve organic sediments predating the last glaciation that provide a window on earlier environmental conditions.

The morphology of the lake floor is influenced by the deposition of glacial till and pre-glacial silty muds that occurred during the last retreat of ice. The extensive drumlin field of southern Cape Breton Island extends across much of the central and western parts of the lake. Remaining ice appears to have been centred on the western part of Bras d'Or Lake, and a series of recessional moraines are visible on the floors of East Bay, St. Andrews Channel, and Great Bras d'Or, with pre-glacial silty muds thickening eastward.

Post-glacial History

The shallowness of the links between the Bras d'Or Lake and the Atlantic Ocean have resulted in a complex post-glacial history. Final melting of glacial ice probably occurred about 10,000 years after the Younger Dryas climatic oscillation. The first sediments deposited above glacial till in the central part of the lake, probably 10,000 to 9,000 years ago, contain dinocysts that indicate some penetration of marine water into the lake. The relatively high sea level inferred at this time reflects the continuing depression of the land from loading by glacial ice. Rebound from this depression cut off marine-water influx from about 9,000 to 4,500 years ago and the Bras d'Or Lake was fresh. Late Holocene subsidence resulted in a renewed influx of marine water in the last 4,500 years. The effects of this subsidence are seen in the transgressive character of many of the shoreline features and the extensive shoals of upper Whycocomagh Bay, Nyanza Bay, and Denys Basin, which lay at the mid-Holocene lake shoreline.

SEDIMENTS

Sediment distribution in the Bras d'Or Lake is similar to that found in many of the larger coastal inlets on the southern shore of Nova Scotia. Deeper areas of the lake are floored by mud, except for the sands found in some areas flushed by tidal currents. More exposed shallow areas of the western part of the lake are commonly floored by gravelly, sandy mud that resulted from the erosion of glacial till. Coastal erosion of glacial sediments has led to the formation of many sandy and gravelly barrier beaches and spits.

OCEANOGRAPHY

Bras D'Or Lake is a fiordal system connected to the sea via two restricted channels. This restricted access causes the tidal amplitude to be reduced and, in combination with high freshwater runoff, results in relatively low salinity. The salinity of surface waters vary from about 29 p.p.t. at the entrance to Great Bras d'Or, to 25–26 in the deep water basins, to 20–21 in surface waters at the east end of East Bay. Lower salinities are found in sheltered bays off the larger rivers that drain into the western part of the lake. A thermocline and halocline develop at 10–20 m during the summer and probably deepen in the winter. Measurements of oxygen and salinity indicate that lake water is a mix of Atlantic water and local runoff, with an insignificant contribution from groundwater. Most of the lake is covered by ice in winter, with temperatures warming by more than 10°C from May to July.

The Bras d'Or Lake shows a typical estuarine circulation, with brackish near-surface waters tending to flow seawards, and deep saline water tending to flow into the lake. Tidal currents in the entrance to Great Bras d'Or are normally 4–5 knots but reach 6 knots or more when the lake level is elevated by up to 30 cm during spring runoff or after northeast gales. Non-tidal flows in the lake proper tend to be very weak but in narrow passages between basins may reach about one knot. The long fetches in the eastern arms of the Bras d'Or Lake allow sizeable waves and swells to develop during northeast gales.

PLANTS

Seaweed species are similar to those of the Gulf of St. Lawrence. In both areas, seaweeds usually found in intertidal zones occur only in deeper water as the result of winter ice activity, and the rockweed *Ascophyllum nodosum* is found subtidally. Sheltered bays have marginal salt to freshwater marsh vegetation.

ANIMALS

The Bras d'Or Lake is one of the areas where the American Oyster is found, owing to warmer water temperatures suitable for growth and reproduction. A significant population of sand shrimp, a southern species, exists here. The polychaete fauna is Virginian in character but also includes some arctic-boreal species. A varied fish fauna includes Blueback Herring, Black-spotted Stickleback, and a southern population of Greenland Cod. A feral population of Rainbow Trout is present in the lake as well. These support strong populations of Great Blue Heron, Double-crested Cormorant, and Bald Eagle.

CULTURAL ENVIRONMENT

Most cultural use of the Bras d'Or Lake is related to shore-based activities. The whole area is of high cultural significance to the Mi'kmaq people and is a centre of Scottish heritage in Nova Scotia. The marine area has some natural fisheries, but aquaculture for oysters and salmonids is most important. The area is important for recreational boating.

Associated Coastal District and Unit
560 Submerged Lowland, 585 Iona Uplands.

Associated Topics
T3.3 Glaciation, Deglaciation and Sea-level Changes, T6.2 Oceanic Environments, T6.4 Estuaries, T10.9 Algae, T11.4 Birds of Prey, T11.7 Seabirds, T11.12 Marine Mammals, T11.14 Marine Fishes, T11.17 Marine Invertebrates, T12.2 Cultural Landscapes, T12.11 Animals and Resources, T12.12 Recreational Resources.

Associated Habitats
H2 Coastal.

**916
Bras d'Or
Lake**

920 MIDDLE SHELF

The Middle Shelf District has been divided into three Units:

921 Middle Shelf Banks
922 Middle Shelf Basins
923 Valley and Plains

GEOLOGY AND SEABED MORPHOLOGY

The Middle Shelf extends roughly from a depth of 110 m near shore to the inner edges of the major offshore banks (Baccaro, LaHave, Emerald, Western, Sable Island, Banquereau, and Georges). Definition of the Middle Shelf District is based on the physiography of the Scotian Shelf but has been extended to include the Gulf of Maine within the same depth ranges. It belongs to the submerged Atlantic Coastal Plain, and its topography was determined by erosional and tectonic processes while it was above sea level. On the Scotian Shelf (the continental shelf south of Nova Scotia), the inner margin of the Middle Shelf is a trough from 145–180 m deep and 40–50 km wide. Outside the trough is a zone that has three broad basins (Roseway, LaHave, and Emerald) and contains isolated deep banks (Roseway and Sambro) on the western end (of 80–100 m depth), and on the east several banks (Middle, Canso, Misaine, and Western Banquereau) separated by valleys and intervening ridges. The banks have a cover of Quaternary and Cretaceous material over a Meguma basement (see Figure 31).

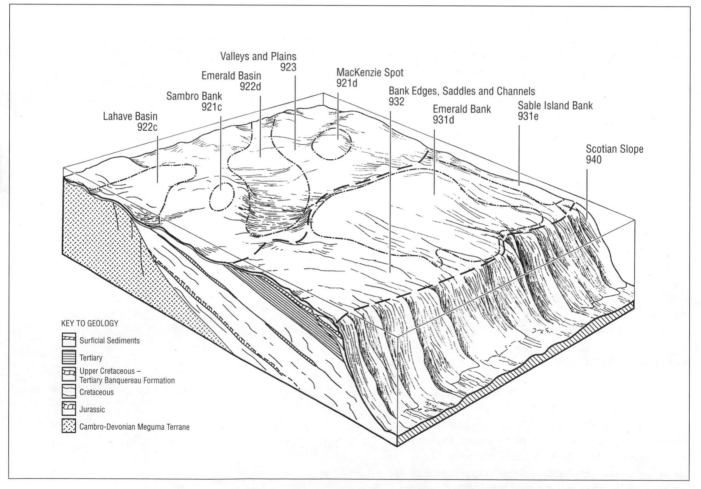

Figure 31: Emerald Basin and Emerald Bank area of the Offshore/Continental Shelf (Region 900). The eroded landscape of the Tertiary and Cretaceous rocks is overlain by glacial deposits.

In the Gulf of Maine, the Middle Shelf includes a series of basins that extend from Northeast Channel (which separates Georges Bank from Browns Bank) through a series of smaller basins to Grand Manan Basin. This section falls into two geological provinces. The northern part is in the Fundian Lowlands, of which the Bay of Fundy is a part; this series of basins may reflect a former drainage pattern which started in the Bay of Fundy and went out over the shelf. The southern part (Georges Basin and Northeast Channel) is part of the Atlantic Coastal Plain (which is similar geologically to the Scotian Shelf).

SEDIMENTS

Middle Shelf areas have sediments derived from glacial activity, and subsequent reworking by an advancing sea level at the end of the glacial period. Bank areas to depths of 110–120 m have coarse sediments of sand, gravel, and occasional boulders. On the bank edges, the bottom is made of sands that have clay and silt. Basins have clay and localized occurrences of silt. The shoreward flanks of the basins have glacial till deposits, and a string of moraine deposits extends from off Country Harbour into the Gulf of Maine.

OCEANOGRAPHY

The Middle Shelf may be subdivided on the basis of water masses into a Scotian Shelf portion and a Fundy/Gulf of Maine portion. Both have the general seasonal pattern described elsewhere for continental shelf areas. Temperatures and salinities in the Middle Shelf tend to be intermediate between those for the Inner Shelf and the Outer Shelf. The influence of the Nova Scotia Current is felt all along the Middle Shelf into the Gulf of Maine. In the Gulf of Maine, there are frontal zones at the northern edge of Georges Bank and a front is induced by tides at the outflow of the Bay of Fundy just offshore. These zones have led to high biological productivity and have an important effect on the distribution and movement patterns of several fish species.

PLANTS

Phytoplankton are the main plants in the Region and are found chiefly in the upper or "mixed" layer of the ocean where turbulence keeps them suspended. Coralline algae form pale to pinkish crusts on rock and gravel surfaces on the banks. Productivity is generally not as great as nearer to shore or closer to the edge of the continental shelf, but several locations have significant production (e.g., the northern edge of Georges Bank and the eastern side of the Gulf of Maine off southwestern Nova Scotia). Much of the productivity of the Middle Shelf takes place in a "bloom" in the spring from late March to May. The abundance of plants stabilizes at a lower concentration during the summer and usually peaks in the fall. Over the winter, concentrations drop as the mixed layer dissipates. The Middle Shelf also contains occasional drifting seaweeds derived from interactions with slope water and the Gulf Stream much further offshore.

ANIMALS

The Middle Shelf has fewer organisms than the Inner Shelf and a relative absence of filter feeders (except on banks and shallow areas) and animals that graze on seaweeds (e.g., sea urchins). Bottom sediments are also generally finer in the Middle Shelf, especially in the basins, and soft-bottom animals are relatively more important than on the Inner Shelf. Animal communities are diverse and contain a broad range of species and types typical of continental shelf oceanic environments of the Northwest Atlantic.

Animals on the Middle Shelf receive their energy either directly or indirectly from sunlight captured by phytoplankton in the surface waters. Zooplankton are adapted almost exclusively to feeding on phytoplankton and are represented principally by copepods such as *Calanus, Metridia*, and *Oithona*. Several kinds of zooplankton, including hyperiid amphipods, krill, arrow worms, and jellyfish feed on copepods and other zooplankton. Several of these groups have representatives which feed on the seabed, but they are a minor component.

Most bottom-dwelling invertebrates spend their early life stages in the water column, where they feed on phytoplankton and in many cases shift to a diet of zooplankton before they return to the seabed. The shift to the warmer temperatures of the surface waters enhances growth. Some lobster stocks occur on the Middle Shelf. Lobster commonly move into the basins of the Middle Shelf and to the Outer Shelf banks and continental slope.

Many of the fish species feed directly on zooplankton during their early life stages. The eggs of species such as cod and haddock float and are in surface waters when they hatch. The young fish stay near the ocean surface for a time before they shift to living near the bottom. The young of many of the so-called groundfish are often distributed over or near banks, suggesting that spawning takes place there.

920
Middle
Shelf

Various fish and whale species may pass through the Middle Shelf en route to areas just beyond the boundaries of the Region, and octopuses may occur in the deep basins.

CULTURAL ENVIRONMENT

Fishing banks in this District (e.g., Sambro Bank and Roseway Bank) are important bottom fishing grounds for summer inshore fishing. Some banks at the western end are included in the "offshore" lobster fisheries. The area contains submarine cables. Some localities have been used for the dumping of munitions.

• • • • • • • •

Associated Topics
T2.2 The Avalon and Meguma Zones, T3.5 Offshore Bottom Characteristics, T6.1 Ocean Currents, T6.2 Oceanic Environments, T11.7 Seabirds, T11.12 Marine Mammals, T11.14 Marine Fishes, T11.17 Marine Invertebrates, T12.11 Animals and Resources.

Associated Habitats
H1 Offshore.

**920
Middle
Shelf**

921 MIDDLE SHELF BANKS

Banks on the Middle Shelf include:

921a   Grand Manan Bank
921b   Roseway Bank
921c   Sambro Bank
921d   MacKenzie Spot
921e   Middle Bank
921f   Canso Bank
921g   Misaine Bank
921h   Artimon Bank

GEOLOGY AND SEABED MORPHOLOGY

The Middle Shelf Banks are generally underlain by bedrock features in the Meguma formation and overlain by Quaternary and Cretaceous material. Middle Shelf banks vary in depth, surface sediments, and morphology. The Roseway and Sambro banks, which separate the Roseway, LaHave, and Emerald basins in Unit 922, are steep-sided, flat-topped mesas at 80–100 m depths. Other banks (Middle, Canso, Misaine, and the western part of Banquereau) appear to be cuestas with more gradually sloping margins. The western part of the Middle Bank is part of the Country Harbour moraine, one of a series of submarine glacial features found on the inner edge of the Middle Shelf (see T3.3 and Unit 922). The surface of Misaine Bank on the northeast end of the Scotian Shelf is extensively incised by channels believed to have resulted from the melting of the ice sheet. Other bank tops were levelled during the post-glacial sea-level advance as they became successive beach zones.

SEDIMENTS

Bottom sediments on the tops of the banks are a coarse deposit known as Sable Island Sand and Gravel, which contains sand and rounded gravel in various mixtures at the surface and has glacial till (Scotian Shelf Drift) beneath. Most of the smaller banks (Sambro, Roseway, The Patch) have a cover of predominantly gravel containing various proportions of sand at depths shallower than 110 m. In contrast, the larger Middle and Misaine banks have, in addition to areas of gravel bottom, a surface cover of chiefly sands with gravel mixed in. Both types of bottom are part of the Sable Island Sand and Gravel formation. The gravel can form a protective pavement of rounded stones embedded in the bottom. The sand tends to be smooth, hard, and flat and to have a variety of surfaces.

The margins of the banks at depths below 110 m have principally sandy sediments that contain small amounts of clay and silt, and frequently gravel. The surface may be flat and smooth to undulating and hummocky. These deposits are called Sambro Sand.

OCEANOGRAPHY

Currents derived from tides form a gyre around the banks and provide a potential though yet unproven means of keeping the larvae of fish species in the vicinity as they mature. Tidal action also tends to produce a mixed water column on banks. The water column on the shallower banks may be well mixed through much of the year, while the deeper banks have a stratified water column.

PLANTS

Plant life follows that of the District description. There does not appear to be a difference in plant production on banks and adjacent basins and channels.

ANIMALS

The coarse sand and gravels of bank tops favour large bivalve species such as the Ocean Quahog and Stimpson's Surf Clam which are less abundant on the Roseway and Middle banks. Concentrations of Sea Scallop also occur on some of the banks of the eastern Scotian Shelf. Bottom invertebrate communities characterized by the Horse Mussel, the Brittle Star *Ophiopholis aculeata*, Sea Scallop, lobster, and the Toad Crab are expected to occur on the coarse substrate in these areas. Sandier areas such as Canso Bank include organisms such as the sand dollar *Echinarachnius parma* and the amphipods *Unciola irrorata* and *Leptocheirus pinguis*. Sand Lance also favour this type of substrate.

Storm-petrels, shearwaters, jaegers, and phalaropes are found in the summer, and murres and kittiwakes are present in the winter.

921
Middle
Shelf
Banks

CULTURAL ENVIRONMENT

Small banks on the Middle Shelf are important for trawling and line fishing from vessels from many small ports. The various local names (e.g., Mackenzie Spot, The Patch, The Bull Pen) come from long use. Some of the earliest records of molluscs reported by J.R. Willis in the 1860s were brought to him from Sambro Bank by local Halifax fishermen.

• • • • • • • •

Associated Topics
T3.3 Glaciation, Deglaciation and Sea-level Changes, T3.5 Offshore Bottom Characteristics, T6.1 Ocean Currents, T6.2 Oceanic Environments, T11.7 Seabirds, T11.12 Marine Mammals, T11.14 Marine Fishes, T11.17 Marine Invertebrates, T12.11 Animals and Resources.

Associated Habitats
H1 Offshore.

921
Middle
Shelf
Banks

922 MIDDLE SHELF BASINS

Basins on the Middle Shelf include:

922a	East Jordan Basin
922b	East Georges Basin
922c	LaHave Basin
922d	Emerald Basin
922e	St. Anns Basin

GEOLOGY AND SEABED MORPHOLOGY

These basins are extensive depressions in the Middle Shelf and are similar to lowlands. They have been extensively filled and smoothed by sedimentation and the action of the ocean. Collectively, their landward edges form a trough that runs parallel to the Atlantic coast of Nova Scotia and is analogous to lowland areas of the emerged coastal plain south of New Jersey.

Basins in the Gulf of Maine tend to be larger and deeper, and are frequently separated by sill-like features typified by the Truxton Swell between Jordan and Crowell basins. Other prominent basins in the Gulf of Maine are Grand Manan Basin (at the mouth of the Bay of Fundy) and Georges Basin (off the northern edge of Georges Bank).

Submarine glacial end moraines occur on the landward flanks of the Middle Shelf basins on the Scotian Shelf, and in the form of the Fundian Moraine that reaches between Crowell and Georges basins in the Gulf of Maine. This complex of moraines extends more than 800 km, from the Gulf of Maine to the Laurentian Channel. These moraines differ from those found on land because they were formed while an ice sheet floated over seawater, and the morainic material was deposited into marine conditions. Some of these moraines have furrows from ancient icebergs that grounded when the water was shallower.

SEDIMENTS

The main sediment of the basins is a grey clay known on the Scotian Shelf as LaHave Clay, which formed during glacial retreat and settled to the seabed in the reduced currents and waves of the basins. Occasionally boulders pierce the cover where they were dropped from the bottoms of melting glaciers, and crater-shaped depressions known as pockmarks are found where natural gas from subsurface rock formations bubbles to the surface. Beneath the clay are layers of silt (Emerald Silt) carried by meltwater from the advancing glaciers and spread throughout the basins. In some places, Emerald Silt has been exposed at the surface. The upper levels of the basins frequently have deposits of glacial till, which also occurs in the moraines in the inner flanks of the basins. The glacial till is classed as Scotian Shelf Drift and was not modified by the last advance of the sea across the continental shelf.

OCEANOGRAPHY

Middle Shelf basins are connected with the Outer Shelf (District 930) and the edge of the continental shelf through "saddles," areas of intermediate depth which separate the banks of the Outer Shelf. The saddles are at depths of less than 200 m but generally more than 100 m and form an entrance to the basins for subsurface water masses. Frequently, storms will force warmer, deeper slope water from the shelf edge into the basins. Middle Shelf basins in the Gulf of Maine have a deeper connection with the Outer Shelf through the Northeast Channel between the Browns and Georges banks, at depths over 200 m. Owing to the greater influence of the tides in the area, significant currents and a larger transport of water occurs through the Northeast Channel into the basins.

PLANTS

Movements of water through the Outer Shelf saddles into the basins of the Middle Shelf bring periodic influxes of nutrients which help to sustain phytoplankton populations. Basin bottoms are too deep to sustain plant growth. Plant productivity in the water over the basins is similar to that over the banks.

ANIMALS

The deep basins on the Scotian Shelf contain high concentrations of the copepods *Calanus glacialis* and *C. hyperboreus* at depths below 200 m, and the populations are greater than on the adjacent shelves. These basins make it possible for *C. finmarchicus* to dominate the shelf zooplankton for most of the year. Two of the largest basins, Emerald and LaHave, contain large populations of Silver Hake, and a large euphausiid (krill) population occurs in Emerald Ba-

922
Middle
Shelf
Basins

sin. The juvenile Silver Hake feed principally on young euphausiids (*Meganyctiphanes norvegica*). Red Hake are common in deeper portions of the southwestern Scotian Shelf and the Gulf of Maine, and Witch Flounder occur in deep holes and channels between the coastal banks and along the deep edges of the banks where water temperatures are suitable.

Invertebrates on the soft bottom of the basins include the Brittle Star *(Ophiura sarsi)*, the Heart Urchin, the Mud Star *(Ctenodiscus crispatus)*, Northern Shrimp, the anthozoan *Pennatula aculeata*, Snow Crab, Jonah Crab, and Tusk Shell (*Dentalium* spp.). Polychaete worms which live in bottom sediments of the basins are part of the Labrador faunal group, while those in shallower water are Acadian, or warmer water forms.

Snow Crab occur on muddy or sandy mud bottoms at depths of 45–245 m around Cape Breton Island. Significant populations of shrimp (*Pandalus borealis* and *P. montagui*) occur over deep muddy bottoms in the basins between Middle, Canso, and Misaine banks, and in basins north of Misaine Bank).

The endangered Northern Right Whale is often seen on the Scotian Shelf, especially in or near Roseway Basin (Unit 923) between Browns and Baccaro banks.

CULTURAL ENVIRONMENT

The deeper basins are used to some extent for fishing, including for Northern (Pink) Shrimp. The most important fishery is that for Snow Crab around Cape Breton Island. There are munitions dumping areas (e.g., sub-Unit 922d, Emerald Basin).

• • • • • • • •

Associated Topics
T3.5 Offshore Bottom Characteristics, T6.1 Ocean Currents, T6.2 Oceanic Environments, T11.7 Seabirds, T11.12 Marine Mammals, T11.14 Marine Fishes, T11.17 Marine Invertebrates, T.12.11 Animals and Resources.

Associated Habitats
H1 Offshore.

**922
Middle
Shelf
Basins**

923 VALLEYS AND PLAINS

GEOLOGY AND SEABED MORPHOLOGY

This zone occurs between depths of 100 and 200 m. It contains the intervening areas of bottom between the Middle Shelf banks and the basins. No distinctions have been made between the bedrock geology of this zone and that of the two previous Units, but this Unit contains various glacial features associated with the basin flanks, including submarine moraines and relict iceberg scours. Because of the sloping terrain, the area is probably subject to phenomena such as slumping.

SEDIMENTS

The upper levels of the basins frequently have deposits of glacial till, which also occurs in the moraines on the inner flanks of the basins. This Unit also frequently contains sands mixed with clay and silt, in contrast to the well-sorted deposits of the banks. These deposits may be flat and smooth to undulating and hummocky, and on the Scotian Shelf are called Sambro Sand.

OCEANOGRAPHY

Oceanographic features are as in the regional description.

PLANTS

This Unit occurs below the depth of seaweed growth, and phytoplankton is the principal vegetation.

ANIMALS

Fauna in the water column reflect that in adjacent basins and banks.

CULTURAL ENVIRONMENT

These intermediate areas between the banks (Unit 921) and basins (Unit 922) are used for bottom trawling and line fishing for species such as American Plaice, Witch Flounder, and Yellowtail Flounder.

• • • • • • • •

Associated Topics
T3.5 Offshore Bottom Characteristics, T6.1 Ocean Currents, T6.2 Oceanic Environments, T11.7 Seabirds, T11.12 Marine Mammals, T11.14 Marine Fishes, T.12.11 Animals and Resources.

Associated Habitats
H1 Offshore.

923
Valleys and
Plains

930 OUTER SHELF

930
Outer
Shelf

This District has been divided into two Units:

931 Outer Shelf Banks
932 Bank Edges, Saddles, and Channels

GEOLOGY AND SEABED MORPHOLOGY

The Outer Shelf is a broad zone (50–75 km wide) consisting of banks and intervening areas (saddles, channels, and one major submarine valley, The Gully) extending from Banquereau on the east to Georges Bank on the west. The main banks (Banquereau, Sable, Emerald, LaHave, Browns, and Georges in Unit 931) are relatively large, shallow (30–80 m), and more or less flat-topped. They represent features in the ancient bedrock that were overlain with glacial till and then levelled by the advancing sea following the last glaciation. Sable Island (District 890) protrudes to a height of 26 m above the surface of the Sable Island Bank and is the furthest offshore island. The relief of the banks relative to other features of the Outer Shelf is comparable to areas of the mainland today—the elevations of the outer banks are generally less than those of the Cobequid Mountains in the Wentworth area of Cumberland County and much less than the Cape Breton highlands. However, The Gully—a submarine canyon between Sable Island Bank and Banquereau—is about half as deep as the Grand Canyon in the United States.

SEDIMENTS

The bank tops contain sand and gravel deposits and, in the case of Sable Island, have been reworked and moved around to form extensive sand fields. Below a depth of about 110 m, the bottom sediment consists of sand with silt and clay mixtures. The Outer Shelf contains no basins, and the only clay deposits are found in the Laurentian Channel, which borders the eastern end of the District.

OCEANOGRAPHY

The shelf break front is a sharp boundary between cool, less salty coastal water and warm, more saline slope water. Shelf break fronts occur in response to tides, winds, and fluctuating offshore currents. Currents from tides can form gyres that encircle the banks and may provide a "retention area" for larval fish. Tidal action also tends to produce a mixed water column on the banks. The water column on the shallower banks may be well mixed through much of the year, while the deeper banks have a stratified water column.

PLANTS

The plant life is primarily phytoplanktonic, but encrusting algae may occur on suitably hard substrates in some of the bank areas. The outer edge of the continental shelf has enhanced plant productivity because of the interaction of shelf and slope waters which brings nutrients to the surface.

ANIMALS

This District sustains a diverse fauna. The offshore banks are inhabited by many species of fish. Several species of large burrowing molluscs occur in the sandy substrate of offshore banks.

Lobster commonly move from the Inner Shelf to the Outer Shelf banks and continental slope and can occur along the Outer Shelf and upper slope from Browns Bank to southeast of Sable Island.

CULTURAL ENVIRONMENT

The Outer Shelf includes some of the most important fishing grounds for shellfish, especially scallops, and groundfish as a result of high production at the edge of the deep water. The area was heavily fished by many nations until Canada introduced the 200-mile fishing zone in 1977. Rock formations beneath the Outer Shelf and the Scotian Slope have provided most of the interest in the search for offshore hydrocarbons. Natural gas was discovered in the vicinity of Sable Island in the 1970s; the first wells to produce hydrocarbons (condensate) commercially in the early 1990s are located there. The seasonal concentration of whales, large pelagic fish, pelagic seabirds, and varied oceanic marine life offers great potential for adventure tourism. The area is traversed by several submarine cables, and two munitions dumping areas are identified on marine charts.

• • • • • • • •

Associated Topics
T3.5 Offshore Bottom Characteristics, T6.1 Ocean Currents, T6.2 Oceanic Environments, T11.7 Seabirds, T11.12 Marine Mammals, T11.14 Marine Fishes, T12.3 Geology and Resources, T12.11 Animals and Resources.

Associated Habitats
H1 Offshore.

930
Outer
Shelf

931 OUTER SHELF BANKS

The Outer Shelf Banks include:
931a   East Georges Bank
931b   Browns/Baccaro Banks
931c   LaHave Bank
931d   Emerald Bank
931e   Sable Island Bank
931f   Banquereau Bank

GEOLOGY AND SEABED MORPHOLOGY

The Outer Shelf Banks were initially bedrock features known as cuestas, typically formed in coastal-plain environments by erosion during early geological periods when they were not submerged. A modern example of a cuesta is Prince Edward Island. Their appearance has been transformed by deposition of glacial till, which has been reworked by the sea to form the present-day surfaces. The banks have moderate relief, generally between 100 and 150 m, and are thus comparable in range to the elevations found on the mainland today. For comparison, the elevations of the Cobequid Mountains in the Wentworth area of Cumberland County are between 200 and 300 m above the surrounding coastal lowland; and North Mountain, between the Annapolis Valley and Bay of Fundy, reaches elevations of about 200 m.

The sandy components of the sand and gravels that are found on the bank tops can be shaped by wave and current activity into a variety of seabed features, including sand ridges, sand waves, ripples, and megaripples. Significant sand-wave fields are found on the western and eastern bars of Sable Island, and megaripples, sand ridges, and ribbons occur on the west Sable Island Bank (sub-Unit 931e) and Middle Bank (sub-Unit 921e). Browns Bank (sub-Unit 931b) has sand waves with megaripples on their sides. Sand waves and megaripples also occur in parts of Georges Bank (sub-Unit 931a), and large tidal ridges are found on the bank tops. Sand ridges are the largest of the features and migrate over long periods of time. Various ridges on Sable Island Bank mark the "footprint" of Sable Island moving to the east.

Patches of gravel, shell beds, and even boulders occur. Many of the surface features change with each storm or tidal event, and many of the smaller features are erased during intervening periods.

The northern edges of Sable Island Bank and Banquereau (sub-Unit 931f) have many steep-sided hanging valleys formed by glacial meltwater running over their edges. These extend onto the bank under the cover of surface sediments and are called tunnel valleys. Sediments moving off the edge of the shelf in these areas contribute material which maintains The Gully, a major submarine canyon and a probable remnant of an early drainage system. Similar movements on the outer edges of the Outer Shelf Banks, particularly during low sea level, have led to the formation of distinctive submarine canyons.

SEDIMENTS

The surfaces of the Outer Shelf Banks shallower than about 110 m consist chiefly of sands and gravels in various combinations in a layer generally less than 15 m deep. In some areas (such as the top of Emerald Bank, sub-Unit 931d), gravel predominates, but Sable Island Bank is mostly covered in sand. Where gravel is found, it can form a protective pavement of rounded stones embedded in the bottom. The sand tends to be smooth, hard, and flat with a variety of surface bedforms. Both types of bottom are classified as Sable Island Sand and Gravel.

The margins of Outer Shelf Banks deeper than 110 m have sediments that are principally sand and contain small amounts of clay, silt, and frequently gravel. The surface may be flat and smooth to undulating and hummocky. Called Sambro Sand, these deposits cover the saddles adjacent to the Outer Shelf Banks in many cases.

OCEANOGRAPHY

Currents derived from tides can form gyres that encircle the banks and may provide a "retention area" for larvae. Tidal action tends to produce a mixed water column on banks. The water column on the shallower banks may be well mixed through much of the year, while the deeper banks have a stratified water column. It is in these areas that shelf-break mixing processes occur.

PLANTS

The biomass of phytoplankton, the productivity, and the seasonal pattern of the waters over the shelves are similar to those found between the banks. Thus there is no greater food supply for other organisms here than over adjacent banks and saddles. The outer edges of the banks are an exception, as phytoplankton productivity is greater in the zone of interaction of shelf and slope waters.

ANIMALS

More plant material reaches the seabed on the banks than in the adjoining areas and, consequently, vertebrate and invertebrate animal populations, including groundfish which feed near the bottom, are more significant on the offshore banks than in adjoining areas.

Cod stocks from Banquereau and the Sable Island Bank migrate during the summer to the outer coast of Nova Scotia and northern Cape Breton. Some of the fish also go into the Gulf of St. Lawrence.

Southern Scotian Shelf cod overwinter in deeper water around LaHave and Browns banks. Some of the cod move from deeper water to the shallower areas of the banks in summer. On Georges Bank, Atlantic Cod occur principally on the eastern portion.

Concentrations of Atlantic Halibut occur along the edges of Georges Bank, Sable Island Bank, and Banquereau, and Witch Flounder have localized areas of high abundance in the deep holes of Banquereau. Haddock aggregate around the offshore banks at the beginning of the year and move onto the banks to spawn as the water temperature rises. The sand and gravel bottom typical of the banks is suitable for haddock spawning. Pollock (Boston Bluefish) spawn on the northeastern parts of the Georges and Browns banks, at several locations on the Scotian Shelf, and on Jeffries Ledge in the Gulf of Maine and migrate as juveniles to inshore areas.

Plate 9: Region 900, Offshore/Continental Shelf. This is an oblique aerial view looking east from Sable Island Bank (sub-Unit 931e) towards Sable Island (District 890) showing a jack-up drilling platform in the foreground. A glaciated Tertiary seabed covered with reworked sand and gravel deposits lies 60 m below the water surface (see Figures 31 and 32). Photo: A. Wilson.

Eggs and larvae of cod, haddock, pollock, and Silver Hake are abundant on the Western and Sable Island banks; those of cod and pollock are found there during midwinter and early spring, and those of Silver Hake during midsummer.

Sea Scallop occurs on the Georges and Browns banks, particularly where the bottom consists of firm gravel, shells, and rock. Two large bivalve species—the Ocean Quahog, and Stimpson's Surf Clam—are found typically on most of the offshore banks, but they are locally abundant. The Ocean Quahog is the main species on Georges Bank and concentrations have been found on the Western and Sable Island banks. Stimpson's Surf Clam occurs on Banquereau.

Sandy areas that make up much of Sable Island Bank include organisms such as the sand dollar *Echinarachnius parma* and the amphipods *Unciola irrorata* and *Leptocheirus pinguis*. Sand dollars are extremely abundant in some locations. Areas of coarse substrate on the banks support the Horse Mussel, the brittlestar *Ophiopholis aculeata*, Sea Scallop, lobster, and Toad Crab. Whales occur in the offshore waters, and mass strandings of Atlantic Long-finned Pilot Whale have occurred on Sable Island. Humpback Whales are often associated with offshore banks, where they take advantage of spawning fish such as Capelin, herring, and Sand Lance, as well as larger zooplankton. The area of Browns Bank 60 km south of Cape Sable is visited by about 200 Northern Right Whales each year.

Common Terns, Herring Gulls, and Great Black-backed Gulls have colonies on Sable Island and use adjacent waters for feeding.

CULTURAL ENVIRONMENT

The fishing banks have been heavily used for ground (bottom) fishing with both trawl and line since the seventeenth century. In the period following the Second World War, there was a deadly increase in fishing by many nations under the international regulations of the ICNAF (International Commission on Northern Atlantic Fisheries). However, declining stocks resulted in the establishment of a 200-mile fishing zone in 1977. Cod stocks on Banquereau (sub-Unit 931f) have declined severely and cod fishing is now closed in most areas. Main products include scallops, offshore lobsters, and ocean clams. The Georges Bank scallop stock is the largest scallop resource in the world. Concentrations of Stimpson's Surf Clam on Banquereau formed the basis for a fishery in the late 1980s.

The banks are also being intensively explored for natural gas and oil with some trial production under way in the early 1990s (see Plate 9). Plans, which include production platforms and seabed pipelines to the Nova Scotia coast, require suitable economic conditions.

There is one recorded munitions dump site (on Emerald Bank, sub-Unit 931d), and the Unit is crossed by several submarine cables.

● ● ● ● ● ● ● ●

Sites of Special Interest
- Sable Island Bank and Sable Island, Georges Bank scallop areas also produce quantities of tertiary fossils, shells of molluscs and crustaceans as well as remains of mammoths, mastodons, walruses and whales
- Sable Island is a distinctive feature of Sable Island Bank (see Region 890)

Associated Coastal District
890 Sandy Island.

Associated Topics
T3.5 Offshore Bottom Characteristics, T6.1 Ocean Currents, T6.2 Oceanic Environments, T11.7 Seabirds, T11.12 Marine Mammals, T11.14 Marine Fishes, T11.17 Marine Invertebrates, T12.3 Geology and Resources, T12.11 Animals and Resources.

Associated Habitats
H1 Offshore.

931
Outer
Shelf
Banks

932 BANK EDGES, SADDLES, AND CHANNELS

GEOLOGY AND SEABED MORPHOLOGY

The banks of the Outer Shelf are bordered by intervening deeper-water areas which include saddles and channels, submarine canyons, and the continental slope. Saddles generally have gentle relief and are shallower than about 200 m, and channels are deep, broad lowland features occurring at the depths of basins on the Middle Shelf. Saddles occur between Sable Island Bank/Western Bank, Emerald Bank, and LaHave Bank. Northeast Channel separates the Browns and Georges banks, and Laurentian Channel separates Banquereau and the eastern Scotian Shelf from banks off the coast of Newfoundland.

Submarine canyons occur along the outer edges of the Outer Shelf and extend down the continental slope. These are narrow, deep, and steep-sided features and include The Gully, and the Verrill, Dawson, Bonnecamps, Logan, Shortland, and Haldimand canyons (see T3.5). The Gully is a submarine canyon that approaches the Colorado River's Grand Canyon in depth, extending from 100 m to more than a kilometre between Sable Island Bank and Banquereau (by comparison, the Cape Breton highlands are roughly 500 m high). The Gully probably originated as a drainage channel and later developed into a canyon. The river and submarine canyon system at the mouth of the Hudson River on the east coast of the United States is an analogous feature.

The Northeast Channel joins the Outer Shelf between the Browns and Georges banks with the basins of the Gulf of Maine at depths between 200 and 300 m. Megaripples occur on the northern and eastern flanks of Northeast Channel at depths of 100–150 m, and sand waves on the bottom of Northeast Channel at depths of 230–260 m are evidently caused by tidal currents. These are some of the deepest recorded sand waves on the continental shelf, caused by strong tidal currents in the Bay of Fundy and Gulf of Maine.

The Laurentian Channel is the most impressive of these features, arising as a former river valley deepened by glacial ice, and having a sill (a shallower portion near the outer edge). This channel extends 700 km from the junction of the Saguenay and St. Lawrence rivers in Quebec to the edge of the continental shelf between Nova Scotia and Newfoundland and was cut 300 m below the rest of the shelf by the advancing ice. Down the slope from the Laurentian Channel is the Laurentian Fan, a delta-like feature containing sediments from the ancestral St. Lawrence River and from recent sediment flows.

At the edge of the Scotian Shelf, the bottom plunges downward to the continental slope. The shelf edge is marked by submarine canyons and glacial features which demonstrate the furthest extent of the ice sheets.

SEDIMENTS

Saddles between Outer Shelf Banks (Unit 931), parts of Northeast Channel, and The Gully generally have a cover of sand containing clay and silt, and frequently gravel (Sambro Sand and Gravel; see above and T3.5). The outer and inner ends of Northeast Channel also have a cover of glacial till, consisting of mixtures of significant amounts of silt and clay in addition to sand, gravel, and boulders. The glacial till is classed as Scotian Shelf Drift.

The bottom in the Laurentian Channel consists of glacial sediments, mainly clay, but silt has been exposed in some places. Flows of sediment down the slope from the channel can leave coarse deposits.

OCEANOGRAPHY

Saddles occur at depths of less than 200 m and form an entrance to the basins of the Middle Shelf (District 920) for subsurface water masses, typically the warmer, deeper slope water from the shelf edge. The Northeast Channel between the Browns and Georges banks, at depths of more than 200 m, is profoundly influenced by tides in the area, and significant currents occur. The deep Laurentian Channel permits incursions of deep water from the Atlantic into the Gulf of St. Lawrence.

PLANTS

The biomass of phytoplankton, the productivity of the waters in saddles, channels, and canyons, and seasonal patterns are similar to those of the adjacent shelves. The outer margin of the continental shelf, however, has greater plant productivity because of the interaction of shelf and slope water masses in a "frontal zone" whose position changes from year to

932
Bank Edges,
Saddles, and
Channels

year. The elevated productivity is used by, and is believed to enhance, populations of fish and other organisms in the area.

The edge of the Outer Shelf is exposed periodically to water masses derived from the Gulf Stream, which flows to the south. Occasionally masses of the seaweed *Sargassum* can be found floating in the area.

ANIMALS

Witch Flounder is associated with deep holes and channels between the coastal banks, along the deep edges of the banks where water temperatures are suitable, and in gullies where bottom is usually clay, muddy sand, or mud. This species has localized areas of high abundance along the edge of the Laurentian Channel, between Sable Island and Banquereau, and in deep holes of Banquereau. Notable concentrations of Atlantic Halibut occur along the edges of the Georges and Sable Island banks and Banquereau. Various flatfish species occur in areas bordering the banks. Owing to the warmer water there, the outer margin of the shelf is a principal area of concentration for Silver Hake, which move onto the Scotian Shelf as temperatures rise in summer. The main known overwintering area for Atlantic Mackerel is the continental shelf south and southwest of Georges Bank.

Short-finned Squid are usually most common along the outer edge of the Scotian Shelf in June, usually between the Emerald and LaHave banks, and in some years along the entire edge of the shelf. They spread over the shelf later in the summer and later migrate southwest down the North American east coast. The young are brought back into the area by the Gulf Stream. Juveniles live in the Gulf Stream frontal zone and slope water off the edge of the continental shelf until they reach about 10 cm in length.

Deep-sea Red Crab is abundant along the shelf edge from the Fundian Channel to Sable Island at depths of 180–550 m. Significant quantities of lobster occur at the shelf edge from Browns Bank to Sable Island Bank.

One of the two best-known areas of concentration of the Northern Bottlenose Whale is in The Gully. Sperm Whales are usually found along the edge of the continental shelf or over canyons and deep basins between banks.

Seabird concentrations are greater in the shelf edge owing to the elevated productivity there. Wintering dovekies are most common over the edges of the Scotian Shelf. On Georges Bank, Wilson's Storm-petrel is most common over the shelf break.

CULTURAL ENVIRONMENT

Like Unit 931, the major marine activities on the shelf edge are fishing and oil and gas exploration. The Northeast Channel includes the area known as the "Hell Hole," where tuna is caught in notoriously difficult sea conditions. Harvestable concentrations of deep-sea Red Crab occur along the Scotian Shelf edge from the Fundian Channel to Sable Island. In the 1960s, whalers out of Blandford caught 67 Northern Bottlenose Whales.

• • • • • • • •

Sites of Special Interest
- The Gully—a deep canyon cut into the continental slope that is an ancient landscape feature and currently the habitat of the rare Northern Bottlenose Whale
- Montagnais structure—a circular structure in mesozoic rocks bounded by faults, just west of LaHave Bank (43.0°N 64.3°W), possibly a meteor impact site

Associated Topics
T3.5 Offshore Bottom Characteristics, T6.1 Ocean Currents, T6.2 Oceanic Environments, T11.7 Seabirds, T11.12 Marine Mammals, T11.14 Marine Fishes, T11.17 Marine Invertebrates, T12.11 Animals and Resources.

Associated Habitats
H1 Offshore.

940 SCOTIAN SLOPE

The Scotian Slope District is a very large area extending from the outer limit of the Outer Shelf (District 930), at approximately 200 m deep, to the political and resource management boundaries at depths of 4,000–5,000 m. This is a fully oceanic environment.

GEOLOGY AND SEABED MORPHOLOGY

The District includes the continental slope and rise, but as the boundary between them is not distinct, no attempt has been made to separate them as Units. The slope is indented by canyons and channels, including The Gully and the Laurentian Channel, both of which originate in District 930 (see Figure 32).

The area is underlain by thick post–Atlantic Rift sediments which accumulated continuously in the Scotian Basin since the Mesozoic. The Jurassic and Cretaceous rocks are mildly folded and faulted along the continental margin. Both the Shelburne sub-basin in the southwest and the Sable sub-basin in the northeast have extensive salt deposits. Late Tertiary and Quaternary deposits are horizontally bedded, and some outcrop in canyons and scarp features on the continental slope. The area is subject to high seismic activity with main stress in a southwest-northeast direction with earthquakes of up to magnitude 6.0. The Newfoundland earthquake of 1929 registered 7.2 on the Richter Scale.

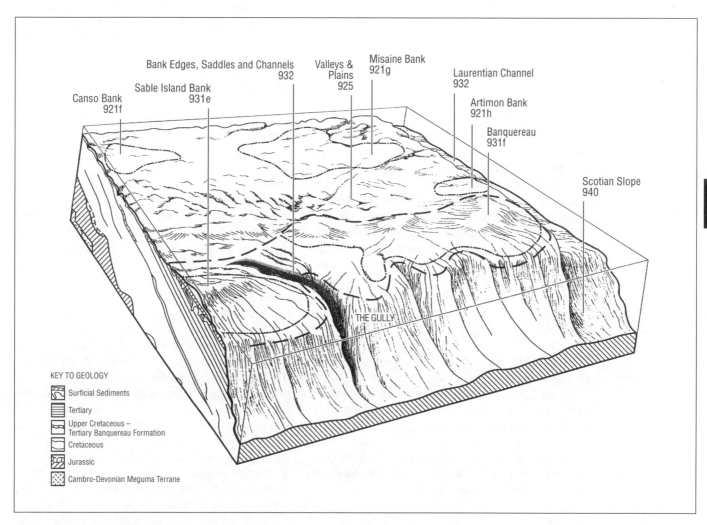

Figure 32: The Gully and Banquereau area of the Offshore/Continental Shelf (Region 900). The strong seabed features of the continental slope (District 940) and Laurentian Channel (Unit 932) can be seen.

SEDIMENTS

Recent sediments accumulating on the continental shelf are slumped along the shelf break and travel down the slope, often in the canyons, as turbidity currents. Thick accumulations of these slumped sediments are found on the slope between 200 and 2,000 m in depth. This talus material includes sand (Sable Island Sand and Gravel), marine silty clay (LaHave Clay), glaciomarine silty clay (Emerald Clay), and diamicton Till. The surfaces of these deposits are marked with pockmarks, paleo-iceberg scour marks, and sand ridges (Laurentian Fan). From the base of the slope towards the deep water is a gradation of surficial sediments: discontinuous, stratified mud series; muds alternating with silt and sand; and finally a sand sheet of Late Pleistocene or Holocene age. These deposits are cut by erosion channels of the same age. The deepwater sediments are covered with a thin layer of pelagic or hemipelagic sediment which includes fine mineral particles and the shells and spicules of marine organisms, for example, Radiolaria.

OCEANOGRAPHY

The District is oceanic in character. Surface waters are generally characterized as slope water derived from the Gulf Stream as warm-core rings diluted about 20 per cent with coastal water. In the area of the shelf break, this water mixes with coastal water of the continental shelf and, with mixing caused by tidally induced "shelf-break fronts," maintains nutrient-rich water at the surface. This effect diminishes with distance, so that nutrients are lower in the Gulf Stream and central Atlantic waters. Deep water at the foot of the slope is clear water derived from the Labrador Current moving along the bottom in a west-southwest direction.

PLANTS

Phytoplankton in the surface water is responsible for the primary productivity that occurs in the District. However, this is only significant in the area of the shelf break because the level of nutrients available diminishes rapidly towards deep water. Some floating patches of *Sargassum* weed occur; these are of relatively little ecological significance, even though they support a distinct community of animals and may rarely reach the Nova Scotia coast.

ANIMALS

The deepwater and oceanic conditions of District 940 support communities of animals not normally encountered in continental shelf waters. The two habitats of the Offshore, open-water and benthic, will be treated separately.

Open-water animals depend upon the primary productivity of the surface waters. Phytoplankton is grazed by herbivorous zooplankton—copepods, cladocerans, euphausiids, and a wide range of larval forms. There are also many carnivorous species, including crustaceans, medusae, and the larvae and juveniles of fish.

The nekton, or free-swimming animals, range in scale from jellyfish to whales, but the predominant forms are crustaceans, cephalopods, and fish. In the deep water these animals are grouped into vertically zoned communities: epipelagic (top), mesopelagic (middle), and bathypelagic (bottom). The mesopelagic community is characterized by a diurnal vertical migration—rising to the surface at night and descending to the depths at day. This migration of several hundred metres allows the deep-water species to take advantage of surface productivity. The epipelagic community includes surface-swimming molluscs (*Janthina* and *Argonauta*), cnidarians (*Valella* and *Physalia*), and fish (swordfish and flying fish). A number of species of invertebrates and fish are associated with *Sargassum* seaweed, and goose barnacles (*Lepas*) are associated with floating objects. The mesopelagic community is composed of crustaceans (shrimps and amphipods), cephalopods (squid and pelagic octopus and fish, particularly the distinctive Lanternfish, Viperfish, and Hatchetfish). These species are all predatory carnivores, are often darkly coloured, and may have reflective plates and photophores (light-producing organs). Lanternfish are found at a depth of 700–1,200 m during the day but rise to within 100 m of the surface to feed at night. The bathypelagic community lives in close association with the bottom and includes economically important types such as Grenadier that occur down to 2,500 m in depth. Many of the species that occur in the bathypelagic zone, such as the Giant Squid, which appears on a 30-year cycle, are poorly known.

The benthic habitat includes communities that live in or on the ocean bottom. In District 940 this is an environment without light. The generally soft sediments support an infauna of worms: Pogonophora and Polychaeta, cnidarians, sea pens, whip corals, solitary corals (*Flabellum*), a wide variety of scaphopod, pelecypod, and gastropod molluscs, and echinoderms. The crinoid (sea lily) *Rhizocrinus*

940
Scotian
Slope

lofotensis has been found on the slope at a depth of 1,700 m. Epifauna includes any animal that roams around the sea bottom or attaches itself to a solid object. Old ice-rafted boulders are colonized by sponges, cnidarians, bryozoa, and brachiopods, while crustaceans, sea spiders, and brittle starfish are vagrants. A variety of bottom-feeding fish occur, including the Atlantic Batfish, Deep-sea Anglerfish, and chimaeras. Blue Hake occurs at a 1,300–2,500 m depth.

CULTURAL ENVIRONMENT

Though the deep water off Nova Scotia is distant from most common human experience, there are some cultural aspects of note. The open sea is fished for pelagic species such as swordfish and sharks which occur along the edges of the Gulf Stream. There is high potential for oil and gas development when technology, economic climate, and environmental considerations make this feasible. Deep water in The Gully has been voluntarily closed to tanker traffic by oil companies to protect the Northern Bottlenose Whale population. Many shipwrecks lie on the bottom, including some vessels that were intentionally disposed of. The freighter *Suerte*, which came ashore at Three Fathom Harbour, Halifax County, was towed out to be sunk off the continental slope in 1962. Munitions have been dumped south of Georges Bank in 2,000 m of water. The area is traversed by several submarine cables, some of which were damaged by the slumping of sediments caused by the Newfoundland earthquake. Cables recovered for repair or replacement are usually covered with growths of deep-sea animals. It is reasonable to presume that wrecks or any other objects of human origin that are placed on the bottom will become colonized by epibenthic animals.

• • • • • • • •

Associated Topics
T3.5 Offshore Bottom Characteristics, T6.1 Ocean Currents, T6.2 Oceanic Environments, T11.14 Marine Fishes, T11.17 Marine Invertebrates, T12.6 The Ocean and Resources.

Associated Habitats
H1.1 Offshore Open Water, H1.2 Offshore Benthic.

**940
Scotian
Slope**

Glossary

Glossary

GLOSSARY

This glossary contains words or phrases used throughout one or both volumes of the *Natural History of Nova Scotia*. Words or phrases that appear only within a specific context in the document are generally not included in this glossary, because their definitions can usually be found under the relevant Topics or Habitats.

ablation till

A surface deposit of loose, permeable, somewhat stratified sandy and stony till overlying denser till.

Acadian Forest

A transitional zone within the Southeastern Mixed Forest defined by Rowe in 1972 as the area between the coniferous Boreal Region to the north and the Deciduous Region to the south. This forest is characteristic of the Maritime Provinces and, being transitional in nature, includes a variety of forest associations.

Acadian Orogeny

A time of mountain building during the Devonian period.

accretion or aggradation

Natural accretion is the buildup of land on a beach by natural deposition of waterborne or airborne material. The process may be managed or accelerated by human action.

acidification

The lowering of pH in soils or water. Commonly associated with changes caused by external processes such as acid precipitation and acidic run-off.

acid precipitation

Rain water or snow containing sulphur and nitrogen compounds and other pollutants associated with industrialization.

acritarchs

An apparently unicellular microfossil of unknown biological affinity ranging in age from Precambrian to Holocene.

aeolian

See *eolian*.

aerobic

Environmental condition where oxygen is present; usually applied to the condition of water or soil.

Alleghanian

Referring to species associated with deciduous forests to the south.

allies

A non-specific term indicating groups of organisms closely related by likeness, etc.

alluvial deposits (alluvium)

Material such as clay, silt, sand, and gravel deposited by modern rivers and streams.

altered rock

A rock whose nature has been changed by geological processes.

amphibolite

A metamorphic rock composed mainly of silica-based rock-forming minerals.

amphipods

A group of crustaceans that includes freshwater shrimps.

amygdaloidal

Containing gas bubbles trapped in lava that were subsequently filled with (often semiprecious) minerals, for example, in basalt.

anadromous

Used to describe fish that spawn in fresh water after spending most of their lives in the sea.

anaerobic

Environmental condition where oxygen is absent or in limited supply; usually applied to the condition of water or soil.

andalusite

A brown, yellow, green, red, or grey mineral (an aluminum silicate) associated with regionally metamorphosed shales.

angular discordance

See *angular unconformity*.

angular unconformity

An unconformity in which younger sediments rest upon the eroded surface of tilted or folded older rocks.

anhydrite

Anhydrous calcium sulphate; a common mineral in evaporite deposits, usually occurring in massive beds.

anorthosite

A coarse-grained igneous rock composed almost entirely of soda lime–based feldspar, distinctive in its lack of quartz.

anticline

A fold in the layers of rock caused by deformation of the earth's crust. The older strata are found towards the centre of the fold.

antimony

A native metallic element, and mineral, that occurs in silvery or tin-white granular, platy, or shapeless masses.

aplite

Generally refers to a dyke rock made almost entirely of light-coloured minerals and with a characteristic fine-grained granitic texture.

Appalachian

A name derived from the Appalachian mountain system of northeastern North America and applied to the Appalachian geological region of North America, of which Nova Scotia is a part.

aquifer

A layer of wet sand or porous rock below the earth's surface capable of producing water, as for a well.

arable soil

Soil suitable for ploughing and cultivation.

arctic-alpine

Referring to a geographic range for plants and animals. Includes those typically found north of the tree-line and at high elevations; found in habitats with climatic conditions resembling those of the arctic or high elevations.

arctic-boreal

Referring to a range of plants and animals. Includes those found in climatic conditions resembling that above the tree-line (tundra) or within the northern coniferous forest just south of the tundra.

arsenopyrite

A mineral of iron, sulphur, and arsenic commonly associated with metamorphism around igneous intrusions as in the quartz veins of the Meguma Zone of Nova Scotia.

arthropods

Members of a major group or phylum of invertebrate animals with hard exoskeletons, segmented bodies, and jointed appendages; includes crustaceans, insects, spiders, etc.

association

A group of species living in the same place.

Aufwuchs

A German word applied by ecologists to small organisms found on the surfaces of aquatic vegetation, etc., in freshwater habitats.

aureole

An area surrounding an igneous intrusion where changes to the original rock have been caused by heat from intruding magma; synonymous with contact zone.

autotrophic

Said of organisms that use sunlight to create food.

avifauna

All bird species.

baleen whales

Whale species that use a hairy plate to sieve small fish and invertebrates from water.

banks, offshore

Generally a large elevated area on the sea floor surrounded by deeper water; a submerged plateau or shelf.

bar

Submerged or emerged embankment of sand, gravel, or other unconsolidated material built in shallow water by waves and currents.

barachois pond

A small lagoon formed when spits created by currents that meet on a straight shoreline coalesce into an enclosing triangular beach.

barite

An industrial mineral, the principle ore of barium, used in textiles, paints, drilling muds, and pharmaceutical products.

barrier beach

A stretch of sand dune or cobble bar that separates a coastal body of water from ocean waters in all but exceptionally high tides, or during storms.

basal till

The bottom layer of glacial till deposited on an eroded bedrock surface.

basalt

A fine-grained, sometimes glassy, basic (i.e., low in silica content) igneous rock.

basement rocks

Older igneous and metamorphic rocks (mainly Precambrian) that are generally covered unconformably by younger sedimentary rocks.

batholith

A large intrusion of igneous rock, usually granite, with 100 km^2 or more of surface exposure.

bathymetric

Data on the depth of a body of water obtained through the measurement and charting of the topography of the bottom.

baymouth bar

A bar extending partially or fully across the mouth of a bay.

beach

A gently sloping area of unconsolidated material, typically sand, but also cobble or shingles, that extends landward from the water to where a marked change in material or form occurs, or to the line of permanent terrestrial vegetation.

beach terrace

A terrace or flat, horizontal surface formed when an old shoreline has been isolated by lowering sea levels.

bedforms

Any deviation from a flat bed, generated by the flow of an alluvial channel.

Glossary
Ab–Be

bedrock

Any solid rock exposed at the surface of the earth or overlain by unconsolidated material.

bench

See terrace.

benthic

Living at the bottom of a fresh or salty body of water.

benthos

Plants and animals that live on, in, or attached to the sea bottom.

berm

A low, incipient, nearly horizontal or landward-sloping area, or the landward side of a beach, usually composed of sand deposited by wave action.

bioclimate

A small-scale climatic condition generated by living organisms.

biodiversity

The variety of life in all its forms contained within a given space at a particular time.

biomass

1. The quantity of living and/or dead organic matter in an ecosystem. 2. A measure of the dried weight of all organic matter in an ecosystem.

biophysical

Refers to a hierarchial land classification system with units characterized by distinct biotic and abiotic elements.

biotite

A widely distributed rock-forming mineral of the mica group. It is generally black, dark brown, or dark green and forms a component of crystalline rocks (either as an original crystal in igneous rocks, or as a product of metamorphic origin in gneisses and schists) or a detrital component of sedimentary rocks.

bivalve

A mollusc with two shells, for example, a clam or mussel.

bloom

Rapid growth of a population of planktonic organisms, usually, but not limited to, phytoplankton.

bluff

A cliff with a broad face, or a relatively long strip of land rising abruptly above surrounding land or water.

boreal

Refers to species characteristic of the biogeographical area that extends across northern Canada south of the tundra.

boulders

Rock fragments larger than 60 cm in diameter.

brachiopods

Marine animals with two unequal shells or valves that are normally bilaterally symmetrical. They range in age from lower Cambrian to Present.

brackish water

Salty water with less salt than seawater.

brownwater lake

See *dystrophic.*

bryophytes

A division of the plant kingdom that includes mosses and liverworts. Plants with rhizoids rather than roots, and little or no vascular tissue.

Bryozoa

A phylum of tiny colonial animals that build calcareous structures of many kinds, mostly marine, ranging in age from Ordovician to Present.

buffering capacity

Ability to neutralize acidic input.

buoyancy

Ability of things to float in a liquid; applied to the tendency of less-dense water to remain above denser water in the ocean.

calcareous

Containing salts of calcium, for example, calcium carbonate as limestone rock or derived soil.

Cambrian

The period that extended from at least 580 million years ago to 500 million years ago.

canopy

The top layer formed by the tallest trees in a forest.

capability class

A rating that indicates the capability of land for some use such as agriculture, forestry, recreation, or wildlife. In the Canadian system, it is a grouping of lands with the same relative degree of limitation or hazard. The degree of limitation or hazard is nil in Class 1 and becomes progressively greater to Class 7.

carbonate

A rock (e.g., limestone, dolostone) consisting of carbonate minerals, e.g., calcite, dolomite.

carbon cycle

The cycle whereby carbon dioxide is fixed in living organisms by photosynthesis or chemosynthesis; is consumed in carbohydrate, protein, and fat by most animals and plants that do not carry out photosynthesis; and ultimately is returned to its original state when freed by respiration and by the death and decay of plant and animal bodies.

Carboniferous

A geological period extending from 370 to 270 million years ago.

Carboniferous sea

A marine incursion during the early Carboniferous Period that formed an inland sea where deposition of limestone, salt, gypsum, and anhydrite occurred.

carnivores

Animals and a few plants that consume dead or living animal food.

catchment basin

See *drainage basin*.

catena

A non-taxonomic group of soils about the same age, derived from similar parent materials and occurring under similar climatic conditions but having unlike characteristics because of variations in relief and drainage.

centripetal

A force that makes a moving body move in a circular manner towards the centre.

cephalopod

One of the Cephalopoda. A marine invertebrate characterized by a head surrounded by tentacles and, in most fossil forms, by the presence of a straight or spirally coiled, calcareous shell divided into numerous interior chambers; ranges in age from Cambrian to present.

chain lakes

A series of connected lakes.

chlorite

A group of platy, usually greenish minerals associated with and resembling micas. Chlorites are widely distributed and are often found in low-grade metamorphic rocks.

Cladocera

Order within the class Crustacea that includes the water flea.

clastic

Usually refers to rocks composed of pre-existing rock fragments produced from weathering and erosion.

clay

1. A mineral soil particle less than 0.002 mm in diameter. 2. A soil textural class containing 40 per cent or more clay, less than 45 per cent sand, and less than 40 per cent silt.

cleavage

The tendency of a mineral to break along planes of weak bonding.

climax forest

A forest whose composition is more or less stable and is in equilibrium with existing environmental conditions.

coal seam

A stratum or bed of coal.

coastal fresh marsh

A tidal marsh moderated by the effects of freshwater runoff.

coastal plain

An area of relatively low land of variable width lying between uplands and the sea. In northeastern North America much of the coastal plain has been submerged as a result of post-glacial sea-level change. The term is often used in connection with distinct associations of plant species—coastal-plain flora—whose range extends from Nova Scotia to Florida at sea level. In Canada, their range is limited to the Great Lakes Basin and southwestern Nova Scotia.

coastline

The boundary between the coast and shore, or land and water.

cobbles

Water-worn rock fragments 7.5–25 cm in diameter.

co-dominant

Forming part of the main structure of a plant community, e.g., the canopy of a forest; sharing in the controlling influence of a biotic community.

colluvial deposit

Weathered material deposited by gravity; e.g., a talus slope.

community

An association of interacting populations, usually defined by the nature of their interaction with the place in which they live.

conductivity

A measure of the ability of waters to conduct electricity. It increases as the amount of dissolved minerals (ions) increases. The micromho is the inverse of the measure of resistance, the ohm.

conglomerate

A coarse-grained (greater than 2 mm), clastic sedimentary rock containing rounded fragments set in a fine-grained matrix that is often cemented with calcium carbonate.

contact

The place or surface where two types of rock come together.

contact zone

See *aureole*.

Glossary
Be–Co

contour

A line drawn on maps that joins points of equal elevation.

convection

Movement of portions of a fluid as a result of density differences produced by heating. Applied to circulation in the atmosphere, lakes, and oceans.

copepods

A group of mostly free-living planktonic crustaceans that forms an essential link in the food chains of lakes and ocean.

Cordilleran flora

Plants characteristic of boreal deciduous woods, which are common on the Pacific coast and in the Rocky Mountains.

cordierite

A common mineral in metamorphic rocks, considered an indication of intensive heat and pressure. A magnesium-iron-aluminum silicate.

Coriolis effect

The tendency of all particles in motion on the surface of the earth to be deflected to the right in the Northern Hemisphere and to the left in the Southern Hemisphere.

COSEWIC status

The status or rank (e.g., extinct, extirpated, threatened, endangered, or rare) given to species of wildlife by the Council on the Status of Endangered Wildlife in Canada (COSEWIC).

country rocks

Generally refers to rocks invaded by igneous intrusions.

Cretaceous

The geological time period between 140 and 65 million years ago.

crinoids

Any of various marine invertebrates of the class Crinoidea, ranging in age from Ordovician to Present, which includes sea lilies and feather stars. They are characterized by feathery, radiating arms and a stem attached to a surface.

crustacean

An invertebrate animal with a hard exoskeleton and at least five pairs of jointed legs on the thorax, includes crabs, lobsters, copepods, amphipods, and isopods.

crustal plates

Major regions of the earth's crust that move relative to each other.

cryoboreal

Refers to species characteristic of the colder parts of the Boreal Zone.

cryogenic action

Disturbance of surface rock, sediment, or soil by alternate freezing and thawing; a daily or seasonal cycle in cold temperate and arctic regions.

crystalline rocks

1. Rocks consisting of minerals in an obviously crystalline state. 2. An inexact term for igneous and metamorphic rocks, as opposed to sedimentary rocks.

cuesta

An asymmetrical ridge with one steep face (an escarpment slope) and an opposite, gently inclined face (a dip-slope).

cultural landscape

A landscape that strongly reflects the past and present land uses of the people who live in it; usually includes cultivated land with patches of natural or managed land.

cupola

A small, dome-like rock formation projecting from an igneous intrusion.

current

Movement in a body of water caused by major ocean circulation or tides, by waves along shorelines, and by gravity-induced flow in rivers.

decollement

The independent disruption by folding or faulting of sedimentary rocks when they slide over underlying rocks.

decomposer

An organism (often bacteria or fungi) responsible for the breakdown of organic material, releasing water, carbon dioxide, and nutrients in an ecosystem.

degradation

The decline in a soil's fertility as a result of loss of organic matter, erosion by wind or water, compaction, salinization, contamination, or acidification.

degree-days

The highest temperatures recorded for each of the days of the year at a particular place, totalled together to estimate the length of the growing season.

delta

A large alluvial deposit, roughly triangular in shape, formed at the mouth of a river.

dendritic drainage

A river or stream tributary pattern resembling the branching of certain hardwood trees.

denudation

The combined action of all the processes that wear away and lower the land, including weathering, mass wasting, stream action, and groundwater activity.

deposit

Any matter laid down; a mineral deposit is generally a natural occurrence of a mineral that is sufficiently abundant or useful to warrant exploitation.

deposition

The laying down of potential rock-forming materials; synonymous with "sedimentation."

deranged drainage

Drainage patterns associated with impermeable, poorly jointed rocks such as slate, granite, and greywacke where surface water is retained in a disorganized series of streams, lakes, and wetlands.

detrital

Referring to minerals in sedimentary rocks that were derived from igneous, other sedimentary, or metamorphic rocks.

detritivore

Animals that feed primarily on fragments of organic matter (detritus) found in soil and bottom sediments.

detritus

Dead or decaying organic matter from plants and animals.

Devonian

The geological time period between 415 and 370 million years ago.

diabase

An intrusive rock, usually occurring in dykes or intrusive sheets; characterized by lath-like feldspar minerals oriented in all directions, with darker minerals in the spaces between.

diatoms

A large and diverse division of microscopic and unicellular algae found in both fresh and salt water. The cell wall is heavily impregnated with silica, and dead cells accumulate on the seabed and eventually form deposits of diatomaceous earth. Living diatoms are abundant among the plankton and are an essential part of food chains in the sea.

differential erosion

Occurs when rocks are not uniform in character and are softer or more soluble in places; causes an uneven surface to develop from erosion or weathering.

dinoflagellates

Microscopic unicellular algae with bodies encased in tough, sculptured cellulose plates and with a whip-like flagellum that facilitates movement. Most are marine and seasonally form an important part of the plankton. Some species are so abundant that they form the basis of red tides and the associated paralytic shellfish poisoning.

diorite

A plutonic rock formed from an intrusion; salt and pepper in colour with dark and light crystals.

dip-slope

A slope of the land surface which approximately conforms to the angle at which the underlying rocks are inclined.

disjunct

An occurrence or population widely separated from the main geographic distribution.

dissected

Refers especially to plains or peneplains in the process of erosion after an uplift, resulting in an area cut into hills and valleys, or into flat uplands separated by valleys.

diurnal tide

A tide in which high water occurs only once a day at intervals of 24–27 hours.

dome

An anticline that is inclined downwards in all directions.

dominant

Refers to the principal species in a group of organisms.

downdraft

Downward movement of air as a result of convection.

drainage, soil

1. The rapidity and extent of the removal of water from soil by runoff or flow downward to underground spaces. 2. As a soil condition, the usual moisture condition of the rooting zone.

drainage basin

The land area that contributes water to a stream or lake system or directly to the ocean; also referred to as a catchment basin.

drainage divide

A boundary between adjacent drainage basins or watersheds.

droughty

Dry conditions in the ground related to long periods of dry weather.

Glossary
Co–Dr

drowned estuary

An estuary that has become submerged under the sea by geological processes.

drumlin

A smooth hill formed from deposits of glacial till; the long axis parallels the direction of flow of the former glacier.

dune

A mound, ridge, or hill of windblown sand.

dyke

1. A tabular body of igneous rock that cuts across the structure of adjacent rocks. 2. A structure with a wall to keep water out and a ditch, used to drain intertidal wetlands.

dykelands

Lands impounded by dykes and commonly used for agriculture.

dystrophic

Refers to acidic fresh water that is strongly coloured by tannins and humic derivatives; also called a brownwater lake. Typified by high oxygen consumption and deficient bottom fauna.

ebb tide

The falling tide.

echinoderms

The phylum of invertebrate animals that includes starfish, sea urchins, sand dollars, and sea cucumbers.

ecology

The study of relationships between organisms and their environment.

ecosystem

The relationships among a particular assemblage of living organisms and the environment in which they live.

ecotone

An area of transition from one habitat to another.

edaphic

Factors pertaining to, or influenced by, soil conditions.

edge habitat

The area of transition from one wildlife habitat to another; an ecotone at the habitat level.

eluviation

The transportation of material in suspension or solution by the downward or lateral movement of water within soil.

embayment

An indentation in a shoreline that forms an open bay.

emergent coastline

A coast where land formerly below sea level has been exposed by crustal uplift, rise in sea level, or both.

emergent plant

A plant rooted in shallow water with much of the stem and most of the leaves above water.

encrusting algae

Species that forms a hard surface on the substrate.

end moraine

Ridge-like accumulation of till along the terminal margin of a glacier.

endemic

Confined to a specific geographic area.

eolian

Referring to the erosive action of the wind and the deposits such as sand, which are arranged by the wind. *Subaerial* is often used synonymously.

epibenthic

Living on the bottom surface of lakes or the ocean.

epifauna

Animals that live attached to or rove over the surface of a sea or lake bottom.

epiphyte

A plant that lives wholly but non-parasitically on other plants, usually above ground.

ericaceous

Species of woody (often evergreen) shrubs commonly associated with bog and barren habitats belonging to the Ericaceae, the blueberry family.

erosion

The wearing away and removal of material on the earth's surface by forces such as running water, wave action, moving ice, or winds.

erratic

A large rock or boulder that has been transported some distance from its source, usually by glacial action.

escarpment

A steep slope.

esker

Long, winding ridges of sand and gravel which originated within or beneath glacial ice.

estivate

A period of dormancy in cold-blooded animals during dry conditions; the metabolic rate is not decreased, but metabolism may become anaerobic, creating an oxygen depth.

estuary

A bay at the mouth of a river formed by subsidence of the land and/or a rise in sea level. Fresh water from the river mixes with the salt water of the sea, giving brackish or low salinity conditions.

euphotic zone

A zone of surface water in a sea or lake where sufficient light penetrates to allow photosynthesis to occur. The depth of the zone is limited by the clarity of the water.

eutrophication

The process of increasing the nutrient concentration of a freshwater environment. This process occurs naturally as a part of the system's successional sequence. The rate of eutrophication can be accelerated by the introduction of artificial nutrients or pollutants.

eutrophic

Referring to fresh waters: high productivity as a result of an abundant supply of nutrients.

evaporite

A rock composed of minerals derived from the evaporation of mineralized water; examples are rock salt and gypsum.

evapotranspiration

The release of water from the surfaces of plants, soil, and other objects; an essential part of the hydrological cycle.

exotic species

Species that do not normally occur in an area.

extirpated

Locally extinct.

facies

1. Part of a rock body differentiated from other parts by appearance or composition; can refer to one part of a rock body, different kinds of rocks, or stratigraphic bodies. 2. A lateral subdivision of a stratigraphic unit.

fault

A fracture or zone of fractures in the earth's crust along which movement has taken place.

fault block

A mass or body of rock bounded on at least two opposite sides by faults; it may be elevated or depressed relative to the adjoining land.

faulting

Movement which produces relative displacement of adjacent rock masses along a fracture.

feldspar

A group of rock-forming minerals, considered to be the most abundant of all minerals. All are aluminum silicates of soda, potash, or lime and all are closely related in structure and composition. Feldspars are the principal constituents of igneous and plutonic rocks.

felsite

A general term used to describe a light-coloured igneous rock.

ferro-humic

Typically acidic, stony, and well-drained soils with a high organic content; associated with upland igneous or metamorphic rocks and deciduous forests.

fetch

The distance in a given direction over which wind can generate waves in water.

filter feeder

An organism that obtains its food by straining particles from the water.

first-order stream

The main, unbranched section of a river or stream.

floodplain

The land bordering a stream, built up of sediments from stream overflow and subject to inundation when the stream floods.

flood tide

The rising tide.

floral element

A component of the vegetation of a region that has a distinct assemblage of species determined by climate and site conditions. For example, in the highlands of Cape Breton Island, the association of Black Spruce, Balsam Fir, White Spruce, poplar, and birch forms a Boreal element of the Acadian Forest Zone.

fluvial

Pertaining to rivers.

fluvial deposits

All sediments, past and present, deposited by flowing water, including glaciofluvial deposits.

fluvioglacial deposits

See *glaciofluvial deposit.*

flux

Continuous motion or change, applied to the rate of flow in fluids.

fold

A bend in strata or any plane surface.

**Glossary
Dr–Fo**

foliated

A layered appearance in a metamorphic rock that results from the parallel segregation of minerals.

foraminifera

Unicellular animals, mostly microscopic and marine, that secrete hard coverings composed of calcium carbonates or build them of cemented sedimentary grains. They range in age from Ordovician to Present.

forb

An herbaceous plant other than grasses; a broad-leaved herb.

foreshore

That part of the shore between the upper limit of wave-wash at high tide and the ordinary low water mark.

formation

A mappable rock unit.

fossiliferous

Containing fossils.

fossil

Any evidence preserved in rock of a once-living organism.

fragipan

A natural subsurface horizon having a higher density than the soil above; cemented when dry but showing brittleness when moist. This layer is low in organic matter and slowly permeable to water; it usually has polygon-shaped bleached cracks.

front

A sharp boundary between water masses of different properties.

frost pocket

A low-lying area of land that collects cold air flowing from surrounding elevated areas and is usually subject to early and late frosts.

garnet

A family of minerals—silicates of aluminum, iron, manganese, chromium, calcium, and magnesium—occurring as accessory minerals in a wide range of igneous rocks and as the finest crystals in some metamorphic rocks.

geochemical

Referring to alterations in the earth's crust as a result of chemical changes; focused on the distribution of the elements.

geodetic

Referring to the shape and dimensions of the earth.

geomorphology

The form of the earth, the general configuration of its surface, and the changes that take place in the evolution of land forms.

geosyncline

A large, generally linear trough that subsided deeply over a long period of time during which a thick succession of stratified sediment accumulated; the strata may have been folded into mountains. Also refers to the stratigraphic surface that subsided in such a trough.

glacial lake

A lake formed either from a basin scoured out by glacial ice or from the damming of natural drainage by glacial till.

glacial till

Nonsorted, nonstratified sediment carried or deposited by a glacier.

glaciofluvial deposit

Material moved by glaciers and subsequently sorted and deposited by streams flowing from the melting ice. These deposits are stratified and may occur in the form of outwash plains, deltas, kames, eskers, and kame terraces.

gleyed soil

An imperfectly or poorly drained soil modified by reduction, or alternating reduction and oxidation. These soils have lower chromas or more prominent mottling, or both, in some horizons than the associated well-drained soil.

gleying

A soil-forming process that operates under poor drainage conditions and results in the reduction of iron and other elements, and in grey colours and mottles.

gleysols

An order of soils developed under wet conditions and permanent or periodic reduction. These soils have low chromas or prominent mottling, or both, in some horizons.

gneiss

A coarse-grained metamorphic rock with a characteristic discontinuous layered structure and a composition generally similar to granite.

graben

A steep-sided, flat-bottomed valley formed between parallel faults.

gradient

A gradual change with distance.

granite

An intrusive rock consisting mainly of alkali feldspar and quartz. The term may be loosely used for any light-coloured, coarse-grained igneous rock.

granodiorite

An igneous rock intermediate in composition between a granite and a diorite.

graptolite

An extinct colonial organism that produced enclosing or supporting structures from a nitrogenous substance similar to fingernails.

gravel

Rock fragments 2 mm to 7.5 cm in diameter.

gravitational

Controlled by the effect of gravity.

greywacke

An impure sandstone consisting of rock fragments and grains of quartz and feldspar in a matrix of clay-sized particles.

ground cover

Those herbaceous plants, small shrubs and non-vascular plants growing beneath the tree and shrub canopy.

ground moraine

Rolling plain that has gently sloping swells, sags, or basins made of till.

groundfish

Fish that feed on or near the sea bottom.

groundwater

Water in the zone of saturation where all open spaces in sediment and rock are completely filled with water.

groundwater recharge

The intake and quantity of water added to the zone of saturation below the land surface.

groundwater seep

A spot where groundwater oozes from the earth, often forming the source of a small stream or spring.

gypsum

Commonest sulphate mineral ($CaSO_4 \cdot 2H_2O$). Associated with halite and anhydrite in evaporite deposits.

gyre

A gyration, or circular or spiral movement, within a medium; applied to movement at the margins of ocean currents.

habitat

The natural home or environment of a plant or animal.

halite

A mineral commonly associated with evaporates; rock salt.

halophyte

A plant tolerant to saline conditions, for example, in a salt marsh.

hardpan

A layer of strongly cemented material that occurs in unconsolidated sediments.

hardwood

A forestry term for deciduous, broad-leaved trees such as oak, maple, and birch and the forests they form.

headland

A high, steep-faced promontory extending into the sea.

hematite

The principal ore of iron, with the composition Fe_2O_3.

herbaceous

Descriptive of non-woody plants with no above-ground persistent parts.

herbivore

An animal which feeds on living plant material.

heterotrophic

Dependent on organic matter for food.

highwater line

The level of highest water on a shore; the high-tide line of the sea and the high-flood line of streams or lakes.

hornblende

A common member of the amphibole rock-forming minerals; usually black, dark green, or brown and found in igneous and metamorphic rocks.

hornfels

A dense, compact rock produced from slate by contact with an intrusion, especially of granite.

humo-ferric

Of soils associated with rolling plains, till features, and forest cover on coarse-textured, iron-rich parent material. Typically moderately well to rapidly well drained and very acidic, with less organic matter accumulated in the mineral layer than in ferro-humic soils.

humus

Organic detritus in soil.

hydric

Characterized by abundant moisture.

hydrocarbons

Naturally occurring hydrogen- and carbon-based complex liquids and gases created through the burial and heating of fine-grained rocks rich in organic matter.

hydrography

The mapping of the characteristics of oceans, lakes, and rivers.

hydrology

The study of the occurrence and properties of water.

Glossary
Fo–Hy

hydrophytic

Refers to plants whose habitat is water or very wet places.

hydrosere

The natural zonation of vegetation at the edges of freshwater habitats.

hydrothermal

Referring to processes, solutions, rocks, deposits, and springs associated with heated or hot materials that are rich in water.

IBP Proposed Ecological Site

A reserve proposed by the Canadian Committee for the International Biological Programme. An ecological reserve is a legally protected natural area where human influence is kept to a minimum. Its purpose is to preserve characteristic or regionally rare ecosystems. Ecological (Nature) Reserve sites are protected in Nova Scotia under the Special Places Act.

ice-contact drift

Any rock material deposited in contact with melting glacier ice.

ice-plucked

Moved from its original site by glacial ice.

igneous rock

One of the three main groups of rock. Igneous rocks characteristically appear crystalline and were formed by the crystallization of magma.

ignimbrite

Rock consolidated from volcanic material which was so hot that the fragments welded together.

illite

A general term that refers to the group of minerals that is abundant in sediments composed mostly or entirely of clay.

impoundment

A structure built to maintain desired water level; commonly used in waterfowl management.

infauna

Benthic animals that burrow into the substrate.

infiltration rate

The maximum rate at which soil can absorb surface water.

interbedded

Occurring between beds or lying in a bed parallel to other beds of a different material.

interglacial

Refers to the time between glaciations.

intermontane

Lying between mountains.

intertidal zone

The area between low- and high-tide marks, alternately covered by water and exposed to air during each tidal cycle.

intolerant

See *shade-intolerant*.

introduced species

Non-native species brought into an area intentionally or accidently by humans.

intrusion

A body of igneous rock that has forced itself into pre-existing rocks.

invertebrate

An animal without a backbone.

ironpan

A compact layer in the soil horizon with a platy structure and very low permeability that impedes drainage and root penetration.

isobar

A line drawn on atmospheric charts to connect points of equal barometric pressure and determine the locations of high and low pressure areas.

isopods

A group of crustaceans that includes wood lice.

isostatic

Related to the state of equilibrium, resembling flotation, in which segments of the earth's crust stand at levels determined by their thickness and density. During the last ice age, the ice depressed the earth's crust, upsetting the isostatic equilibrium.

joint

A fracture in a rock along which there has been no movement.

Jurassic

The geological period between 210 and 140 million years ago.

kame terrace

A terrace-like body of material deposited at the side of a valley by melted water that flows along the surface of a glacier.

kames

Steep-sided mounds of stratified material deposited against an ice-front.

kaolinite

A common clay mineral.

karst topography

A landscape typical of gypsum and limestone areas, where sinkholes have formed as a result of the dissolution of rocks by rainwater; narrow, crumbling ridges separate the sinkholes.

kettle hole

A bowl-shaped depression created when blocks of ice become lodged in glacial deposits and melt, leaving a depression.

knoll

1. A submerged, rounded elevation rising from the sea floor. 2. A small, rounded hill, often associated with resistant rock.

krummholz

A condition where trees growing in exposed areas exhibit an asymmetrical outline and stunted growth. Occurs as a result of extreme conditions such as high wind and salt spray.

lacustrine

Of lakes.

lacustrine deposits

Material deposited by or settled out of lake waters and exposed by the lowering of water levels or the elevation of land. These sediments range in texture from sand to clay and are usually varied (layered annual deposits).

lagoon

See *barachois pond*.

landscape

A heterogeneous land area composed of interacting systems repeated in similar form throughout. Landscapes vary in size.

landscape ecology

A study of the structure, function, and change in a heterogeneous land area composed of interacting ecosystems.

landscape element

The basic, relatively homogeneous ecological unit, whether of natural or human origin, on land at the scale of a landscape; includes matrix, patch, and corridor elements.

lava

Fluid rock, or magma, such as from a volcano or a fissure in the earth's surface; also, the same material solidified by cooling.

leaching

The process by which rain and the substances dissolved in it gradually break down and decompose rocks. Materials may be removed from soil by leaching.

lentic

Related to slow-moving water, such as in lakes and bogs.

limestone

A bedded sedimentary deposit consisting chiefly of calcium carbonate.

limnetic

Related to the environment of lakes and ponds.

lithosphere

The crust of the earth, up to 100 km.

lithostratigraphic

Consisting of stratified and mainly sedimentary rocks grouped on the basis of physical rather than biological characteristics or time.

littoral

The zone between the extreme high-tide and extreme low-tide levels in the sea; also the zone from the shore to the light-compensation level of the sea and lakes.

loam

A soil mix of coarse sand, silt, clay, and organic matter.

loess

Deposits composed primarily of windblown silt and lacking visible layers.

lotic

Related to fast-moving water, such as in most streams and rivers.

lumbricid

A general term for the oligochaete worms of the Lumbricidae which include familiar earthworms.

Luvisols

An order of soils that have a clay accumulation in the B horizon. These soils develop under forests or forest-grassland transition areas in a cool climate.

macrophyte

Large plants (e.g., seaweeds, herbs, trees), in contrast to small plants such as lichens and mosses.

macrotidal

An ocean system which features a large tidal range, as in the Bay of Fundy.

magma

Molten rock material, including dissolved gases and crystals, generated within the earth and capable of intrusion and extrusion; considered the source of igneous rocks.

magnetite

Magnetic iron ore, frequently associated with igneous rocks; a black iron oxide with a metallic lustre.

marine

Associated with the sea.

marine transgression

The advance of the sea over coastal land areas as a result of rising sea levels or the subsidence of the land.

massif

A massive block of bedrock; usually a large landscape feature.

mature soil

A naturally produced soil with well-developed horizons.

Glossary
Hy–Ma

meander

A loop-like bend in a stream or river that develops when a watercourse flows through level land and erodes its floodplain.

mean high or low water

The average height of the high- or low-tide mark on seashores, determined over a 19-year period.

mean sea level

The average height of the surface of the sea for all tidal stages over a 19-year period, usually determined from hourly height readings.

meiofauna

Microscopic aquatic animal life of bottom and shoreline sediments.

meltwater

Water resulting from the melting of snow or glacial ice. Glacial meltwater often forms streams and carries rock material beyond active glaciers.

meromictic (meromyxia)

The condition in permanently stratified lakes.

mesa

Flat-topped hills, or mountains, cut off on one or more sides by steep escarpments.

mesic

Refers to habitats with plentiful rainfall and well-drained soils.

mesopelagic

Related to the mid-depths of the open ocean.

mesophyte

A plant which grows in conditions of average water supply.

mesothermal

Climate with a middle temperature range, a roughly warm and cold climate, as opposed to a more extreme tropical or arctic climate.

mesotrophic

Refers to fresh waters with moderate nutrient concentrations and productivity.

Mesozoic

The geological era between 247 and 65 million years ago.

metamorphic rocks

Rocks whose physical and chemical properties have been changed by elevated temperature and pressure.

mica

A group of minerals characterized by perfect cleavage in one direction and by the thinness, toughness, and flexibility of their elastic flakes.

micro-

Refers to microscopic organisms, including animals, plants, bacteria, and fungi, that are primarily single-celled, although some colonial and multi-celled organisms are included.

microclimate

The climate of a microhabitat.

microflora

Microscopic plant life, including bacteria and some fungi.

microhabitat

The parts of a habitat an individual organism encounters in the course of its activities.

micromhos/cm

See *conductivity*.

midden

A prehistoric garbage dump generally found along the coast in Nova Scotia, typically consisting of a pile of shells of predominantly shellfish species and other discarded items of bone, stone, and pottery deposited during prehistoric times by aboriginal peoples.

minerotrophic

Descriptive of a habitat where nutrients are intruded from ground water flow as opposed to exclusively rainwater (ombotrophic).

mixis

The process and pattern of annual water circulation in lakes; used as a classification scheme for lakes, e.g., a monomictic lake has one regular period of water circulation during a year.

molluscs

Unsegmented invertebrate animals that possess an external or vestigial calcium carbonate shell; they include clams, snails, sea slugs, and squid.

molybdenum

A metallic element of the chromium group. It resembles iron in its white colour, malleability, difficult fusibility, and capacity for forming steel-like alloys with carbon.

monadnock

An isolated hill that stands above the general level of a peneplain; erosion remnants of the original surface.

moder

A non-matted forest humus derived from plant remains.

monzogranite

A subdivision of the granites, typically pink in colour.

mor

A well-defined matted layer of organic deposits resting on mineral soil.

moraine

Accumulations of material, mainly till, deposited directly by glaciers.

morphology

1. The form of a living organism. 2. The external forms of rocks and landscape features.

mottles

Irregularly marked spots or streaks, usually yellow or orange, but sometimes blue. Mottles in soils generally indicate poor aeration and impeded drainage.

mudstones

Dark-grey, fine-grained shales that decompose rapidly and convert to mud when exposed to the atmosphere; they include clay, silt, and siltstone.

mull

A rich soil developed under mixed forests where a suitable supply of calcium is available.

Myriapoda

A group of diverse, many-segmented, and appendaged terrestrial arthropods, including centipedes, millipedes, and isopods.

neap tide

A tide near the time of quadrature of the moon with the sun. The neap tidal range is usually 10–30 per cent less than the mean tidal range.

nearshore

An indefinite zone that extends seaward from the shoreline to well beyond the breaker zone. It defines the area of nearshore currents.

nekton

Free-swimming pelagic animals in the ocean and large freshwater lakes; they include many invertebrate species but also fishes and whales.

nematodes

A large, widespread, and diverse group of free-living and parasitic unsegmented worms. They are particularly important in the soil and can be important pests of plants and parasites of humans and domestic animals.

nitrogen-fixing

Applied to bacteria that can facilitate the incorporation of atmospheric nitrogen into organic compounds. Classically associated with the root nodules of legumes such as beans.

nutrient

Any substance required by organisms for normal growth and maintenance.

offshore

In beach terminology, the comparatively flat zone of variable width that extends from the breaker zone to the seaward edge of the continental shelf; also used to describe the continental shelf and slope, as in "offshore hydrocarbon exploration."

offshore wind

A wind blowing from the land onto the water.

old-growth forest

A phase in forest development characterized by a multi-layered structure, old climax tree species, snags, and large amounts of coarse woody debris.

oligochaetes

The group of annelid worms that includes the earthworm.

oligotrophic

Refers to fresh waters with poor nutrient supply and low productivity.

ombrotrophic

Condition of an ecosystem that derives its nutrient input largely from rainwater; for example, raised bogs.

omnivore

An animal that can feed on almost anything, including living and dead plant and animal material.

onshore wind

A wind blowing from the water onto the land.

oolitic

A textural term for sedimentary rocks consisting largely of oolites, which are small spherical or ellipsoidal accretions resembling a fish egg. Oolites are calcareous, siliceous, and ferruginous.

Ordovician

The geological period from 500 to 435 million years ago.

organic carbon

Carbon derived from plant and animal residues.

organic matter

The organic fraction of the soil; includes plant and animal residues at various stages of decomposition, cells and tissues of soil organisms, and substances synthesized by the soil population.

orogeny

A period of mountain building, lasting tens of thousands of years.

ortstein

A type of hardpan that consists of organic matter cemented with iron and aluminium oxide.

Ostracoda

A class of crustaceans; small bivalve animals that live in both salt and fresh water.

outcrop

The place where a particular rock unit is exposed at the surface.

outwash

Sediments "washed out" beyond a glacier by flowing water and laid down in thin beds or strata; the particle size may range from boulders to silt.

Glossary
Me–Ou

overburden

The layers of surficial sediments that cover bedrock and need to be removed before mining can take place.

ovipositor

An elongated structure on some female insects that allows the precise placement of eggs.

oxbow lake

A lake formed when river meanders are cut off from the main channel.

paleo-

A combining form meaning old, ancient, early, primitive, or archaic.

paleo-environment

The environment of the geologic past.

paleo-Indians

The people who lived in Nova Scotia between 10,000 and 11,000 years ago.

Paleozoic

The geological era between the end of the Precambrian (600 million years ago) to the beginning of the Mesozoic (225 million years ago).

paludification

The transformation of land into marsh.

Pangaea

A hypothetical supercontinent of past eras that was later fragmented by continental drift.

parent material

The unconsolidated and more or less chemically unweathered mineral or organic matter from which soil has developed.

parallel drainage

A drainage pattern in which streams flow nearly parallel to one another over an area; commonly associated with a pronounced slope.

particle size, soil

The grain-size distribution of the whole soil, including the coarse fraction. It differs from *texture*, which refers to the fine earth (less than 2-mm) fraction only.

passerines

Perching birds.

peat

A dark-brown or black organic material produced by the partial decomposition and disintegration of mosses, sedges, and other plants which grow in marshes and wetlands.

pedology

The aspects of soil science that involve the constitution, distribution, genesis, classification, and mapping of soils.

pedon

The smallest three-dimensional unit at the surface of the earth that is considered to be a soil.

pegmatites

Coarse-grained igneous rocks usually found as dykes associated with a large mass of fine-grained plutonics. Unless specified otherwise, the name usually means granite pegmatites.

pelagic

Living and feeding in the water column, as opposed to living associated with a sea or lake bottom.

Pelecypoda

A class of the phylum Mollusca; bivalves including mussels, clams, and oysters.

peneplain

A smooth, rolling erosion surface that develops late in the cycle of erosion.

perhumid

A type of climate that has humidity values of +100 and above; the wettest type of climate.

permafrost

Permanently frozen ground.

permeability

The ability of a substrate to allow a solution to pass through it.

Permian

The geological period between 290 and 247 million years ago.

pH

The intensity of acidity and alkalinity, expressed as the negative logarithm of the hydrogen ion concentration. A pH of 7 is neutral; lower values indicate acidity and higher values alkalinity.

phyllite

A fine-grained, foliated metamorphic rock intermediate between mica schist and slate; not as tough as slate. Mica crystals give a silky sheen to the cleavage surface.

physiography

Description and interpretation of landforms.

phytogeographic

Referring to the distribution of plant species.

phytoplankton

Microscopic plants that float or drift almost passively in oceans, lakes, or rivers.

pillow lava

Basaltic lava that solidifies under water and develops a structure that resembles a pile of pillows.

pioneer

Refers to species that colonize bare substrate.

Pleistocene

A division of the Tertiary period of geological history during which glaciation occurred, ranging from 0.1–1.8 million years ago.

placer

An alluvial or glacial deposit containing particles of gold or other valuable minerals.

planation

The grading of an area by any erosive process, subaerial or marine.

plankton

Suspended, free-floating, and microscopic aquatic organisms.

plate tectonics

The theory that the earth's outer shell consists of plates which interact in different ways to produce earthquakes, volcanoes, mountains, and the crust itself.

plucked

See *ice-plucked*.

pluton

A large igneous intrusion.

pocket beach

A small beach formed in an indentation of a coastline.

pockmark

A feature of the offshore sea-bottom that resembles a round, crater-like depression up to 300 m across and 1–30 m deep

podzols

Soils formed in cool, wet conditions, with a strongly developed leached zone.

podzolic

An order of soils having accumulations of amorphous combinations of organic matter, aluminum, and iron in the B horizon.

polychaetes

Worms with true body segments and hard spines; mainly marine.

pothole

A circular feature worn into solid rock by sand, gravel, and stones that have been spun around by water currents.

Precambrian

The period of time between the consolidation of the earth's crust and the beginning of the Cambrian period; about 4 billion years in duration.

primary production

The rate at which energy from light is absorbed and used with carbon dioxide to produce organic matter in photosynthesis.

primitive plants

Species that developed early in the evolutionary history of plants.

productivity

Rate of production of new biomass by populations of organisms.

profile, beach

The intersection of the ground surface with a vertical plane; may extend from the top of the dune line to the seaward limit of sand movement.

profundal

The deepest parts of lakes and the ocean.

progradation

A seaward advance of the shoreline that results from the deposition of sediments nearshore by rivers.

protozoa

A large, diverse, and widespread group of mostly microscopic non-cellular animals, including both free-living and parasitic forms.

provincial park

A legally established park administered by a province.

pyrite

A brass-yellow mineral with a bright metallic lustre that usually occurs in veins of all classes of rocks; often associated with gold mining and referred to as fool's gold.

quartz

A very hard, glassy-looking mineral; crystallized silicon dioxide; constituent of all acidic igneous rocks and some intermediate and basic rocks; common in metamorphic rocks, as a veinstone, and as a dominant constituent of sandstone (the sand grains are quartz).

quartzite

A granulose metamorphic rock made essentially of quartz.

radial drainage

The drainage pattern where streams radiate from a central area, in particular from a rounded upland area.

raised beach

A wave-cut platform raised above the present sea level.

Glossary
Ov–Ra

range

1. Applied to tides: the difference in height between consecutive high and low waters. The "mean range" is the difference in height between mean high and mean low water marks. 2. Applied to animals: the area around an animal's nest or burrow used for feeding and other daily activities ("home range"); also the larger area used by migratory species. 3. With reference to plants: Complete distribution for a given landmass.

rare

Applied to a species infrequently seen in a suitable habitat. The term is usually qualified to reflect the area observed; for example, a species "rare in Nova Scotia" is not necessarily "rare in Canada."

rectangular drainage

A drainage pattern characterized by right-angle bends in both the main stream and its tributaries; common in permeable, well-jointed rocks such as limestone, sandstone, and gypsum; also referred to as *trellised drainage*.

red bed

Term applied to red sedimentary rocks, usually sandstones and shales.

refugium

A locality that has escaped drastic alteration following climatic change, in contrast to the region as whole (plural *refugia*).

regeneration

The recovery of vegetation after natural or human disturbances such as cutting or fire. Succession proceeds towards the climax state as far as site conditions will permit.

rejuvenation, stream

Occurs when a mature river encounters a geological obstacle such as resistant rock and renews erosive activity, producing a waterfall or rapids.

relative sea level (RSL)

Position of sea level relative to the land. RSL change measures the land movement versus the water movement over time.

relict

An occurrence that represents localized remains of an originally much wider distribution.

remnant population

See *relict*.

remote forcing

Referring to currents that arise as a result of a force or forces from a non-local or remote area.

reserve

Crown land reserved for park development.

rhyolite

An extrusive igneous rock equivalent in composition to granite, in which the crystalline constituents are too small to be distinguished with the unaided eye.

riffle

A shallow section in a river or stream where the water flows swiftly; may be less turbulent than rapids.

rift

An area of the earth's crust along which divergence is taking place, allowing a fault plane to intersect with the surface.

riparian

Ecological term associated with riverbanks; used in connection with plant and animal habitat.

rotifers

Members of the invertebrate phylum Rotifera. Important among freshwater plankton and in nutrient recycling in aquatic systems. They are minute, less than one millimetre in length, and usually transparent.

runoff

Water that flows over land rather than infiltrating into the ground.

saddle

The area between marine banks.

salinity

The "practical salinity unit" measures the amount of salt in marine waters. It has the same numerical value as the old measure of parts per thousand (by weight), except in very saline and very dilute waters when the difference is, at the most, 0.06 units.

salmonid

Any member of the family of fish Salmonidae, which includes salmon and trout.

salt marsh

Marshland periodically flooded by saline tidal water and characterized by organisms tolerant to saline conditions.

sand

1. A mineral soil particle between 0.05 and 2.0 mm in diameter. 2. A soil textural class containing more than 85 per cent sand and less than 10 per cent clay.

sand ridge

A long, sinuous offshore feature that stretches over wide areas of the seabed and is formed in extreme conditions, such as by subsurface tides.

sandstone

A sedimentary rock composed predominantly of sand-sized quartz grains.

sand wave

An offshore bottom feature caused by storms and tidal currents. Sand waves on the Scotian Shelf can be from 0.5–12 m high and from 12 m to 1 km long.

saprophyte

A plant that derives nutrients from organic material and cannot photosynthesize.

scarp

A steep slope.

schist

A medium- to coarse-grained metamorphic rock with strong foliation that results from a parallel orientation of platy minerals such as micas.

scour

Removal of material by waves and currents, especially at the base of a shore structure.

scree

See *talus*.

second-order stream

Tributary initiated by the confluence of two first-order streams.

sedimentary

One of the three main groups of rock; rocks formed of material derived from pre-existing rocks by processes such as weathering, erosion, and precipitation.

seepage site

A place where water oozes from the earth, often forming the source of a small trickling stream.

semi-diurnal tide

Tide in which high water occurs twice daily with intervals averaging 12.4 hours.

seral stage

A stage of development in the successional process (sere) recognized by distinct soil and water conditions and associations of plants and animals.

sessile

Attached directly to a base without a flexible joint; used when describing parts of organisms, such as leaves or flowers.

shade-intolerant

Refers to trees that require full sunlight to reproduce and thrive.

shade-tolerant

Refers to trees that can reproduce and thrive in partial sunlight or shade.

shale

A laminated sediment composed predominantly of clay-sized particles.

shell midden

See *midden*.

sill

A sheet-like body of igneous rock which conforms to bedrock or other structural planes.

sillimanite

An aluminum silicate mineral usually found in fine fibrous masses and associated with intensely metamorphosed mica schists and gneisses and contact-metamorphic deposits.

silt

1. A mineral soil particle between 0.002 and 0.05 mm in diameter. 2. A soil texture class containing more than 80 per cent silt and less than 12 per cent clay.

siltstone

A very fine-grained consolidated clastic rock composed predominantly of particles of silt.

Silurian

The geological period between 436 and 415 million years ago.

sinkhole

A depression occurring in karst topography, often the result of the collapse of a cavern roof.

slate

A fine-grained metamorphic rock easily split into flat, smooth plates.

slope water

A band of water consisting of Gulf Stream water diluted by approximately 20 per cent coastal water near the edge of the continental shelf and separated from the coastal water by a sharp front.

slumping

The formation of a landslide that develops where strong, resistant rocks overlie weak rocks.

smectite

A greenish variety of clay mineral.

softwood

A forestry term for coniferous, needle-leaved trees and the forests they form.

soil survey

The systematic examination, description, classification, and mapping of soils in an area.

solution lake

A lake formed in soluble material such as salt, limestone, and gypsum; water in these lakes is often alkaline.

Southern Upland

A physiographic area that comprises the southwestern half of mainland Nova Scotia.

spit

A low tongue or narrow embankment of land, usually composed of sand or gravel, formed by wave and current action, with one end attached to the shore and the other ending in open water.

Glossary
Ra–Sp

spring tide

A tide that occurs at or near the time of the new or full moon and rises highest and falls lowest from the mean sea level.

staging area

An area where migrating birds congregate to rest and refuel.

staurolite

A crystallized iron-aluminum silicate mineral that occurs in regionally metamorphosed rock.

stibnite

A sulphide compound associated with arsenic and antimony minerals; the principal ore of antimony.

stones

Rock fragments greater than 25 cm in diameter.

storm surge

The rise above normal water level on the open coast that results from wind stress on the water surface.

stratification

1. Applied to rocks: the presence of layers, or strata; typical of sedimentary rock. 2. Applied to water: division of the water column into layers of different temperature or salinity.

stratigraphic

Refers to the formation, composition, sequence, and correlation of stratified rocks as part of the earth's crust.

stratum

A layer of rock (plural *strata*).

striae

Small grooves on the surface of a rock, formed by glacial action.

strike

The compass direction of the line of intersection created by a dipping bed or fault and a horizontal surface.

strike-slip fault

A fault along which movement is horizontal.

subaerial erosion

Erosion that occurs at or near the surface. See *eolian.*

submarine valley or canyon

1. The seaward extension of a valley cut on the continental shelf during low sea level. 2. A steep, valley-like depression carved into the outer margin of the continental shelf and slope by turbidity currents.

submerged coastline

A coast which has been partially drowned as the result of a rise in sea level, a subsidence of the crust, or both.

substrate

The surface on which organisms grow; usually providing physical support and a supply of nutrients.

subtidal

Pertaining to the marine environment below the lowest level of low tide.

succession

The progressive change in the composition of a community of organisms towards a largely stable climax.

superimposed drainage

A natural drainage system established on underlying rocks independently of their structure.

surface water

All moving and standing water naturally open to the atmosphere.

surficial

Characteristic of, pertaining to, formed on, situated at, or occurring on the earth's surface; especially consisting of unconsolidated residual alluvial or glacial deposits lying on bedrock.

surf zone

The area between the outermost breakers and the limit of wave uprush on the seashore.

suspension feeder

A freshwater animal that feeds on materials suspended in water.

syenite

A wholly crystalline rock resembling granite but containing little or no quartz.

sylvite

A potassium-chloride mineral associated with sedimentary salt beds and volcanic features; the principal ore of potassium.

syncline

A fold in layers of rock caused by deformation of the earth's crust. Synclines are basin-shaped and have the younger strata towards the centre of the fold.

taiga

Derived from Russian, meaning *boreal.* In Nova Scotia the term refers to a transition area in the Cape Breton highlands with boreal to tundra-like conditions and supporting windswept dwarf vegetation.

talus

Rock fragments that result from the mechanical weathering of rocks.

tartigrades

A phylum of tiny, highly specialized aquatic invertebrates commonly known as "water bears," mainly less than one millimetre in length and commonly found in water film on the leaves of terrestrial mosses and lichens.

taxa

A group of any size used in the classification of things, particularly plants and animals.

tectonic

Refers to deformation of the earth's crust or to the forces that cause it; controlled by a process such as orogeny.

temperate

1. Refers to species characteristic of mixed forest that have their northern extension in Canada in Cape Breton. 2. The Temperate Forest, composed predominantly of deciduous species, extends west along the St. Lawrence to the Great Lakes and south into the mid-eastern United States.

terminal moraine

See *end moraine.*

terrace

A nearly level surface or bench bordering a steep slope, such as a stream terrace or wave-cut terrace.

terrane

1. A formation or group of formations. 2. The area or surface over which a particular rock or group of rocks is prevalent.

Tertiary

That geological period which elapsed between 65 and 36 million years ago.

texture, soil

The relative proportions of particles less than 2 mm in diameter (sand, silt, and clay) in a soil.

thallus

The vegetative structure of algae and fungi, which may be leaf-like or stem-like, but is not vascular tissue.

thermo-

Description of a condition in seawater, based upon measurement of haline temperature and salinity.

thermodine

A zone of rapidly changing temperatures observed in the vertical profile of a body of water such as a lake.

third-order stream

Tributary initiated by the confluence of two second-order streams.

tholeiites

A general term for basalts textured with isolated crystals in the general mass.

thrust fault

A fault in which the material above the fault plane moves up in relation to the material below; characterized by a low angle of inclination.

tidal amplitude

Vertical tide; the amplitude of the vertical tide (in metres) is half the range between low water and high water.

tidal currents

Horizontal tide; the vertical tide has different amplitudes and phases at different locations and these differences produce slopes in sea surface, giving rise to tidal currents.

tidal flat

A marshy or muddy land area covered and uncovered by the rise and fall of the tide.

tidal gyre

A gyre formed by oscillating tidal currents washing back and forth around the edge of a bank, where the depth is increasing rapidly.

tidal mixing

Occurs when strong tidal currents mix the water column.

tidal rectification

The process of extracting energy from an oscillating tidal current (where the mean velocity is zero) to produce a non-zero mean unidirectional flow.

tide

The periodic rise and fall of water that results from the gravitational attraction of the moon and sun upon the rotating earth.

till

Unstratified glacial and fluvioglacial deposits left after the retreat of glaciers and ice sheets; consists of clay, sand, gravel, and boulders intermingled in any proportion.

tolerant

See *shade-tolerant.*

tombolo

A beach formed in the sheltered lee of an island, often connecting the island to the mainland.

toothed whale

A whale of the sub-order Odontoceti, having teeth rather than plates of baleen. They grasp and swallow prey whole, unlike the sub-order Mysticeti which are filter feeders.

topography

Description of the geographical surface features of a region.

transgression

The gradual expansion of a shallow sea, resulting in the progressive submergence of land, as when sea levels rise or land subsides.

Glossary
Sp–Tr

transition zone

An area linking two series of sediments formed in contrasting environments.

transverse fault

A fault whose strike is at a right angle to the general structure.

trellised drainage

See *rectangular drainage*.

Triassic

The geological period between 247 and 212 million years ago.

trilobite

Animal fossil from the class of arthropods Trilobita, now extinct but abundant from the Cambrian to Silurian.

tuff

Rocks consolidated from volcanic material containing a predominance of fragments not greater than 2 cm in diameter.

tungsten

A rare element of the chromium group contained in certain minerals associated with high-temperature quartz veins and isolated as a hard, brittle, white or grey metal.

tunicates

Primitive vertebrates; the adults are sessile and the larvae planktonic; also called sea squirts.

turbidite

A downslope movement of dense, sediment-laden water created when sand and mud on the continental shelf and slope are dislodged and thrown into suspension.

unconformity

A surface of erosion that separates younger strata from older rocks.

understory

The intermediate layer of trees and shrubs within a forest structure.

uplift plain

An eroded and levelled area of land which has been uplifted, thereby forming a raised, generally uniform upland.

upwelling

A vertical movement of water, usually near coasts and driven by onshore winds, that brings nutrients from the depths of the ocean to surface layers.

vascular plants

Seed-bearing plants, ferns and their allies that use vessels to conduct water, salts, and nutrients.

Virginian species

Faunal element of eastern North America found from Cape Cod to Florida living in warm and temperate marine waters. Nova Scotia has a disjunct population.

volcanic bombs

Detached masses of lava shot out by volcanoes, which, as they fall, assume rounded forms like bombshells.

volcanics

One of the main groups of rocks that form the earth's surface.

washover

A small delta formed on the landward side of a barrier beach or bar, resulting from storm waves breaking over low or fragile parts and depositing sediment.

water column

Description of the character of ocean or lake waters based upon a vertical profile that recognizes differences related to depth.

watershed

A planning term that refers to the area from which surface water drains into a common lake or river system or directly into the ocean; also referred to as a *drainage basin*.

water table

The upper level in the saturated zone of groundwater.

wave

1. One of the ridges which alternates with depressions (troughs) on the surface of water and breaks on the shore as surf. 2. More generally applied to ridge and trough oscillation within a fluid (e.g., internal waves in the ocean) and the transmission of light, sound, and electricity through a medium.

wave climate

The nature of incident waves, including the characteristic wave height, period, length, and direction.

wave-cut platform/terrace

A bench or shelf along the coastline at sea level; cut by wave erosion.

wildlife

Any non-domesticated living organism, including plants, lower animals, and vertebrates.

wind gap

A low depression or notch in a ridge where streams formerly flowed; often used for highways.

Wisconsinan glaciation

The last of four glacial stages in the Pleistocene of North America.

xenolith

Fragments of rocks of extraneous origin that have been picked up by magma and are therefore foreign to the igneous rocks in which they occur.

xeric

Refers to habitats in which plant production is limited by availability of water; a dry site.

xerophyte

A plant which grows in a dry habitat and is able to withstand conditions of prolonged drought.

zeolite

A generic term for a group of hydrous alumino-silicate minerals that occurs in cracks and cavities of igneous rocks, especially the more basic lavas.

zonation

The occurrence of species or communities in specific zones, each with a characteristic dominant species; commonly used to define aquatic environments.

zooplankton

Animals that drift or weakly swim in the ocean, largely at the mercy of prevailing currents.

Index

INDEX

Index

Index

Index

Index

Index

Index

Index

Index

Index

LIST OF ILLUSTRATIONS

FIGURES

PLATES

TABLES

List of Illustrations